# Heidegger's
# Atheism

# Heidegger's Atheism

## The Refusal of a Theological Voice

Laurence Paul Hemming

University of Notre Dame Press
*Notre Dame, Indiana*

Copyright © 2002 by
University of Notre Dame
Notre Dame, Indiana 46556
http://www.undpress.nd.edu


Manufactured in the United States of America


A record of the Library of Congress Cataloging-in-Publication Data
is available upon request from the Library of Congress

ISBN 0-268-03058-8


∞ *This book is printed on acid-free paper.*

*for Ferdinand and Susan*
*and my Parents*

*gifts of God*

*Ausserdem bin ich von Hause aus katholisch.*
—Martin Heidegger to Pastor W. D. Zimmermann,
30 June 1968

# Contents

# Foreword

This work has come to fruition over much time and has traversed three universities, with many friends and supporters along its way. It has emerged as an engagement with the often troubled experience of thinking with and writing about Martin Heidegger, especially for men and women of faith. I am one among many who might have some claim to have been taught the discipline and practice of thinking by studying Martin Heidegger. Though I would count myself no Heideggerian, yet his thought continues to amaze and captivate me.

The translations in this volume are my own, though heavily informed by the now many published translations of Heidegger's texts. The notorious difficulty of translating Heidegger's German has meant that I have deliberately erred on the side of the literal, and I have provided the original German in the footnotes. The reader should always refer to the German for the inner sense of the texts quoted. I have eschewed the usual rendering of *das Sein* as 'Being with a big B' (as John Macquarrie used to say in Oxford) in favor of just 'being.' *Das Seiende*, which can also mean 'being,' and has often been translated as 'whatever is', I have distinguished in English by tending to render in the plural: 'beings.' Where I have deviated from this convention I have made clear in the text why.

I have sought to translate as inclusively as possible and would ask the reader kindly to bear with me when I have reluctantly resorted to use of male terms for the sake of simplicity to denote the whole of humanity. Other solutions seemed too labored, in particular the use of female pronouns in place of male. As a male author this seems to me to be colonization under another guise, and I have eschewed it. I would ask you always to assume that I have intended translations to be understood in an inclusive sense even where you are dissatisfied with the compromises I have made.

Within quotations and translations, I have added words indicated by square brackets, [. . .], for the sake of clarification of the sense or for grammatical completeness. Perspicacious readers may be perplexed by some spelling or grammar in foreign-language quotations. Wherever possible, I have used critical editions and authoritative texts and retained the original spelling and format found there. Thus apostrophes creep into Nietzsche's genitives, Descartes's Latin has accented vowels, and Leibniz's French and St. Catherine's Italian are different from our own. Some of the constructions from the Heidegger *Gesamtausgabe* are questionable; however, in the absence of a critical edition of his work I have not sought to correct them myself.

With origins in study begun at the University of Oxford in 1992, a good part of the research reproduced here was carried out as doctoral work at the University of Cambridge between 1995 and 1998. More latterly it has benefited from time at Heythrop College of the University of London, where I now work and have my intellectual home.

I would like to record my debt of gratitude to the late Cardinal Basil Hume, who, as Archbishop of Westminster, made my going to Cambridge possible, and the Archbishop of Birmingham, Vincent Nichols, who in his time at Westminster and afterward has encouraged my work. I would also like to thank John McDade, S. J., Heythrop's Principal since 1999, who has ensured I have had time and opportunity to develop my work.

Graham Ward, my supervisor at Cambridge, has been a friend to these researches, and I would also like to thank David Burrell, C. S. C., for his support and encouragement and Fergus Kerr, O. P., who since 1999, has from time to time made good and helpful suggestions. I am indebted as well to Nicholas Boyle of Magdalene College, Cambridge, for his many corrections and improvements of my translations. If the improvements are his, the persisting errors are entirely mine. I would like to thank John Milbank for encouraging publication of this work, despite our very different understanding of Heidegger. I must also record my thanks to Richard Price for his help with the weakness of my Greek, and Gemma Simmonds, I. B. V. M., for her perspicacious help with my French. I would like to thank Julian Goman for his work on the index.

Earlier fruits of the research of which this book is the latest form have appeared in print elsewhere. Some of the questions around Jean-Luc Marion's reading of Martin Heidegger were raised in *New Blackfriars* in 1995.[1] A preliminary discussion of Heidegger's approach to analogy and nihilism appeared in the collection *Radical Orthodoxy* under the title "Nihilism" in

---

1. "Reading Heidegger: Is God without Being?" in *New Blackfriars*, vol. 76 (1995).

1998,[2] and questions concerning Heidegger's understanding of God which formed the basis for what has become chapter 6 appeared in *The Thomist* under the title "Heidegger's God" in the same year.[3] Two other publications in 1998 arose out of research which went on respectively to become, in the first instance, chapters 3 and 4, and in the second chapter 7. My earlier views on Heidegger's turn appeared under the title "Speaking out of Turn: Martin Heidegger and Die Kehre" in the *International Journal of Philosophical Studies*,[4] and a preliminary discussion of Heidegger's reading of the figure of Zarathustra appeared as "Who is Heidegger's Zarathustra?" in *Literature and Theology*.[5] Readers who are bothered to look in these places will see how much my thought has developed, and I hope matured, in the time that has passed.

Finally, I must acknowledge the people to whom this work is dedicated, without whose untiring loving friendship and support this work would neither have begun, nor been undertaken, nor carried to fruition. Deo gratias.

Feast of St. Catherine of Siena,
29 April 2001

---

2. "Nihilism: Articulating Nihilism and Redemption in a Post-Modern Context" in *Radical Orthodox*, Milbank, J; Ward, G., and Pickstock, C. (eds.), Routledge, London, 1998.

3. "Heidegger's God: A Reading of Heidegger's Critique of Aquinas' Assertion Deus est suum esse" in *The Thomist*, vol. 62 (1998).

4. "Speaking out of Turn: Martin Heidegger and Die Kehre" in *International Journal of Philosophical Studies*, vol. 6 (1998).

5. "Who is Heidegger's Zarathustra?" in *Literature and Theology*, vol. 12 (1998).

# Heidegger's Atheism

Chapter One

# Introduction

---

## HEIDEGGER'S ATHEISM

Martin Heidegger says that "philosophical research is and remains atheism".[1] Even before this he said that only when philosophy is properly atheistic, "only then is it honest . . . before God".[2] What did he mean by the term 'atheism'? Heidegger's silences appear, sometimes to perplex, perhaps even to appall us, and yet it is my contention that more often the silences claimed for him are not his, but meet our own hermeneutical and interpretative difficulties with his work. So often Heidegger's retorts are the teasing responses of the pedagogue who forces me to answer my own questions in his presence, so that I could almost overlook the fact that it is to him I had turned for an answer. What kinds of access must we have to a thinker's thoughts? The viewpoint of this book is that it will be sufficient to understand what Heidegger understood by the terms 'atheism' and 'God' to listen to what he himself said, and what he said about himself. This is not to say that I intend to have the last word on the matter. It will become clear, I hope, that, for me, at least, final resolutions of anything are impossible—strictly speaking—for as long as I must breathe. This is not in itself a personal view but one supported by the whole history of inquiring into what is eternal and what possible.

To what extent is Heidegger's own biography an issue for his understanding of atheism? Let me reassure the reader, I am no biographer. The facts of Heidegger's early life, his connections with the Catholic

---

1. *Prolegomena zur Geschichte des Zeitbegriffs* (GA20), p. 109 f. "Philosophische Forschung ist und bleibt Atheismus."
2. *Phänomenologische Interpretationen zu Aristoteles* (GA61), p. 246. "Damit allein aber steht sie ehrlich . . . vor Gott."

Church, and the degree and extent of his break from it have been laid out in other places.[3] My contention is that Heidegger's biography is not particularly helpful in unraveling his understanding of atheism, which is his strictly philosophical concern.

Like memory itself, the researches yet to come concerning Heidegger must confront what already has arrived, both in Heidegger's published work and how it has been understood and in what has been forgotten and what distorted. No memory is pure: traumas have a way of pressing in on us to assert themselves more forcibly than matters which seemed of no great account at the time. The way back in to memory can be hard and marked with shapeless shadows. Things which require an understanding now had no meaning at the time. This book concerns itself with the memory of Heidegger. It concerns itself with the memory of Heidegger because the very phrase splits in its ambiguities: uniquely his was a form of remembering of the whole of the Western tradition. How good or bad a memory it is, and what the character was of the person who remembered, have in part determined how we continue to remember Heidegger. How adept we are at remembering ourselves affects how the memory lives.

Did Heidegger remember God, and if he did, whose God or gods did he remember—Christian, pagan, or some new one or ones unknown to us? Was Heidegger silent about God? Any claim about Heidegger's silence must confront this strangeness: that there is hardly a text of Heidegger's, long or short, that does not mention God, gods, or divinity—not only once, but on almost every page. Heidegger reeks of God, and yet at no point does he say who or what God is. Heidegger—this man routinely taken to be *the* philosopher of being—refuses to tell us not only who or what God or divinity is, but what being is either. In other words, is there a sense in which Heidegger's silences are concerned with our capacity to hear?

Why is it possible to find a silence concerning God in Heidegger's work? One of Heidegger's earliest doctoral students, Karl Löwith, whose understanding of Heidegger I shall consider in detail, made the persistent accusation that in carrying out a 'turn' in his thought, Heidegger had supplanted God with being, a view that both creates the supposed silence and accounts for it.[4] Löwith goes so far as to suggest that Heidegger is nothing other than

---

3. See in particular: Safranski, R., *Ein Meister aus Deutschland* (1994), chapters 1, 2, 3, and 7; and Ott, H., "Heidegger's Catholic Origins" (1995).
4. Cf. Löwith, K., *Heidegger—Denker in dürftiger Zeit* (1984).

a latter-day follower of the medieval metaphysician John Duns Scotus. This unoriginal taunt bases itself on the fact that Heidegger's *Habilitationsschrift* concluded research on a text that (at the time of writing) was believed to have been authored by Scotus, although it later turned out otherwise. To have followed Scotus (whose work so often seems to contradict and question Thomas Aquinas) is tantamount to saying that in contradistinction to earlier Scholasticism, which appeared to be saying God and being were the same, for Heidegger, being and God are the same in a God-denying reversal.[5] For Löwith, this question of Heidegger's silence over God is already grounded in how to read and interpret Heidegger and who to read him against. What concerns me here is that Löwith inaugurated a way of reading Heidegger which persists to this day, and which, as I shall show, simultaneously indicates and conceals the place of God in Heidegger's thought.

In the course of this study the question of Heidegger's atheism will in part ask to what extent Heidegger is still in dialogue with the Christian tradition which arises out of Scholasticism, a tradition he knew and understood well, and—certainly early on—believed to be central to his thinking. Referring to the "later" Heidegger in particular has assumed an importance in such a way that the *naming* of periods in the work of Heidegger has become a mark of ways of thinking about his work. Is there a later Heidegger who stands over against the earlier, and if so, why should this periodization have a significance? What if there is no later Heidegger in the sense of one whose thoughts are different to the earlier, and this very claim to a later and earlier itself is open to question? Perhaps if I can trace in Heidegger's work a development and a ceaseless re-asking of the same questions in differing ways (particularly with regard to the question of God) the idea that there was once a Heidegger I followed by a Heidegger II can be seen as no longer adequate to address the question of what Heidegger thought and how he thought it.[6] Indeed, what if the very idea that there might be a Heidegger I and Heidegger II arises directly out of an attempt by Karl Löwith and to a lesser extent William Richardson to confront Heidegger with a question about God?

---

5. Löwith, K., *Heidegger—Denker in dürftiger Zeit* (1984), footnote on p. 139 referring to pp. 348–351 of Heidegger's 1916 Habilitationsschrift, *Die Kategorien- und Bedeutungslehre des Duns Scotus* (*Frühe Schriften* [GA1]).

6. This is the schema proposed by Richardson, W., in *Heidegger: Through Phenomenology to Thought* (1963), to explain Heidegger's turn. I will consider this schema in detail in chapter 3.

Heidegger has—justly or otherwise—been named a precursor of the postmodern in such a way that he (and to some extent Nietzsche) name what it is to think *into* and so perhaps *after* the end of metaphysics, the end of Modernity, or whatever end is currently announced, so that he is (to paraphrase Jacques Derrida) a signpost to the apocalypticism of the moment, the moment's coming in to its finitude and end, and so actually coming to be.[7]

What role does the apocalyptic play in Heidegger's thought? Heidegger's relation to Nietzsche is central to this question. If, as Heidegger says (citing Nietzsche in making the claim): "No one with any insight will still deny today that nihilism is in the most varied and most hidden forms the 'normal state' of humanity", is Heidegger a nihilist?[8] What is his concern with nothing? An abiding concern is the character and tone of Heidegger's voice, a voice that reaches to speak of *das Nichts*, 'the nothing.' Heidegger's voice appears to move in a tense province bounded by the prophetic and a kind of withdrawal. The voice itself is to some extent always concerned with silence, and so with the how, when, and why of speaking and not speaking, of language itself. Derrida's observation "Isn't the voice of language . . . always that of the last man? . . . there is apocalypse *without* apocalypse" points out that the apocalyptic voice is always a voice addressing some*one*.[9] Who is being addressed and in what tone? Might it be that the apocalyptic I often find when reading Heidegger in particular is the tone of voice that the self adopts when it—I—bring myself to face myself *as finite?* It is, if you like, the voice of finitude speaking in the face of the universality and anonymity of the subject. It is that voice which brings me home to my finitude, a sort of shock. The apocalyptic voice confirms the moment and makes it what it most is. It is not, however, a voice which I simply utter in an

---

7. Smith, G. B., *Nietzsche, Heidegger, and the Transition to Postmodernity* (1996), p. 281. "Nietzsche and Heidegger are the primary philosophical progenitors of contemporary postmodernism . . . we can ignore their thought but will not thereby transcend them—quite the opposite." Smith's point is that postmodernism, a term with which he is ill at ease, arises as a marker for a whole panoply of positions (often mutually contradictory) because of something which is thought to have been done *elsewhere*, out of range, somehow, by Heidegger and Nietzsche. In short, the postmodern situation is not explained by postmodernism.

8. *Zur Seinsfrage* (*Wegmarken* [GA9]), p. 392, citing Nietzsche, *Der Wille zur Macht* (1996), §23. "Kein Einsichtiger wird heute noch leugnen wollen, daß der Nihilismus in den verschiedensten und versrecktesten Gestalten der 'Normalzustand' der Menschheit ist."

9. Derrida, J., "Of an Apocalyptic Tone" (1992), pp. 49, 67.

act of volition—of the will—but is rather that voice in which I speak (above all to myself) when I find what I have most *been* given to say: given—by something hidden from myself and emerging which is yet *still* myself. One might almost say, it is myself in the mode of reply, of '*after . . .*', of *my* calling me into a future. Yet I asked about Heidegger's voice and now am speaking only of my own. How often have any of us read a text of Heidegger's and been shocked by it, so much so that we assumed the shock we found was the intended voice of the text? How often have I returned to a text looking for the tone of shock I remembered there and missed it entirely, so that I almost wondered what all the fuss was about? The fuss was surely mine alone.

Hearing Heidegger's voice is not easy. Too much is written of what Heidegger *says*, ignoring the patience he demanded and the willingness to remain with what he attempts to speak *of*. But is Heidegger not a nihilist, an apocalyptic conjurer, and an iconoclast? Or is his voice a voice of 'the' nothing that clears the way for something to be said? What could that something be?

The apocalyptic voice of *Dasein* is a voice Heidegger claimed he had already found in Nietzsche, a tone of horror. It is not for nothing that Derrida calls it the voice of the last man—this man who is figured in *Also Sprach Zarathustra*, the man whom Zarathustra comes to teach. Can this voice be reserved to a man alone? In that it is the voice of withdrawal, of departure, of opening up a space, a span in distance, yes. For as the voice of the last *man*, other gendered voices too have come to speak—a matter about which Heidegger himself spoke, albeit fleetingly. Can the language of *Dasein* give voice to being? This, I might suggest, is a question Heidegger struggled to answer throughout.

If "Heidegger" is to some extent the mark of the voice of the nothing and the apocalyptic in much current thinking, it is perhaps because the apocalyptic voice is one that has been drained of God, a voice without God (in the sense that I might stand without a city wall), a voice overpowered by presence and the presence of everything extant before it. Does this voice not have to overcome the presence of the extant in order to come again to presencing, to come again to God? This is, as I shall argue, the authentic voice of *Dasein:* of Heidegger's *Dasein* of *Sein und Zeit* and beyond, of *Dasein* translated as existence, of *Dasein* understood as the meaning of being-the-there. Even here, there is to be found an intimation of how Heidegger has been misheard in his talk about *Dasein*, an intimation that once again concerns Karl Löwith. Jean Beaufret records an exchange between Heidegger and Löwith in Heidelberg in 1969, where Löwith explained his differences from his former teacher at great length. At the conclusion, Heidegger is reported to have asked: "But *Dasein* in *Sein und Zeit* . . . how do you understand it?" Löwith replied: "The there of being". Heidegger retorted: "*No!* . . . being has no *there*".[10] Heidegger laid the blame for this interpretation at the feet of Sartre, who translated *Dasein* into French as *être-là*. Beaufret notes that Heidegger had dealt with the same question in a seminar conducted together with Eugen Fink two years earlier. There we find him addressing the same issue in almost identical words. His exasperation with Löwith is therefore no stunt, nothing conjured for the moment to prod his wayward pupil, but rather is marked by the way he returned again and again to the issues and problems surrounding the interpretation of his work.

In this seminar with Fink conducted almost at the end of his life, Heidegger discusses at some length the meaning of the term *Dasein* before referring his auditors again to the work that he always returns to in his public utterances, the work that provides the basis for understanding him until the very end, the book that guides his own interpretations, *Sein und Zeit*. In many ways, *Sein und Zeit* is the only book he ever published himself. Everything else he published were lectures and short essays. His other books have been published posthumously. Even now, they are only two, and both are incomplete.[11]

Two things stand out in the exchange to which Beaufret draws our attention: first, that in 1967 (when the seminar took place) Heidegger still sees himself as thinking through the perspective he outlined in *Sein und Zeit*, which he describes even forty years on as a new position and historical step and therefore different from anything that preceded it. Second, Heidegger still understands what is elaborated in *Sein und Zeit* as describing the structures that make possible other, earlier philosophical determinations, the understanding of human being that precedes him, determinations like, for instance, consciousness:

> Consciousness is only possible on the basis of the *Da*, as a mode derivative of it. From here one must understand the historical step that is taken in *Sein und Zeit*, which takes as its departure *Dasein* as opposed to consciousness.[12]

10. Beaufret, J., "En chemin avec Heidegger," in *Cahier de l'Herne: Heidegger* (1983), p. 212. "HEIDEGGER: Aber *Dasein* in *Sein und Zeit* . . . Wie meinen Sie das? LÖWITH: *Das Da des Seins*. HEIDEGGER: *Nein!* . . . L'Être n'a pas de *là*" (author's italics).

11. *Beiträge zur Philosophie (Vom Ereignis)* (GA65), and *Besinnung* (GA66).

12. *Seminare* (GA15), pp. 204, 205. "HEIDEGGER: Im Französischen wird Dasein mit être-là übersetzt, so z. B. bei Sartre. Doch damit ist alles das, was in *Sein und Zeit*

*Dasein* means, Heidegger tells us, the standing open of humans to whatever is, *ek-stasis*. What he means, as I shall examine in much greater detail later, is that through what *Dasein* is present to, it also takes its understanding of being from, but what it is present to is not in any sense its being. The *Da* of *Dasein* does not refer to my being 'there', but the there that anything is, through whose presence I become present to myself. I am not the there of being.

This discussion in Freiburg arises out of a question about the gods: already it is concerned with our topic. Fink notes that "the gods understand their blessedness of being in the ricochet back of the frailty of mortals".[13] It is at *this* point that Heidegger has opened a question of the there of *Dasein*, a point concerning the gods. The gods become intelligible at the point where they take their blessed-being from mortals, which is the same as saying that when mortals attain to the understanding and being of the blessed-there of (the place occupied by) the gods, *Dasein* discovers them.[14] The *there* of this being is with the highest beings, the gods, and not any there of my embodiment—and yet my embodiment is included in this, for I can know this, as Fink points out, only through my frailty, which is another way of saying my being embodied.

What does Heidegger mean by gods here? To understand what Heidegger means by gods (in a seminar which takes as its topic the fragments of Heraclitus) it is necessary to turn to his interpretations of Aristotle, from the period immediately before the publication of *Sein und Zeit*. Heidegger opens his lectures on Plato's *Sophist* with a long excursus on Aristotle's understanding of the modes of truth. He is concerned to elaborate the relation of σοφία, 'wisdom', to φρόνησις, commonly translated as 'practical wisdom'. The term 'practical' (πρακτική) here does not have the sense we commonly give it, but rather refers to things which undergo change, τὰ πράγματα. Φρόνησις means 'practical wisdom' insofar as it

---

als neue Position gewonnen wurde, verlorengegangen. Ist der Mensch so da, wie der Stuhl? . . . das Bewußtsein ist nur möglich auf dem Grunde des Da als ein von ihm abgeleiteter Modus. Von hier aus muß man den geschichtlichen Schritt verstehen, der in *Sein und Zeit* mit dem Ansatz beim Dasein gegenüber dem Bewußtsein gemacht ist." Cf. Beaufret, "En chemin avec Heidegger," p. 212, where several of these points are repeated, almost word for word.

13. *Seminare* (GA15), p. 201. "Die Götter verstehen ihr seliges Sein in der Rückbetroffenheit von der Hinfälligkeit der Sterblichen."

14. *Seminare* (GA15), p. 202. "FINK: Die Götter können ihr Sein nur haben, sofern sie offenständig sind für die Sterblichen."

concerns matters and affairs that undergo change and through whose handling of them a human being becomes transparent to him- or herself and takes him- or herself in hand. Σοφία, on the other hand, refers to θεωρεῖν, to pure contemplation, not of the things that change—of matters of everyday life—but of the ἀεί, 'the always', the things that always remain the same. Heidegger notes that "the *Dasein* of human being is not ἀεί, not always; the being of humans arises and passes, it has its determinate time, its αἰών".[15]

Heidegger argues that for Aristotle σοφία takes precedence and is understood as higher than φρόνησις in relation to truth and to νοῦς because of the way in which the Greeks understand being. Heidegger uses the example of a doctor, who may restore himself to health. This taking oneself in hand and restoring oneself is φρόνησις. However, for the Greek outlook, simply to be healthy is higher than making oneself grow into health—knowing what health is in itself is given in θεωρεῖν, contemplating it through presence to it. He concludes "θεωρεῖν *is a way of being in which a human attains his or her highest way of being: his or her own spiritual health*".[16] What does 'highest being' mean here? He argues that for Aristotle, "human *Dasein* comes into its own only if it *always is what it can be in the highest sense,* that is, when it remains in the highest measure, as long as possible, and most nearly always, in the pure pondering of the beings that are always".[17]

This highest being, however, means for Aristotle being divine. Already in the lectures I have been quoting, Heidegger had pointed out that σοφία was taken to be divine. He mentions Aristotle's citation of poetry from Book I of the *Metaphysics* that says that the gods are jealous of humans who strive for θεωρεῖν, pointing to how Aristotle rejects this poetic view. Aristotle, says Heidegger, rejects the view that the gods can be jealous because to be in the mode of existence of the divine is to reject all affects, all possibility of being. Aristotle, he says, cautiously advances the view that perhaps a god would most of all have σοφία and therefore that σοφία is an attribute of

---

15. *Platon: Sophistes* (GA19), p. 137. "Das Dasein des Menschen ist nicht ἀεί, nicht immer; das Sein des Menschen entsteht und vergeht, es hat seine bestimmte Zeit, seinen αἰών."

16. *Platon: Sophistes* (GA19), p. 170. "*Das* θεωρεῖν *ist eine Seinsart, in der der Mensch seine höchste Seinsart hat: sein eigentliches geistiges Gesundsein*" (author's italics).

17. *Platon: Sophistes* (GA19), p. 171. "Das menschliche Dasein ist dann eigentlich, wenn es *immer so ist, wie es in höchstem Sinne sein kann,* wenn es sich also in höchstem Maße, möglichst lange und immer, im reinen Betrachten des Immerseienden aufhält" (author's italics).

divinity, or as Aristotle argues in the *Nicomachean Ethics* "the object of σοφία is a θεῖον, a being-always".[18] What Heidegger shows is how the Greek conception of being indicates how *Dasein*'s highest possibility is understood through divinity. He summarizes this in the following way:

> Therein lies *the accommodation of human Dasein's own characteristic tendency of its being-timely to the world as the being-always*. This abiding with the eternal, θεωρεῖν, is not anyhow or for a while, but it should remain unbroken throughout the whole length of life. Therein occurs for humanity a certain possibility of ἀθανατίζειν [being-without-death], a way of being for humans in which they have the highest possibility of not coming to an end. This is the extreme position to which the Greeks carried human *Dasein*.[19]

Heidegger analyzes the highest being of human being as being-godly; indeed, he notes that Aristotle is not tempted to side with the poets cited in the *Metaphysics* in order to strip away the mythology of godishness, so that what we are left to understand are pure possible structures of *Dasein*. And yet Heidegger draws attention to the caution Aristotle exercises. For surely the way into this highest possibility of being is not easy, else why would the gods be jealous of it? Might not the poet be better placed to make progress on the way in to θεωρεῖν than the brash philosopher? Surely it is with this Aristotelian caution that Heidegger himself proceeded into the realm opened up by Hölderlin.[20] Moreover, if in *Sein und Zeit* being-toward-death takes a central place, is it not possible to see that even this question of the

---

18. *Platon: Sophistes* (GA19), p. 133. "Der Gegenstand der σοφία [ist] ein Immersein, θεῖον."

19. *Platon: Sophistes* (GA19), p. 177f. "Darin liegt *die eigentümliche Tendenz der Anmessung des menschlichen Daseins hinsichtlich seines Zeitlichseins an das Immersein der Welt.* Dieses sich Aufhalten beim Immersein, das θεωρεῖν, soll nicht beliebig, zuweilen sein, sondern es soll ununterbrochen durch die Dauer des Lebens sich durchhalten. Darin besteht für den Menschen eine gewisse Möglichkeit des ἀθανατίζειν, eine Seinsart des Menschen, in der er die höchste Möglichkeit hat, nicht zu Ende zu gehen. Das ist die äußerste Position, auf die das menschliche Dasein durch die Griechen getragen wurde" (author's italics).

20. See, in particular, Heidegger's two lecture courses on Hölderlin: *Hölderlins Hymne 'Andenken'* (GA52), and *Hölderlins Hymne 'Der Ister'* (GA53). See esp. §43 of *Hölderlins Hymne 'Andenken'* with its comparison of Greek and German as banks of the same historical river.

place of death in Heidegger's thought already refers itself to divinity, because Heidegger is in such close conversation with Aristotle?

The understanding of the world as eternal and the concern that σοφία has with the ἀεί, the things that are always the same, indicates that the Greeks had no concern with origins and movement for its own sake in beings.[21] If the philosopher is not concerned with how human being comes into being, then, Heidegger argues, this means that what philosophy considers in itself (that is, as its very matter) delivers no broader meaning for human existence. It is for this reason that for Aristotle, the gods have nothing to do with human *Dasein*. What the gods make available to *Dasein* is not human self-concern but the abandonment of every changeable human concern for the sake of the ἀεί, the things which *of their very essence* could not be human, because they never change—they are always the same. It is for this reason, Heidegger says, "that Aristotle couldn't be further removed from a religious worldview or anything like it".[22] He emphasizes this by saying that "if Aristotle characterizes σοφία as a θεῖον, this occurs as a purely *ontological* intention: metaphysics is not theology".[23] Here theology is clearly intended to be taken in its modern sense, as a concern of faith. This means that when we discover the term θεολογική in Aristotle it has precisely and only an ontological determination.[24] As a purely ontological determination it is ordered to the science that considers beings *as* being (ὄν ᾗ ὄν), first philosophy (πρώτη φιλοσοφία), which is at the same time theology (θεολογια).[25]

Each of these two determinations, what later comes to be known as ontology, and theology as it is named by Aristotle, take the whole of beings as their theme and form the science of being. Each is a particular way of being ordered to the whole. A note Heidegger added to the manuscript of

21. Cf. *Platon: Sophistes* (GA19), p. 167. "Σοπία *is indeed autonomous, but what is thematic in it is the* ἀεί, hence that which has nothing to do with γένεσις, whereas the being of human *Dasein* intrinsically involves γένεσις, πρᾶξις, κίνησις" (author's italics). ("*Die* σοφία *ist zwar eigenständig, aber das, was bei ihr im Thema steht, ist das* ἀεί, also das, was überhaupt nichts mit der γένεσις zu tun hat, während doch das menschliche Dasein sein Sein darin hat, γένεσις, πρᾶξις, κίνησις zu sein.")

22. *Platon: Sophistes* (GA19), p. 168. ". . . daß Aristoteles von nichts weiter entfernt ist als von einer religiösen Weltanschauung oder dergleichen."

23. *Platon: Sophistes* (GA19), p. 134. "Wenn Aristoteles die σοφία als ein θεῖον kennzeichnet, so geschieht das in rein *ontologischer* Abzweckung; die Metaphysik ist nicht Theologie" (author's italics).

24. Cf. Aristotle, *Metaphysics:* VI, 1 (1026a20 f.); XI, VII (1064a41).

25. *Platon: Sophistes* (GA19), p. 221.

this lecture course, reproduced in the *Gesamtausgabe* edition, says that first philosophy and theology correspond to his own delimitation of 'beings as a whole' (*Seiendes im Ganzen*) and 'beings as such' (*Seiendes als solches*).[26] Heidegger is also making a distinction between theology as reflection on Christian faith and theology as part of the philosophical science of being. Heidegger points out that this distinction is maintained right up until the Middle Ages and beyond. Indeed, the distinction can be found in Aquinas, with an allusion to Book VI of Aristotle's *Metaphysics*.[27] Aquinas elsewhere distinguishes between God known through natural reason and how God is known as Trinity, within God's self.[28]

Have we not, therefore, answered the question which this book attempts to thematize in its entirety at the very outset? Will it not be sufficient to say that Heidegger interpreted Aristotle in particular and the Greek conception of being in general, by an appeal to the gods as thematic representations of highest being, and therefore simply as a structure of *Dasein*? Does Heidegger's atheism, therefore, not simply operate as something like the demythologizing of his friend Bultmann, applied to the history of ontology instead of the history of the construction and reception of the New Testament? Although the gods are nothing human, they belong to *Dasein* as the possibility of *Dasein*'s utmost 'ek-stasis', standing out of itself, that means that the gods (for the Greeks at least) are worked out through an orientation toward the world. What is at issue in these lectures on Aristotle in the winter of 1924–25 is only a preliminary clarification, indicating the working out of a fundamental position that was to remain with Heidegger's thinking to the end (as his remarks over forty years later in discussion with Eugen Fink clearly demonstrate).

What of the God of faith? How did it come to be that the God of faith was taken to be included in the structures of being-human, which is to ask, how does the religious worldview to which Heidegger refers arise, and what does it intend? In fact, for Heidegger, even the medieval synthesis of theology

---

26. *Platon: Sophistes* (GA19), p. 223, n. 3.
27. Aquinas, *Summa Theologiae*, Ia, q. 1, a. 1, resp. ad 2. "Hence theology included in sacred doctrine differs in kind from that theology which is part of philosophy." ("Unde theologia quae ad sacram doctrinam pertinet, differt secundum genus ab illa theologia quae pars philosophiae ponitur.")
28. Aquinas, *Quaestiones Disputatae: de Veritate*, q. 10, a. 13. The title of the article is: "Whether the the Trinity of persons can be known by natural reason". ("Utrum per naturalem rationem possit cognosci trinitas personarum.")

in its two provinces, as a natural knowledge of God and as a knowledge of faith, is itself a distortion of the Greek understanding of being. The natural understanding of God is itself not just a Christian but a Christianizing interpretation, which while claiming to belong to the realm of philosophy and metaphysics in fact relies on an understanding of the cosmos's being-caused and so having an origin in God. In fact the very arising of such a view is the mark of Christianity's attempt to reconcile itself with the ancient cosmologies and so demonstrate its rationality and consonance with non-Christian wisdom. At the heart of this consonance is the tension between the ancient understanding of eternity of the world and the Christian notion of its having been brought into being by God. The Christian conception of creation de-divinizes the cosmos, which means that the way in which *Dasein* stands out toward τό θεῖον and experiences divinity changes profoundly.

'Natural' now comes to mean, not Greek φύσις, but what of God is to be known or deduced prior to faith. This understanding was above all taken up by Descartes, Leibniz, and Kant, in unfolding the history of being, so that the original separation of theology (understood as *sacra doctrina* and reflection on faith) and philosophy that is a feature of thinking in the Middle Ages is reconfigured as a unity which nevertheless moves entirely in the province of metaphysics: faith is now subsumed under philosophy, but philosophy is now infected with faith.

The atheism which Heidegger announces is therefore a purging of these understandings of God from philosophy. Is there, therefore, some pure understanding of being to which Heidegger seeks return? Surely, rather, Heidegger's atheism is an attempt to show the genealogy of thinking itself, unfolding as it does through successive encounters with God. Atheism in this sense means bringing these encounters into relief. This does not mean, as I shall show, that there is no room in *Dasein*'s self-conspection for faith, rather, that faith must be faith in something of my own.

What for Heidegger is the effect of the transformation of the Greek understanding of being to the medieval and the modern periods? Heidegger unfolds these transitions in outline through his reading of Anselm's supposed ontological proof for the existence of God in the 1927 lecture course later published as *The Basic Problems of Phenomenology*.[29] Here we have a

---

29. *Die Grundprobleme der Phänomenologie* (GA24). This was one of the few volumes of the *Gesamtausgabe* to have been edited and planned with Heidegger's explicit cooperation and was published in the year before his death.

clear statement of the meaning of Heidegger's atheism: "It is not the question of the proofs of God's existence here that interests us, but the problem
of the interpretation of being".[30] It is impossible to unfold the interpretation
of being at work here without reference to God, but it is not God that is at
issue here. God, insofar as God is discussed at all, acts as a marker for particular interpretations of being. As I shall demonstrate in the later chapters
of this book, it is only when philosophy itself addresses the place of God in
its interpretation of being, which means it is only when Nietzsche and to a
lesser extent Hegel each proclaim that God is dead, that the question of God
can emerge at all. Unless we have prepared ourselves adequately by understanding what in *philosophy* is intended by atheism, we will be unprepared
for the meaning of the phrase God is dead.

What Heidegger demonstrates in analyzing Kant's critique of the ontological proof is that his assertion that being is not a real predicate works
through the distinction established in medieval theology between the real
and the actual, between essence and existence. Heidegger argues that for
Kant, to say that something is real means that it is possible and not that it
is necessarily extant, so that the term corresponds to the medieval *essentia*.
The proof fails because being is not (in these terms) a real predicate but
would have to refer to something actual to be a proof. Something possible
(in Kant's sense of real) need not exist: existence would have to be added to
it for it in fact to be actual and so extant. To take a thing, say God, with all its
real predicates (which might include omnipotence, omniscience, and the
like), and say that it exists is to argue nothing about the thing itself, which
would have its predicates whether it existed or not (just in order for it to be
a concept). By asserting that it exists, I add nothing to it in and of itself (as
a concept) but express only its relation to me. To co-posit the self alongside
the thing in positing its actuality is, as Heidegger quotes Kant as saying, "nothing but a miserable tautology".[31] This is a different order of assertion to that
of predication. Heidegger says that for Kant "what is posited in existential-
asserting and is added to bare representation, to the concept, is 'a relation
of the actual thing to myself'."[32] The conclusion which Heidegger implies

30. *Grundprobleme* (GA24), p. 58. "Uns interessiert hier nicht die Frage der
Gottesbeweise, sondern das Problem der Interpretation des Seins."
31. *Grundprobleme* (GA24), p. 56. "[ist] nichts als eine elende Tautologie."
32. *Grundprobleme* (GA24), p. 54. "Das, was gesetzt wird in der Existenz-Aussage
und was hinzugesetzt wird zur bloßen Vorstellung, zum Begriff, ist 'ein Bezug des wirklichen Dinges zu mir selbst'."

but does not draw out is that the primary referent of existential assertion is to myself and not to what is asserted. Thus saying God exists or God does not exist does not refer to God at all but to myself and the interpretation of being which is operative as the basis of what(ever) I say.

Having demonstrated how this kind of speaking about God is actually determined out of an interpretation of being, Heidegger then proceeds to demonstrate what interpretation of being is operative within it. The distinction between essence, quiddity, or whatness, of a thing and existence (*that* it is), emerges from the medieval appropriation of the Greek understanding of being. Heidegger demonstrates this by reference to its most extreme appearance in the mystical theology of Eckhart: "It is characteristic of medieval mysticism that it seeks to fasten on God, ontologically posited as its own proper essential being, God, in God's very essence". This is a transformation of the meaning of essence, because, instead of essence being an ontological determination *of* a being, it itself becomes understood as itself *a* being. Heidegger says that for Eckhart, what interests him most is "not actually God—God is for him a provisional object—but divinity".[33] Heidegger cites Eckhart's expression "if it were said of God that God is, that would be added on"[34] to show how existence cannot be added to God, since this would add myself to God. God is, in this sense, simultaneously strictly speaking nothing at all and the most universal being. This position is entirely in virtue of God understood as the origin of being, as creator, and as the one to whom being, strictly speaking, is alone reserved. It is for this reason that God's unknownness to human being is thematized metaphysically by Aquinas as God's simultaneous transparency to God's self: God alone knows God.

Heidegger's question here—a question that concerns being and not God—is how do the terms 'quiddity' (medieval *essentia*) and 'existence' (*existentia*) become constitutive for the interpretation of being in the West, both during and after the Middle Ages? He says that the way we understand the relation can be explained through the relation between the Greek terms μορφή and εἶδος, shape and form. In understanding the meaning of the

---

33. *Grundprobleme* (GA24), p. 127. "Es ist das Charakteristische der *mittelalterlichen Mystik*, daß sie versucht, das ontologisch als das eigentliche Wesen angesetzte Seiende, Gott, in seiner Wesenheit selbst zu fassen ... d.h. ihn interessiert nicht eigentlich Gott— Gott ist für ihn noch ein vorläufiger Gegenstand—, sondern die Gottheit."

34. *Grundprobleme* (GA24), p. 128. Quoting Eckhart: "Spräche man von Gott er ist, das wäre hinzugelegt".

term εἶδος, however, Heidegger is always careful to draw attention to the fact that εἶδος does not mean form, but the look that a thing has.[35] In normal perception, the appearance or look that something has is understood to be grounded in its form. The shape it has gives it its look. Heidegger argues that "for *Greek ontology*, however, the founding connection between εἶδος and μορφή, appearance and form, is exactly the reverse: the appearance is not grounded in the form, but the form, the μορφή, is grounded in the appearance.[36] Heidegger concludes that this can only be understood through the mode of production: what is formed is a product. The potter, he says, forms a vase out of clay. All such forming and producing of things use an image as the guide against which a thing is produced. The guiding image is the image that exists before the thing is formed, so that the thing is *con-formed* to its prior image: "The thing is produced by looking to the anticipated look of what is to be produced by shaping, forming. It is this anticipated look of the thing, sighted beforehand, that the Greeks mean ontologically by εἶδος, ἰδέα".[37] The εἶδος can therefore be interpreted as both idea and form because in modern interpretation of Greek ontology we take it for granted that the preexistent idea of a thing is also its form. For the Greeks, however, a thing is produced according to the idea which exists for it in advance of itself, in advance of its actualization.

What is the mark of this shift whereby we now presume the appearance of a thing to spring from its shape or form? The medieval understanding of perception that is exemplified in Aquinas in fact attempts to conform itself to what Heidegger names as Greek ontology in its structure, with one important difference. For Aristotle (and Plato, for both are here intended by Heidegger's references to the Greeks), any given *Dasein* or human being produces the knowing (and therefore being) of a thing through having regard to the

---

35. For a fuller discussion of why Heidegger interprets εἶδος in this way, see Heidegger, *Platons Lehre von der Wahrheit* in *Wegmarken* (GA9), esp. p. 214. Εἶδος and μορφή are routinely translated with the same term, form, in the overwhelming majority of English renderings of Aristotle's and Plato's texts.
36. *Grundprobleme* (GA24), p. 149. "Für die *griechische Ontologie* aber ist der Fundierungszusammenhang zwischen εἶδος und μορφή, Aussehen und Gepräge, gerade umgekehrt: nicht das Aussehen gründet im Gepräge, sondern das Gepräge, die μορφή, gründet im Aussehen" (author's italics).
37. *Grundprobleme* (GA24), p. 150. "Alles Bilden von Gebilden vollzieht sich am Leitfaden und am Richtmaß eines Bildes im Sinne des Vorbildes. Im Hinsehen auf das vorweggenommene Aussehen des Dinges ist es, was die Griechen mit εἶδος, ἰδέα, ontologisch meinen."

anticipated look of a thing. For Aquinas, however, the prior cause of the being of all things is given by God, not any human intelligence. To God alone is reserved the prior ideas of all things, because God, as creator, is the producer of all that is. Aquinas says "the ideas existing in the divine mind are neither generated nor generating, but in the sense of the word [ideas], are the creation or production of things".[38] In consequence of this, the perceiving creature receives the look that God anticipates for the thing through the form that God has given it. The anticipated idea, prior in God, is now only subsequently in the creature. Moreover, insofar as the subsequent look received by the creature is identical with the prior anticipated idea intended for the thing in its form, the knowledge that the creature has of the thing is true. So Aquinas says:

> A natural thing stationed between two intellects is said to be true inso-
> far as it conforms to each. It is said to be true in conformity to the divine
> intellect insofar as it fulfills that to which it is ordered by the divine
> intellect . . . according to its conformity to a human intellect insofar as it
> gives rise to a true estimate of itself.[39]

Precisely that power of anticipation in production ascribed by Heidegger to the potter, Greek τέχνη, is ascribed by Aquinas to the divine intellect in the whole order of nature. Humanity only has this prior productive power insofar as it makes artifacts. Indeed, for Aquinas this is the entire basis for how we might have knowledge of God naturally and not through faith.

The mark of the shift from the ancient ontology to an ontology which distinguishes between the essence and the existence of a thing is therefore to be found in the natural articulation of God. By showing how the ontology that Kant and Descartes take up has already been unfolded through a distinction made in medieval philosophy that itself reconfigured the ancient ontology, Heidegger traces the genealogy of how God has been thought. However, the genealogy that he traces turns out to be the genealogy of the

---

38. Aquinas, *Quaestiones Disputatae: de Veritate*, q. 3, a. 1, ad 5. "Quod ideae existentes in mente divina non sunt generatae, nec sunt generantes, si fiat vis in verbo; sed sunt creativae et productivae rerum." See also q. 10, a. 4, resp.

39. Aquinas, *Quaestiones Disputatae: de Veritate*, q. 1, a. 2, resp. "Res ergo naturalis inter duos intellectus constituta, secundum adaequationem ad utrumque vera dicitur; secundum enim adaequationem ad intellectum divinum dicitur vera, in quantum implet hoc ad quod est ordinata per intellectum divnum . . . secundum autem adaequationem ad intellectum humanum dicitur res vera, in quantum nata est de se formare veram aestimationem."

question about being, since it should be clear that if Aquinas in particular has projected the ancient understanding of human being onto the divine, then the supposed natural articulation of the divine turns out to be a transformation of the ancient articulation of what it means to be human. This genealogy comes to light in virtue of Heidegger's question about being. More clearly put, Heidegger's question of being will have an outcome for any understanding of God. This outcome, for Heidegger, however, is always negative, in that he refuses to investigate any positive meaning of God for the sake of the question of being.

Through this preliminary investigation into Heidegger's understanding of the ancient ontology and its relation to medieval and modern conceptions of being, it has been possible to give an outline of what Heidegger understands by atheism and why he appears both to be silent and to speak constantly of God. Indeed, it should be clear in a preliminary way what Heidegger means by atheism. In explaining what this book is about, therefore, it should be clear that in this negative investigation into God, a place remains for the God of faith. This place only opens out, however, in unfolding what it is that Heidegger is asking *about* when he asks the question of being. The argument of this book is therefore very simple. The place that Heidegger reserves for faith answers the question about God, but to understand this place requires simultaneously asking the question he asked: the question of being. The place Heidegger holds open, he holds open for anyone who follows the path he has opened up. To have filled this place himself, however, would have been to close off the possibility of following him down the path he opens.

## Heidegger's God

In being concerned with Heidegger's atheism, surely I must also be concerned with Heidegger's understanding of God. In fact this text will only tangentially deal with the question of God for Heidegger—indeed it decidedly overlooks the understanding of the holy that Heidegger develops, particularly in relation to Hölderlin. In his analysis of the two poems "Der Ister" and "Andenken" Heidegger explains how the gods of themselves "persisting in their essence, are incapable of comporting themselves toward beings".[40]

---

40. *Hölderlins Hymne 'Der Ister'* (GA53), p. 194. "In ihrem eigenen Wesen beharrend, vermögen sie nie zum Seienden sich zu verhalten."

In order for the gods to so comport themselves and for the heavenly ones both to achieve unity and to be disclosed in relation to beings, the gods must be related "to the 'holy' that is 'beyond' them".[41] The 'holy' is the relation of the gods to beings, but through an other, who as the place of the holy, takes up this relation between human beings and the gods, unequal to either of them. Insofar as this other one is not equal either to gods or humanity, it is not Christ, who is the identity of both, and so this understanding is not a Christian understanding. Nor should it be: this does not make a pagan out of Heidegger, but rather is his unfolding of the holy within the thinking of the Greeks, even when it relates to Hölderlin and to German myth. Heidegger understands the holy in Western thinking to move in a province thought essentially by the Greeks, even when articulated by others.

Heidegger's atheism, on the contrary, is an explicitly Christian affair, and it is for this reason that I concern myself primarily with Heidegger's relation to the Christian tradition. Does Heidegger therefore refuse the Christian God? Or rather, does he refuse the way the Christian God has been woven into human thinking? Is his atheism not precisely *this* refusal? He tells us that "the whole situation of modern metaphysics" arises out of "the Christian representation of beings as *ens creatum* and the fundamental mathematical character (of thinking about beings)".[42] Irrespective of the assumed atheism of modern science, this is exactly the universe as both Newton and Descartes conceive it, an intensification of the medieval insistence of the origins of the cosmos in God. He adds: "Nature, or the cosmos have, since the rulership of Christendom in the West, been considered as created, not only in the Middle Ages, also through the whole of modern philosophy. Modern metaphysics from Descartes to Kant, and also the metaphysics of German Idealism after Kant, is unthinkable without basic Christian conceptions".[43] Yet these Christian conceptions do not escape the force of the fundamentally mathematical character of modern thinking. Heidegger concludes:

---

41. *Hölderlins Hymne 'Der Ister'* (GA53), p. 194. "Zum 'Heiligen', das 'über' ihnen ist."

42. *Die Frage nach dem Ding* (GA41), p. 85. "Der ganze Sachverhalt der neuzeitlichen Metaphysik . . . 1. die christliche Vorstellung vom Seienden als dem ens creatum; 2. der mathematische Grundzug."

43. *Die Frage nach dem Ding* (GA41), p. 84. "Die Natur oder der Kosmos gelten aber seit der Herrschaft des Christentums im Abendland als das Geschaffene, nicht nur im Mittelalter, sondern auch durch die ganze neuzeitliche Philosophie hindurch. Die neuzeitliche Metaphysik seit Descartes bis zu Kant, und über Kant hinaus auch die Metaphysik des Deutschen Idealismus, ist ohne christlichen Grundvorstellungen nicht zu denken."

God as creator, the world as created, humanity and its eternal salvation—
are the three domains defined by Christian thought within beings as a
whole. Since metaphysics asks about beings as a whole, in that it is and
why it is, metaphysics properly, understood as Christian, is concerned
with God (theology), the word (cosmology), and humanity and the salvation of souls (psychology). But, in accord with the fundamental mathematical character of modern thinking, metaphysics is also formed out of
the basic principles of pure reason, *ratio*. Thus, the metaphysical doctrine
of God becomes a theology, but a *theologia rationalis*, the doctrine of the
world becomes cosmology, but a *cosmologia rationalis*, the doctrine of
humanity, psychology, but a *psychologia rationalis*.[44]

This intensification of the presence of Christian ideas at the same time as
the mathematical redetermination of what beings are is itself the turning-
about, *Umwendung*, from "the earlier knowledge of nature to modern thinking".[45] The importance of this turn-about will become clear in chapters 3
and 4, but already it is possible to see how closely related all Heidegger's
later talk of the turn and the talk about Heidegger's turns will be to his atheism and his relation to Christianity. This reconfiguration is a process that
is in consequence of Christianity, though as Heidegger himself held, with
disastrous consequences for faith. For this reason I am concerned with
Heidegger's atheism as a primarily Christian question.

For Heidegger, the atheism he was proposing was a way into faith;
indeed, in early lectures from 1921 he expressly says so, and there is no
reason to think that he deviated later from this view. If, on the one hand,

---

44. *Die Frage nach dem Ding* (GA41), p. 85. "Gott als der Schöpfer, die Welt des
Geschaffenen, der Mensch und sein ewiges Heil, sind die drei aus dem christlichen
Denken her bestimmten Bereiche innerhalb des Seienden im Ganzen. Da die Metaphysik
nach dem Seienden im Ganzen fragt, was es sei und warum es so sei, wie es ist, handelt die
eigentliche Metaphysik—christliche verstanden—von Gott (Theologie), von der Welt
(Kosmologie), vom Menschen und seinem Seelenheil (Psychologie). Sofern nun gemäß
dem mathematischen Grundzug des neuzeitlichen Denkens auch die Metaphysik aus den
Grundsätzen der bloßen Vernunft, der ratio, sich gestaltet, wird die metaphysische Lehre
von Gott eine Theologie, aber eine theologia rationalis, wird die Lehre von der Welt
Kosmologie, aber eine cosmologia rationalis, wird die Lehre vom Menschen Psychologie,
aber eine psychologia rationalis."

45. *Die Frage nach dem Ding* (GA41), p. 84. "[Die] Umwendung des früheren
Wissens von der Natur zum neuzeitlichen Denken."

philosophy must in its very radical questioning character be atheistic,[46] on the other hand "I do not comport myself religiously in philosophizing, even if I can as a philosopher be a religious man".[47] Is Heidegger's atheism simply concerned with a personal view, privately held, outside the public sphere of (philosophical) debate—the very atheism that becomes possible after Newton, Descartes, and Kant—the presumed atheism of modern science? Or is it rather that philosophy, because it is concerned with being and the being of beings, can say nothing of God, and so part of the task of philosophy—why Heidegger's atheism is so much a concern with the Christian God and that God's entanglements with metaphysics—is to undertake the disentanglement, so that a more genuine philosophy, a concern again with the question of nature, can appear? This would allow a more genuine attunement to the question of God, while saying nothing of God. It would be to discover the meaning of the flight of the gods and the last god which preoccupies Heidegger in the *Beiträge zur Philosophie*, the central work of the 1930s.

Early on in the *Beiträge* Heidegger says that "the flight of the gods must be experienced and endured".[48] Such an endurance and experience prepare for the nearness of the last god, against the "prolonged Christianizing of god"[49] so that "the nearness to the last god is the keeping of silence. This must be set into work and word in the style of reservedness".[50] Heidegger's atheism is therefore in play with his understanding of God but in ways that are not immediately evident—indeed a certain reserve, a certain invisibility and silence is of the very essence of their being in play. This silence has perplexed some readers. George Kovacs, in considering the question of God in Heidegger's work, speaks of "thinking becoming free for God", and adds: "Whatever the final status of this 'being free for God' may be, it is quite

---

46. Cf. Heidegger's restatement of this in *Phänomenologische Interpretationen zu Aristoteles* (GA61), p. 197. "Philosophy must in its radical, in-and-of-itself principles of questionability be *atheistic*" (author's italics). ("Philosophie muß in ihrer radikalen, sich auf sich selbst stellenden Fraglichkeit prinzipiell *a-theistisch* sein.")

47. *Phänomenologische Interpretationen zu Aristoteles* (GA61), p. 197. "Ich verhalte mich nicht religiös im Philosophieren, wenn ich auch als Philosoph ein religiöser Mensch sein kann."

48. *Beiträge zur Philosophie* (GA65), p. 27. "Die Flucht der Götter muß erfahren und ausgestanden werden."

49. *Beiträge zur Philosophie* (GA65), p. 24. "Die lange Verchristlichung des Gottes."

50. *Beiträge zur Philosophie* (GA65), p. 12. "Die Nähe zum letzten Gott ist die Verschweigung. Diese muß im Stil der Verhaltenheit ins Werk und Wort gesetzt werden."

puzzling though not incompatible with [his] 'methodological atheism'".[51] I want to go much further than this: the question is not one of compatibility; rather, the methodological atheism, which in the modern period especially is the systematic concern with the way in which philosophy has become entwined with Christianity, actually allows the question of God to reappear. For the Christian theologian the meaning is complex but no less urgent. Precisely the exposure of the extent to which this Christianizing has occurred re-releases the theologian for a concern with matters of faith, with faith in Christ himself. There is nothing anti-Christian in this thought; indeed, it shows how much this atheism is an almost entirely Christian affair.

This book is therefore unconcerned, directly, with Heidegger's God, or rather, it serves to point toward a concern with God for Heidegger, for me, and for theologians more generally. In the matter of God, Heidegger asks us to hold ourselves in reserve, to be drawn in the direction of keeping silence. Is not God in God's very self kept in silence?

## CHRISTIANITY'S PAST CONCERN WITH HEIDEGGER

What of the successive taking up of Heidegger by theologians—Rudolf Bultmann, Karl Rahner, Heinrich Ott, and to a lesser extent Paul Tillich? There has been a long-standing intuition that Heidegger's researches must have a profound impact on the question of God as far as it is taken up in theology as a formal discipline. In fact theological appropriations of Heidegger's work have never opened up Heidegger's thought as a question, preferring to reserve for him a place strictly as philosopher. In this sense, rather than raising Heidegger's work as a problem for theologians and for theology in general, it was assumed that an encounter with Heidegger would provide an impetus for fresh theological work.

Rudolf Bultmann's engagement with Martin Heidegger in Marburg in the years 1923–29 certainly allowed him to raise hermeneutic theology to an entirely new level. John Macquarrie describes the engagement by saying:

> The existential approach to the New Testament lays bare not another philosophy of existence but a kerygma, the proclamation of God's saving acts in Christ. This kerygma is entirely different from a philosophy.

---

51. Kovacs, G., *The Question of God in Heidegger's Phenomenology* (1990), p. 202.

The existentialist philosopher may know that man's existence is a fallen one, he may even be able to conceive of an authentic existence, but it is the New Testament which knows of God's gracious act which can lift men out of their fallen state, and of the divine love which can empower men to love. Theology cannot be absorbed into philosophy because it knows and proclaims what God has done about that human situation which philosophy can only analyze. Thus Bultmann draws the dividing line between theology and philosophy, and sets an immense distance between them.[52]

Anthony Thiselton, who provides perhaps the best English-language explication of Heidegger's influence on Bultmann, quotes the latter as saying: "I learned from (Heidegger) not *what* theology has to say but *how* it has to say it".[53] Thiselton describes in some detail how Bultmann took over the language of Heidegger's *Sein und Zeit* to the point where "Heidegger's role is to offer a conceptuality which seems almost to have been designed to achieve the very task with which Bultmann was already grappling".[54] Commentators whose verdict on Bultmann has been negative have remained neutral when indicating Heidegger's influence, reserving their criticism for the theologian alone.[55] Bultmann is not actively involved in unfolding the question with which Heidegger is engaged; rather, he is dependent on Heidegger's results. If Bultmann says in different places that "in speaking of God, theology must at the same time speak of man" and "every assertion about God is simultaneously an assertion about man and vice versa", he intends these as statements as strictly preparatory to understanding the hermeneutical possibilities of being addressed kerygmatically by preaching in the name of Jesus (both in the New Testament and in a modern situation) and not in Heidegger's sense of how being human is thrown into question by asking the question of being.[56] In

52. Macquarrie, J., "Philosophy and Theology in Bultmann's Thought" (1966), p. 131. Macquarrie carries out a far more extensive survey of the relationship between Heidegger and Bultmann in *An Existentialist Theology: A Comparison of Heidegger and Bultmann* (1955).

53. Thiselton, A., *The Two Horizons* (1980), p. 28, citing Bultmann's "Reply" in Kegley, C. W., *The Theology of Rudolf Bultmann* (1966), p. 276 (author's italics).

54. Thiselton, A., *The Two Horizons* (1980), p. 232.

55. Cf. for instance Bockmühl, K., *The Unreal God of Modern Theology* (1988). Bockmühl, while accusing Bultmann of laying the foundation for Christian atheism, cites Heidegger only in passing.

56. Cited by Thiselton, A., *The Two Horizons* (1980), p. 39.

other words, the problem here is one of interpretation of the kerygma and not of the self-interpretation of being-interpretative, which, as I shall consider, might function as a way of understanding what Heidegger means by *Dasein* and as a way of thinking about the hermeneutic circle. Rather, Bultmann's setting apart of theology and philosophy does not ask how they belong together but takes this being set apart as given, confirmed in every sense by the philosopher to whom he makes appeal.

In recalling Bultmann's comment that it was *how* and not *what* that is at stake in his appropriation of Heidegger's thought, the question is left open as to the *how* in which *Dasein* knows that it is by God that *Dasein* is kerygmatically addressed. In this sense the question about *what* comes once again to the fore, because the mode, character, and content are constitutive of *Dasein* itself. For Bultmann, *Dasein* is never thrown ontologically into question by the address of God; he appears to rest content that God (and Heidegger) knows already who *Dasein* is. Bultmann therefore never opens up the deeper and harder question of why I might just take it for granted that God knows whom it is that God will address. Such an assumption takes away every power the address has that it might in its very addressing, its essence, constitute the one to whom it speaks. This is the gratuity of address. For Heidegger, who *Dasein* 'is' is more disclosed in all being-addressed than in what any *Dasein* has to say of itself.

If Bultmann's engagement with Heidegger exemplifies one way in which theologians have made appeal to his work, Karl Rahner's has been of quite a different order. Rahner said of Heidegger: "I might very simply and modestly acknowledge that although I had many good professors in the classroom, there is only *one* whom I can revere as my *teacher*, and he is Martin Heidegger".[57] There have been several scholarly attempts to analyze the relationship between Rahner's and Heidegger's thought;[58] however, each in differing ways make a common point, well summed up by Jack Bonsor:

---

57. Imhof, P., and Biallowons, H. (eds.), *Karl Rahner im Gespräch* (1983), vol. 1, p. 49. "Soll (ich) ganz einfach und schlicht dankbar bekennen, daß er zwar viele gute Schulmeister des mündlichen Wortes hatte, aber doch nur *einen*, den er als seinen *Lehrer* verehren kann, eben Martin Heidegger?" (author's italics).

58. See in English, for instance, Bonsor, J. A., *Rahner, Heidegger, and Truth* (1987); Hurd, R. L., "Heidegger and Aquinas: A Rahnerian Bridge" (1984); Masson, R., "Rahner and Heidegger: Being, Hearing, and God" (1973); Sheehan, T. J., *Rahner* (1987), especially chapters 3 and 4 and the last section; and the substantial analysis in Tallon, Andrew, "Personal Becoming: Karl Rahner's Christian Anthropology" (1979).

Rahner's interpretation of Heidegger is not seeking to restate what Heidegger explicitly held, but is seeking new possibilities within Heidegger's fundamental ontology. As a result his interpretation is not fully Heideggerian.[59]

Rahner's reluctance to engage directly with Heidegger is perhaps indicated by Johannes Metz's substantial reediting of the second (1963) edition of Rahner's *Hörer des Wortes*. This text, which at times speaks in ways remarkably reminiscent of Heidegger's lectures of the mid-1930s, contained in its original 1941 edition several references to Heidegger, in chapters 5 and 7 in particular. In Metz's edition the references disappear.[60] Rahner himself has stated on more than one occasion that while Heidegger taught him how to think, what he taught him was in some sense secondary. He goes so far as to say that

Heidegger's philosophy that was characteristic of the years 1934 to 1936 was quite distinct from his later philosophy. The Heidegger I learned was the Heidegger of *Sein und Zeit*, the Heidegger of the battle cry, perhaps just about the Heidegger of metaphysics . . . insofar as it is philosophical, my theology does not really show the systematic and thematic influence of Heidegger . . . I would say that Heidegger had little influence on my philosophy or even my theology.[61]

The question of Heidegger's influence on Rahner actually obscures the question of whether or not for Rahner what Heidegger has to say of God is raised as a problem. Rahner himself acknowledges this when he explicitly points to the difference in the ways in which he and Heidegger each speak of God. In the collection of interviews with Rahner published as *Karl Rahner im Gespräch* the

---

59. Bonsor, J. A., *Rahner, Heidegger, and Truth* (1987), p. 187, note 20.

60. Several of them are preserved in the English translation of excerpts of *Hörer des Wortes* made by Gerald McCool as the first chapter of his *A Rahner Reader* (1975).

61. Imhof, P. and Biallowons, H. (eds.), *Karl Rahner im Gespräch* (1983), vol. 2, p. 151f. "Und ich würde zweitens sagen, daß die eigentliche Philosophie Heideggers ja 1934–36 immer noch etwas ganz anderes war als der spätere Heidegger. Dieser Heidegger, den ich mitbekommen habe, das war der Heidegger von 'Sein und Zeit', war der Heidegger meinetwegen des Kampfrufs, vielleicht gerade noch der Metaphysik . . . es handelt sich sicher nicht so sehr in meiner Theologie, soweit sie philosophisch ist, um eine systematische, inhaltliche Beeinflußtheit von Heidegger . . . und insofern möchte ich sagen, daß meine Philosophie nur wenig, meine Theologie auch wenig mit Heidegger zu tun hat."

interviewer on one occasion asks whether Heidegger speaks rather of gods than God. Rahner replies: "It is all the same whether someone wants to speak as a philosopher explicitly of God or gods or of the divine or of a numinous being or anything like that . . . the theologian will appeal to Sacred Scripture as God's word; the theologian will work with an understanding of revelation".[62] In this, Rahner speaks with similar reservations to those of Bultmann— philosophy and theology stand apart, they are two enterprises separated by a gulf. Sheehan suggests: "Because Rahner, before encountering Heidegger, had already formulated his own problematic as the Scholastic issue of beingness (*esse*) in its general and its highest form, and because he already 'knew'—or at least held on faith—that the ultimate reality was God as pure self-presence, he could not accept, or perhaps even fully understand, Heidegger's position on the phenomenological 'ultimacy' of atelic movement".[63] Just what Sheehan might mean by atelic movement I will come to consider (using rather different language) later, but Rahner has in a sense decided the question of God from the vantage point of faith prior to any phenomenological inquiry, which as I shall indicate, is precisely a move Heidegger seeks to overcome, and is precisely *that move* which both would yield Rahner's understanding of *esse* as formulated in consequence of ontotheology and protects it (for faith) from the ontotheological consequences of its being subsumed under metaphysics. It is this deciding in advance that for Heidegger has already foreclosed the question of theology in relation to philosophy, already discovered them to be apart before ever asking why. In this sense, Heidegger's holding apart of philosophy and theology differs from those of his theological interlocutors in that he does not take it for granted but rather makes it the subject of genuine phenomenological inquiry. The task of philosophical atheism is just the methodological face of that inquiry in its being undertaken.

Sheehan concludes: "From the viewpoint of scholarship the issue is whether Rahner's theology of man and cognition, and his grounding of metaphysics on that base do or do not fall under Heidegger's account of ontotheology and the forgetfulness of the hiddenness of 'being'".[64] This is

62. Imhof, P. and Biallowons, H. (eds.), *Karl Rahner im Gespräch* (1983), vol. 2, p. 222 f. "Es ist gleichgültig, ob jemand als Philosoph ausdrücklich von Gott oder Göttern oder von einem Göttlichen oder von einem Numinosen oder von irgend so etwas reden will oder nicht . . . der Theologe wird sich auf die Heilige Schrift als Wort Gottes berufen; der Theologe wird mit einem Offenbarungsverständnis arbeiten."

63. Sheehan, T. J., *Rahner* (1987), p. 118.

64. Sheehan, T. J., *Rahner* (1987), p. 309 f.

precisely the same question that will reappear in inquiring into Heidegger's explication of Aquinas's understanding of *esse* and analogy. I will carry this out therefore, not as an inquiry into the relationship between Rahner and Heidegger, but rather into Heidegger's own presentation of his reading of that tradition on which Rahner also draws, which will appear precisely as placing into question the meaning of the word *esse*. In this sense, the complicating question of whether Rahner's metaphysics is more influenced by Heidegger, Maréchal, or Kant need not be raised here at all. The question is not whether, but why and how Rahner interpreted the word *esse* in a way different from Heidegger, and in this sense the answer cannot simply lie in an internal investigation of Rahner's engagement with his teacher. Rahner had noted in his only piece of writing specifically on Heidegger, that in the 1929 essay *Vom Wesen des Grundes* Heidegger argues that the necessary finitude of being is the human (understanding of) being, not being in and of itself (*esse*).[65] What I intend to show is that for Heidegger it is simply not possible ever to posit the *esse* of anything (and here, of course, I am explicitly referring to *ipsum esse*, which is understood to be God) in and of itself, even the *esse* of *esse*, or the essence of essence, but rather that in the unfolding of the *esse* of God within Christian theology it is always a question concerning salvation and not metaphysics that is at issue.

One further remark needs to be made in order to illustrate both that Rahner never in any thematic way problematizes Heidegger's position with respect to God and that Rahner himself is content to appeal to a conventional reading of Heidegger. I have already indicated that the Heidegger whom Rahner says he knows is broken out from the rest of Heidegger's work, the Heidegger of *Sein und Zeit* and of the lecture courses and seminars he attended between 1934 and 1936.[66] This is conventional enough to allude to the turn in Heidegger's work that will play so important a part in my discussion of Heidegger's atheism.

---

65. Rahner, K., *Einführung in den Begriff der Existentialphilosophie* (*Sämtliche Werke* [1996]), p. 341. This article was first published in France in 1939, and the original German appears to have been lost. In Rahner's *Sämtliche Werke* the French and a reconstructed German text lie side by side, with the German clearly marked as a "translation (*deutsche Übersetzung*)". The English text, "The Concept of Existential Philosophy in Heidegger," was translated from the French. Cf. *Vom Wesen des Grundes* in *Wegmarken* (GA9).

66. There is some evidence from Rahner's *Geist in Welt* (1957) to suggest he also had access to notes and transcripts of lecture courses that precede these years and

In addition Rahner states in 1939: "If, as some are afraid is the case, radical atheism is the last word of this anthropology, then finitude and nothingness must be the last word of its coming ontology".[67] Immediately it should be clear that Rahner is interpreting the word atheism very differently from how I have begun to suggest it needs to be taken, even before I have formally clarified in what sense Heidegger intends it. Heidegger, as we shall see, precisely associates the 'last' with God.[68] Rahner is largely content to argue that the consequences of what Heidegger might have to say of God will in turn invalidate any formal (Christian) theological project that tries to speak out of his work as such. Robert Masson interprets *Hörer des Wortes* as an "implicit refutation of Heidegger's alleged 'nihilism'", where, unlike Heidegger, Rahner wishes to assert that the meaning of being, or man's transcendence, is not nothing (*das Nichts*), but God.[69] Both Masson and Sheehan agree that Rahner misunderstood Heidegger's elaboration of the meaning of the nothing, a point apparently confirmed by Honecker's problems with the doctoral thesis that eventually became *Geist in Welt*. Masson notes that the misunderstanding leads Rahner to interpret Heidegger in such a way that "if he wanted, Heidegger could . . . advance his thought beyond fundamental ontology to the question of God—which of course is what Rahner does as a follower of Aquinas".[70] Rahner's assumption is that his question of the meaning of being, *esse*, is the same as Heidegger's. Heidegger, however, is not interested in *esse* as in consequence of God (as I have already shown in outline and argue in greater detail in what follows), but rather, insofar as there is a question to be asked about being, asking *that* question will have consequences for any talk about God.

Rahner, like Bultmann before him, never problematizes the thought of Heidegger in relation to theology as such. Rahner's appeal to Heidegger, like Bultmann's, is to the philosopher who might usefully provide clarification

---

specifically the 1929–30 course on finitude that was later published as volume 29/30 of the *Gesamtausgabe*. This is not unlikely, not least because it was commonplace among Heidegger's students to circulate more or less accurate transcripts of his earlier lectures amongst themselves: many of these transcripts have formed the basis for corrections to later published volumes of the *Gesamtausgabe*.

67. Rahner, K., *Einführung in den Begriff der Existentialphilosophie*, p. 345. "Athéisme radical, si comme il est à craindre, le dernier mot de cette anthropologie: finitude, néant, doit être aussi le dernier mot de l'ontologie à venir."

68. See pp. 266–267 below.

69. Masson, R., "Rahner and Heidegger" (1973), p. 473.

70. Masson, R., "Rahner and Heidegger" (1973), p. 487.

and a philosophical basis for further, fruitful, but strictly theological work. Heidegger's understanding of God *as such* is indeed never a thematic or systematic question for Rahner.

Heinrich Ott's discussion of Heidegger is well documented in English and has largely now faded from active consideration.[71] Although Heidegger himself seems to have approved and encouraged Ott's work to some degree,[72] criticism of it came from another quarter. Hans Jonas, participating in a conference at Drew University in 1964, specifically attacked Ott for not raising as problematic Heidegger's critique of theology. As a nontheologian, he said: "Instead of theology's finding validation or corroboration for itself in what has been borrowed from itself, the real case is that philosophy must examine the philosophical validity of Heidegger's borrowing from theology".[73] While there are significant problems with Jonas's suggestion that Heidegger hypostasizes being (in a fascinating way Jonas preempts Jean-Luc Marion's later reading of Heidegger in *Dieu sans l'être* almost to the letter and for the same reasons), Jonas is correct to indicate that Ott takes over in an unquestioning way much of Heidegger's analysis of language and being without ever opening up what Heidegger says about theology. Ott does this by restricting the limits of what can be said solely to statements of faith: "As philosophical thinking is related to being, when being speaks to thinking, so faith's thinking is related to God, when God is revealed in his word".[74] Jonas points to the fact that Ott's appropriation takes for granted that Heidegger's philosophical position can underpin a theology of faith. Jonas notes that his own investigations of Heidegger's statements (statements which Ott had used to confirm his conclusions) revealed them to be "hypothetical and for argument's sake, rather than as a statement of (Heidegger's) own position".[75] Ott's attempt to

---

71. See Robinson, J. M., and Cobb, J. B. (eds.), *The Later Heidegger and Theology* (1963), especially the section entitled "The German Discussion," and Ott's own piece in this volume entitled "What Is Systematic Theology?"; also Deely, J., "The Situation of Heidegger in the Tradition of Christian Philosophy" (1967), esp. pp. 163–168.

72. See, for instance, Heidegger's letter to Ott on the publication of *Denken und Sein: Der Weg Martin Heideggers und der Weg der Theologie* (1959), quoted in part in an English translation in Robinson, J. M., and Cobb, J. B. (eds.), *The Later Heidegger and Theology* (1963), p. 110.

73. Jonas, H., "Heidegger and Theology" (1964). The published version of the paper notes that it was delivered at Drew University in a slightly abridged form.

74. Reported by Ott in Robinson, J. M., and Cobb, J. B. (eds.), *The Later Heidegger and Theology* (1963), p. 43.

75. Jonas, H., "Heidegger and Theology" (1964), p. 222 f., note 10.

reconstruct a hermeneutics closer to Barth's than to Bultmann's does not resolve the meaning and status of faith.

As before, I am not concerned with the position which Ott is trying to elaborate, but rather with Ott's resistance to raising Heidegger's critique of theology as a problem in itself, so that he never really asks the question of how and in what way Heidegger is relevant for Christian theology. The vigor of Heidegger's critique of theology, especially that of the 1930s, is glossed over. Rather, in the same way as Bultmann and Rahner before him, Ott takes it for granted that what Heidegger says in his philosophical inquiries can provide a basis for theology that will be fruitful. All of these thinkers enforce a form of distinction between the provinces of theology and philosophy that result in theology only ever being informed by Heidegger's thought and never self-tested against what that thought concludes.

Ott presupposes that Heidegger has resolved the question of the being of being-human, or *Dasein*, and so never opens up the question of how any revelation of God in itself throws human being into question. Alluding to my earlier point about the apocalyptic voice, neither he nor Bultmann and certainly not Rahner ever questions the self-discovery of the finitude of being human. For both Ott and Bultmann, the finitude of *Dasein* is taken strictly as a philosophical problematic and one which is to be addressed by God, not fundamentally altered in the carrying out of an understanding of address in and of itself.

In a sense, each of the three moments I have outlined, exemplified by Bultmann, Rahner, and Ott, takes for granted that there is philosophy and there is theology, and that they stand apart. To problematize Heidegger, however, would be to open up the question of their standing apart *as* their belonging together. This forms a fundamental part of my topic.

Otto Pöggeler asks the question "did Heidegger, together with Rudolf Bultmann, direct theology into the formative role of exegesis and find a new path for this task through existential interpretation? Or did he, by means of Nietzsche's talk about the death of God, bring all theology into question?"[76] In a sense, this could be taken as a preliminary statement of the scope of this book. Yet concealed in Pöggeler's question is an assertion about the turn

---

76. Pöggeler, O., *Neue Wege mit Heidegger* (1992), p. 465. "Hat Heidegger, zusammen mit Rudolf Bultmann, die Theologie auf die fundierende Rolle der Exegese verwiesen und für diese mit der existentialen Interpretation neue Wege gefunden? Oder hat er mit Nietzsches Rede vom Tode Gottes alle Theologie in Frage gestellt?"

from the early to the later Heidegger—if you like, Heideggers I and II—for it suggests that either Heidegger's existential interpretation gave a new path for theology to tread or (in Heidegger's confrontation with Nietzsche) the whole of theology was thrown into question. The question needs to take into account the meaning of Heidegger's existential interpretation only when the engagement with Nietzsche is fully worked out. In order to do this, I show how the question which besets Heidegger from the very beginning remains the same and so come to a renewed understanding of what the turn actually is. What will become clear is that the existential horizon, far from disappearing (as one Heidegger supposedly supersedes another), actually offers theology the opportunity to *place itself* into question all over again in the very engagement with Nietzsche, experienced in the explication of the meaning of the madman's proclamation of the death of God. Why is the term experience at issue here? As I demonstrate in Heidegger's reading of Nietzsche, the death of God is a *Grunderfahrung*, a basic experience (rather than a basic thought) of Western thinking. It is nothing thought, yet is what provides for thinking to think of (the) nothing. It is nothing thought, because it is what thinking takes most for granted.

## HEIDEGGER AND CONTEMPORARY CHRISTIAN THEOLOGY

In the course of unfolding Heidegger's atheism, I want to show how there are indeed profound implications for Christian theology. Heidegger cannot be adjunct to any given theological project—hermeneutics, transcendental Thomism or radical systematics—but rather his atheism, properly understood, will bring us into confrontation with *that* tradition from out of which theology has also worked. In this way, it will become possible to understand why Heidegger believed that a path could be revealed along which theology can become self-questioning, without rendering either philosophy or theology into objects or discrete domains of inquiry.

Especially in much contemporary Catholic theology or theology which appeals to Catholic sources, a strong appeal is often made not just to ontology but to its history. This history has on occasion been described as ontology's inherent narratability. Heidegger's understanding of the *Seinsgeschichte*, or history of being, has brought into philosophy and theology that thinking, and so thinking of being has a history and unfolds, especially in the West. Pope John Paul II's recent Encyclical *Fides et Ratio* has itself made an appeal precisely to this in his talk of the "crisis of rationalism"[77] as the culmination of a long series of developments in philosophy. This crisis refers to the failure of reason to provide a ground of all things and the exposure of and reflection on that failure initiated by Nietzsche and Heidegger. The commonplace that being has a history, that philosophy is historically located (as opposed to Hegel's understanding of the history of philosophy as the triumph of metaphysics) has opened the way to more serious readings of ancient and medieval texts. The presumed self-evident transparency of philosophical discourse, which took the view that reason and truth were simply convertible, has given way to more careful evaluations of the way in which the history of ideas is always constituted genealogically. In consequence Descartes is no longer read simply as an epistemologist, and Aristotle (insofar as we have been invited to take him seriously at all) is not concerned solely with ethics and the philosophy of mind.

I want later to consider what Heidegger means by ontotheology, but as a name and a hermeneutic it has now established itself, often without particular reference to Heidegger, as the mark of a certain way of thinking about the trajectory of philosophy in the West. Merold Westphal has commented that "without too close a look either at how Heidegger uses the term or at the specifics of the discourse to be discredited, 'ontotheology' becomes the abracadabra by which a triumphalist secularism makes the world immune to any God".[78]

Conceived in this way, ontotheology refers to the inherent narratability of ontology. The history of being just *is* the story of the development of thinking from Parmenides to Nietzsche, or, if we are being more inclusive, Heidegger himself. Understood like this, philosophy simply becomes the process of retrieval of these great figures from the past, while all the time weighing-up and discriminating between their competing views. Theology, correspondingly, becomes the putting-to-use of this weighing-up and discriminating of theology's self-appointed task, so that the correct theological view becomes the one guaranteed by the thinker who turns out to be the best in the weighing and discriminating. In this way, the task of theology both authenticates philosophy and is itself vindicated by what it authenticates. If, supposedly, we

77. John Paul II, *Fides et Ratio* (1998), p. 53. "Discrimen rationalismi."
78. Westphal, M., "Overcoming Onto-theology" in Caputo, J.D., and Scanlon, M.J. (eds.), *God, the Gift, and Postmodernism* (1999), p. 148.

are being discriminating (along with Heidegger), then we admit that it is Heidegger who opens up and introduces this grand narrative of Western thought in its splendid sweep from the Eleatic stranger to the present day.

In an essay on the reception of Heidegger, Anthony Godzieba notes that "contemporary Catholic theological reflections occur within an era whose thought is strongly influenced on the one hand by the on-going reception of Heidegger's overcoming of metaphysics and on the other by the continuous critique of modernity".[79] He analyzes this with respect to "reactions to Heidegger's argument within Catholic philosophical theology and the Catholic theology of God" as a range of reactions which most recently has been "attempts to read biblical narratives of creation and redemption in dialogue with the claim of ontological difference".[80] Godzieba notes a still further example of contemporary engagement in the work of Walter Kaspar.

Theologians, and Catholic theologians especially, have often seized gleefully on the possibilities opened up by the broad acceptance of Heidegger's sustained critique of rationalism and the Enlightenment (without particular regard for its origin), seeing in this critique a possibility for a return to more ancient sources, especially Aquinas, uncomplicated by the need to accommodate this return to the epistemological rigors of scientific knowledge and the philosophy of subjectivity. It is perhaps for this reason that what looked like the triumph of transcendental Thomism in the immediate postwar period now seems so dated and methodologically obscure. That Heidegger has been so influential for so many contemporary Catholic theologians is an often unacknowledged (or even unrealized) debt, which, in remaining unacknowledged, allows for trivial and distorted interpretations of Heidegger's fundamental positions to predominate as normative. Moreover, too quickly accepting Heidegger's conclusions without proper attention to what took him to them has sometimes resulted in an extravagant rashness. Jean-Luc Marion's now infamous denunciation of Aquinas (which I consider in detail) in the name of following limits set by Heidegger is a case in point. There is no quick route to what Heidegger spent a lifetime in unfolding. Let me sound an urgent caution: quick aping of Heidegger's fundamental positions is a sure path to disaster.

---

79. Godzieba, A., "Prolegomena to a Catholic Theology of God between Heidegger and Postmodernity" (1999), p. 318.
80. Godzieba, A., "Prolegomena to a Catholic Theology of God," p. 323.

In an essay on Heidegger and theology, George Connell writes that "the unwavering intent of Heidegger's thought is to recall us from forgetfulness to a reawakened awareness of Being. What Heidegger has in mind by this 'awareness of Being' is so maddeningly elusive . . . because it is more experiential than conceptual".[81] What this statement brings to light in its incomprehension, together with what I have already said about the inherent narratability of ontology, is that for Heidegger the history of being is anything but a narrative of ontology, but rather the history of the forgottenness of being itself. As early as *Sein und Zeit* Heidegger had argued that "the being of beings 'is' not itself a being. The first philosophical step in understanding the being-problem consists in, not μῦθόν τινα διηγεῖσθαι, not in 'recounting a history', that is not determining beings as beings through tracing them back to another being, as if being itself might have the character of some possible being".[82] Being, as that which is to be asked about and brought about as a question, cannot be brought to light and questioned in the way that beings themselves can. Ontology, in other words, is inherently *not* narratable.

The elaboration of the history of being is the elaboration, not of being's narratability, but its concealment. Heidegger expands on this point, made first in *Sein und Zeit*, in the elaboration of this history of being at the opening to a section of the *Nietzsche* lectures written in 1941 but not published until 1961:

One could take the following as a historical report concerning the history of the concept of being.

The essential would then be unheard.

But the essential lets itself be said at times in hardly any other way.[83]

---

81. Connell, G., "Against Idolatry: Heidegger and Natural Theology" in Westphal, M. (ed.), *Postmodern Philosophy and Christian Thought* (1999), p. 146.

82. *Sein und Zeit* (GA2), p. 6. "Das Sein des Seienden 'ist' nicht selbst ein Seiendes. Der erste philosophische Schritt im Verständnis des Seinsproblems besteht darin, nicht μῦθόν τινα διηγεῖσθαι, 'keine Geschichte erzählen', d.h. Seiendes als Seiendes nicht durch Rückführung auf ein anderes Seiendes in seiner Herkunft zu bestimmen, gleich als hätte Sein den Charakter eines möglichen Seienden."

83. *Die Metaphysik als Geschichte des Seins* (*Nietzsche* [GA6.2]), p. 399. "Das Folgende könnte man als einen historischen Bericht über die Geschichte des Seinsbegriffes aufnehmen. Das Wesentliche wäre dann überhört. Aber das Wesentliche läßt sich zur Zeit vielleicht noch kaum anders sagen."

In this sense, it is metaphysics, and not being, which immediately lends itself to narration, as the history of the concealment, the very forgetting of being, but this concealment is itself a speaking of something essential which at the same time hides and withdraws. In contradistinction to Connell, Heidegger does not seek an awareness as an experience of being in contrast to its being thought. This supposed maddening aspect to Heidegger's work has nothing to do with the privilege of experience over thinking, but rather is the very mark of inattentiveness, to letting something be unheard, which is yet an unfolding of an understanding. The pedestrian history of ontology which has become common coinage in much contemporary theology completely overlooks and refuses to hear that what is at issue for Heidegger is no grand narrative, no overarching account of the West (the question would otherwise have to be asked: what came before Parmenides and Heraclitus anyway, else how arbitrary a beginning they would represent for such an all-encompassing account) but rather what is *essential*, which means, what essences: being itself.

It is not the narratability of ontology that is at issue, but the question of the narrating: who narrates, and why? In the self-disclosure of the narrator to him- and herself, the narrator becomes an issue for the narrative, the narrative becomes his and hers, *mine*. The narrative gives the narrator to be—it is what goes in advance of him or her and has to be discovered, and yet insofar as it is *essential*, insofar as it really constitutes and gives being to the narrator, it is already at work in her and him—the narrator has already been made-narratable by being. This disclosure of the narrative is therefore a self-disclosure which, nevertheless, must perforce account for the world out of which the narrator is given. If ontology is ever inherently narratable, it is because—if it really is ontology—it is already narrating. The inherence refers to the narrator, not to being.

It is in this sense that the French theologian Jean-Luc Marion, whose work I discuss, is so important. Marion has raised the question of Heidegger's understanding of being as having significance for Christian theology. His engagement with Heidegger has been made possible by the unique place that Heidegger has assumed in the postwar philosophical situation in France, a situation so heavily influenced by Kojève and Beaufret.[84] Marion has, as a theo-

---

84. Tom Rockmore has documented this reception in a slightly one-sided and somewhat journalistic approach in *Heidegger and French Philosophy* (1995). He notes: "It is fair to say that the vast majority of French philosophers since the war have been marked by their encounter with Heidegger" (p. 135). Rockmore is not untypical of North American scholar-

logian rather than as a philosopher, sought to engage with Heidegger (hence my decision not to examine the more strictly philosophical work of thinkers like Jean-François Courtine). Moreover, Marion has now been extensively translated into English and has in a particular way raised specific questions about Heidegger's relevance for an understanding of God and Christian theology in a modern context that concerns itself with nihilism. I am, however, strictly concerned with his engagement with Heidegger as one which will open up the path of theology's self-questioning, and in no sense do I intend to elaborate fully or thematically his wider project.

There is a further reason for Marion's importance. As editor of the Parisian journal *Revue Métaphysique* he has been at the center of a number of theologians' attempts to engage with Heidegger.[85] While Marion is arguably the most important figure among this group, he represents in a particularly exemplary way the assumptions that have more generally been adopted in order to engage theologically with the matters with which Heidegger is understood to be concerned.

Each of these theologians I have considered in their different ways highlights two concerns that allow Heidegger's significance for Christian theology to be unlocked as a question in its own right and not as propaedeutic to a study which is only informed by his thinking. The first of these has already been hinted at by Rahner. Ghislain Lafont makes a more explicit formulation when he says Heidegger's "approach to 'being' has something nihilistic about it".[86] To put the question more starkly, if for Heidegger being and nothing are the same—belong together—then how might the nothing be understood in relation to God and theology? Moreover, for Heidegger, being human is only understandable in this belonging together of being and nothing. In elaborating this belonging together he says:

> The human essence belongs itself to the essence of nihilism, and therewith to the phase of its fulfilment. Man, as the essence put into use in

---

ship in being troubled by the extent to which Heidegger's political engagement has not been a central concern for many French writers, despite very serious attempts to address it by thinkers of the stature of Derrida and Lacoue-Labarthe, among others.

85. For example, note the positions developed by Jean-Yves Lacoste and Ghislain Lafont (to name only two).

86. Lafont, G., *Dieu, le temps, et l'être* (1986), p. 280. "[Heidegger's] démarche vers l'"être' a quelque chose de nihiliste."

be**x**ng helps to constitute the zone of be**x**ng and that means at the same time of nothingness.[87]

In the second place is the question of analogy. Lafont and Marion have both made appeal to analogy in order to overcome Heidegger's atheistic destructuring of metaphysics. As I discuss in relation to Heidegger's understanding of Aquinas' interpretation of *esse*, the question of analogy can provide no refuge from, or easy resolution of, Heidegger's destructuring of metaphysics; rather, for Heidegger analogy already is the very mark of the impasse of thinking which metaphysics most *is* in itself. Another way of saying this is that analogy, in the way it has been taken up into Christian thinking, has become the very mark of the Christianization of God and the rationalism of metaphysics. It is no accident that every attempt to instantiate Christian thinking as a renewal of metaphysics in contemporary theology makes a strong appeal to analogy—the work of Graham Ward and John Milbank are cases in point.[88] Courtine has indicated that (in what he calls the *analogia entis*): "Heidegger appears to have suspected it assumes the status of something *unthought* . . . a blind spot", and so became both a blind spot for metaphysics and its decisive trait.[89] I demonstrate in detail how Heidegger actually unfolded this view in a lecture course on Aristotle in 1930. It is Heidegger's very unfolding of the question of analogy which makes it possible to show both what *esse* becomes the marker for, and what, as only a marker, it also conceals. In unfolding Heidegger's reading of analogy, it becomes clear how the existential interpretation named by Pöggeler is not overcome by the proclamation of the death of God, but rather belongs with it in pointing forward to the very way in which Heidegger's work can be argued to be significant for Christian theology at all.

87. *Zur Seinsfrage* (*Wegmarken* GA9), p. 412. "Das Menschenwesen gehört selber zum Wesen des Nihilismus und somit zur Phase seiner Vollendung. Der Mensch macht als jenes in das Se**x**n gebrauchte Wesen die Zone des Se**x**ns und d.h. zugleich des Nichts mit aus."

88. See just for two examples: Ward, G., *Cities of God* (2000), esp. pp. 39, 129–130, 165, and *passim;* Milbank, J. "Intensities" (1999), p. 482, and *passim.*

89. Courtine, J.-F., *Suárez et le système de la métaphysique* (1990), pp. 534f., 538. "Heidegger semble l'avoir soupçonné, partageait avec celle-ci son statut d'*impensé*" (author's italics). Courtine makes no mention of where he believes Heidegger to have formulated his suspicion. In fact the suspicion is first alluded to in *Sein und Zeit* and more clearly worked through in *Aristoteles Metaphysik* Θ 1–3 (GA 33).

## THE SHAPE OF THIS INVESTIGATION

Does Heidegger's atheism have significance for Christian theology? This question may now be asked as follows: how does nihilism, figured in Nietzsche's proclamation that God is dead, belong together with the current situation of human being? To think through this question means to think through the question of the being of beings, the ontological difference, and it means to think it through by returning to the very tradition from out of which Heidegger spoke and with which he engaged. This investigation therefore constitutes an attempt to think through a question that Heidegger himself raised.

Part of the delineation of this topic must be Heidegger's political engagement in the period 1933–45. I propose neither to solve the question of why Heidegger became a Nazi in 1933 nor to resolve his silence on the matter from 1945 until his death in 1976. I am neither an apologist for Heidegger, nor do I seek a role as one of his accusers. It is neither possible nor desirable to gloss Heidegger's political engagement on the basis that his politics and his philosophy were two separate arenas which either did not overlap, or at least if they did, only very slightly. It may eventually be the case that the opening of the Heidegger archive at Marbach will resolve many of the questions for which historical answers in particular have been sought, questions, for instance, concerning Heidegger's actual relationship with the Hitler regime in the crucial periods of 1933–34 (the Rectorate) and 1942–45 (when Heidegger claimed he was under suspicion)—or of Heidegger's attitude to the biologism of the Nazis. These are not my questions here. Others have engaged themselves with these matters.[90]

How should this question be raised within this topic? Twice in *Das Rektorat 1933/34, Tatsachen und Gedanken,* Heidegger mentions the death of God as the figure of nihilism.[91] Hermann Heidegger's preface to this piece (which includes the so-called *Rektoratsrede*) says it was written in 1945, shortly after the end of hostilities, and was, on his father's instructions, to be published only posthumously. It concerns Heidegger's thoughts in particular about his assumption of the rectorate of Freiburg University after Hitler came to power and until 1934, and the situation of the Nazis in general. Here Heidegger says:

90. Cf. among others Safranski, R., *Ein Meister aus Deutschland* (1994); Sluga, H., *Heidegger's Crisis* (1993); Ott, H., *Martin Heidegger: Unterwegs zu seiner Biographie* (1988).
91. In *Die Selbstbehauptung der deutschen Universität,* pp. 25 and 39.

This reality of the will to power can be expressed, with Nietzsche, in the proposition 'God is dead.' Essential reasons led me to cite this proposition on my rectorial address. This proposition has nothing to do with the assertion of vulgar atheism. It means: the supersensible world, especially the world of the Christian God, has lost its effective force in history . . . if things had been different, would the First World War have been possible? And especially, if things had been different, would the Second World War have become possible?[92]

Michael Zimmerman rightly places Heidegger's own reading of his Nazi engagement at the center of the question. He cites Lacoue-Labarthe's belief that the Holocaust represents a radical caesura between God and humanity, "from which the West has not recovered". He concludes, commenting on this passage, "Heidegger, however, believed that the real caesura had *already occurred* in the death of the biblical God and the Christian-platonic table of values . . . subsequent events, including world wars and death camps . . . were symptoms of it".[93] Heidegger concludes: "What is essential is that we are in the midst of the fulfilment of nihilism, that God is 'dead' and every time-space for godhead is buried".[94] What is a time-space? As I shall indicate, it is the place of being-human. God is dead, and so the very place of godhead, being-human, is buried too. That God is dead means that the human being is in some sense also dead to God. Heidegger makes these remarks in light of his own commentary on his Nazi engagement, placing this issue as one that needs to be thought through and that stands in the very center of my topic. Just how the burial of possible godhead in nihilism might be understood, I make fully clear.

How therefore, do I intend to treat the topic I have unfolded? In chapter 2 I show how Heidegger's earlier thought both springs out of and con-

---

92. *Die Selbstbehauptung der deutschen Universität*, p. 25. "Diese Wirklichkeit des Willens zur Macht läßt sich im Sinne Nietzsches auch aussagen durch den Satz: 'Gott ist todt'. Diesen Satz habe ich aus wesentlichen Gründen in meiner Rektoratsrede angeführt. Der Satz hat nichts zu tun mit der Behauptung eines ordinären Atheismus. Er bedeutet: Die übersinnliche Welt, insbesondere die Welt des christlichen Gottes, hat seine wirkende Kraft in der Geschichte verloren . . . wäre, wenn es anders wäre, der erste Weltkrieg möglich gewesen? Und vollends, wäre, wenn es anders wäre, der zweite Weltkrieg möglich geworden?"

93. Zimmerman, M., "The Death of God at Auschwitz?" (1996), p. 247 (author's italics).

94. *Das Rektorat*, p. 39. "Das Wesentliche ist, daß wir mitten in der Vollendung des Nihilismus stehen, daß Gott 'todt' ist und jeder Zeit-Raum für die Gottheit verschüttet.

fronts his original theological horizon. This leads in chapters 3 and 4 to an extended consideration of the meaning of the turn in response both to how Heidegger's work has been received and as a demonstration of the inner unity of Heidegger's thought as a thoroughgoing phenomenology in the elaboration of the term *die Kehre*. In chapter 5 I intend to show the origin of the term *das Ereignis* both in its phenomenological roots and as an experience of Nietzsche's word that God is dead, contrasted with Heidegger's elaboration of the term *das Geschehnis*, or happening, as well as an analysis of Heidegger's reading of Plato and the meaning of the term that later becomes a name for God, τὸ ἀγαθόν, the Good. Chapter 6 then lays out in a preliminary, negative sense Heidegger's understanding of God and how God has been interpreted in Christian doctrinal theology. Here it becomes necessary to show what Heidegger understands by the Scholastic term *esse* and the medieval appeal to the doctrine of analogy and so bring Heidegger into debate with St. Thomas Aquinas and to ask how *esse* becomes a name for God by examining Heidegger's interpretation of Aristotle. In chapter 7 I examine Heidegger's interpretation of Nietzsche's figure of Zarathustra in order to demonstrate how the existential horizon of his earlier work is fulfilled through an elaboration of the meaning of Nietzsche's nihilism. Here it is also necessary to raise the question of Heidegger's Nazi engagement and his subsequent articulation of that engagement. In chapter 8 I then bring Heidegger into confrontation with the French theologian Jean-Luc Marion to indicate both the problematization of Heidegger's thought in contemporary (and especially French) theology and the reasons for the failure to clarify with sufficient depth Pöggeler's allusion to why Heidegger's work is able to bring the whole of theology into question. Finally I turn the issue of the question of Heidegger's later work for contemporary theology on its head and point to the challenge Heidegger issues to theologians in light of his thinking, the challenge that is the real meaning of his atheism. This, I argue, is the importance of his later work for Christian theologians: how what he argues about theology and the death of God points toward an overcoming of any attempt by theologians to carry out a metaphysics.

Chapter Two

# The Basis of
# Heidegger's Atheism

## Heidegger's Relation to Christian Theology

I have already indicated that Heidegger asserts the atheism of philosophy very early on in his work, as least as early as 1921, and that this atheism is profoundly connected with the Christian God. Nevertheless, Vincent Vycinas notes in *Earth and Gods* that "Heidegger does not encounter God in the Christian sense" and concludes his penetrating study of Heidegger's understanding of world with an appendix entitled *Heidegger and Christianity*.[1] Vycinas adds "the fact of such non-encountering is not a judgement against the existence of God. Neither is it a testimony for Him in the explicit sense: 'Philosophy is a finite assertion of man and not the voice of God'".[2] This is correct, in that it explains the position Heidegger himself takes up with regard to God and theology, and most particularly Christian theology.

Heidegger's biographical origins in and separation from theology have been extensively researched.[3] Both Rüdiger Safranski and Hugo Ott have drawn attention to Heidegger's Catholic upbringing and his willingness to take up conservative positions, not so much because of any fanaticism, but, as Safranski notes, simply because Catholicism

---

1. Vycinas, V., *Earth and Gods* (1961), pp. 312 ff., p. 313.
2. Vycinas, V., *Earth and Gods*, p. 313, quoting Eugen Fink.
3. See: van Buren, *The Young Heidegger* (1994), esp. chapters 6 and 8; Kisiel, T., *The Genesis of Heidegger's Being and Time* (1993), chapters 2 and 4; Ott, H., *Martin Heidegger: Unterwegs zu seiner Biographie* (1988), Second Division, and "Heidegger's Catholic Origins" (1995); Safranski, R., *Ein Meister aus Deutschland* (1994), esp. chapter 7; Schaeffler, R., *Frömmigkeit des Denkens? Martin Heidegger und die katholische Theologie* (1978).

was part of the stuff and makeup of his and his family's life.[4] Safranski notes that Heidegger's admission to the Catholic seminary (to train as a priest) in the Schwabian town of Konstanz in 1903 began a financial dependency on Catholic sources that continued until the completion of his formal education in 1916, with the publication of his *Habilitationsschrift*.[5] What has perhaps sometimes been overlooked is Heidegger's deep knowledge of the texts central to the neo-Scholasticism which formed so much a part of a German Catholic seminary education in the early years of the twentieth century. Heidegger would have been familiar with the texts of Aquinas— in particular the two *Summas* and the *Quaestiones Disputatae: de Veritate*, as well as Aquinas's commentaries on Aristotle's *Metaphysics, Physics, Nicomachean Ethics*, and *de Anima*. It is clear from his earlier (Marburg) lecture courses in particular that he was also familiar with the work of Augustine, Anselm, Eckhart, Bonaventure, Scotus, and Occam, as well as Bernard of Clairvaux, Suárez, and other figures formative of the Scholastic tradition. Bultmann is said to have described Heidegger (during his time at Marburg) as "our foremost Luther man".

Safranski adds that "what fascinates [Heidegger] about theology is not the theological but the philosophical aspect", and indeed, Heidegger records in 1915 that his lectures in theology had driven him to conduct his own readings of the scholastics, because the philosophical training available to him failed to give him what he sought.[6] Despite Ott's attempts to locate Heidegger's break from formal Catholicism in political intrigues around his failure to secure a senior academic post, it is clear from what he writes (and Ott's liberal citations of Heidegger's correspondence with his friend Laslowski), that Heidegger was already, even by 1913, questioning the neo-

---

4. See Safranski, R., *Ein Meister aus Deutschland* (1997), p. 23. For examples of Heidegger's early conservative positions, see in particular the various short writings and book reviews published as chapters 1, 5, 6, 9, and 10, in *Reden und andere Zeugnisse eines Lebensweges* (GA16).

5. Safranski, R., *Ein Meister aus Deutschland*, p. 24.

6. Safranski, R., *Ein Meister aus Deutschland*, p. 57; *Lebenslauf (Zur Habilitation 1915)*, chapter 15 in *Reden und andere Zeugnisse eines Lebensweges* (GA16), p. 37. "Nach Absolvierung des Gymnasiums bezog ich im Wintersemester 1909 die Universität Freiburg im Breisgau, wo ich ununterbrochen bis 1913 blieb. Zunächst studierte ich Theologie. Die damals vorgeschriebenen philosophischen Vorlesungen befriedigten mich wenig, so daß ich mich auf das Selbststudium der scholastischen Lehrbücher verlegte. Sie verschafften mir eine gewisse formale logische Schulung, gaben mir in philosophischer Hinsicht nicht das, was ich suchte."

Scholasticism that was then current as the interpretative access to the earlier texts.[7]

Writing of this period later (in 1922), Heidegger observed that with the beginning of his activity as a teacher, it became impossible for him to undertake philosophical research while remaining bound to a Catholic faith.[8] Safranski's conclusion is surely correct: that what mattered in all of Heidegger's theological concerns was the engagement with philosophy. Theology was a way into philosophical research. Ted Sadler, Thomas Sheehan, Theodore Kisiel, and John van Buren have all conducted extensive research into how Heidegger's early lectures on religion and in particular how the 'kairological time' of early Christian communities actually pointed him in the direction of a description of human being which enabled him to develop a critique of Aristotelian ontology, demonstrating the degree to which it also was only possible on the basis of an understanding of being which remained undisclosed.

Sadler is not wrong to see in this an earlier form of "what [Heidegger] will later call '*Seinsvergessenheit*'".[9] Sadler draws attention to Karl Lehmann's essay on the younger Heidegger's work and its concern with Christian themes, although he misses the crucial point, omitting to mention that it is Lehmann's stress on the originary Christian experience of history—that history at any moment is subject to its own end through Christ's second

7. See Ott, H., *Martin Heidegger: Unterwegs zu seiner Biographie*, esp. pp. 81–95. Ott quotes on p. 90 a letter from Laslowski which counsels Heidegger in 1915, in the run-up to a professorial appointment that he failed to attain, saying: "*Please* be careful especially *now*, in what you say about scholasticism" (author's italics). Indeed, Ott's charge of opportunism as Heidegger's motive for receiving financial support from Catholic sources only succeeds if, as Safranski supposes, Heidegger had entertained doubts about the direction of Catholic scholarship since at least 1913. The school of interpretation that was emerging in Catholic circles was driven by ideological concerns: Leo XIII had restored the place of Aquinas in Catholic thought in 1873 with the publication of his Encyclical Letter *Aeterne Patris,* and Pius X had in 1907 issued the condemnation of Modernism in the Encyclical Letter *Pascendi.* What emerged from this taut intellectual engagement with the modern world and simultaneous recovery of medieval sources was a systematization of thought, a neo-Scholasticism, that was itself unwitting prey to all the forces it was resisting.

8. *Vita* (chapter 17), in *Reden und andere Zeugnisse eines Lebensweges* (GA16), p. 43. "Schon bei Beginn der akademischen Lehrtätigkeit wurde mir klar, daß eine echte wissenschaftliche Forschung frei von jeglichem Vorbehalt und versteckter Bindung nicht möglich sei bei wirklicher Festhaltung des katholischen Glaubensstandpunktes."

9. Sadler, T., *Heidegger and Aristotle* (1996), p. 172.

coming—that enables the earliest Christian communities to have a unique access to the question concerning the meaning of being. Lehmann compares this to the Aristotelian ontology by saying: "*The experience of the original-Christian understanding of history is perhaps the only possible 'standpoint' from which the limitation of the former ontology in its understanding of the meaning of being and also the persistence of this limitation could stand out*".[10] This makes the reference to the forgetfulness of being the more prescient—this forgetfulness is not just a feature of time, it is what the history of being is. Sadler points out that after 1921 Heidegger moved beyond these earliest Christian links with the question of being: "He came to think of this as too restrictive a context in which to situate his ontological enquiries, and as too susceptible to misinterpretations along doctrinal lines".[11] Nevertheless, it is a persistent concern with going back into the roots of the Christian experience itself which provides the basis for a philosophical critique of the whole history of ontology.

It is worth noting in connection with this research Hugo Ott's emphatic view that (interpreting some remarks of Heidegger's made to a private circle in 1954) throughout, the God with whom Heidegger is concerned is "definitely the Christian God".[12] My whole argument is an attempt to demonstrate philosophically the truth of what for Ott is a statement made in the light of his (strictly speaking) historiographical research. On the other hand, Ott is keen to remind us of Heidegger's strongly felt and expressed anti-clericalism, with the implication that it has a significance for his atheistic philosophical work. Ott misses the point of what Heidegger's atheism is about.[13] This atheism is an address in the wake of Nietzsche's declaration of the death of God, a way of taking up a position with regard to the whole of the history of Western philosophy and the way in which it has articulated God, both Christian and before Christ. Heidegger's own view, his refusal to undertake a theology, is part of this address, not (as indeed Vycinas tells us) because he either has or does not have a view on faith or belief, but because his address springs from a strictly philosophical motive. Philosophy has nothing to say of the Christian God—which means that Heidegger's discus-

10. Lehmann, Card. K., "Christliche Geschichtserfahrung und ontologische Frage beim jungen Heidegger" in Pöggeler, O. (ed.), *Heidegger: Perspektiven zur Deutung seines Werkes* (1984), p. 154 (author's italics).

11. Sadler, T., *Heidegger and Aristotle* (1996), p. 172.

12. Ott, H., "Heidegger's Catholic Origins" (1995), p. 154.

13. Ott, H., *Martin Heidegger: Unterwegs zu seiner Biographie*, p. 95.

sion of the tradition of Western philosophy, whenever it has believed itself able to say something about God, and in particular the Christian God, takes on an interpretative urgency. If Vycinas says that Heidegger does not come to the problem of God, he also notes that this has nothing to do with atheism taken in the conventional sense.[14] My argument is that Heidegger's refusal to come to the problem of God is a way of bringing his interlocutor, *me*, to the problem of God. Heidegger's atheism is a vibrant pedagogy, indicating the extent to which so much which claims to speak of God does not do so, and which forces me to confront the question of who the God is who might lie silent behind all that has been said. If Heidegger does not come to the problem of God, as Vycinas says, he is not indifferent to what it means. Even the anticlericalism was a stance.

The charge has been made that Heidegger's use of terms like fallenness[15] and guilt[16] (following comments of Karl Löwith's that we will examine later) suggest that it is possible to interpret the language of *Sein und Zeit* as a masked Christian theology.[17] Fergus Kerr repeats the charge when he says "Heidegger's attitude to Christian theology, hostile at one level, overtly and explicitly so, attributing the monstrous invention of the transcendental subject to Christian theology, is also proprietorial, indeed exploitative of and even parasitical upon Christian theology".[18] He concludes "it may be said, without much exaggeration, that almost every philosophical innovation in *Sein und Zeit* may easily be traced to a theological source".[19] Immediately the difficulties in reading Heidegger become clear. For Heidegger, the question is not whether he has interpretatively and imaginatively

---

14. Vycinas, V., *Earth and Gods*, p. 315.

15. *Verfallenheit.* Cf., for an earlier working out of this term in particular, the section entitled *Ruinanz* in *Phänomenologische Interpretationen zu Aristoteles* (GA61), esp. p. 155. Here *Ruinanz* is understood as a decline (*Verfall*) into an objectifying (*Objektivierung*).

16. *Schuld.* Kisiel notes that this term appears briefly in 1924 and 1925, but does not give references: Kisiel, T., *The Genesis of Heidegger's Being and Time*, p. 504.

17. Löwith makes this point on more than one occasion, but in particular he suggests: "Heideggers existenziale Ontologie ist weder imstande, die Naturphilosophie der Antike zurückzuholen, noch kann sie auf die christliche Spaltung eines geborenen und wiedergeborenen Menschen, eines 'eigentlichen' und 'uneigentlichen' Daseins verzichten" (*M. Heidegger und F. Rosenzweig* [1984], p. 84). The extent to which such a reading of *Eigentlichkeit* is unwarranted will, I hope, become clear in what follows concerning coming to my-self.

18. Kerr, F., *Immortal Longings* (1997), p. 47.

19. Kerr, F., *Immortal Longings* (1997), p. 47.

internalized a Christian theology which is now reproduced in philosophical form—indeed that is (loosely described) his very charge against metaphysics, as we shall see. Rather, the question is, what is the ontological basis for these ontic descriptions of matters of Christian faith? This is a philosophical question that concerns itself with theology. Heidegger is proceeding back through Christian belief and the Christianization of God to ask how philosophy actually is, and can in the future remain, the ontological basis for an understanding of human being worked out on the basis of faith. Löwith and Kerr entirely miss the point: if Christianity is to speak truly of human being, even though it speaks only *after* God has spoken, what it speaks of must have a basis in the world. Otherwise the contents of Christian doctrine, having no ontological basis (not, in other words, being an address to human being which can be heard by humans and recognized by them as such), would simply be an imaginative fancy. As we shall see, this is no more than what he actually says in his 1927 lecture "Phänomenologie und Theologie".[20]

Hans-Georg Gadamer reports Heidegger speaking in a group of theologians in Marburg in the early 1920s on the task of theology: "After evoking the Christian scepticism of Franz Overbeck, he said it was the true task of theology, to which it must again find its way back, to seek the word which is capable of calling to faith and keeping in faith".[21] It was, Gadamer notes, a pure Heidegger-sentence, full of ambiguousness. He adds that this sentence was only fulfilled in the later "talk about the turn" where he says that "the call to faith, the summons that challenged the self-sufficiency of the 'I' and made it necessary that the 'I' become an issue for itself in faith is to be found".[22]

Heidegger's concern with philosophy over theology does not mean he privileges philosophy over theology in general, but rather that he saw it as his own task to think philosophically. This task commits him to a methodological atheism, precisely because it indicates the extent to which the Christianization of God has subsumed philosophy under Christian doctrine,

20. *Phänomenologie und Theologie* (*Wegmarken* [GA9]), pp. 45–78.
21. Gadamer, H.-G., "Marburger Theologie" (1964) in *Heideggers Wege* (1983), p. 29. "Er sagte nämlich, nachdem er die christliche Skepsis Franz Overbecks beschworen hatte, es sei die wahre Aufgabe der Theologie, zu der sie wieder finden müsse, das Wort zu suchen, das imstande sei, zum Glauben zu rufen und im Glauben zu bewahren."
22. Gadamer, H.-G., "Marburger Theologie," p. 37. "Rede von der Kehre" . . . "der Anruf des Glaubens, der Anspruch, der die Selbstgenügsamkeit des Ich herausfordert und es zur Selbstaufgabe im Glauben nötigt."

above all the doctrine of the *ens creatum*. Kerr has already indicated where this concern is most centrally located, both for Heidegger and for modern metaphysics generally: in the working out of the meaning of the 'I', the self. For modern metaphysics, exactly as Kerr notes, the self is worked out through the *cogito* of Descartes and the transcendental subject of German Idealism. For Heidegger, the self is worked out through the phenomenological description of *Dasein*.

## HEIDEGGER'S CRITIQUE OF THE SUBJECT OF METAPHYSICS

What is the relationship between subjectivity and the *ens creatum?* In speaking of the Greek understanding of human being, Heidegger always reminds his reader that the Greeks understood the human being uniquely as the ζῷον λόγον ἔχον, the being that has language. This having language is speaking, λέγειν, which is the basis for human beings' concern with truth, ἀλήθεια. Ἀληθεύειν means "*to be disclosing,* to remove the world from concealedness and coveredness".[23] Speaking, therefore, is concerned with world, so that the human being is both "in the sphere of other existing beings (*Daseienden*) with it in the mode of living (plants, animals) and indeed as a being which has language (λόγον ἔχον), which addresses and discusses its world . . . its *concern* in the wider sense".[24] This understanding of *Dasein*'s being in the world undergoes a transformation in the development of what Heidegger calls Christian *Dasein,* in the developments of the medieval period. At the same time the translation of ζῷον λογον ἔχον from Greek thought into the Latin mentality which understands human being as *animal rationale* means that the original Greek sense is lost. Humanity is now understood strictly in terms of the *ratio,* reason, rather than speaking. It becomes a theological definition, determined out of biblical revelation. Heidegger says: "The guide taken from this is Genesis Chapter One, verse twenty-six, 'and God said, Let us make man according to our image and likeness'. Humanity is, according to the measure of faith, predetermined

23. *Platon: Sophistes* (GA19), p. 17. "ἀληθεύειν meint: *aufdeckendsein,* die Welt aus der Verschlossenheit und Verdecktheit herausnehmen" (author's italics).

24. *Ontologie (Hermeneutik der Faktizität)* (GA63), p. 27. ". . . im Umkreis von anderem mit ihm in der Weise des Lebens Daseienden (Pflanzen, Tiere), und zwar als ein Seiendes, das Sprache hat (λόγον ἔχον), seine Welt anspricht und bespricht; seine Welt . . . des *Besorgens* im weiteren Sinne" (author's italics).

as being-created in God's image".[25] The effect of this is that the essence of what it is to be human is made entirely dependent on God as such, something which is added to the Greek definition. The meaning of ζῷον λόγον ἔχον therefore undergoes a multiplicity of changes while appearing to say the same thing. The *ratio* of speaking, λέγειν, becomes the *ratio Dei* of medieval thought. From being determined out of the condition of its being with other beings (this is what speaking is), human being is now determined out of its foundation on God. Heidegger makes the same point in *Sein und Zeit*, noting, however, that "the Christian definition in modern times becomes de-theologized".[26] The same process occurs both for the world, which is transformed from Aristotle's view that it is eternal to the Christian concern that "in the beginning God created the heavens and the earth",[27] and for God as well, in that the ancient ontology is also used to work out the Christian understanding of God, and so "the being of God becomes interpreted ontologically".[28]

When, therefore, in *Sein und Zeit*, Heidegger sets out to demonstrate the way Descartes transforms the interpretation of world in the inception of modern metaphysics, he notes that "the considerations which follow will not have been grounded in full detail until the 'cogito sum' has been phenomenologically destructured".[29] The text points to the section of *Sein und Zeit* which was never published.[30]

What concerns me in this discussion is not Heidegger's analysis of the way in which the consequence for understanding world is transformed by Descartes from Aristotle's place (τόπος) into geometrical, spatial, *res extensa*

---

25. *Ontologie (Hermeneutik der Faktizität)* (GA63), p. 27. "Der hinaus entnommene Leitfaden ist Genesis 126: και εἶπεν ὁ θεός · Ποιήσωμεν ἄνθρωπον κατ᾽ εἰκόνα ἡμετέραν καὶ καθ᾽ ὁμοίωσιν". Heidegger quotes the Greek Septuagint version of the text.

26. *Sein und* Zeit (GA2), p. 48, with the same biblical reference. "Die christliche Definition wurde im Verlauf der Neuzeit enttheologisiert".

27. Genesis 1:1.

28. *Sein und Zeit* (GA2), p. 49. "Das Sein Gottes [wird] ontologisch . . . interpretiert."

29. *Sein und Zeit* (GA2), p. 49. "Ihre ausführliche Begründung erhält die folgende Betrachtung erst durch die phänomenologische Destruktion des 'cogito sum'."

30. Heidegger has three extended discussions on the *cogito* elsewhere: in sections of the 1927 lecture course *Grundprobleme der Phänomenologie* (GA24), the 1935/36 lecture course *Die Frage nach dem Ding* (GA41) and in the 1940 lecture course *Der europäische Nihilismus* (*Nietzsche* [GA6.2]).

(an important enough subject in itself). Rather, the question is how what Heidegger calls the Christianization of God becomes the basis for a fundamental redescription of human being. The persistent question has remained whether Descartes himself was an atheist. Zbigniew Janowski has shown in detail that Descartes's fundamental motive and impulse were exactly the same as that also identified by Heidegger (although he makes no reference to Heidegger's work). In emphasizing the novelty of Descartes's work and its freedom from antecedents, Janowski says "for Descartes the question is . . . is there anything that does not depend on God? . . . Descartes' [question] is about the *ontological* relation between God and the creation".[31] In the determination of human being, Janowski shows how the ontological dependence of humanity on God is worked out through the human being's likeness to God.[32] Heidegger indicates, but does not discuss in detail, the way in which Descartes, having established the *cogito*, asks 'whether there be a God' and what character such God might have.[33] Descartes concludes: "By the term 'God' I understand a substance: a substance infinite, independent, most highly intelligent, most highly powerful, and which both I myself and everything else that is extant—if indeed something else is extant—have been created".[34]

Two things are significant about what Descartes says. First, Descartes invokes the divine names (as indeed he does elsewhere) precisely in order to establish the priority of God. God is infinite substance as opposed to human finite substance, although, as Heidegger notes, this leaves the question of the meaning of substance unclarified in Descartes. This has the effect that "'being' itself does not 'affect' us, and therefore cannot be interrogated. 'Being is not a real predicate' according to a remark of Kant's, who is only repeating Descartes' principle".[35] In this sense, what Descartes carries through with regard to metaphysics is both further grounded and established by Kant.

---

31. Janowski, Z., *Cartesian Theodicy* (2000), p. 104.

32. Janowski, Z., *Cartesian Theodicy* (2000), p. 130, citing the fourth of the *Meditationes de Prima Philosophia* in Descartes, R., *Descartes* (1996), VII, p. 62.

33. Descartes, R., *Meditationes de Prima Philosophia* (*Descartes*, VII, 1996), p. 36. (Third meditation) "Examinare debeo an sit Deus."

34. Descartes, R., *Meditationes de Prima Philosophia* (*Descartes*, VII, 1996), p. 45. (Third meditation) "Dei nomine intelligo substantiam quandam infinitam, independentem, summe intelligentem, summe potentem et a quâ tum ego ipse, tum aliud omne, si quid aliud extat, quodcumque extat, est creatum."

35. *Sein und Zeit* (GA2), p. 94. "Das 'Sein' selbst 'affiziert' uns nicht, deshalb kann es nicht vernommen werden. 'Sein ist kein reales Prädikat' nach dem Ausspruch *Kants*, der nur den Satz Descartes' wiedergibt."

Second, a double temporal movement in the order of being is inaugurated with regard to God, a movement that nevertheless lies hardly recognized or explicated in Descartes's commentators. Descartes establishes the 'I' of the *cogito* as the first indubitable thing the self may know. In so doing, the *cogito* comes to something of which it may be even more certain—not because there are degrees in the order of certainty, but because of a certain priority with regard to time. God is discovered *subsequent* to the establishment of the self but is discovered in the manner of *already needing to have been,* in order to be the indubitable cause of the self and everything else that is (insofar as it is). God already is, but this is dependent on my knowing in virtue of who I am.

The important point here is that this is the temporal mode of procedure of faith: I come to believe in a God who (in faith, I discover) first gave me to be. However, the proper temporal priority of faith is transposed improperly to the order of being, of philosophy itself, so that God lies at the origin as the philosophically accessible cause of all things, in virtue of the structure of the self, the subject. This priority of God as most real being and the creator and cause of all things is precisely the understanding which Heidegger's atheism is intended to destructure. Heidegger describes this move in the following way: "Modern philosophy made a total turnabout of philosophical inquiry and started out from the subject, the I".[36]

This word—turnabout (*Umwendung*)—will be critical in understanding Heidegger's entire philosophical work. Yet this turnabout already proves to be entirely in consequence of the Christianization of God. It is necessary, therefore, to see the intimate connection between Heidegger's critique of subjectivity and his methodological atheism. In order to do this, I want to sketch, albeit briefly, four moments in the phenomenological description of *Dasein* from the period prior and immediately subsequent to the publication of *Sein und Zeit:* first, the existential analytic of *Dasein;* second, the hermeneutics of facticity; third, the worlding of world; and fourth, the nothing as the ground of interpretation, which itself is an abyss or no ground at all. In each case it is possible to see how the analytic of *Dasein* is worked out in relation and opposition to Descartes's subject.

Understanding what coming to the self means arises from considering the questionableness that opens the project of *Sein und Zeit* and Heidegger's

---

36. *Die Grundprobleme der Phänomenologie* (GA24), p. 174. "Die neuere Philosophie vollzog eine totale Umwendung des philosophischen Fragens und ging vom Subjekt, vom Ich aus."

critique of subjectivity. This will allow the turn, or turnabout, to be elaborated in relation to Heidegger's own understanding of *die Kehre* in chapters 3 and 4.

## The Phenomenological Description of *Dasein*

In chapter 1 I noted how, in connection with Bultmann's failure to problematize Heidegger's thinking, being-interpretative might function as a name for *Dasein*. To understand how this already might be the case by the time of Heidegger's involvement with Bultmann in Marburg in the 1920s, it is necessary to understand how the facticity of *Dasein* as such and *Dasein* as self-questioning is precisely established as what Heidegger calls atheism. István Fehér suggests that Heidegger's fundamental perspective can be understood to have arisen out of his continual inquiry into what philosophy actually is.[37] This very inquiry brings questionableness to the fore, so that Heidegger says "thrust within absolute questionableness and thus seeing, to have it, that's what's really grasping philosophy".[38]

What Heidegger names in *Sein und Zeit* and elsewhere as the existential analytic of *Dasein* is the multiplicity of structures in which, through questioning as the very approach and procedure for doing so, *Dasein* comes to an understanding of its character as existing.[39] This questioning, as a placing of the 'I' into question, is the means whereby the ontological difference is brought to light:

> If the questioning is genuine, then it has to be adequate to what it asks for, to the degree that this is possible. The questioning must therefore rightly understand what it asks when it asks about being. What it asks for here as such refers back to the very questioning, inasmuch as this questioning is *a* being. In asking about being, however, we do not raise the question of the being of the being which the questioning itself is;

---

37. Fehér, I., "Heidegger's Postwar Turn" (1996), esp. p. 17f. Fehér also makes the point in "Heidegger's Understanding of the Atheism of Philosophy" (1995), p. 207.

38. *Phänomenologische Interpretationen zu Aristoteles* (GA61), p. 37. "In die absolute Fragwürdigkeit hineingestoßen und sie sehend haben, daß heißt Philosophie eigentlich ergreifen."

39. Cf. for instance: *Sein und Zeit* (GA2) §1; *Prolegomena zur Geschichte des Zeitbegriffs* (GA20), p. 202ff; *Logik* (GA21), §§16, 17, and 37; *Grundprobleme der Phänomenologie* (GA24), p. 322.

but we do satisfy the sense of the question of being when we first uncover the questioning as *a* being simply in what it is . . . as what is this being, of which we say that it questions, looks upon, considers as, relates, etc.—already given? It is *that* being which we ourselves are; this being, which I myself am in each particular instance, we call the *Dasein*.[40]

*Dasein* is therefore the place of the ontological difference: "To grasp the understanding of being means to understand *that* being to whose being-constituted the understanding of being belongs, *Dasein*".[41] The whole force of this explication of the structural analytic of *Dasein* is, however, to unfold the structures of *Dasein* as that being for whom world worlds. It is, in other words, a radical critique of any attempt to represent a transcendental structure of subjectivity—it is the critique of subjectivity as such (indeed, it is elaborated specifically as a critique of Kant and Husserl).[42] In a 1925 lecture course Heidegger stresses the fact that "*Dasein* . . . is . . . *not* a subject or con-

---

40. *Prolegomena zur Geschichte des Zeitbegriffs* (GA20), p. 199 f. "Wenn das Fragen echtes ist, dann hat es möglichst seinem Erfragten angemessen zu sein, d.h. das Fragen muß recht verstehen, was es fragt, nach dem Sein nämlich. Das Erfragte schlägt hier als dieses Erfragte auf das Fragen selbst zurück, sofern dieses ein Seiendes ist. Aber im Fragen nach dem Sein stellen wir nicht die Frage nach dem Sein des Seienden, das das Fragen selbst ist, sondern wir genügen dem Sinn der Frage nach dem Sein, wenn wir das Fragen als Seiendes zunächst lediglich in dem, was es ist, aufdecken . . . Als was ist dieses Seiende, von dem wir sagen: fragen, hinsehen auf, ansprechen als, beziehen— vorgegeben? Es ist *das* Seiende das wir selbst sind; dieses Seiende, das ich je selbst bin, nennen wir das *Dasein*" (author's italics).

41. *Grundprobleme der Phänomenologie* (GA24), p. 322. "Das Seinsverständnis begreifen heißt aber *das* Seiende zunächst verstehen, zu dessen Seinsverfassung das Seinsverständnis gehört, das Dasein" (author's italics).

42. The sharpness of this critique cannot be underestimated. In *Prolegomena zur Geschichte des Zeitbegriffs* (GA20), §4, β, Heidegger concludes by elaborating a point against Husserl he will repeat in 1937 concerning any attempt to establish a universal theory of knowledge. It is, he argues, simply not possible to deduce a universal knowledge which could then subsequently be passed on, perhaps pedagogically, without having been primarily or originarily experienced by those who will receive it. Why this should be I will examine in full later. Heidegger says (*Grundfragen der Philosophie* [GA45] p. 87): "The knowledge of the essence, therefore, if it is to be shared, must itself be accomplished anew by the one who is to assume it. More precisely, it cannot be communicated in the sense of the passing on of a proposition, whose content is simply grasped without its foundation and its acquisition being accomplished again." ("Die Wesenserkenntnis muß daher—soll sie zur Mit-teilung kommen—von dem, der sie aufnehmen soll, selbst

sciousness, which only incidentally provides itself with a world".[43] This contradicts Löwith's assertion that only in the later Heidegger does one find the claim that his work is an attempt to overcome the notion of the subject, illustrating the extent to which the overcoming of subjectivity lies at the very origin of the whole project of *Sein und Zeit* and the years which precede it.[44]

World comes into view therefore, precisely by putting the 'I' into question. It has as its primary target the *ens certum* which Descartes attempts to secure through the *cogito*. In the putting of the self into question that is the structural analytic of *Dasein*, Heidegger shows that to be in the place of questioning is to bring before the self the there that being is: *Da-sein*. In a lecture course in 1929 Heidegger contrasts this there-being with subjectivity and asks how the subject first came into view (through the *cogito*), and if that is not a self-questioning. He remarks that in the coming-about of the subject the *only thing* that is not put into question is myself: "Descartes . . . begins philosophizing with *doubt*, and it seems everything is put into question. Yet it only seems so. *Dasein*, the I (the ego) never comes into question at all . . . all that is ever put into question . . . is knowledge, consciousness of things".[45] The structural analytic of *Dasein* is, from the outset, and in its very working out, the reversal of the Cartesian order of questioning. Questioning will be used to challenge the method of doubt as a way of bringing the 'I' to the fore instead of questioning everything except the 'I'. In consequence nothing like a subject can be established in virtue of it, nothing independent of world, nothing mathematically founded.

---

wieder neu vollzogen werden. Genauer gesagt, sie kann nicht mitgeteilt werden im Sinne der Weitergabe eines Satzes, dessen Gehalt einfach erfaßt wird, ohne daß die Gründung und Gewinnung nachvollzogen ist.")

43. *Prolegomena zur Geschichte des Zeitbegriffs* (GA20), §32, p. 422. "*Dasein* . . . ist . . . *nicht* ein Subjekt oder Bewußtsein, das sich gelegentlich erst eine Welt zulegt" (author's italics).

44. *Heidegger—Denker in dürftiger Zeit* (1984), pp. 148–154. In particular, Löwith argues that the later Heidegger abandons the "subjectival, *Dasein*-oriented foundation of truth" ("subjekthafte, daseinsmäßige Fundament der Wahrheit") of *Sein und Zeit* (p. 148) and speaks of Heidegger's attempt to speak of being without "subjectivity as the point of departure" ("Ausgangsstellung bei der Subjektivität") (p. 151).

45. *Die Grundbegriffe der Metaphysik* (GA29/30), p. 30. "*Descartes* . . . beginnt das Philosophieren mit dem *Zweifel*, und es sieht so aus, als werde alles in Frage gestellt. Aber es sieht nur so aus. Das Dasein, das Ich (das ego) wird gar nicht in Frage gestellt. . . . es wird in Frage gestellt . . . nur immer das Wissen, das Bewußtsein von den Dingen" (author's italics).

## The Hermeneutics of Facticity

What preceded the elaboration of the analytic of *Dasein* in the period between 1919 and 1924 was the thoroughgoing working out of the hermeneutics of facticity, exemplified in a lecture course of 1923 entitled *Ontologie (Hermeneutik der Faktizität)*. Here in the *Supplement*, Heidegger raises the notion of destructuring which in itself *is* the hermeneutics of facticity.[46] Destructuring will be "a penetrating, dismantling, going-back to the motive-sources of explication". This will reveal the "hidden motives"[47] which drive the ruling interpretations that have precisely taken over and formed a world independent of my being through the structures of subjectivity, and so left me as alienated from what world is. Even earlier than this in 1922, Heidegger had stressed that philosophy's ability to explicate the fundamental movements of life itself: its capacity "to make factical life speak for itself on the basis of its own factical possibilities" only if it is "fundamentally atheistic".[48] Fehér notes that in the course of elaborating the character of the hermeneutics of facticity, Heidegger demonstrates that "the present is . . . thoroughly permeated and dominated by traditional conceptual schemes, dragged along through the centuries without any effort at an original re-appropriation—conceptual schemes and habits whose roots in lived experience, from which they once emerged, have long withered away".[49] Destructuring actually brings the tradition before me in an entirely new way, for it forces me to question its reception and interrogate it into its very roots—to know it, precisely in order to understand and so overcome it. To overcome—a term I shall use often—does not mean to exceed, but rather to bring before the self and stand within whatever is overcome for its own sake, properly. Such an interrogation reveals the very lived-experience of its origins, in that in order to be able to interrogate it with regard to its

---

46. *Ontologie* (GA63), a Freiburg lecture course of the summer semester of 1923, p. 106. The point is repeated in *Phänomenologische Interpretationen zu Aristoteles* (1922/23), p. 249. The notion of *Destruktion* appears as early as the *Anmerkungen zu Karl Jaspers 'Psychologie der Weltanschauungen'* (*Wegmarken* [GA9]), p. 3 f.

47. *Phänomenologische Interpretationen zu Aristoteles* (1989), p. 249. "Im abbauenden Rückgang zu den ursprünglichen Motivquellen der Explikation vorzudringen . . . verdeckte[n] Motive[n]".

48. *Phänomenologische Interpretationen zu Aristoteles* (1989), p. 246. "Das faktische Leben von ihm selbst her aus seinen eigenen faktischen Möglichkeiten auf sich selbst zu stellen", "wenn [die Philosophie] grundsätzlich atheistisch ist."

49. Fehér, I., "Heidegger's Postwar Turn" (1995), p. 16.

roots means already to understand that what now are the shards and hints of meaning once were the very stuff of interpretation; they were the very material of the common expression of lived-experience. Again, such a lived-experience presupposes a world—just that world which, *as* lived-experience worlded *Dasein*, but which has since been covered over and forgotten. In the covering over and forgetting, what gets left behind are objectifications that in their turn take over as markers for an experience that is no longer available to be articulated.

To undergo the separation from the lived-experience that produced an interpretative way of being reproduces the world as objects. Such a reproduction at the same time displaces me from standing in the worlding of lived experience: I come now to be explained as the subject who knows the objects of a world in which I no longer live. The worlding of world becomes so many objects (objectifications) against which a subject is made to stand. Hence Heidegger's concern with objects—literally ob-jects, things that stand against (the German is *Gegenstand*), displacing me from where I would stand to be in lived experience. Heidegger analyzes this decay of meaning as, for instance, in the epistemology of the theoretical sciences, a *"demand for a standpoint-free observing"* which is itself in consequence of the coming about of the subject-object distinction.[50]

## THE WORLDING OF WORLD

This working through of *Dasein* reveals it as that being who, through a factical, worlded hermeneutics and explication of the meaning of lived experience, in its very structures, in being worlded, occurs as an abyss, an ungrounded being, and so not originarily caused by God in the order of being. Heidegger indicates that this being ungrounded is the very constitution of *Dasein*'s freedom. *Dasein* would, for instance, be free to discover itself (through God's revelation, in faith) as caused by God precisely and only because its originary freedom is that it discovers itself in its world as ungrounded by anything other than its being in the world ontologically. However, this freedom brings with it attendant dangers, dangers which are part of the structure of *Dasein* and of its freedom. The question of meaning

---

50. *Ontologie* (GA63), p. 82. Cf. p. 81. *"Forderung eines standpunktfreien Betrachtens"* (author's italics).

is posed for *Dasein* precisely because meaning is not given in advance of (i.e., prior to) *Dasein*, but *Dasein* has to advance toward what meaning is: *Dasein* must discover meaning for itself and make it its own. This advancing-toward is a temporal phenomenon.

In the phenomenology of *Ruinanz* that Heidegger explicated in lectures in 1921 and 1922, he defines the whither of ruinance precisely as the nothing.[51] The consequence of this coming to the self as worlded, through factical interpretation, is that in lived experience there is always an undergoing of the loss of meaning. This is what ruinance is and how it occurs. Ruinance is the passing of time, or 'timing' of factical, lived, existing, *as* the taking away of that sense of time which would otherwise reveal that the separation of meaning was taking place from its lived roots or origins. In other words, ruinance is a forgetting, a decay which, in decaying, destroys even the remembrance of its occurring, so that it renders what it destroys invisible, and it renders itself invisible at the same time: "Factical, ruined, living 'has no time', because its basic movement, ruinance itself, takes away 'time', an erased time which as itself factically ruined living in itself erases. Ruinance erases time, which means that it seeks to delete the historical from out of facticity".[52] Ruinance is, in a sense, the forgetting that belongs to being-factical. To be factical is to be finite in a world. To be worlded means to be gaining and erasing, and so being worlded has a driven aspect which in its very negating allows a driving-forward, but as a being-driven into the impersonal and the static realities of the impersonal *das Man* that is no one or nobody in particular; the anonymous. Ruinance disembodies me as something whose lived experience is subordinated to the objectifications of meaning in ruinance.[53]

How can this be? Which is to ask, how can ruinance, which is timely, have no time and yet can only be understood as a phenomenon which is concerned with time? This may be explained in two ways. First, in that *Dasein* is something I know myself to be, I move in time by an orientation toward the future which may include the past as a remembering of it, or as a forgetting. My existence is, however, altered by my experience of time whether I

---

51. *Phänomenologische Interpretationen zu Aristoteles* (GA61), p. 143.

52. *Phänomenologische Interpretationen zu Aristoteles* (GA61), p. 139 f. "Das faktische, ruinante Leben 'hat keine Zeit', weil seine Grundbewegtheit, die Ruinanz selbst, die 'Zeit' wegnimmt, eine wegnehmbare Zeit, die faktisch ruinantes Leben für sich selbst in sich selbst wegnimmt. Die Ruinanz nimmt die Zeit weg, d.h. aus der Faktizität sucht sie das Historische zu tilgen."

53. Cf. *Ontologie* (GA 63), p. 32.

remember or forget, and in this sense I still change, whether in moving I know it and can explain it, or not. My projecting forward into a future is not something I will as such, but rather is how I could even know myself at all, how I could have the view that driving forward is the driving of my will. I am driven into the future because the present, through ruinance, decays into the past and leaves me with an absence, a nothing, which demands to be filled. Ruinance gives the semblance of being overcome only when I enter into the reflection on my timeliness as such. I take up the future as existing, which is also always a certain laying aside of the past *in order* to take up the future. I can be aware of ruinance or not, but even becoming aware of ruinance implies a certain taking hold of it in a particular way, a 'how' of bringing it to the fore. Whether I take hold or not, ruinance occurs. In taking hold in a particular way, everything that is not taken in in this taking hold is itself lost to ruinance, so that memory itself takes form as a particular memory, as *this* memory, which is not (but could have been) *that* memory.

The second sense has to do, not with my *Dasein* as constituted as *mine*, but as its being-constituted: what I take up in order to understand my taking up; what I take for granted, in that it explains all the taking-up of the future I do. This is the very possibility of my knowing that I am oriented toward the future, as a knowing that also contains a lag, a stretching out (*intentio*) as a space for reflecting or failing to reflect in being timed. Ruinance has no time because it is my losing of myself, and I am timely.

## THE NOTHING AS THE GROUND OF INTERPRETATION

There is then a negating in ruinance which allows life to be as such, but which is always alienative. Heidegger describes this as a drop or crash. Where does ruinance end up—where does it plunge down into? Nowhere—it is its own whither. The erasing and negating is revealed in its very negating-character as *the* nothing. Finally, Heidegger concludes, the nothing of facticity as such is "of and for itself timingly enlivening environing *not coming to the fore in ruinance of existence itself* (facticity)".[54] Nothing itself is structural to facticity.

---

54. *Phänomenologische Interpretationen zu Aristoteles* (GA61), p. 148. "Von ihm für es selbst gezeitigtes lebensmäßiges umweltliches *Nichtvorkommen im ruinanten Dasein seiner selbst* (Faktizität)" (author's italics).

In 1921–22 Heidegger uses the phrase 'the empty' to illustrate the sense of nothing in factical life. It is this emptiness and nothing-character which constitutes "the how of '*yet existing*'" which he had already pointed out was the very *Da-* of "*Da-*sein of facticity".[55] It is only a short step, therefore, from this factical explication of 'ruinance' to describing the very freedom of *Dasein* as an abyss in the essay *Vom Wesen des Grundes* in 1929.[56]

Negation as such is the very actuality of *Dasein* as both finite and temporalizing, which is what Heidegger means when he says that *Dasein* is time itself. Here the inquiry into care is explained: "In what sense is the structure of being of *Dasein*—care—characterized by time? These structures are not different to what they themselves are, neither as time nor as something of a relation to time, but rather care is in a way determined 'through' time, in the sense that it is itself time, the facticity of time itself".[57] There are two further ways in which Heidegger investigates the nothing in relation to *Dasein*. The first is through the phenomenology of mood, specifically anxiety. The second is in his description of the finitude of *Dasein* as "being-toward-death".[58] In *Dasein*'s being-toward-death *Dasein* first overcomes the everydayness of being objectified and comes to itself as being for itself. In its finitude *Dasein* discovers its own *Da-*, that it is there, the place of its being which is wholly its own. In the phenomenon of anxiety, *Dasein* most discovers its questionableness, its inability to secure itself against the world. Anxiety is always that mood of being where *Dasein* discovers itself unable to totalize itself, where its incompleteness as temporal being brings itself before itself as negated, as a not.

Questioning, which appears as a hermeneutical task, is just that possibility of bringing the self to the self as a being, of coming about, of discovering being to be through a particular being, this being, *my* being. I am most myself when I most discover myself as constituted, *given*, by what I most am

---

55. *Phänomenologische Interpretationen zu Aristoteles* (GA61): p. 148, "(das) Wie des '*noch Daseins*'"; p. 142, "*Da-*sein (der) Faktizität" (author's italics).

56. *Vom Wesen des Grundes* (*Wegmarken* [GA9]), p. 174, and *passim*.

57. *Logik* (GA21), especially the concluding section, §37, p. 409, *Zeit als Existential des Daseins—Zeitlichkeit und Sorgestruktur*. In this section we find: "In welchem Sinne ist die Seinsstruktur des Daseins—Sorge—durch die Zeit charakterisiert? Diese Strukturen sind nicht außer dem, was sie selbst sind, noch in der Zeit, noch in irgendeiner Beziehung zur Zeit, sondern die Sorge ist in der Weise 'durch' die Zeit bestimmt, daß sie selbst Zeit, die Faktizität der Zeit selbst ist."

58. Although *Angst* is described in *Sein und Zeit*, Heidegger most fully elaborates its relation to the nothing as such in the inaugural lecture *Was ist Metaphysik?* (*Wegmarken*, [GA9]). With regard to being toward death, see esp. *Sein und Zeit* (GA2), §§51–53.

not. Constituted by what? Nothing. Nothing as the ground (which is no-ground) of meaning-giving. Put another way, the very inquiry into ground reveals there to be no ground at all: ground, appearing through groundlessness. This is the factical understanding of myself as given, rather than any causal explanation which I can be given through faith. Nevertheless this groundlessness is the ontological grounding possibility of discovering (in faith) myself to have been created by God. In order truly to discover myself as created (in the order of faith), I must first take myself as groundless (in the order of being). The factical givenness of myself has no explanation, it needs no why, it is the one thing about which I *need* never ask, but whose meaning is only disclosable in that I alone ask about it. Every asking is a projection into the future, even when the question itself concerns the past. Every causal explanation of this why is a conjecture which might explain but does not expose the structure of this given; every *why* is an advancing toward, a genuine orientation toward a future, not something which I must discover as already having been. Even Descartes's argument in the *Meditations* has this structure, because (in the order of being) the *cogito* is discovered and grounded first, although this priority is transgressed in what it subsequently discovers already to have been in the order of being. Part of the atheism required to expose this factical understanding is the refusal to adduce causes to my being before understanding what else those causes mean and represent. My very givenness *to myself* has no cause; it is my being, my *Dasein*. It is the one thing which, however I explain it, will not yield its meaning through this explanation.

What is at issue here is the carrying through of a critique of Descartes. If the order of procedure of the analytic of *Dasein* is reversed with regard to Descartes, this is the abandonment, *philosophically*, of any attempt to ground the self in God as the prior cause of the self. I can find no cause for myself prior to myself, because in the order of being, even something which (say, through faith) I subsequently discovered to have caused me (say, God), nevertheless is a *subsequent* discovery.

## THE QUESTION OF ANALOGY

Having clarified, albeit briefly, some of Heidegger's concerns with regard to atheism in the phenomenological analysis of *Dasein*, I raise in a preliminary way, solely as a problem, the question of analogy, which I will consider again in more depth in chapter 6, precisely because of the way it also relates to

Descartes for Heidegger. In what follows, I wish only to outline the problem as Heidegger prepares it in *Sein und Zeit,* and only insofar as it refers to Heidegger's atheism. Descartes's consideration of the world as *res extensa* and Aristotle's understanding of place, τόπος, lie outside the concerns of this book (as I have noted), although any thoroughgoing treatment of the question of analogy in relation to Heidegger's work would also have to take them extensively into consideration.

Descartes is able to found the whole of being (*substantia finita*) on God (*substantia infinita*) for three reasons: first, because, as I have already noted, for Heidegger, Descartes evades the question of the interrogability of being; second, Descartes founds the whole of created being on increate being, the being of God; and third, however, and most importantly, and despite the turnabout of prior philosophical thinking that his fundamental position represents, Descartes founds modern metaphysics in the way he does only because the inherent possibility of doing so already lay with Aristotle. These three matters conspire to bring the question of analogy to the fore as a seeming solution to the problem of being insofar as modern theology makes an appeal through modern metaphysics to speaking of God. What appears as so appealing a solution is in fact the incapability of modern metaphysics to resolve the question of being at all, which means its inability to make the self, the 'I', questionable in its very structures. The suggestion in *Sein und Zeit* is that the problem of analogy would have to be destructured to its very roots in order properly to undertake a phenomenological description of *Dasein.* From the point of view of Heidegger's atheism, this would mean that speaking of God would also undergo a certain transformation, one which did not entangle God in the structures of *Dasein,* where the mark of this entanglement is that the structures of *Dasein* appear to be worked out through a question concerning God.

Herman Philipse suggests that a major part of Heidegger's critique of Aristotle's understanding of being as such is that "even though Aristotle's ontology aimed at raising the question of bring, he did not succeed in doing so because he reduced the *being* of entities to yet another entity, the Deity".[59] Certainly Heidegger's description of the relation of the divine to the modes of ἀληθεύειν worked out in the *Nicomachean Ethics* shows how σοφία, for Aristotle, is the highest mode of ἀλήθεια. Σοφία is primarily the mode of being of the divine ("κτῆσις of a θεός")[60] and by implication therefore not

59. Philipse, H., *Heidegger's Philosophy of Being* (1998), p. 97.
60. *Platon: Sophistes* (GA19), p. 134. "Κτῆσις eines θεός."

determined as properly a mode of being of *Dasein*. Heidegger notes that the working out of the divinity of σοφία, by which all the modes of ἀληθεύειν then fall into an ordering structure, makes the gods—divinity itself—into a philosophical thematic and so is "a very early anticipation of Aristotle's *Metaphysics*".[61] Heidegger immediately adds a footnote to the printed text, pointing the reader to the place in the *Metaphysics* where Aristotle's understanding of the divine is laid out: "We hold, then, the divine is a being, living, without change, the best; and therefore life and unceasing ages and unchangedness are proper to the divine".[62]

Because σοφία is determined as properly the mode of divinity, all the other modes of ἀληθεύειν (τέχνη, ἐπιστήμη, φρόνησις, and νοῦς) are transformed so that they become dependently modes of divinity too, because they constitute a framework by which divinity and nondivinity (mortality) are coordinated. The whole structure of ἀλήθεια in the understanding of human being is simultaneously not worked out on the basis of being-human but being-divine. This has far-reaching consequences for philosophy, in that it represents, from the very beginning, a reversal in the order of working out of the being of beings, the ontological difference itself. From the outset, in other words, the being of beings is worked out on the basis of a being which is not the being of *Dasein*, but of something else, the divine, or what we now call God.

It is possible to see, therefore, how Heidegger interpreted Descartes, not as making the fundamental move to determine the being of beings out of the divine, but rather, through an intensification of a Christianizing process begun in the Middle Ages, of converting an ontological dependence on the divine already established in Aristotle to its most extreme possibility, which (on the basis of philosophy's taking over something preferred by faith in revelation) is the possibility demanded by the interpretation of the being of the world (and of human being) as *ens creatum*.

The problem of analogy arises, therefore, from "Aristotle, in whom this problem is foreshadowed in prototypical form just at the outset of Greek ontology"[63] and is worked out in varying ways in the theology of

61. *Platon: Sophistes* (GA19), p. 134. "Das weist weit voraus in die 'Metaphysik' des Aristoteles."

62. Aristotle, *Metaphysics*, XII, vii (1072b30). "φαμὲν δὴ τὸν θεὸν εἶναι ζῷον ἀΐδιον ἄριστον, ὥστε ζωὴ καὶ αἰὼν συνεχὴς καὶ ἀΐδιος ὑπάρχει τῷ θεῷ"

63. *Sein und Zeit* (GA2), p. 93. "Aristoteles, bei dem wie im Ansatz der griechischen Ontologie überhaupt das Problem vorgebildet ist."

Scholasticism. Frequently Heidegger reminds his readers that Descartes worked out his ontology on the basis of the categories laid down and investigated by the tradition of Scholasticism.[64] Indeed, Heidegger remarks: "With regard to the working out of this problem ontologically, Descartes remains always far behind the Scholastics".[65]

In the problem of analogy the signification 'being' is taken to be capable of signifying any particular beings with which one may be concerned. Thus "in the assertions 'God is' and 'the world is' we assert being".[66] However, in this asserting of being, the being of human being has already been referred in its fundamental ontological properties to something other than the human being or *Dasein*. Analogy arises as a solution to this problem, in that it appears to make transparently possible the signification of the being of all beings, including God. Heidegger's point is this: *Dasein* is the being who is properly concerned with being as such, being is an issue for it. This makes the being of beings and above all the being of *Dasein* interrogable, capable of being questioned: above all, I can inquire into the character and ways of my own being. When, however, the being of beings is determined no longer by and out of the being for whom its being is an issue, being is, strictly speaking, no longer interrogable.

Put another way, God's self-questioning or even God's self-transparency philosophically are no concern of mine, because they can *never* be a concern of *mine*. As Aquinas tirelessly reminds us, God alone knows God in God's self. We only know God in God's effects. If God is made the determinant of the interrogability of the being of beings, then human beings would depend for their knowledge of being on revelations from God. When this is thematized in a formal, philosophical way, something like the *cogito* would have to emerge, because every cognition now becomes a revelation from God. Thus not only is the meaning of being left unclarified in modern metaphysics, but the way into clarifying it—by questioning, the self-questioning of *Dasein* as the inherent possibility of the interrogability of being, is blocked off. The

---

64. See, for more contemporary investigations of this relation: Janowski, Z., *Cartesian Theodicy* (2000); Secada, G., *Cartesian Metaphysics: The Scholastic Origins of Modern Philosophy* (2000); and Des Chene, D., *Physiologia: Natural Philosophy in Late Aristotelian and Cartesian Thought* (1996).

65. *Sein und Zeit* (GA2), p. 93. "*Descartes* bleibt hinsichtlich der ontologischen Durcharbeitung des Problems weit hinter der Scholastik zurück."

66. *Sein und Zeit* (GA2), p. 93. "In den Aussagen 'Gott ist' und 'die Welt ist' sagen wir Sein aus."

*cogito* doubts—questions—absolutely everything except itself. There is a corollary to this, one that will be decisive for the conclusions of this book. If God's self-transparency can never be a philosophical concern of *mine*, in what ways can I be concerned with it? Does faith have an access to this self-transparency, and if so, how?

In virtue of a possibility initiated by Aristotle and thematized in an extreme form by Descartes, in saying 'God is' within the province of metaphysics, such a saying already presupposes the occlusion of the being of *Dasein:* the being of *Dasein* has not been determined out of its own self-questioning and bringing of itself to the fore, and so it is no longer free to come across other things that are. Analogy is the very marker of this occlusion, or as Heidegger refers to it in the text we consider in chapter 6, an impasse.

## THEOLOGY AS THE SCIENCE OF FAITH

It has remained a persistent question what Heidegger meant, in *Sein und Zeit* and elsewhere, by the terms *Eigentlichkeit, eigentlich, Uneigentlichkeit,* and *uneigentlich.* Both Stambaugh's and the Robinson and Macquarrie translations of *Sein und Zeit* render these terms as authenticity/authentic and inauthenticity/inauthentic. Heidegger's introduction of the terms in *Sein und Zeit* comes with a warning for their difficulty:

> As modes of being, *authenticity* and *inauthenticity*—these expressions have been chosen in the strictest sense of the word—are based on the fact that *Dasein* is in general determined by mineness. However, the inauthenticity of *Dasein* does not signify a "lesser" being or "lower" degree of being. Rather it is the case that even in its fullest concretion *Dasein* can be characterized by inauthenticity when busy, excited, interested, ready for enjoyment.[67]

---

67. *Sein und Zeit* (GA2), p. 42 f. "Die beiden Seinsmodi der *Eigentlichkeit* und *Uneigentlichkeit*—diese Ausdrücke sind im strengen Wortsinne terminologisch gewählt—gründen darin, daß Dasein überhaupt durch Jemeinigkeit bestimmt ist. Die Uneigentlichkeit des Daseins bedeutet aber nicht etwa ein 'weniger' Sein oder einen 'niedrigeren' Seinsgrad. Die Uneigentlichkeit kann vielmehr das Dasein nach seiner vollsten Konkretion bestimmen in seiner Geschäftigkeit, Angeregtheit, Interessiert, Genußfähigkeit" (author's italics).

These two terms can better be translated as ownliness/ownly and disowned-ness/disowned if only because, while accurately rendering the Greek sense of τὸ αὐτὸ to which Heidegger alludes (as well as all the German resonances of *eigen*), yet to the English-speaking ear the word *auth*entic does not stress sufficiently the particularity of selfhood in what is meant by *Je-meinig, my*-own.

It was the very working through of this coming-to-the-self of facticity in the period from 1919 up to and just beyond the publication of *Sein und Zeit* (in fact up to the inaugural lecture for Heidegger's professorial chair at Freiburg in 1929, *Was ist Metaphysik?*) that enabled Heidegger to demonstrate the extent to which theology itself had become inauthentic—literally, had disowned and become dissociated from its roots. John van Buren quotes from Heidegger's winter semester lectures of 1919–20 where Heidegger says that:

> The ancient Christian achievement was distorted and buried through the infiltration of classical science into Christianity. From time to time it reasserted itself in violent eruptions (as in Augustine, in Luther, in Kierkegaard). Only from here is Medieval mysticism to be understood . . . [after Augustine] the struggle between Aristotle and the new "feeling for life" continued in Medieval mysticism and eventually in Luther.[68]

He notes that in the same lecture course Heidegger called for the "destructuring of Christian philosophy and theology".[69] Van Buren has demonstrated with great effectiveness the way in which Heidegger's reading of Augustine, the mystical tradition (especially Eckhart), and the early Luther in his lecture courses of 1919, 1920, and 1921, illustrated the extent to which Christianity had delivered itself over into an alien thinking: "To use Heidegger's terminology in his 1919 course, the Greek conceptuality of the Patristic and Scholastic periods brought about a 'theorizing' of primal Christianity and more particularly a designifying, deworlding and mytholo-

---

68. Cf. van Buren, J., *The Young Heidegger* (1994), p. 146, referring to *Grundprobleme der Phänomenologie* (GA58), p. 205.

69. van Buren, J., *The Young Heidegger* (1994), p. 147, citing *Phänomenologie der Anschauung und des Ausdrucks* (GA59), p. 12. "Die radikale Explikation der phänomenologischen Problematik, deren Sinn gewonnen werden soll, wird die griechische Philosophie (Platon und Aristoteles) und ebenso die neuzeitliche seit Descartes in dem destruktiven Aspekt zu nehmen wissen, so zwar, daß damit die positiv entscheidende Destruktion der christlichen Philosophie und Theologie sich erst klar vorbereitet."

gizing of its concrete historical content-sense". The result, in Scholasticism especially, is that "the believer/God relation is forced into the foreign Aristotelian notion of '*theion*', the divine, as first cause and '*noesis noeseos*, thought of thought' . . . (which) 'does not have the slightest thing to do with the God of Thomas'".[70]

It is from this background that the 1927 lecture published as *Phäno-menologie und Theologie* has to be understood, with its opening refusal to discuss philosophy and theology as an opposition, while at the same time trying to bring into discussion the question of their relation. Heidegger explicitly clarifies what the object of the ontic science of theology is: not God, but rather, "*theology is the science of faith*".[71] This is so in four ways: first, not as a set of propositions; second, as a believing comportment toward revelation; third, because it arises out of faith; and fourth, because theology as an objectification of faith has no other purpose than to advance faith. This ontic science has only to do with an investigation into faith, which is a way of being of *Dasein*. It is in no sense concerned with a disclosure of the essence of God or of God's being as such, but only *my* being in its comported faithfulness to God. Why this should be so important will become clear in my consideration of *esse* in chapter 6.

A term which Heidegger employs in this discussion and which has the potential to be very confusing is pre-Christian. One is apt to think of the pre-Christian as what occurs before Christ's coming, or to interpret all time subsequent to the birth of Christ as Christian time. For Heidegger, however, the question of the pre-Christian is entirely related to faith and so not to any universal time but my time, the time of this *Dasein*. The pre-Christian is therefore what is before *my* human existence's faith in Christ. This in Christian terms might be inferred to have two moments—as prior to baptism (or conversion) and prior to formation as a Christian person. It may even have a third moment as that structure of existence which makes conversion possible, which might bear conversion, baptism, or being-in-Christ. Such a figuration is included in the subsequent life of faith: "So it is part of the Christian happening of rebirth that therein a pre-faithful, that is, unfaithful (unbelieving) existence of *Dasein* is sublated . . . in faith is the

---

70. van Buren, J., *The Young Heidegger* (1994), p. 159, quoting *Phänomenologische Interpretationen zu Aristoteles*, pp. 250, 263, and *Logik* (GA21), p. 123.

71. *Phänomenologie und Theologie* (*Wegmarken* [GA9]), p. 55. "*Theologie ist die Wissenschaft des Glaubens*" (author's italics).

existential-ontic pre-Christian existence indeed overcome . . . 'overcome' does not mean disposed of, but possessed in a new way".[72]

In the same lecture ontology is envisaged as acting as a corrective to the ontic sciences, among which must be included theology: "Ontology functions therefore only as a corrective of the ontic, and to be precise, the pre-Christian content of theological basic-concepts . . . here one must note this correction is not grounding".[73] Ontology here therefore does not mean some generalized science, some abstract knowledge which, suitably clarified and so clarifying, can ground anew a whole theoretical or abstract theology. Ontology is just that being of knowing which, as knowing, brings me to 'be' myself for myself for the first time. Ontology is just that coming to the self which is yielded by the hermeneutics of facticity; it is *Dasein* coming to itself as an entity, a being, in questioning, owning itself, becoming *authentic*. Such an ontology is not grounding, because it is already ungrounded—it comes about through taking into understanding the violent plunge into nothing. It is possible to see how Heidegger developed the strongly existential language that characterized *Sein und Zeit* and yet also how it was that *Sein und Zeit* was itself so little understood. Is there not, after all, a danger here—precisely that danger which misled Heidegger's earliest critics into believing him to be advancing a decisionism or voluntarism or existentialism, where I can will myself to be authentic? Is this questioning which gives *Dasein* to itself as a being something I can just decide to do? Is not this strong existential language nothing other than the *existentialism* that Heidegger always repudiated as a creation above all, of Sartre?

How can this investigation be characterized, this question which brings me before myself in concern, or care, for the first time, and which in doing so throws up the need for that coming to the self which entails and demands a destruction of philosophy and theology to its roots, as just that destructuring of those very things which first brought me to myself?[74] In 1919 Heidegger

72. *Phänomenologie und Theologie* (*Wegmarken* [GA9]), p. 63. "So liegt doch im christlichen Geschehen als Wiedergeburt, daß darin die vorgläubige, d. i. ungläubige Existenz des Daseins aufgehoben ist . . . im Glauben ist zwar existenziell-ontisch die vorchristliche Existenz überwunden . . . überwinden besagt nicht abstoßen, sondern in neue Verfügung nehmen."

73. *Phänomenologie und Theologie* (*Wegmarken* [GA9]), p. 64. "Die Ontologie fungiert demnach nur als ein Korrektiv des ontischen, und zwar vorchristlichen Gehaltes der theologischen Grundbegriffe. Hier bleibt aber zu beachten: diese Korrektion ist nicht begründend."

74. See *Sein und Zeit* (GA2), esp. §§57, 64–65. Care translates *die Sorge*.

introduced a term which was prescient for any understanding of *die Kehre*, the turn. Specifically discussing the character of hermeneutics, he made the observation "through tipping-over of understanding and appearance (application of negation?) phenomena come to expression. Philosophical intuition is not then the most adequate if it *reproduces* happenings".[75] The term tipping-over is repeated in a lecture series of 1925–26, specifically in relation to Kant.[76] If, as von Herrmann suggests, this term is the origin of the term *die Kehre*, it is specifically so in relation to the understanding of phenomena themselves.[77] In other words, the tipping-over which must always be a possibility for philosophy (i.e., when it becomes a questioning) also occurs as a question about the *what* and *how* of knowing phenomena—things. A turnabout— a tipping-over—in the order of thinking will have profound consequences for the understanding of phenomena or beings.

If tipping-over is prescient of *die Kehre*, still more so is Heidegger's naming of phenomenological research as an atheism, which belongs intimately to *die Kehre* when it is fully elaborated. So far, I have traced two parallel movements, albeit briefly. Each functions as a preliminary indication—a hint, perhaps, of how *die Kehre* will come to be understood, in an understanding to be elaborated in the later chapters of this book. The first revealed Heidegger's analysis of *Dasein* to be grounded in the nothing. The second culminated in just that clarification sought when, as Gadamer notes, Heidegger's question for theology can be formulated as "whether there was no more appropriate way for Christians to understand themselves than the way offered by contemporary theology".[78] Gadamer's conclusion here is of particular importance, for it demonstrates well how Heidegger's project of destructuring is required both in the fields of philosophy and theology: "that the theology, which he had studied and which found its support in

---

75. *Grundprobleme der Phänomenologie* (GA58), p. 263 (appendix). "Durch die Umkippungen des Verstehens und Anschauens (Verwendung der Negation?) kommen die Phänomene zum Ausdruck—philosophische Intuition ist nicht dann am adäquatesten, wenn sie das Geschehen *nachbildet*" (author's italics). The appendix was compiled from Oskar Becker's notes of the lecture course.

76. *Logik* (GA21), p. 269.

77. *Wegmarken* (GA9), p. 487. "Sie [die Marginalien] sind aus der sich vollziehenden Kehre, die Heidegger früher schon mit dem Kantischen Wort 'Umkippung' bezeichnet hat, gedacht und gewähren uns oft einen jähen Einblick in die Bewegung des sich kehrenden Denkens."

78. *Heidegger's Wege* (1983), p. 145. "Ob es nicht ein angemesseneres Selbst-Verständnis des Christen gibt als das durch die zeitgenössische Theologie angebotene?"

Aristotle's metaphysics did not correspond in the least bit to the true motives of Greek thinking must have been sharpened by his exchange with this thinking".[79] If the theology he had studied did not correspond to what he had come to learn was the Greek understanding of being, neither did this theology correspond to what I have described as reflection on the lived experience of faith. His study of St. Paul, St. Augustine, and Luther pointed toward a destructuring purgation of the matter of theology; his study of Aristotle (and through Aristotle, Plato), in contrast, pointed to the need for a destructuring of philosophy. The destructuring at issue would reveal both philosophy and theology in their originary grounds.[80]

## THE MEANING OF HEIDEGGER'S ATHEISM

When Heidegger said that philosophical research is and remains atheism he described that research as new. This philosophical research is, therefore, phenomenology, a new and changed field in the procedures of philosophical research. This new research is, he tells us, explained "out of the retrospective and past situation of philosophy".[81] In this sense, philosophical research is now and will remain atheism but was not always so. Already the question of what philosophical research is can be shown as belonging to a historical unfolding, something that has come to pass in a particular form in consequence of what it was before and where it came from. Heidegger is, however, arguing that phenomenology is in its very self-descriptiveness atheistic. Why is this so? Further on, Heidegger says of philosophy: "And precisely in this atheism (it) becomes what a great man once called the 'Gay Science'".[82] The capitalization of *Fröhliche* explains who the great man is—Nietzsche, in whose *Die Fröhliche Wissenschaft* is to be found the story of the madman's

---

79. *Heidegger's Wege* (1983), p. 145. "Daß die Theologie, die er gelernt hatte und die sich weithin auf die aristotelische Metaphysik stützte, nicht einmal den wirklichen Motiven des griechischen Denkens entsprach, mußte für ihn die Auseinandersetzung mit diesem Denken nur noch verschärfen."
80. In his lectures on Plato in the winter of 1924/25, Heidegger stressed that the way into Plato was through Aristotle (see *Platon: Sophistes* [GA19], esp. pp. 12–14).
81. *Prolegomena zur Geschichte des Zeitbegriffs* (GA20), p. 108. "aus der rückwärtigen und vergangenen Lage der Philosophie."
82. *Prolegomena zur Geschichte des Zeitbegriffs* (GA20), p. 110. "Und gerade in diesem Atheismus wird sie zu dem, was ein Großer einmal sagte, zur 'Fröhlichen Wissenschaft'."

proclamation of the death of God. Phenomenology, this atheism, can and does come about only after Nietzsche and what he has to say about the proclamation of the death of God.

At this point, about the only meaning for the word atheism that can be ruled out, as Vycinas pointed out above, is that Heidegger was or is what is meant by the commonplace term an atheist. What is clear is that in 1925, long before the lectures on Nietzsche of 1937–44 (where, it is commonly understood, Heidegger first elaborated his understanding of the history of being) and before the so-called turn out of the existential analytic of *Dasein* toward the meaning of being as such, Heidegger was already unfolding the place of God in the context of a historical inquiry into what he himself constitutes as the philosophical tradition, precisely because Nietzsche had proclaimed the death of God. In other words what it is routinely claimed he is doing in the later, wartime, and postwar work (as against his earlier work), he is already doing in outline even before the publication of *Sein und Zeit*.[83] What does this mean? Immediately, there is no later Heidegger *as opposed to* the earlier (and so by implication, no hermeneutic turn from the structural analytic of *Dasein* to the analysis of being as such) as far as what later has conventionally been taken to indicate. Moreover, as I intend to show, the terms that are later fully named and worked out as *das Ereignis* and *die Kehre* and the philosophical positions that they indicate are already, as early as 1919 and certainly by 1925, working as directives in his thinking.

How might this atheism be understood? This question might better be asked: how is the self (subject) normally grounded? As we have seen, in modern metaphysics the self as subject is either simply taken to be caused by God or discovered to be causally grounded by God, subsequent to the self-grounding maxim *cogito ergo sum*. Here both God and the self occur apart from the world.

---

83. An example of this can be found in Michel Haar's "Critical Remarks on Heidegger's Reading of Nietzsche" in Macann, C. (ed.), *Critical Heidegger* (1996 [1995]) pp. 121–133. Haar suggests that Heidegger's elaboration of Nietzsche as a negative theologian is in consequence of the Nietzsche lectures after his analysis there of the Eternal Return and the Will to Power. In similar vein John Caputo traces Heidegger's opposition to Catholic students in Freiburg to his becoming an "enthusiastic reader of Nietzsche" while simultaneously putting aside "Kierkegaard, Aristotle, and Luther", and proposes a still further shift in the postwar years where Heidegger is said to become "anti-nietzschean" (*Heidegger and Theology* [1993], pp. 277, 281). I remain unconvinced that Heidegger's Nietzsche interpretation underwent these particular alterations.

For Heidegger this is expressly the effect of the Christianization of God, which, through methodological atheism, he expressly seeks to challenge. For metaphysics the self, grounded by God, is grounded in certitude. It either is caused by or is substance. But *Dasein* is grounded by nothing and discovers itself to be a being not in certainty but through questionableness. Finally, the subject, caused or cogitating, wills, and as willing, knows. But questionable *Dasein* occurs and comes authentically to itself as a being only because of an unwilled event, the death of God.

This coming-to-the-self in questioning comes about as a de-divinization, neither caused, willing, certain, nor even thinking, and as insubstantial; existence: without God, other than God, and knowing itself as other than God. The self that Heidegger secures phenomenologically is without God, atheistically.

## THE FUTURITY OF GOD

If God as the cause and origin of everything, as the origin of *ens creatum*, is a production of modern metaphysics, I ask for the first time a question to which I return repeatedly, the question indicated by Heidegger's atheism: what has God to do with philosophy? When Leibniz announced his principle *nihil est sine ratione*, nothing is without reason, he announced what might almost be called the high-water mark of metaphysics. Leibniz concludes his thoughts on the principle of sufficient reason with the statement "and this final reason of things is called God".[84] What he rejoiced in, what Galileo, Descartes, and Newton in different ways all wanted as an absolute ground of reason is God. Each in his separate way announced the same thing, not as a proof, but as the presupposition to every proof: in his *General Scholium* to the third edition of the *Principia Mathematica*, Newton argues: "This most elegant system of the sun, planets, and comets could not have arisen without the design and dominion of an intelligent and powerful being".[85] He adds: "He rules all things, not as the world soul, but as the Lord

---

84. von Leibniz, G. W., *Principes de la Nature et de la Grace* (1954), p. 46/47. "Cette Raison suffisante . . . cette derniere raison des choses est appellée Dieu."

85. Newton, *Philosophiae Naturalis Principia Mathematica* (1972), II, p. 760. "Elegentissima haecce solis, planetarum et cometarum compages non nisi consilio et dominio entis intelligentis et potentis oriri potuit."

of all, and because of his dominion he is called Lord God *Pantokrátor*.[86] Here the transition from the ancient cosmos through to its Christianization is named. Armed with this knowledge the court philosopher and Newton's theologian Samuel Clarke announced in his Boyle lectures of 1704 that "the being and attributes of God are not only possible or barely probable in themselves, but also strictly demonstrable to any unprejudiced mind from the most incontestable principles of right reason".[87] Here again is ample demonstration of the Christianization of God, in the roots of modern physics as well as metaphysics.

Heidegger asks how God got into philosophy "not only in the modern period, but in philosophy as such".[88] In a lecture course from 1942–43 on Heraclitus, Heidegger considers the Greek word τὸ δαιμόνιον. He cites a passage from Aristotle's *Nicomachean Ethics* which says: "One says (the thinkers) indeed know the effusive, and so astounding, and thereby difficult and hence in general 'demonic'—but also unusable, because they do not seek what according to straightforward popular opinion, is useful for humanity".[89] He notes, therefore, that the word demonic here cannot have the meaning to which we have become accustomed, but means rather, the uncanny, something which is neither monstrous nor immense nor minute, but simply that which cannot be measured, calculated, or reasoned about or away; nothing, Heidegger says, that can be "grasped by the fangs of the will",[90] but rather the way being itself shines out into the everyday—something so simple that it "belongs so immediately to the 'canny'[91] that it can never be explained on the basis of the familiar".[92] The uncanny—the demonic—

---

86. Newton, *Principia*, II, p. 760. "Et propter dominium suum, dominus deus Παντοκράτορ dici solet."

87. Clarke, S., Vailati, E. (ed.), *A Demonstration of the Being and Attributes of God and Other Writings*, Cambridge, Cambridge University Press, 1998 [1704], p. 7.

88. *Identität und Differenz* (GA11), p. 46. "Nicht nur in die neuzeitliche, sondern in die Philosophie als solche?"

89. *Parmenides* (GA54), p. 148. Cf. Aristotle, *Nicomachean Ethics*, VI, vii (1141b7ff). "καὶ περιττὰ μὲν καὶ θαυμαστὰ καὶ χαλεπὰ καὶ δαιμόνια εἰδέναι αὐτοὺς φάσιν, ἄχρηστα δ', ὅτι οὐ τὰ ἀνθρώπινα ἀγαθὰ ζητοῦσιν. Man sagt, sie (die Denker) wissen zwar Überschwengliches und also Erstaunliches und somit Schwieriges und deshalb überhaupt 'Dämonisches', aber dies sei auch das Unbrauchbare, weil sie nicht das suchen, was so geradehin nach der Menschen Meinung für den Menschen das Taugliche ist."

90. *Parmenides* (GA54), p. 150. "für die Greifzange des Willens Ungreifbare."

91. In the English dialect sense of the pleasant and familiar, as in 'he's a canny lad'.

92. *Parmenides* (GA54), p. 150. "Was zum Geheuren so unmittelbar gehört, daß es nie aus dem Geheuren erklärt werden kann."

is therefore what surrounds everywhere and makes possible the familiar, which, before it became familiar was proffered as uncanny. Heidegger proceeds in these lectures to consider that kind of looking which is not what in modern philosophy we would know by intentionality, the being-directed-toward, the gazing-at as a self-direction and self-accomplished activity, but rather the looking that he takes from the Greek verb θεάω, which, he notes, strictly speaking only appears in the medial form θεάομαι, meaning contemplate, spectate. This 'looking' Heidegger describes as a self-pointing, which he relates to his translation of the Greek verb δαίω as: I point. Thus τὸ δαιμόνιον has to do with a pointing or pointing-out. Such a self-pointing is an indicating of the self with respect to what appears together with it, so that through looking, the one looking also in a sense appears (the verb here is *erscheinen*, shining forth) and takes up and is as a there, the there that *Dasein* takes up.[93] This look, θέα, he says, "is not looking as an activity and act of a 'subject', but the arising and coming-toward of the 'object' . . . self-pointing".[94]

This is the very opposite of God as absolute presence, as being as such, where being is taken as a synonym for full-presence, or where, as Aquinas puts it, God alone is the plenitude of existence.[95] Here God is understood as what enters and disturbs presence through becoming, which is not an already, but a coming-into, a from-out-of-what-is-ahead. Heidegger shows how the concealed is the basis for what emerges and can be seen and known and that this concealed now speaks. God, or the divine, is therefore to do with world and speaking, λέγειν, the speaking which the human being also has. In this speaking the concealed emerges and gives rise to what is unconcealed and so lies present: it belongs to it and yet separates itself and is at work in the presencing and presentedness of everything extant, including myself, indeed, precisely because I encounter myself as also included in this unfolding event.

In metaphysics and in the thinking that flows from the Enlightenment, revelation is excluded or becomes problematic because it must be accounted for within the extantness of everything present, and insofar as immediate presence cannot account for revelation, it must be excluded. Moreover, as I

---

93. *Parmenides* (GA54), p. 152. "Da ist."
94. *Parmenides* (GA54), p. 153. "Der Blick, θέα, ist nicht das Blicken als Tätigkeit und Akt des 'Subjekts', sondern der Anblick als Aufgehen und Entgegenkommen des 'Objekts' . . . sich-zeigen."
95. Cf. Aquinas, *Summa Theologiae*, Ia, q. 8, a. 1, resp.; q. 20, a. 2, resp.

have indicated, revelation has been taken over into the province of meta-physics proper, so that, insofar as it is admitted at all, it is now determined according to reason, the *ratio*. In contrast, however, here with Heidegger, the opposite is true, and the familiar *is* and everyday *occurs* on the basis of the uncanny and unfamiliar and what that points out. This is still unconcerned with revelation, only because in thematizing this looking, we are looking at the looking of ourselves and not at what it is that might be available for us to see, once we have a sense of what it was for the Greeks to look at all. He con-cludes by saying: "Humanity itself is that being whose particular appoint-ment is to be addressed (in the sense of spoken to) from being itself in such a way that in the self-pointing of humanity, in its looking and in its sight, the uncanny itself, the god, appears".[96] Being is the possibility of being-addressed but not the address itself.

To conclude, therefore, what in thinking through an origin of the way in which God is thought as an absence that looks, that calls me forward in the looking, opens up here an unfolding of the separation of faith and philosophy, by showing how philosophy is concerned with being, but God is simultane-ously nothing being and nothing known. Nothing can be said of God's enter-ing being—until God speaks. Thought in a Christian way, when God speaks, *this* speaking belongs, not to philosophy, but faith. Thought in a Greek way, the speaking of the gods is the content of the pointing-out. What becomes of issue in philosophy is therefore not a forestalling of the content of revelation, but of its receipt, its being possible, its being received by humanity, and its being understood in its receipt. The content of revelation, the matter of what God says, and so who God is, is reserved alone to faith. *Dasein* does not find God as an always-already, but must wait for God and points itself out to the future in order, in waiting, to know who God is who may speak or flee from *Dasein* or remain silent. When God speaks, this is an event in being. What *event* means here will be a matter for consideration in what follows.

---

96. *Parmenides* (GA54), p. 155. "Der Mensch selbst ist dasjenige Seiende, das seine Auszeichnung darin hat, vom Sein selbst angesprochen zu sein, so daß im Sichzeigen des Menschen, in seinem Blicken und seinem Anblick das Ungeheure selbst, der Gott, erscheint.

# Chapter Three

# Reading Heidegger's Turn

## The Turn and Heidegger's Atheism

In chapter 2 I indicated how, for Heidegger, the question of being only opens up as a question if it brings *Dasein* before itself as a being within being. This is the same as saying that *Dasein* discovers itself as the place of the ontological difference. Already in a preliminary way I indicated that something which was named as *die Umkippung,* tipping-over, is at work in Heidegger's thought from as early as 1919.[1] I have suggested that tipping-over is prescient of *die Kehre,* the turn. Robert Bernasconi argues that in Heidegger there are "'sayings of a turning (*Kehre*)'. *Kehre* here does not refer to an ostensible shift in Heidegger's own intellectual development, but to an event in the history of being . . . the *Kehre* is the turning from metaphysics to another beginning".[2] I examine in detail what he means by this in the next two chapters by unfolding the structure of the turn through the various ways in which it is brought to light. Before I do this, however, it is necessary to gain an understanding of how the

---

1. That this idea is not so very revolutionary is to some extent confirmed by Gadamer and Kisiel, both of whom have argued that the turn actually took place in 1919 or 1920. Gadamer says, "The turn seems to me to have actually taken place in the year 1920" ("Wilhelm Dilthey nach 150 Jahren" [1985], p. 159). Kisiel argues that his work on the *Kriegsnotsemester* (GA56/57) "adds further credence to Gadamer's thesis that the groundwork for all of Heidegger's later thought after the 'turn' was already laid in 1919" (*Das Kriegsnotsemester 1919* [1992], p. 105). In discovering Gadamer and Kisiel to hold a view apparently so close to the one I begin with here—that the turn as defined by Löwith and Richardson is not explained as fracture between the work of *Sein und Zeit* and what comes after it—leaves me with a question: why do they then not abandon all talk of turns altogether? What, in any significant sense (if we are not concerned with Heidegger's juvenalia) is the turn *from?*

2. Bernasconi, R., *The Question of Language in Heidegger's History of Being* (1985), p. 66.

turn has been understood by Heidegger's interpreters. It will become clear that what Heidegger means by the turn and how it is understood by his commentators is marked by a disjuncture, which is itself the mark of the failure of many of Heidegger's commentators to take seriously the radicality of the understanding of being he announces and the parallel failure to interpret how he brings that understanding to light. It is the methodological atheism that Heidegger develops that brings this understanding to light, an atheism which he finds connected with Nietzsche's proclamation of the death of God. In this way talk of method gives way to an event he discovers to be taking place.

How does the turn relate to Heidegger's atheism? Precisely in carrying out the analytic of *Dasein* as an atheism, I demonstrated in chapter 2 that there are matters in Heidegger's thought that are most commonly supposed to be the work of the later Heidegger and not the earlier. Recently Bernasconi has cautioned that "Heidegger scholars should be used by now to finding what had seemed to be late developments firmly located in earlier texts".[3] This therefore draws attention to how it is that Heidegger came to be understood through the schema of later and earlier. The relationship of the later to earlier work is almost always explained through some reference to a turn, which is said to have taken place in Heidegger's thinking after the publication of *Sein und Zeit*. Is this turn in Heidegger's thinking the same thing that Heidegger himself meant when talking of *die Kehre?* The tipping-over, as a precursor to the turn, was discussed (as I indicated) through seeking to gain an orientation on the past situation of philosophy. This orientation is brought to light through Heidegger's methodological atheism: it indicates how Descartes redefines the task of philosophy in the emergence of the subject, but even more, it provides a way into the destructuring of Aristotle's first philosophy as an ontology that from the outset conceals the meaning of the question of being in the being of the divine.

I ask how Heidegger's work is divided, not simply as a matter of Heidegger's biography, but rather in a way that will allow me to read myself into what it is of which Heidegger is speaking. It is my own biography, as my own *I*-being, that I want to put into question, not simply Heidegger's. This is because in suggesting that the question of being concerns a question about the self, Heidegger is already asking about something with which I am intimately concerned: my-self. Already a second connection between this

---

3. Bernasconi, R., "The Greatness of the Work of Art" in Risser, J. (ed.), *Heidegger toward the Turn* (1999), p. 115, note 4.

methodological atheism and what I am proposing is at work, since I already demonstrated, at least in a preliminary way, that Heidegger's claim that a methodological atheism is necessary to bring this question about the self— my-self—to the fore means that this question is not simply a question concerning me, but about the whole history of thinking which gives me to be, which occurs in advance of me, and to which I must gain an orientation in order to become questioning and questionable. The method brings the whole history concealed in being before me.

That the key to reading Heidegger is a turn or reversal has become so much of a commonplace that the turn seems to have been here from the very beginning, always enabling the clarification of Heidegger's work. I can come upon some as yet unread piece and find myself able to say that this piece predates the turn or comes after it but is always somehow related to and so unlocked by it. The turn is taken as the common currency of reading Heidegger, so that even when considering what was written before it is supposed to have happened, the turn is already operative.

The turn, described like this, is not an issue in his philosophical work, but rather the mark of how Heidegger has been received in the literature about him, particularly in the postwar period. The literature which appeals to the turn like this is now so great that it is impossible to survey or even suumarize it adequately. István Fehér comments that "it has become more customary and even fashionable . . . to speak about more periods or more turns on Heidegger's path of thinking . . . the turn has been taking on ever more complex and differentiated meanings, undergoing, as it were, a certain proliferation".[4] In short, the turn has acquired a life of its own.

Turns, therefore, have become so much part of the scholarly business of understanding Heidegger that they crop up everywhere, and in doing so become ever more distant from what they promise to explain. Hugo Ott suggests that Edmund Husserl's appointment of Heidegger as an *Assistent* in 1919 concluded a series of events which leads him to say "the years 1918/19 also saw the institutional 'turn' or change of direction, whereby Heidegger, who was still formally attached to the department of Christian philosophy . . . now openly switched, in effect, to a different philosophical discipline".[5] John van

---

4. Fehér, I., "Heidegger's Postwar Turn" (1995), p. 9.
5. Ott, H. (1992), *Martin Heidegger—Unterwegs zu seiner Biographie*, p. 115. "Es war also auch die institutmäßige Wende vollzogen, d.h. Heidegger, eigentlich dem Bereich der christlichen Philosophie . . . zugeordnet, wechselte gewissermaßen die philosophische Disziplin auch augenfällig nach außen."

Buren, in contrast, discovers the origins of the turn before the 1927 publication of *Sein und Zeit:* "The first and most decisive 'turn' in Heidegger's thought,
from being to the differentiated temporal giving of being, is to be found in the
silent decade between his 1916 Scotus book and *Sein und Zeit.* But there are
portentous signs of this turn already in two texts from 1915–16".[6] Van Buren
can go further back even than this, asserting more strongly than Ott 'turns' as
an aspect of Heidegger's biography. He says "in his youthful period . . . he
made the first, decisive, and idiosyncratic turns *from* his earlier preoccupation
with being as the static presence of valid logical sense and ultimately as the
eternity of the absolute spirit of God *to* the temporal giving of being. This is
the biographical sense of his talk about the end of philosophy and a new
beginning. All this, as Gadamer has written, was 'the turn before the turn'".[7]

Fehér has argued convincingly that Heidegger's postwar (First World
War) turn was the first, the one where he acquired his own philosophical
voice.[8] But is it a turn to acquire a voice? Surely this is no turn, but an
authentic beginning? If this postwar turn is of the sort that I shall show
was constructed by Karl Löwith, one which explains a split in Heidegger's
thought, has Fehér's 'turn' turned itself inside out and reunited the very
thing it split? As Olafson has observed, "there is no comparable consensus
for what the 'turn' is".[9]

## THE TURN IN READING HEIDEGGER

Why does the need to find turns in Heidegger arise? It seems that relying on
turns allows me to suppose that there is a narrative of Heidegger's develop-

---

6. van Buren, J., *The Young Heidegger* (1994), p. 87.

7. *The Young Heidegger* (1994), p. 242 (author's italics).

8. Fehér, I., "Heidegger's Postwar Turn" (1995). Fehér cannot hold on to what he has
found. Having argued (p. 9) "the young Heidegger can in no way be said to have had a philosophical outlook of his own" and so declaring (p. 23) that the postwar (First World War)
turn is the "fundamental turn", thereby placing the whole language of turns into question
by locating it at the beginning of Heidegger's career. However, he merely re-embarks on the
whole language of turns. He concludes that "the postwar turn foreshadow(s) the . . . turn
more properly called as such", a turn which is "to be accounted for in terms of a passage
from the failure to carry out a total re-appropriation/destruction to a concept of the self-
withdrawal of being". In other words, the postwar *fundamental* turn is just an early indica-
tor of the *later really fundamental* turn, which puts the argument right back where it started.

9. Olafson, F., *Heidegger and the Philosophy of Mind* (1978), p. 153.

ment, which, were I assiduous enough or possessed of enough facts, I could uncover in its entirety, but the turn does it for me, without my having to do anything at all, so that I can rely on the conceptual understanding it gives me in order to interpret what Heidegger is all about. Does the turn not release me from understanding how any particular text of Heidegger's connects to any other? Might it be that the very issue here is the possibility of hearing and reading Heidegger at all? The suspicion is that, after its inception, the turn becomes a device for explaining Heidegger by only brushing past him and positing easy access to the otherwise demanding texts that he leaves in his wake.

Such a reading fragments Heidegger's work into a set of texts with which I can become ever more familiar in their particularity, while having to ask no particular questions about their unity. This has led to the absurdity of speaking of 'many Heideggers' as if this immediately resolved all the hermeneutical difficulties of his texts, something I will touch on again in chapter 5. My contention is that in order to understand the turn it is necessary to inquire not simply into Heidegger's own elaboration of *die Kehre* (although I intend to do that in this chapter and the next), but also to ask why in the literature on Heidegger an almost ubiquitous assumption is that Heidegger can be understood through the notion of a turn and that the way into Heidegger is to understand both why turns arise as keys to Heidegger's work and life and why they fail. These inquiries do not stand apart—as one and the same inquiry, it locates me in relation to Heidegger. It is the inquiry into what it is to read him at all, and it is my questioning into the place that he opens up, the ontological difference. My separation from Heidegger and my closeness to him are therefore precisely posed in this question of the turn. I undertake this in the next two chapters. First, I inquire how the turn arose in Heidegger's commentators. I next ask what Heidegger himself understood the turn to be and what place it has in what his work is about, the question of being.

There is here, however, a more difficult question, a question that touches on the very sensitivities Heidegger drilled into his students time and again: how should you or I approach what a thinker has to think? This is more than just a pedagogical concern. So often, in leading his students (and so himself) to other thinkers, Heidegger lays out the problematic which provides the very basis for entering thought at all. Speaking here specifically of Plato, he says:

> This past to which this lecture seeks access is nothing that lies far detached from us, but rather we are this past itself. And we are it not insofar as we expressly cultivate the tradition and are friends of classical

antiquity, but rather our philosophy and knowledge live from these foundations.[10]

He adds that it is what of our past we do *not* know and that is concealed from us because it has become an everyday matter that is still operative in giving us to think at all. It is this concealment that requires the hardest work to make what is concealed transparent and bring it to speak again. As Heidegger presents this to his students—here in the matter of interpreting Plato—so are we in relation to him in the meaning of the turn. Part of the complexity of this issue is that Heidegger consciously implicated himself in the attempt to understand the turn and his work overall. He undertakes his own withdrawal from those who will not undertake the necessary work to attempt to hear what he is speaking of.

## The Origin of the Turn

In 1951 Heidegger's former pupil Karl Löwith announced the discovery of a turn in Heidegger's thought,[11] with which he begins his characterization of Heidegger's betrayal of the central thesis of *Sein und Zeit* (central, because he did not care for the beginning and the end, believing it to be too much like his later work).[12] The very postulation of this turn arose out of Karl Löwith's

---

10. *Platon: Sophistes* [GA19], p. 10. "Diese Vergangenheit, zu der die Vorlesung Zugang sucht, ist nichts, was abgelöst von uns fern liegt. Sondern wir sind diese Vergangenheit selbst. Und wir sind sie nicht etwa, sofern wir die Tradition ausdrücklich pflegen, Freunde des klassischen Altertums sind, sondern unsere Philosophie und Wissenschaft lebt aus diesen Fundamenten."

11. One of the first places in which Löwith does this is in *Heideggers Kehre*, a piece published in *Die Neue Rundschau* in 1951. As with so many of Löwith's written pieces, the arguments advanced are constantly recycled, and sections are borrowed word for word from other pieces. Almost the entirety of this text is subsequently contained first in the 1952 *Neue Rundschau* edition of *Heidegger—Denker in dürftiger Zeit* and then again in the 1960 expanded edition of the same work published in Löwith's *Sämtliche Schriften*. Given this, and the fact that the arguments do not alter substantially with retelling, I have cited only the version published in 1960. Löwith does not subsequently advert to his writing in 1951 or to his 1952 *Neue Rundschau* edition of *Heidegger—Denker in dürftiger Zeit*, either in the preface to the second (1960) edition already mentioned or in the preface to *Mein Leben in Deutschland*, and so always gives the date of it as 1953, the year of its publication as a single piece.

12. Cf. Löwith, K., *Heidegger—Denker in dürftiger Zeit* (1984), p. 139.

initiation of the first Heidegger controversy, concerning Heidegger's political engagement with Nazism, with the 1946 publication in French of a piece translated as "The Political Implications of Heidegger's Existentialism."[13] Löwith was scandalized by Heidegger's use of his own philosophical language in the *Rektoratsrede*, the speech of accession to the rectorate of Freiburg University after the Nazis had come to power in 1933. Löwith draws our attention to his horror that "the language of this discourse . . . is drawn entirely from the concepts of *Sein und Zeit* and also from the vocabulary of the political movement".[14] The turn he identifies, as a disjunction in Heidegger's thought, functions as a way of splitting the Heidegger of *Sein und Zeit* from the Nazi Heidegger of this speech of accession and the other pandering speeches in praise of Hitler in the year that followed it, before Heidegger's resignation as rector in 1934.

It would be hard to doubt that Löwith was correct to raise questions about Heidegger's political engagement; however, his simultaneous claim that the turn provides a hermeneutic tool to investigate the relationship between Heidegger's biography and his philosophy is far more problematic. It is my contention that Heidegger's *Kehre* remains a phenomenological concern and has bearing on his biography only consequentially.[15] Heidegger's insertion of himself into the question of the turn indicates the extent to

13. "Les implications politiques de la philosophie de l'existence chez Heidegger" in *Les Temps Modernes*, 1946–47, no. 14; later translated as "The Political Implications of Heidegger's Existentialism" by Richard Wolin in *The Heidegger Controversy* (1991). The piece claims to have originated in 1939 and so is contemporary with Löwith's references to Heidegger in his *Mein Leben in Deutschland vor und nach 1933* which, although written in 1939 and submitted for a Harvard prize competition in 1940, was not published in German until 1986, and in English in 1994.

14. Löwith, K., *Heidegger—Denker in dürftiger Zeit* (1984), p. 170. "Die Sprache dieser Rede . . . ist durchaus den Begriffen von *Sein und Zeit* entnommen und zugleich dem Vokabular der politischen Bewegung."

15. Reinhart Koselleck's foreword to *Mein Leben in Deutschland* (1986) suggests that Löwith's critique of Heidegger reflects the more poignantly on Löwith's own biography. He notes (p. xi): "Here above all we find the autobiographical genesis of his critique of Heidegger which appeared later (1953) in *Denker in Dürftiger Zeit*. The unmistakable appreciation of, and decided distancing from, his teacher Heidegger add up to a puzzle, which cannot be solved in purely psychological, sociological, or philosophical terms, as there is always one aspect from each different perspective that cannot be seen". To elucidate this further would require a much fuller investigation, but it confirms my view that Löwith's critique of Heidegger is characterized by an imprecision which is never stabilized or resolved as a strictly philosophical issue.

which his biography, far from being explained by the turn, becomes self-consciously an issue for its explication. How does Löwith describe the turn he uncovers? He considers "whether Heidegger's later talk of 'being' and finally of 'event'(*Ereignis*) is the consequence of his point of departure or the result of a reversal (*Umkehr*)". He concludes: "A critical discussion (of the later published works) in relation to *Sein und Zeit* changes from a biographical detail into a main philosophical theme that concerns nothing less than the question regarding the grounding of human *Dasein:* either on the basis of its own 'authentic' being, or on the basis of 'being' which is wholly other and which from out of itself 'eventuates' (*ereignet*) the *Dasein* of human nature".[16] It is important to note that Löwith explicitly connects the turn with *das Ereignis*. I will examine the real connection between these terms in full in chapter 4, but it is possible immediately to see that Löwith's description of the turn, from the very beginning, is intimately connected with and yet fails to come close to describing what Heidegger himself meant by the turn.

Löwith asks, therefore, whether being belongs to authentic *Dasein* or whether it stands as something over against *Dasein;* by implication therefore, as something which is whether *Dasein* is or is not. The question concerns facticity and *Dasein*'s existence as finite time, or being-toward-death, a major theme of *Sein und Zeit*. Is being finite (in a finitude marked by death) or is it eternal? Löwith counterposes the (then unpublished) 1924 lecture *Der Begriff der Zeit*, where Heidegger says "then philosophy will know nothing of the eternal",[17] to the small text *Der Feldweg* where Heidegger speaks of "a gate to the eternal".[18] Löwith sums up: "*Sein und Zeit* only appears to have dispensed with the question concerning an eternal truth. In actuality Heidegger posed it anew by thinking onward, in a turn, from the finite temporality of *Dasein* to an origin that remains. The existential-temporal standpoint of *Sein und Zeit* is

---

16. Löwith, K., *Heidegger—Denker in dürftiger Zeit* (1984), p. 125. "Ob Heideggers spätere Rede vom 'Sein' und schließlich vom 'Ereignis' die Konsequenz seiner Ausgangsstellung ist oder die Folge einer Umkehr . . . dann wird eine kritische Erörterung dieser Schriften im Verhältnis zu *Sein und Zeit* aus einer biographischen Nebensache zu einer philosophischen Hauptsache, die nichts Geringeres betrifft als die Frage nach der Begründung des menschlichen Daseins: entweder aus seinem eigenen 'eigentlichen' Sein, oder aus dem ganz andern 'Sein', das von sich aus das Dasein des Menschenwesens 'ereignet'".

17. *Der Begriff der Zeit* (GA64), p. 5. "Dann wird die Philosophie die Ewigkeit nie haben."

18. *Der Feldweg* (GA13), p. 40. "Ein Tor zum Ewigen."

thereby 'sublated'".[19] Is Löwith correct? Is the finite being of *Sein und Zeit* later replaced in a turn by a notion of infinite being as a masked figure of the eternal, as a kind of atheism or God-denial? Is this the proper connection between the turn and Heidegger's atheism, as has so often been asserted? If this were correct, would not any question concerning Heidegger's atheism have to reveal it as the attempt to install an immanent description of being as a new god, a god who stands in the place of God? These questions will be considered in more detail later, but it is important to see that they occur at the very beginning of the question concerning the turn.

The questions Löwith raises here do indeed concern God, for in 1924 Heidegger had unfolded the eternal as a matter concerning faith and God, which philosophy, unlike theology, has no access to, because it has no access to faith. This, he says, is an "embarrassment" that cannot be relieved.[20] What Löwith overlooked is that in *Der Feldweg* Heidegger has already explicitly raised a question concerning God by the time he speaks of a gate to the eternal. Moreover, this is in the context of being unable to speak of God. The text reads: "The breadth of all growing things which rest along the pathway bestows world. Only in what remains unsaid in their speech is— as Eckhart . . . says—God only God".[21] The gateway to the eternal is then only a hint toward something which remains unsaid, an embarrassment. It is entirely plausible that the articulation of the eternal in these two texts is the same.

While I have demonstrated that these two texts, one in 1924, the other in 1950, can be read as being consistent with each other, it does not necessarily disprove Löwith's point. It does, however, cast significant doubt on Löwith's claim, since *Der Feldweg* is the *only* text Löwith cites in support of his argument. The burden of proof, therefore, remains firmly with Löwith,

---

19. Löwith, K., *Heidegger—Denker in dürftiger Zeit* (1984), p. 156. "*Sein und Zeit* hat die Frage nach einer ewigen Wahrheit nur scheinbar beseitigt. In Wirklichkeit hat sie Heidegger neu gestellt, indem er in einer Kehre von der endlichen Zeitlichkeit des Daseins zu einem bleibenden Ursprung hinausdenkt. Der existentiale-temporale Ansatz von *Sein und Zeit* ist damit 'aufgehoben'."

20. *Der Begriff der Zeit* (GA64), p. 5. The term *Verlegenheit* conveys well what Heidegger is trying to say, for in *Verlegenheit* I am not only embarrassed, but in a sense held back by embarrassment from saying more.

21. *Der Feldweg (Aus der Erfahrung des Denkens* [GA13]), p. 39. "Die Weite aller gewachsenen Dinge, die um den Feldweg verweilen, spendet Welt. Im Ungesprochenen ihrer Sprache ist, wie der alte Lese- und Lebe-meister Eckehardt sagt, Gott erst Gott."

and the question of what Heidegger means by atheism, by the turn, and by God remains open.

How might Löwith's claim to have discovered two different senses of the same word, being, across Heidegger's work be understood? In the first place it is frequently argued that the analytic of death as revelatory of the finitude of *Dasein* disappears from Heidegger's later work. In fact death as the finitude of *Dasein* corresponds to the nothing as revealing the finitude of being. Thus, in the 1949 lecture *Das Ding*, Heidegger remarks that "death is the shrine of nothing".[22] The analysis of death is only one aspect of the whole discussion of the nothing. Second, while recognizing Heidegger's concern to de-structure subjectivity in his later work, Löwith continues to read the analytic of *Dasein* in *Sein und Zeit* as a form of subjectivity, a reading I have already shown to be false in chapter 2.[23] If Heinrich Wiegand Petzet is to be believed, Heidegger commented on this when referring to Löwith's attendance at his lectures: "He conceals this, just as much as how in the 1927 lecture course, the year *Sein und Zeit* appeared, for four hours every week I dealt with the question of being and not with subjectivity".[24]

Löwith's confusion arises because of his failure to understand the relation between the analytic of *Dasein* and Heidegger's simultaneous concern with being as such.[25] He appears not to have understood that not only *Dasein*, but being also, is finite. This is because being is something which

22. *Das Ding* (*Bremer und Freiburger Vorträge* [GA79]), p. 18. "Der Tod ist der Schrein des Nichts".

23. Cf. *Heidegger—Denker in dürftiger Zeit* (1984), p. 148. Criticizing the later Heidegger, Löwith says: "But what things depend on above all is no longer, as in *Sein und Zeit*, the subjectival and *Dasein* oriented foundation of truth, but rather being itself". ("Worauf es vor allem ankommt ist aber nicht mehr, wie in *Sein und Zeit*, das subjekthafte, daseinsmäßige Fundament der Wahrheit, sondern das Sein selbst.")

24. Petzet, H.W., *Auf einen Stern zugehen* (1983), p. 98. "Dies verschweigt er ebenso wie die Vorlesung von 1927, dem Erscheinungsjahr von *Sein und Zeit*, wo ich vierstündig jede Woche von der Seinsfrage und nicht von der Subjektivität handelte." The reference is clearly to the *Grundprobleme* lectures (GA24).

25. Löwith does at times come close to this understanding, for instance in the opening section of chapter 2 of Löwith, K., *Heidegger—Denker in dürftiger Zeit* (1984), p. 164, when he says: "Even the Ever-extant, thought in Greek terms, which looks like eternity, is in actuality a mere derivative of temporal being". ("Auch das griechisch gedachte Immer-Seiende, das so aussehe wie Ewigkeit, sei in Wirklichkeit ein bloßes Derivat des Zeitlichseins.")

always belongs to *Dasein*, to the being of being-human, not necessarily because 'infinite' is a name for God. For Heidegger to call God infinite is simply to exclude God from the finitude that *Dasein* and being is. The question of being arises for Heidegger through the analytic of *Dasein*, in particular through a phenomenology of finitude which *Dasein* understands most intimately in death. However, the finitude of being is not identical or coterminous or (crucially) contemporaneous with the finitude of *Dasein*. Being is not always only mine, but I can only experience it as mine. It is not mine most of all in the sense that for Heidegger I also belong to being. Löwith failed to understood what Heidegger meant by essence. *Das Wesen*, essence, however, is for Heidegger always pointed toward the future; it is something I do or am 'done as' because I am projecting toward being something that I then am, or because something pulls me into shape from out of what it is. It is not substance, and so does not pre-cede or (as *sub-stans*) underpin or ground me, and much of Heidegger's work is designed to show how this is. 'My' essence is something which I receive from beyond me, and yet it is me in some way. It is me as *a returning to my self*. In this sense, Heidegger later employs the verbal sense of *das Wesen* (essence) as *west*— essences. *Das Sein west:* being essences. Language might supply an example for how this is. I experience language as mine. Language is not mine, however, until I become able to speak. I must learn to speak, learn to make language mine (I am pulled into shape by speaking in a way that can be understood). In coming to language, I make it my own, but I receive it from beyond me, though in receiving it, I become who I am for myself for the first time. Language, however, is also finite, also has a history and with whose history I am concerned, but it is in some sense mine and in another sense other than me.

To return, therefore, to Löwith's opening question, *Dasein* experiences being as its own, and being eventuates *Dasein*. The two belong to each other, as I indicate, in *die Kehre*, but whereas for Löwith the turn is the mark of a fracture in Heidegger's thought, for Heidegger this *Kehre* was not worked out as a fracture in relation to his biography or any changes in his thought but is the working out of the belonging together of *Dasein* and being itself: it is, then, the mark of the unity of his thinking and the event of the belonging together of being and *Dasein*.

Löwith inaugurated a tendency to postulate the turn as a narrative and biographical device. In a footnote to *Heidegger—Denker in dürftiger Zeit* he asserts again the particularity of *Sein und Zeit* as a work by suggesting that the work of the later Heidegger (after *Sein und Zeit*) is in fact only returning to the thesis of his 1916 *Habilitationsschrift*.[26] Löwith suggests the interchangeability of terms from this work of 1916 and others routinely used after 1927. He concludes, alluding (entirely out of context) to Heidegger's own assertion, that great thinkers think only one essential thought, that "the analytic of *Dasein* resolved upon itself, which reaches its acme in the doubly emphasized 'freedom toward death' (*Sein und Zeit*) would signify only an intermediate stage and Heidegger's 'turning' toward being which itself gives, would be a return to his theological beginning".[27] This is consistent with his attempt to postulate the turn as an abrogation of *Dasein*'s existence as finite time in favor of being (*das Sein*) understood as eternity (or in some sense as a figure for God). Löwith does not suggest how the supposedly interchangeable terms are interdependent or point to passages that illustrate their connectedness, but relies for his case only on his undemonstrated claim that Heidegger remains in some sense a concealed theologian, something which could be explained by events in his life, were they but known or able to be brought to light.

Petzet's recollections of Heidegger's comments and observations on the issues surrounding his life provide a record of Heidegger's misgivings about the discussion of the turn, specifically in relation to Löwith. Petzet reports Heidegger's comments that "it's terrible, the abuse of the essential word *Kehre*... Löwith does not inform his readers that the real 'turn' is communicated for the first time in 1930 in the lecture *On the Essence of Truth*".[28]

It would be easy to overlook that according to Petzet's report, Heidegger was well aware from the outset that what is at issue in the invention of the turn is the very notion of distance and closeness to Heidegger himself and how he is to be read and Löwith's self-understanding in relation to that reading. Petzet reports Heidegger as saying: "In 1929 when Löwith was the reddest Marxist—today he has turned Christian . . .—then he wrote of *Sein*

---

26. Löwith, K., *Heidegger—Denker in dürftiger Zeit* (1960), p. 139 (footnote).

27. Löwith, K., *Heidegger—Denker in dürftiger Zeit* (1960), p. 139f. (footnote): "So würde die Analytik des zu sich selbst entschlossenen Daseins, die in der doppelt hervorgehobenen 'Freiheit zum Tode' (Sein und Zeit S. 266) gipfelt, nur ein Zwischenstadium bedeuten und Heideggers 'Kehre' zum sich selber gebenden Sein und Rückkehr zu seinem theologischen Anfang sein."

28. Petzet, H.W., *Auf einen Stern zugehen* (1983), p. 98. "Schmerzlich ist mir der fürchterliche Mißbrauch eines für mich wesentlichen Wortes 'Kehre'. . . . Löwith verschweigt auch seinen Lesern, daß die echte 'Kehre' zum ersten Mal 1930 in dem Vortrag *'Vom Wesen der Wahrheit'* mitgeteilt ist."

*und Zeit* that it was a 'concealed theology'. Later he wrote it's all atheism".[29] Heidegger indicates in this sentence that the issue of who here has been turned around is not at all clear. Is it not Löwith, rather than Heidegger who is at stake, the Marxist-turned-Christian, who has need of explaining himself? Who we are when we read what we read is not an idle matter. For Heidegger, it is only Löwith and his own concerns who are disclosed in his description of the turn and not what Heidegger has to speak *of* at all.

Recall that Löwith—Marxist turned Christian whose Jewish ancestry forced him into exile from Germany from 1933 until after the war— inaugurates the turn in order to remain with the Heidegger of *Sein und Zeit* while jettisoning the Nazi Heidegger. His own biography was at stake in his perplexing relationship with his teacher. Who could not sympathize with Löwith, who sought a way to remain faithful to Heidegger within the traumatic injustices of his own life? Am I bound to do the same, refusing Heidegger's Nazism by taking on Löwith's turn? Is it possible to rescue an earlier Heidegger from the taint of the later? Surely, if this resolves something for Löwith, it does not resolve anything for Heidegger's own thinking, which resists this periodization. As I argue in chapter 7, must I not simply confront the fact of Heidegger's political engagement and come to terms with it? Could Löwith have done this, however, when what Heidegger embraced— however far from the biologism of the Nazis Heidegger believed himself to be—put his pupil so close to death at Nazi hands?

## THE LATER DEVELOPMENT OF THE TURN

Löwith, having established the notion of the turn as a fracture in Heidegger's thinking, ceases to be particularly influential for its development. Far more important for the origin of the turn in the English-speaking literature is the point of intersection between Heidegger's understanding of *die Kehre* and William Richardson's characterization of a reversal that connects Heidegger I and Heidegger II. Reversal is Richardson's term for what I have called the turn, in his large-scale commentary, *Heidegger: Through Phenomenology to Thought,* published in 1963. Heidegger was persuaded by Richardson

29. Petzet, H.W., *Auf einen Stern zugehen,* p. 98. "Im Jahre 29, als Löwith noch rötester Marxist war—heute hat er sich zum Christlichen 'gekehrt'...—damals schrieb er über 'Sein und Zeit', das alles sei 'verkappte Theologie'. Später schrieb er, alles sei Atheismus."

to write a foreword to this work, and it is widely accepted that in it he confirmed Richardson's thesis.

When *Through Phenomenology to Thought* was published the Macquarrie-Robinson translation of *Sein und Zeit* had only been available for two years. Richardson's book was a monumental survey of Heidegger's as yet almost wholly untranslated German works in print and seemed to contain within it the key to the riddle of the apparent lack of any intelligible connection between the author of *Sein und Zeit* and the thinker of the fourfold, first made available to English readers in 1958 in *The Question of Being*, a translation of Heidegger's essay for Ernst Jünger published as *Zur Seinsfrage*.[30] Richardson held that there were not one, but two, Heideggers connected by the reversal, self-evidently a point of fracture in Heidegger's thought. Moreover, Heidegger's own comments in the opening pages of the work seemed sufficiently obscure and cryptic to direct the English reader, not to what he himself said of a turn, but rather to the brilliance and clarity of his expositor, of whose conclusions there seemed to be no particular rejection. The title of the book itself directed how to read this thinker, which is to say that Richardson promised all in Heidegger that seemed obscure would be thematized and clarified in a work that claims in its opening page to be "in as concise a statement as possible the essentials of his entire problematic".[31] Richardson even went so far as to assert the "completeness" of his analysis, noting that with Heidegger's now advanced years there would be little new to come that might challenge his exposition.[32] (The first of the planned 102 volumes of the Heidegger *Gesamtausgabe* would not appear for another thirteen years, and only then in German.) "The method was to trace the development of this problematic out of the author's early work, by considering his writings according to the order in which they were composed rather than that in which they were published."[33]

30. *Zur Seinsfrage* in *Wegmarken* (GA9).
31. Richardson, W.J., *Heidegger: Through Phenomenology to Thought* (1963), writer's preface (*Vorwort*), p. xxv. In references to this *Vorwort* I have given the page number of the German text, which lies side by side with its English translation. The published translation is idiosyncratic, but I have retained it because it appeared so much as part of the original text.
32. Richardson, W.J., *Heidegger: Through Phenomenology to Thought* (1963), p. xxvi.
33. Richardson, W.J., "Heidegger's Way through Phenomenology to the Thinking of Being" (1981), p. 79. This was the preparatory résumé for *Heidegger: Through Phenomenology to Thought* which had been submitted in German to Heidegger.

Richardson provided his readers with the clear way to read Heidegger's obscurity, apparently with the unequivocal backing of the master himself, a reading to which, if anyone aspired to understand the master, he would have to conform. Richardson's two Heideggers, I and II, had differing though complementary concerns. Heidegger I is "the Heidegger principally of *Being and Time*" whose "*status quaestionis*" is "what is the relation between the radical finitude of man and the comprehension of Being as such?"[34] Heidegger II attempts the thinking of being, which is a foundational thinking, and Richardson says "foundational thinking is the process by which human ek-sistence responds to being, not only in its positivity but in its negativity, as the continual process of truth-as-history"[35] The point of relationship between Heidegger I and Heidegger II is the 1930 lecture *Vom Wesen der Wahrheit:*[36] "[it] is the breakthrough. Here [1930], Heidegger II emerges out of Heidegger I . . . it is a genuine transformation of thought".[37] He concludes: "How far have we come? Heidegger I becomes Heidegger II . . . the thinking of Being . . . at last!"[38] Richardson traced the reversal precisely to the point where I have indicated Petzet reported that Heidegger said he had communicated it for the first time.

After all this, who could fail to have been astonished at Heidegger's own comment on Richardson's schema?

The distinction you make between Heidegger I and II is justified only on the condition that this is kept constantly in mind: only by way of what

---

34. Richardson, W. J., *Heidegger: Through Phenomenology to Thought* (1963), p. 84.

35. Richardson, W. J., *Heidegger: Through Phenomenology to Thought* (1963), p. 84.

36. There is an earlier lecture of this title dating from 1926, whose text has not yet been published in the *Gesamtausgabe*. This lecture was delivered at Bremen, Marburg, and Freiburg in 1930 and again at Dresden in 1932. The lecture was first published in a *Sonderausgabe* edition in 1943, with a second *Sonderausgabe* edition in 1949 containing a new first paragraph and a reworked concluding section entitled *Anmerkung*. The 1949 text was included in *Wegmarken* (GA9). The 1943 text altered and revised the 1930/32 version, though Heidegger insisted that the fundamental position and structure of the work remained unaltered. For a fuller treatment of the various developments and alterations of the text see John Sallis's essay "Deformatives: Essentially Other Than Truth" in the work edited by him and entitled *Reading Heidegger* (1993), p. 45. There are various unpublished typescripts of the 1930/32 version in circulation.

37. Richardson, W. J., *Heidegger: Through Phenomenology to Thought* (1963), p. 243.

38. Richardson, W. J., *Heidegger: Through Phenomenology to Thought* (1963), p. 254 (dotted spacing original to the text).

Heidegger I has thought does one gain access to what is to-be-thought by Heidegger II. But (the thought of) Heidegger I becomes possible only if it is contained in Heidegger II.[39]

This is an extraordinary passage: what it says is so astonishing that its meaning might be overlooked altogether, on the assumption that it must say something quite different. Indeed, it has invariably been read as Heidegger's support for Richardson's schematization of the turn. What else could it say?

The first part appears to confirm Richardson's analysis, but only if the second part is overlooked: Heidegger I becomes possible only if it is contained in Heidegger II. For this can only mean that Heidegger II precedes Heidegger I—is thought before it, as what makes it possible and lays the ground for it.

Richardson was so confident of his results that the editor of his later publication of the English text of the résumé on which *Through Phenomenology to Thought* was based (the very résumé whose German translation Richardson had sent to Heidegger in the first place) attached a prescript that said: "In a long, wide-ranging discussion, Professor Heidegger confirmed the validity of the interpretation".[40] But Heidegger does not confirm the validity of the interpretation; he stands it on its head. He reverses it. How can *this* reversal be dismissed at the outset of a work whose central, guiding thought is the analysis of *the* reversal that, it is claimed, will formulate the essentials of Heidegger's entire problematic?

The foreword to Richardson's work is one of the rare times that Heidegger ever comments on the turn as it is presented in the literature. Petzet's report of Heidegger's remarks is one of few others. Richardson is aware of Heidegger's claim that the real turn is found in the lecture *Vom Wesen der Wahrheit*. He is, I suspect, relying on Heidegger's own comment from the foreword that "the thinking of the reversal *is* a change in my thought".[41] There are two things to be noted here: first, that Heidegger

---

39. Richardson, W. J., *Heidegger: Through Phenomenology to Thought* (1963), p. xxiii. "Ihre Unterscheidung zwischen 'Heidegger I' und 'Heidegger II' ist allein unter der Bedingung berechtigt, daß stets beachtet wird: Nur von dem unter I Gedachten her wird zunächst das unter II zu Denkende zugänglich. Aber I wird nur möglich, wenn es in II enthalten ist."

40. Richardson, W. J., *Heidegger's Way through Phenomenology to the Thinking of Being* (1981), p. 79.

41. Richardson, W. J., *Heidegger: Through Phenomenology to Thought* (1963), p. xvi. "Das Denken der Kehre *ist* eine Wendung in meinem Denken" (author's italics).

brings into proximity the two German words that characterize his own discussion of the turn, *die Kehre,* and the noun formed from the verb *wenden* (to
turn), *die Wendung.* Second, Heidegger concedes a change (*Wendung*) in his
thought. Heidegger adds:

> But this change is not a consequence of altering the standpoint, much
> less of abandoning the fundamental issue, of Being and Time. The think-
> ing of the reversal results from the fact that I stayed with the matter-for-
> thought (of ) 'Being and Time,' sc. by inquiring into that perspective
> which already in Being and Time was designated as 'Time and Being'.[42]

Heidegger connects *die Kehre* with the third, unpublished section of the first
part of *Sein und Zeit.* This suggests that Petzet's report about *die Kehre* (communicated for the first time in 1930) must be heard more carefully, for it does
not say that *die Kehre* in 1930 has never been *thought* before. It was, Heidegger
says here, announced in 1927, highlighting in itself a contradiction, for the
very work away from which Heidegger is later said in the literature to turn is
already halfway down the path of carrying that very turning out.

The "change" arises from the fact that "I stayed with the matter-for-
thought of 'Being and Time'". This does not mean that Heidegger changes
his thought, for he says he did not alter his standpoint. If Heidegger did not
change his thought (his standpoint), could it be his thought contains a
change? By remaining with the matter at hand, Heidegger himself unfolded
a change in that thinking which stays with the questioning of being. That
change came about in the thinking through of *that* which in the work *Sein
und Zeit* was to have gone under the title *Zeit und Sein.* How can the thought
of being contain a change? Yet Heidegger says in Richardson's preface that
he will discuss

> your second question. It reads: "Granted *that* a 'reversal' has come-to-
> pass in your thinking, *how* has it come-to-pass? In other words, how are
> [we] to think this coming-to-pass itself?"

42. Richardson, W. J., *Heidegger: Through Phenomenology to Thought* (1963), p. xvii.
"Aber diese Wendung erfolgt nicht auf Grund einer Änderung des Standpunktes oder
gar der Preisgabe der Fragestellung in 'Sein und Zeit'. Das Denken der Kehre ergibt sich
daraus, daß ich bei der zu denkenden Sache 'Sein und Zeit' geblieben bin, d.h. nach der
Hinsicht gefragt habe, die schon in 'Sein und Zeit' (S. 39) unter dem Titel 'Zeit und Sein'
angezeigt wurde."

Your question admits of an answer only if we make clear what 'reversal' means, [or] more precisely, if one is ready to think through in becoming fashion what has already been said, instead of constantly circulating unwarranted assertions.[43]

*Die Kehre* already has something to say which, in the face of making already constantly unwarranted assertions, is in danger of not being heard. The question is how? Moreover, how will the question let itself be answered? Heidegger does no answering; the question lets itself, admits, of an answer. Just that questioning attitude, approach, corresponding, would allow an answer. Heidegger asks how Richardson proposes to overcome the common false reading of the turn to speak the same turn that he, Heidegger, has to speak. Such a speaking of the same is a *nachzudenken*, a thinking through, thinking toward. In the previous paragraph Heidegger had stressed that the phenomenology of Richardson's book's title is itself a process of "allowing the most proper concern of thought to show itself".[44] What Richardson renders as "most proper" I should rather translate as "ownly," "ownmost." In the very thought of the turn, Heidegger is inviting Richardson to say the same. To say the same would be to speak of being, which (in the same paragraph) Heidegger names as "being as such (*das Seyn*)".[45]

The appearance of the Middle High German term *das Seyn* in the text, a common device of Heidegger's, indicates that this is what was earlier named as destructuring at work, a going back into the roots in order to return to what most needs to be said. To speak the same, to correspond, is what is at issue. For Heidegger, it is not that Richardson should speak the

43. Richardson, W. J., *Heidegger: Through Phenomenology to Thought* (1963), p. xvii. "Die zweite von Ihnen gestellte Frage. Sie lautet: 'Zugegeben, *daß* in Ihrem Seinsdenken eine 'Kehre' geschehen ist—*wie* ist dann diese 'Kehre' geschehen—oder, anders gefragt, wie ist dieses Geschehen selbst zu denken?'

"Ihre Frage läßt sich nur beantworten, wenn zuvor geklärt ist, was 'Kehre' besagt; deutlicher gesprochen, wenn man willens ist, dem darüber schon Gesagten entsprechend nachzudenken, statt fortgesetzt grundlose Behauptungen in Umlauf zu bringen."

44. Richardson, W. J., *Heidegger: Through Phenomenology to Thought* (1963). "Sich-zeigenlassen der eigensten Sache des Denkens."

45. Richardson, W. J., *Heidegger: Through Phenomenology to Thought* (1963). "Das Sein als solches (das Seyn)". Richardson here translates Heidegger's use of the older term *das Seyn* by the Old English 'beon'. From the early 1930s at least Heidegger frequently used the form *das Seyn* to indicate when he was speaking (as here) of being as such, or being as he had brought it to light. I have preferred to leave the term untranslated.

same as Heidegger, but that Richardson and Heidegger should both speak out of the same. Heidegger asks: how will you read me? This is not a relativism, but rather the question: will you read the same as I have read? Will *die Kehre* speak to you? When *die Kehre* speaks to you in its ownmost, you will speak *die Kehre*. To understand what that could possibly mean, it will be necessary to ask, not what Richardson thinks changes in Heidegger's thought, but what change Heidegger thought he was undertaking and explaining.

## A CHANGE IN THE TURN

What did Heidegger hold *die Kehre* itself to be? In order to explore this I follow through Heidegger's reading of Richardson and amplify it from other sources to show what Heidegger is referring to when he replies to Richardson. I propose to read Richardson against himself, in the direction Heidegger proposes against Richardson, that will tell us why Heidegger II contains and makes possible Heidegger I. I allow Heidegger to unlock for me the Richardson who decided that he would unlock Heidegger. I inquire into what it is Heidegger has to speak *of,* in order to see if it is possible that I might speak *of the same* as Heidegger.

Already, however, the perspective for understanding *die Kehre* has changed, from something which occurs *in* Heidegger's work to something Heidegger believes to have *occurred.* Almost unnoticed I find I am pressed into listening for Heidegger's turn, listening for what Heidegger himself listened, in the face of articulating Richardson's reversal. Unwittingly, the turn is undergoing a change.

In chapter 2 I noted that Heidegger used the term turnabout, *Umwendung,* in relation to Descartes. There he said: "Modern philosophy made a total turnabout of philosophical inquiry and started out from the subject, the I".[46] If it is no longer possible to interpret the turn in Heidegger's thought as, strictly speaking, a change in his thought, but rather that his thinking explains the character of what change is in itself, does his use of the term turnabout in relation to Descartes provide any clue to what the turn actually is? It is not just in Descartes alone that turnabouts occur, but rather, for Heidegger, all previous philosophy is forced into a position of turning about in its attempt to carry out the proper task of philosophy and its incapability

---

46. See p. 50 above.

of doing so. For Heidegger, the reason for that failure is philosophy's inability to determine itself out of the proper being of the *Dasein,* so that philosophy ends up producing worldviews and not ontology. Heidegger opened his lectures with the attempt to "establish philosophy on its own basis" by saying that "it can be shown historically that at bottom all the great philosophies since antiquity more or less explicitly took themselves to be, and as such sought to be, ontology. In a similar way, however, it can also be shown that these attempts failed over and over again".[47] Heidegger then notes that his previous two lecture courses, one on ancient philosophy and the other on the history of philosophy from Aquinas to Kant, had demonstrated the historical reasons for this.

The question Heidegger seeks to answer in tracing both these attempts and their failure is: what is the character of philosophy as such? This question must be asked through the various attempts of philosophers to bring an ontology to light. Nevertheless, something else is sought, namely what both explains the various turnabouts that these former attempts in philosophy themselves were, and what makes them possible, as their ontological basis. What makes them possible is both what explains them and their failure and explains something else too: the fundamental ontological structure of *Dasein* and of being as such. The method for proceeding, however, is the atheism of philosophy, precisely because every former attempt of philosophy to carry out an ontology fails precisely because of the way in which it refers the fundamental ontological constitution of the human being to a being other than the human, namely that of the divine. This failure has precisely been brought to light in virtue of Heidegger's atheism. The change in Heidegger's thought, therefore, is not the attempt to describe the fundamental constitution of *Dasein,* but the fundamental constitution of *Dasein* in its being—the being of beings, therefore, the ontological difference as such.

As Heidegger has indicated, this change he announces in the character of philosophy, that as phenomenology so will it carry itself out as ontology, is *die Kehre.* The turn is therefore not connected with Heidegger's atheism, but rather is itself the formal, historical condition of the appearance of that atheism, since the fundamental form of the being of *Dasein* is atheistic, pre-

47. *Grundprobleme der Philosophie* (GA24), p. 16. "Die Philosophie aus sich selbst zu begründen"; "Daß sich im Grunde alle großen Philosophien seit der Antike mehr oder minder ausdrücklich als Ontologie verstehen und als solche sich selbst gesucht haben, läßt sich historisch zeigen. Ebenso läßt sich aber auch zeigen, daß diese Versuche immer wieder scheiterten und warum sie scheitern mußten".

cisely in that it is the possibility of the *Dasein* being open toward the divine and so available to the divine address. This availability, however, is not a reserve in advance of the address, since it is only in the event of the address that any being-available comes to light. The address, as an event, constitutes and discloses the being-available. The event of being-addressed and being-available is constitutive of, and a mode of, the being of *Dasein*. The phenomenological description of the turn will turn out to be Heidegger's atheism as such, no longer as a method, now as an event.

There are three indications concerning *die Kehre* that arise out of the foreword to Richardson's study. The first locates where the original *Kehre* is first communicated, confirmed by Petzet's report, which I have argued says more on closer inspection than first appeared to be the case. The second is Heidegger's statement in the foreword itself: "The first time in my published writings that I spoke of the 'reversal' was in the *Humanismusbrief*",[48] complete with the date (1947) and page reference, page 17 of the *Sonderausgabe*, or edition that published the letter on its own.[49] The third is the 1937 lecture course *Grundfragen der Philosophie*, for reasons that will become clear in the next chapter.[50] By following these hints and finding their amplifications it will become possible to hear what turns in Heidegger's claim:

But Heidegger I becomes possible only if it is contained in Heidegger II.

Heidegger says the turn is communicated for the first time in the lecture *Vom Wesen der Wahrheit*. Immediately this appears to be a contradiction. For Heidegger claims that the first literary mention of *die Kehre* is in the *Humanismusbrief*, and the date given for this by Heidegger is 1947, or at the earliest 1945.[51] In fact in the 1943 text of *Vom Wesen der Wahrheit* the words *die Kehre* do not appear at all. At most, there are a few compounds of the verb *kehren* but these are only in relation to explications of particular issues

---

48. Petzet, H. W., *Auf einen Stern zugehen* (1983), p. 98. "Literarisch habe ich zuerst im 'Humanismusbrief' von der Kehre gesprochen."

49. *Über den Humanismus* (*Sonderausgabe* [1949]), a letter of 1947 to Jean Beaufret. In fact the exact phrase cited on the following page of the *Vorwort*, "Hier kehrt sich das Ganze um" appears on p. 19 of the *Sonderausgabe*.

50. *Grundfragen der Philosophie* (GA 45).

51. Cf. Richardson, W., *Heidegger: Through Phenomenology to Thought* (1963), p. xvii. Heidegger, referring to the publication of the *Letter on Humanism* says "also hat sich in Heideggers Denken seit 1947 eine 'Umkehr' oder gar seit 1945 eine 'Bekehrung' vollzogen".

in the text. Communication and literary mention appear, therefore, to be different things. Recalling, however, that in Heidegger's foreword there are two verbs which turn, *kehren* and *wenden*, the turn as it is intended by Heidegger leaps forth from the text.

In section 7 of *Vom Wesen der Wahrheit*, entitled *Die Un-wahrheit als die Irre*, Heidegger says:

> As insistent, man is turned toward the most readily available beings. But he insists only by being already ek-sistent, since, after all, he takes beings as his standard. However, in taking its standard, man is turned away from the mystery. The insistent turning toward what is readily available and the ek-sistent turning away from the mystery belong together. They are one and the same. Yet turning toward and away from is based on a turning to and fro proper to *Dasein*. Man's flight from the mystery toward what is readily available, onward from one current thing to the next, passing the mystery by—this is erring.[52]

Human being turns to and from "nothing less than the concealing of what is concealed as a whole, of beings as such, i.e. the mystery".[53] The concealment of what is concealed as a whole is described as un-essence, un-truth. This is contrasted with the extantness of one current thing to the next.

The passage ends by speaking of *das Irren*, in the flight from mystery into what is readily available, the extant. This, however, is a determination of time as humanity turns away from mystery into the readily available. In the 1924 lecture *Der Begriff der Zeit*, Heidegger had discussed the past (*vorbei*) in similar terms:

---

52. *Vom Wesen der Wahrheit* (*Wegmarken* [GA9]), p. 196. "Insistent ist der Mensch der je nächsten Gangbarkeit des Seienden zugewendet. Aber er insistiert nur als der schon ek-sistente, indem er doch das Seiende als ein solches Richtmaß nimmt. In seinem Maßnehmen ist das Menschentum weggewendet von Geheimnis. Jene insistente Zuwendung zum Gangbaren und diese ek-sistente Wegwendung vom Geheimnis gehören zusammen. Sie sind eines und dasselbe. Jenes Zu- und Weg-wenden folgt jedoch einer eigentümlichen Wende des Hin und Her im Dasein. Die Umgetriebenheit des Menschen weg vom Geheimnis hin zum Gangbaren, fort von einem Gängigen, fort zum nächsten und vorbei am Geheimnis, ist das Irren."

53. *Vom Wesen der Wahrheit* (*Wegmarken* [GA9]), p. 193. "Nichts Geringeres als die Verbergung des Verborgenen im Ganzen, des Seienden als eines solchen, d.h. das Geheimnis."

This past, as that to which I run ahead . . . scatters all secretiveness and busyness.[54]

He concludes that such a past is the 'how' of my *Dasein.*

The central concern here is *Dasein* as time, either turning the future into the extantness of the past by attempting to reproduce the past in the future, which is an erring; or in being genuinely and ecstatically held out to the future, to what has not yet been (essenced) and is therefore not-yet and so un-true. *Dasein*'s timeliness (in the case of the past) is the scattering of all *Heimlichkeiten,* secretiveness. It would be easy to miss Heidegger's play with the words *heimlich* (secrecy) and *Geheimnis* (which can be translated as "secret", but which I have translated as "mystery"). If the past, as that to which I run ahead, scatters all that is secret and hidden, it is the future which conceals and holds the hidden and secretive, the mysterious. Again the 1924 lecture confirms this, for here Heidegger says: "With regard to time, this means that *the fundamental phenomenon of time is the future*".[55] More importantly even than this "*Dasein* conceived in its most extreme possibility of being, *is time itself,* not in time".[56] The question is therefore how *Dasein* is as time.

## HEIDEGGER'S DESCRIPTION OF THE PHENOMENON OF TIME

The question of the relation of *Dasein* to time, and in particular of time's relation to the turn is central to all the concerns of the next chapter. In order to prepare fully for understanding how the turn is connected with time, I briefly examine Heidegger's treatment of the question of time. What I present here is only a sketch: the full discussion is carried out in a central section of his 1927 lectures *Grundprobleme der Phänomenologie* and the last three sections of Division II of *Sein und Zeit.* It is on the basis of the working out of the phenomenology of time that the full meaning of the turn is developed. Heidegger takes the originator of the understanding of time that is still current in the Western tradition to be Aristotle, who, he says, no one has yet

---

54. *Der Begriff der Zeit* (GA64), p. 17. "Dieses Vorbei, als zu welchem ich vorlaufe . . . jagt alle Heimlichkeiten und Betriebsamkeiten auseinander."

55. *Der Begriff der Zeit* (GA64), p. 19. "Auf die Zeit gesehen besagt das: *das Grundphänomen der Zeit ist die Zukunft*" (author's italics).

56. *Der Begriff der Zeit* (GA64), p. 19. "Das Dasein, begriffen in seiner äußersten Seinsmöglichkeit ist *die Zeit selbst,* nicht in der Zeit" (author's italics).

surpassed, with some exceptions in the work of Augustine and Kant. These two "nevertheless in principle hold fast to the Aristotelian concept of time".[57]

Heidegger undertakes his description of Aristotle's position with an analysis of the term *Umschlag*, change, by showing how Aristotle works out his understanding of time in connection with local motion and change.[58] Change is the fundamental basis on which Aristotle determines time, even though it is not change as such, but something connected with change and motion, κινήσεώς τι. Heidegger concludes "Aristotle says: ἀριθμὸς κινήσεως κατὰ τὸ πρότερον καὶ ὕστερον. We translate this as: time is something counted in connection with encountered motion with a view to the before and after, in the horizon of the earlier and later".[59] This horizon is a συνεχές, a continuum, which also appears in the working out of the ontological determination of the mathematical.[60] As a continuum it also can be understood as stretch. It is in this sense that time both posits and is experienced on the basis of a horizon, of the away-from-there, toward-here. Each of the stages on this continuum constitutes a 'now', so that the 'now's become, in their succession, countable. The obvious comparison for understanding the basis of this is with geometry, where each 'now' corresponds to a point, a θέσις, on the line or stretch, but Heidegger explicitly rules this out, because in the now, in contrast to the counting of points on a line, "there is always a reference to the no-longer and not-yet".[61] Whereas in geometry every point, every θέσις, is complete in itself and like every other point, each now is simultaneously both the same as every other now in its character and different from every other now because of what it indicates. It has, in other words, like number (ἀριθμός)—as opposed to mere sequences of geometrical arbitrary countable points—a genuinely ontological determination. Each now is genuinely differentiated from every other.

57. *Die Grundprobleme der Phänomenologie* (GA24), p. 336. "die dennoch grundsätzlich den Aristotelischen Zeitbegriff festhalten."

58. *Die Grundprobleme der Phänomenologie* (GA24), p. 332. "Wir sprechen vom Fluß der Zeit und sagen: die Zeit vergeht. Für κίνησις sagt Aristoteles auch μεταβολή. Dies ist der allgemeinste Begriff der Bewegung, wörtlich Umschlag."

59. *Die Grundprobleme der Phänomenologie* (GA24), p. 340f. "Aristoteles sagt: ἀριθμὸς κινήσεως κατὰ τὸ πρότερον καὶ ὕστερον. Wir übersetzen: Die Zeit ist ein Gezähltes an der für den Hinblick auf das Vor und Nach, im Horizont des Früher und Später, begegnenden Bewegung."

60. Cf. *Platon: Sophistes* (GA19), §15, esp. p. 114 ff.

61. *Die Grundprobleme der Phänomenologie* (GA24), p. 351. "Im Jetzt als solchem liegt schon die Verweisung auf das Nicht-mehr und Noch-nicht."

The no-longer and not-yet which characterize each now are not added to the now; they belong to the now as part of its very content. It is this which allows the now to have within itself the *"character of a transition"*.[62] The now is therefore in no sense a limit, because as both transition and dimension it is open in what it points toward and in what lies in its no-longer, while at the same time being specific to itself. Heidegger notes again that, as such, the now is understood through number (ἀριθμός), not limit (πέρας). This means that as number the nows are understood through measure, and also that through the appearance of each now, things are measured by time on the basis of their transitional character. The being in time of anything is precisely its measurability with regard to transition. This, Heidegger says, is the common understanding of time. Because it is so closely linked with change and with local motion, time is worked out by Aristotle in the general terms of the Greek cosmos, of which modern determinations are only a modification. In this sense Aristotle's understanding of time corresponds to his general worldview.

Heidegger's principal concern in elucidating the Aristotelian understanding of time is to unfold not Aristotle's common understanding of time, but rather in order to ask the question "from where does that time originate which we know *first of all* and which we know solely?"[63] He resists the Aristotelian worldview in favor of its originary ontological possibility. In other words, Heidegger seeks to ask the question: what is the ontological possibility of time? The answer is that *"Dasein,* expecting its ability to be, *comes toward itself"*.[64] Because it retains or forgets, *Dasein* always comports itself to what it has already been—it is always, in knowing itself, returning to itself. It is in this sense, Heidegger says, that *Dasein* as such can be said to be futural. Its being is always determined from out of the future. The question, therefore, is the manner of its return. The genuine, originary being of *Dasein* is as follows: "That which *Dasein* has indeed already been, its having-been-ness, belongs together with its future".[65]

---

62. *Die Grundprobleme der Phänomenologie* (GA24), p. 352. *"Charakter eines Überganges"* (author's italics).
63. *Die Grundprobleme der Phänomenologie* (GA24), p. 374. "Woher entspringt die Zeit, die wir *zunächst* kennen und die wir *einzig* kennen?" (author's italics).
64. *Die Grundprobleme der Phänomenologie* (GA24), p. 375. "Das Dasein *kommt,* sein Seinkönnen gewärtigend *auf sich zu*" (author's italics).
65. *Die Grundprobleme der Phänomenologie* (GA24), p. 375. "Dasjenige, was das Dasein je schon gewesen ist, seine *Gewesenheit,* gehört mit zu seiner Zukunft."

It is this turning back on itself from out of where it has just been that enables *Dasein* to constitute time at all, as a series of 'now's. This is the structure of the original unity of past, present, and future, which Heidegger names as the temporal-ecstatic horizon. Every possibility of being for *Dasein* occurs out of this originary experience of time, which nevertheless lays the basis for the common understanding of time in Aristotle and those who follow him. *Dasein* stands out of itself in order to return to itself *as,* in a manner determined by whatever it stands out toward. This standing-out is *Dasein*'s openness to the future, to the horizon of the intrinsic possibilities that it can be open for. It is only possible to elicit the structure of the turn which I will describe in chapter 4 on the basis of the originary description of time which Heidegger provides.

If originary time is the basis for Aristotle's conception of time, what is the consequence of what follows from Aristotle's description of time, and what is its connection with Heidegger's atheism? Is Aristotle's description of time a sequence of 'now's? Heidegger says that "the nows appear as intratemporal. They come and pass away like beings".[66] This has the consequence that time is experienced, not in the unity of the ecstases of the past, present, and future, but as extantnesses, as beings-at-hand, and therefore that time will have the appearance of being determined out of the same basic position from which beings themselves are determined: from Aristotle to the present day, time will be determined out of whatever concealment of being is also unfolding the determinations of beings themselves. What this means will become fully clear in chapters 5 and 6. Suffice it to say for the moment that this understanding of time will conceal what being means within it, in favor of the extantness of beings. As far as Heidegger's atheism is concerned, this will indicate that time will be determined out of the being of God. Even time is understood on the basis of Heidegger's atheism.

The experience of time as the being of beings is overcome for the sake of the experience of time as 'now's, as kinds of beings. The privileging of beings over nonbeing is rooted in *Dasein*'s particular orientation with regard to time, common time as opposed to originary time, as described by Aristotle. This means that the infinitude of time is experienced as the totality of 'now's rather than the negative sense of pure openness, of a privation with regard to ecstasis. Heidegger says "the infinity of time is not a positive feature of

---

66. *Die Grundprobleme der Phänomenologie* (GA24), p. 385. "Die Jetzt geben sich als innerzeitig. Sie kommen an und verschwinden wie Seiendes."

time but a privation which characterizes a negative character of temporality".[67] Temporality is finite precisely in virtue of death, because *Dasein* is nothing other than temporality. *Dasein* falls into inauthenticity when it forgets the finitude of (its own) temporality.

Heidegger does not say so explicitly, but the suggestion is that precisely the supposed infinitude of time that marks the being of God itself arises out of *Dasein*'s self-concealment of its inauthenticity from itself. Aristotle frequently determines the outermost of the heavens as the eternal seat of the divine as immortality or, more literally, being-without-death, ἀθάνατος. In chapter 1 I considered how for Heidegger, this in fact corresponds to "ἀθανατίζειν [being-without-death], a way of being for humans in which they have the highest possibility of not coming to an end. This is the extreme position to which the Greeks carried human *Dasein*".[68] This corresponds to Aristotle's definition of time as ἡ σφαῖρα αὐτή, the (outermost) sphere of the heavens itself, the place which is always the same, ἀεί, and eternal or immortal.[69] Heidegger's atheism with regard to the Greek privileging of the permanent over the impermanent, the intransitory over the transitory, and the without-death over death, itself as the means by which the now-character of time is unfolded, forces the unfolding of the originary experience of time in its structures. Time is now no longer worked out on the basis of the unchanging (or even the ever-changing, which is what Nietzsche will transform it into), the symmetrical connection with the working out of (Aristotelian) local motion (and what this itself changes into after Descartes and the *res extensa*), but on the basis of the existential analytic of *Dasein*. Thus what change, motion itself, means for Heidegger is also worked out on the basis of the being of *Dasein*. Change, as the basis for time, is simultaneously the basis for the turn. The turn is the means by which *Dasein* experiences change and Heidegger's account of change on the basis of the being of beings. It is in this sense that Heidegger's thought contains a change—it now describes what change in itself is. Change is the turn.

67. *Die Grundprobleme der Phänomenologie* (GA24), p. 387. "Die Unendlichkeit der Zeit ist nicht etwa ein Vorzug der Zeit, sondern ein Privativum, das einen negativen Charakter der Zeitlichkeit charakterisiert."

68. See p. 9, note 19, above.

69. Aristotle, *Physics*, IV, X (218a33). Cited by Heidegger in *Die Grundprobleme der Phänomenologie* (GA24), p. 331

Chapter Four

# The Event in Heidegger's Turn

## THE CONNECTION BETWEEN *DIE KEHRE* AND *DAS EREIGNIS*

In the last chapter I suggested that the phenomenological description of the turn is Heidegger's atheism as such, no longer as a method, now as event. I have attempted to show how Heidegger develops *die Kehre* as the timing of *Dasein* as turning and the structures within which turning takes place. Now I ask how and why this is, as a way of working out the event of the turn. I want, in short, to show how Heidegger links the turn inextricably with the term *das Ereignis*. This term, often (and painfully) translated as the event of appropriation, propriation, and the like, bears also the simple meaning 'event', a meaning most often eschewed as the least of what Heidegger intends. Speaking and saying belong to *die Kehre*, as I have already suggested. What is to be said also always says *das Ereignis*.

In the 1949 note added to the text of the lecture *Vom Wesen der Wahrheit* Heidegger says: "The question of the essence of truth springs out of the question of the truth of essence".[1] He adds: "*The essence of truth is the truth of essence*".[2] These two statements are explicitly *not* dialectical or tautological, they do not offer a synthesis to something higher, nor do they say nothing at all; rather, they are each "the saying of a turning".[3] For the first time in *Vom Wesen der Wahrheit* the word *Kehre* makes an appearance, in the note added nineteen years after it was given as a lecture. Yet the turn here appears not to have been carried out. For the final paragraph says:

---

1. *Vom Wesen der Wahrheit* (*Wegmarken* [GA9]), p. 201. "Die Frage nach dem Wesen der Wahrheit entspringt aus der Frage nach der Wahrheit des Wesens."
2. *Vom Wesen der Wahrheit* (*Wegmarken* [GA9]), p. 201. "*Das Wesen der Wahrheit ist die Wahrheit des Wesens*" (author's italics).
3. *Vom Wesen der Wahrheit* (*Wegmarken* [GA9]), p. 201. "Die Sage einer Kehre."

Already in the original project the lecture 'On the Essence of Truth' was to have been completed by a second lecture 'On the Truth of Essence'. The latter failed for reasons that are now indicated in the letter 'On Humanism'.[4]

I have already indicated Heidegger's comment that the first *literary* reference to *die Kehre* in his published works is found in the *Letter on Humanism*. This reference says:

Here the whole turns itself about.[5]

What turns itself about is "the adequate imitative and collaborative execution of this other thinking that abandons subjectivity", the guiding thought of *Sein und Zeit*.[6]

This is no longer the turn as such, but rather the saying of the turn. The turn itself was worked out in relation to time, as that turn into and out of the future as secrecy and the past. How did Heidegger make the transition to understanding the turn in relation to language? Indeed, if, as it would appear, *die Kehre* is in fact later worked out in relation to language, rather than time, would this not be precisely a turn of the kind beloved in the literature, a change of Heidegger's mind? Language and time, however, belong together for Heidegger. In a 1942–43 lecture series in a subsection entitled *Being and the Word,* Heidegger notes that: "In *Sein und Zeit,* no matter how strange it must sound, 'time' is the given name of the originary *ground* of the word".[7] Language is the timing of time. Moreover he raises this here with respect to *das Ereignis.*

The third, unpublished division of *Sein und Zeit* was to have been entitled *Zeit und Sein.*[8] Heidegger confirms that it was held back, in the same way

---

4. *Vom Wesen der Wahrheit* (*Wegmarken* [GA9]), p. 201. "Der Vortrag 'Vom Wesen der Wahrheit' sollte bereits im ursprünglichen Entwurf durch einen zweiten 'Von der Wahrheit des Wesens' ergänzt werden. Dieser mißlang aus Gründen, die jetzt in dem Brief 'Über den Humanismus' angedeutet sind."

5. *Über dem Humanismus* (*Sonderausgabe*), p. 19. "Hier kehrt sich das Ganze um."

6. *Über dem Humanismus* (*Sonderausgabe*), p. 19. "Der zureichende Nach- und Mit–vollzug dieses anderen, die Subjektivität verlassenden Denkens."

7. *Parmenides* (GA54), p. 113. "'Zeit' ist in 'Sein und Zeit', so befremdlich das klingen muß, der Vorname für den Anfangs*grund* des Wortes" (author's italics).

8. *Sein und Zeit* (GA2), p. 39. This indicates that of the first book of *Sein und Zeit* only the first two divisions were published: 1. *Die vorbereitende Fundamentalanalyse des*

that the other half of the saying of the turning, that lecture which was to have explicated the second half of the thought that the essence of truth is the truth of essence, which was also held back in 1930. Thus in 1947, in the *Humanismusbrief*, Heidegger claims that the horizon outlined for thinking in 1927 in *Sein und Zeit* remains the same as it was in 1930 with the lecture published in 1943 as *Vom Wesen der Wahrheit*. Indeed, in the *Humanismusbrief* he uses the very words that he repeats in 1963 in the foreword to Richardson's book: this reversal is not a consequence of altering the standpoint, much less of abandoning the fundamental issue, of *Sein und Zeit*. In 1963 (the year after the lecture *Zeit und Sein* was delivered) the horizon remains the same.[9] What horizon? Solely the horizon opened up by undertaking that thinking which abandons subjectivity, the other thinking from which Heidegger's work springs.

Why, then, is the lecture *Vom Wesen der Wahrheit* important? "The lecture . . . thought out and delivered in 1930 but not printed until 1943, provides a certain insight into the thinking of the turning from 'being and time' to 'time and being'".[10] If the departure point for *Sein und Zeit* was *es gibt* (literally it gives, which has the sense of *il y a* in French, that there is no 'it' that gives as such) that leads to *es gibt Sein*,[11] there is being, the guiding thought of the lecture *Zeit und Sein* is *es gibt* that leads to *es gibt Zeit*.[12] The saying of the turning, that pointed first to being and then to time, brings to the fore *es gibt*. In the lecture Heidegger asks the question: what is the "indeterminate" relation indicated by the word *and* in (what is now known to be) a saying of the turning: being *and* time, time *and* being? He answers:"The 'It' that gives".[13] The whole force of the lecture *Zeit und Sein* is to understand *es gibt* as *Ereignis:*

---

*Daseins;* and 2. *Dasein und Zeitlichkeit.* The third unpublished division was to have been entitled 3. *Zeit und Sein.*

    9. Published in *Zur Sache des Denkens* (GA14).

    10. *Über den Humanismus* (*Sonderausgabe*), p. 19. "Der Vortrag . . . der 1930 gedacht und mitgeteilt, aber erst 1943 gedruckt wurde, gibt einen gewissen Einblick in das Denken der Kehre von 'Sein und Zeit' zu 'Zeit und Sein'."

    11. *Sein und Zeit* (GA2), p. 7. "Being lies in the fact that something is, and in its being as it is; in reality, in presence-at-hand; in subsistence; in validity; in *Dasein;* in the 'there is'." ("Sein liegt im Daß- und Sosein, in Realität, Vorhandenheit, Bestand, Geltung, Dasein, im 'es gibt'") See also (p. 212): "Of course only as long as Dasein *is*, which means, the ontical possibility of the understanding of being, 'is there' being" (author's italics). ( "Allerdings nur solange Dasein *ist*, das heißt die ontische Möglichkeit von Seinsverständnis, 'gibt es' Sein.")

    12. "It times."

    13. *Zeit und Sein* (*Zur Sache des Denkens* [GA14]), p. 21. "Das 'Es' das gibt."

Now it's clear: what lets the two matters belong together, what brings the two into their own, and even more, maintains and holds them in their belonging together—the way the two matters stand, the matter at stake—is Ereignis ... accordingly 'it', that 'gives' in "It beings", "It times", proves to be *das Ereignis*.[14]

## SAYINGS OF THE TURNING

It should be noted that *es gibt* also belongs to a further saying of a turning, namely "the essence of language: the language of essence" outlined in the three lectures given between December 1957 and February 1958 and later published in as *Das Wesen der Sprache*.[15] *Die Kehre* has always to do with essence, rather than with meaning, truth, language, or any particular being. Why is this important? Because one consistent interpretation of the turn in the literature is that it was a turn from the meaning of being to the truth of being.[16] What this interpretation fails to understand is that Heidegger is always inquiring not into the *meaning* of being, the *truth* of being, but the meaning of *being,* truth of *being:* in other words, the being of meaning, the being of truth. But you cannot inquire into being as such (*das Sein*), only beings (*die Seienden*). Even truth, meaning, and language are beings. More important still, essence names the unfolding of a being. How do beings unfold? Over time. What is time? *Dasein* is as time. Essence names the way any being comes about in *Dasein*. Not that any *Dasein* brings this or that

---

14. *Zeit und Sein* (*Zur Sache des Denkens* [GA14]), p. 20. "Nunmehr zeigt sich: Was beide Sachen zueinander gehören läßt, was beide Sachen nicht nur in ihr Eigenes bringt, sondern in ihr Zusammengehören verwahrt und darin hält, der Verhalt beider Sachen, der Sach-Verhalt, ist das Ereignis ... Demnach bezeugt sich das Es, das gibt, im 'Es gibt Sein', 'Es gibt Zeit', als das Ereignis." To speak of *das 'Es', das gibt*, the 'It' that gives, is almost impossible in German.

15. *Unterwegs zur Sprache* (GA12), p. 200 ff.

16. For a typical argument of this kind, see Gary Aylesworth's "Translator's Foreword" to his translation of *Gesamtausgabe* 51, as *Basic Concepts* (1993). Aylesworth says (p. xi): "The 'turning' is a transition ... from the problematic of the meaning of being to the question of the truth of being ... a truth whose disclosure is to be won through a confrontation with the history of being itself, instead of the existential analyzes of *Dasein* that constitute his earlier work".

being about, but rather, beings essence *Dasein.* They are what give *Dasein* to be, being.[17]

I inquire into what Heidegger called the real turn, indicated by Petzet's report and in particular how it has to do with time. Do the meanings of these two central terms of Heidegger's, *die Kehre* and *das Ereignis,* belong together? If I can show they do, then the outline for which I have argued is correct. The lecture *Die Kehre* discusses the danger named in two lines of Hölderlin:

> Where there is danger,
> saving also grows.[18]

Heidegger proposes that danger and the saving are the same, that the one is the other. Here again is a kind of saying of a turning. Danger has utterly to do with the essence of technology, with the *Ge-stell,* usually translated as en-framing. So Heidegger says: "The danger is the epoch of being, coming to presence as En-framing".[19] In this lecture and in the essay *Die Frage nach der Technik,* Heidegger outlines technology as that epoch of being where being is most concealed, the forgottenness of being. When danger *is* as danger, being *is* as most concealed, and out of its own concealedness brings itself to pass into its epoch. Moreover, this concealment belongs either to forgotten-ness, in what is past, or to the mystery, as what is future. It has the same time structure as *Ruinance* and its timing in relation to the nothing, and has to do with the occurring of world: "When the danger is as the danger, with the turning about of forgottenness, in the safekeeping of *das Seyn,* world events-itself. That world events itself as world, that the thing things, this is the distant advent of the coming to presence of being itself".[20]

I have indicated that the concealedness of concealment is *das Geheimnis,* the mystery. Now Heidegger argues:

---

17. This is turned about from (is the opposite of) the way in which things occur in valuation, in the Will to Power, as I argue in chapter 7.

18. *Die Kehre (Bremer und Freiburger Vorträge* [GA79]), p. 72. "Wo aber Gefahr ist, / wächst das Rettende auch."

19. *Die Kehre (Bremer und Freiburger Vorträge* [GA79]), p. 72. "Die Gefahr ist die Epoche des Seyns, wesend als das Ge-stell."

20. *Die Kehre (Bremer und Freiburger Vorträge* [GA79]), p. 73. "Wenn die Gefahr als Gefahr ist, ereignet sich mit der Kehre der Vergessenheit die Wahrnis des Seyns, ereignet sich Welt. Daß Welt sich ereigne als Welt, daß dinge das Ding, dies ist die ferne Ankunft des Wesens des Seyns selbst."

The turning of the danger comes to pass suddenly. In this turning, the
clearing belonging to the essence of being suddenly clears itself and
lights up . . . when in the turning of the danger, the truth of being
flashes, the essence of being clears and lights itself up. Then the truth of
the essence of being turns in.[21]

Here *das Ereignis* and *die Kehre* stand as explaining each other and belonging
together. As *das Ereignis* is the delivering over of man and being one to
another, so *die Kehre* is that delivering in the saying of its taking place. But
where is time, the horizon that Löwith said had disappeared from Heidegger's work? Time *as* epoch, and not just one but two epochs in their standing
against each other—the epoch of being as pure presence and the epoch of
the presencing of being (the two opposed possible futures named in the lecture *Vom Wesen der Wahrheit*)—flash, as the conditioning possibility of the
moment of *das Ereignis* in its turning. One epoch turns out of the other, as
the most extreme possibility of it, in a moment.

In *Vom Wesen der Wahrheit*, *Dasein* turns (*wendet*). In the lecture *Die
Kehre*, being turns (*kehrt*). It eventuates itself (*sich ereignet*). A later, marginal
note of Heidegger's to the text of *Vom Wesen der Wahrheit* shows how the
whole movement of the turn takes place and how *das Ereignis* and *die Kehre*
belong together. Here *Dasein*, in *in-sistent* and *ek-sistent* turning turns toward
and from beings, is also turning toward and from being (in just the movement I cited from section 7). The passage of *Vom Wesen der Wahrheit* says:

Letting-be is intrinsically at the same time concealing. In the ek-sistent
freedom of *Dasein* a concealing of beings as a whole events itself, which
is concealment.[22]

Heidegger's marginal note reads:

---

21. *Die Kehre* (*Bremer und Freiburger Vorträge* [GA79]), p. 73f. "Die Kehre der Gefahr
ereignet sich jäh. In der Kehre lichtet sich jäh die Lichtung des Wesens des Seins . . .
Wenn in der Kehre der Gefahr die Wahrheit des Seins blitzt, lichtet sich das Wesen des
Seins. Dann kehrt die Wahrheit des Wesens des Seins ein."
22. *Wegmarken* (GA9), p. 193. "Das Seinlassen ist in sich zugleich ein Verbergen. In
der ek-sistenten Freiheit des Daseins ereignet sich die Verbergung des Seienden im
Ganzen, ist die Verborgenheit."

First edition 1943 between five and six. The leap into the (in *Ereignis* essencing) turning.[23]

An examination of the text of sections 5 and 6 reveals that they are both speaking of ways of being of *Dasein*, in *The Essence of Truth* (section 5) or *Untruth as Concealing* (section 6). The relation between the two is expanded and developed in section 7.

The turning as it is explained here is not the separation of being from *Dasein* (as Löwith had implied), but being itself from beings-as-a-whole, which is the metaphysical determination of being solely as being-ness (Heidegger's name for the God of metaphysics). *Dasein*'s comportment toward either being or beings-as-a-whole takes for granted *Dasein*'s existence as finite time, since each comportment assumes a temporal horizon: determination toward the mystery, as futural; or in flight, as a kind of being seized and consumed by the extantness of what is past.

Heidegger's concern in addressing Richardson directly is that *die Kehre* explains how they are related to him and of what he is trying to speak. This speaking is in consequence of how *Dasein* is toward itself and given as timely. As early as 1928, Heidegger had connected *die Kehre* with a preliminary sketch for what will two years later be called ontotheology. In his lectures on Leibniz and logic he describes the analyses of first *Dasein* and then the temporality of being. He notes:

But the temporal analysis is at the same time the turn, where ontology itself runs back into the metaphysical ontic in which it implicitly always remains. Through the movement of radicalizing and universalizing, the aim is to bring ontology to its latent overturning. Here the turn is carried out, and it is turned over into the metontology.[24]

23. *Wegmarken* (GA9), p. 193. "1. Auflage 1943: Zwischen 5. und 6. der Sprung in die (im Ereignis wesende) Kehre."

24. *Metaphysische Anfangsgründe der Logik* (GA26), p. 201. "Diese temporale Analytik ist aber zugleich die *Kehre*, in der die Ontologie selbst in die metaphysische Ontik, in der sie unausdrücklich immer steht, ausdrücklich zurückläuft. Es gilt, durch die Bewegtheit der Radikalisierung und Universalisierung die Ontologie zu dem in ihr latenten Umschlag zu bringen. Da vollzieht sich das Kehren, und es kommt zum Umschlag in die Metontologie."

Heidegger proceeds to name two horizons, fundamental ontology, and metontology, which constitute the unity of the concept of metaphysics. This coming about of fundamental ontology and metontology is the transformation of *that* basic problem which hitherto was introduced under the dual conception of πρώτη φιλοσοφία and θεολογια.[25] Overturning appears to be playing the same role as the term tipping-over played in 1919.[26] This discussion takes place in the concluding appendix to a section entitled *The Transcendence-Problem and the Problem of Sein und Zeit* and immediately prior to a section entitled *The Transcendence of Dasein. Die Kehre* then, is an overturning of the inner structure and character of the problem of transcendence. In these lectures, having raised the transcendence problem, Heidegger moves on to the problem of grounds. I indicated (in chapter 2) that in 1929 the problem of ground is the working out of the freedom of *Dasein* and that this is understood as *Dasein* transcending into nothing. At the center of transcendence stands *die Kehre;* indeed the turn unlocks transcendence as a change, a tipping-over, of transcendence appearing in one way and now appearing in another. In 1928 the language is indeed different from the language of 1930, but what Heidegger describes in these lectures is an oscillation, a kind of switching between being turned toward the (originary) future—the mystery or the passing away of meaning (a future dominated by the past), a turning of *Dasein* this way and that, which is *Dasein*'s factical concretion, being in the world and the worlding of world. In other words, *die Kehre* does not name a single turn but the oscillation and vibration of coming to the self and losing the self, of owning and disowning that is the character of knowing beings and at the same time disclosing a worlded self, an 'I'. This 'I' belongs either to a genuine, open, and mysterious future, or is driven to replicate the past in the future, which is an anxious resistance of the demands of the future. All of this has to do with being determined toward and away from things in general and things in particular.

---

25. *Metaphysische Anfangsgründe der Logik* (GA26), p. 202.

26. Indeed, the term *Umschlag* seems to have appeared about the same time. Cf. the 1919/20 lecture course published as *Phänomenologie der Anschauung und des Ausdrucks* (GA59), esp. pp. 70–71, where Heidegger speaks in relation to Simmel of a change of vital form ("Umschlag der vitalen Form").

## THE MEANING OF TRANSCENDENCE

The question of transcendence is worked out in relation to beings or things: "As existing, *Dasein* never relates only to a particular object; if it relates solely to one object, it does so in the mode of turning away from other beings that are beforehand and at the same time appearing along with the object. This multiplicity occurs not because there are several objects, but the other way about".[27] There is no way of being without beings: every determination of being is also a 'how' of relating to or comporting to beings. Even in withdrawal from the manifold of beings to concentrate on one, the manifold continues to exert itself: the question is only how. This is what it means to be embodied. To be bodily is to be thrown, which means worlded, and to discover myself as worlded. Thrownness precedes even sexual identity and provides for it to occur and be understood:

> The essentially thrown dispersal of the as yet wholly neutrally understood *Dasein* is demonstrated, among other things, by the fact that *Dasein* is being-with with *Dasein*. This being-with with $X$ does not come about on the basis of factically existing together, it is not clarified only on the basis of a supposedly more originally genus-like being of sexedly differentiated bodily essences, rather this genus-like striving-together and genus-like uniting metaphysically presupposes dispersal of *Dasein* as such, which means being-with in general.[28]

Being-with specifically raises the problem of freedom. This being-factical is also spatially articulated. At this point in the text Heidegger makes it clear

---

27. *Metaphysische Anfangsgründe der Logik* (GA26), p. 173. "Das Dasein verhält sich als existierendes nie je nur zu einem Objekt, und wenn, dann nur in der Weise des Absehens von zuvor und zugleich immer miterscheinenden anderen Seienden. Diese Mannigfaltigung geschieht nicht dadurch, daß es mehrere Objekte gibt, sondern umgekehrt."

28. *Metaphysische Anfangsgründe der Logik* (GA26), p. 174 f. "Die wesenhaft geworfene Zerstreuung des noch ganz neutral verstandenen Daseins bekundet sich unter anderem darin, daß das Dasein *Mitsein* mit Dasein ist. Dieses Mitsein mit . . . entsteht nicht aufgrund eines faktisches Zusammendaseins, es erklärt sich nicht nur auf dem Grunde eines vermeintlich ursprünglicheren gattungshaften Seins der geschlechtlich gespaltenen leiblichen Wesen, sondern dieses gattungshafte Zusammenstreben und die gattungshafte Einigung hat zur metaphysischen Voraussetzung die Zerstreuung des Daseins als solchen, d.h. das Mitsein überhaupt."

that the pre-sexual, free, neutral postulation of *Dasein* "is only possible on the basis of the extreme existentiell *mission* of the one projecting".[29] In *Sein und Zeit* Heidegger had defined *existentiell* in the following terms: "We come to terms with the question of existence always only through existence itself. We call the understanding of oneself that is *dominant* here *existentiell* understanding".[30] *Existentiell* means being factical. This securing of the absolute neutrality and free independence of *Dasein* is the way in which Heidegger describes the structure of transcendence. Transcendence is secured in virtue of beings, but only as a 'how' of being toward them: close, as a losing of the self among them; distant, as a drawing back and reflecting. Being-with with other *Dasein*s alone secures the possibility of considering oneself apart from them. This is again the oscillating and turning I have named. In this oscillating, the horizon of time gets lost, which means it becomes figured spatially. The spatial figuring of transcendence results in the positing, not of the future as a temporalizing of the self, but of a world apart, a transcendent world. Rediscovering facticality means rediscovering the temporal horizon of transcendence *in a return,* a turning-back to the very world from which *Dasein* first transcended. This is precisely what Heidegger believed Nietzsche to be describing with the figure of Zarathustra.

Why is Heidegger able to say this multiplicity occurs not because there are several objects, but the other way about? In this section Heidegger repeats the claim: "The existentiell mission of fundamental ontology brings with it the appearance of an extremely individualistic, radical atheism".[31] Still further he describes the determination of οὐσία as the constitution of the ὄν ἢ ὄν both in Aristotle and in Plato's *Theaetetus,*[32] leading in Aristotle to the distinction between "πρώτη οὐσία, this being as it exists, the that-being, and the δευτέρα οὐσία, what-being, essence".[33] He concludes by investigat-

29. *Metaphysische Anfangsgründe der Logik* (GA26), p. 176. "[Dasein] ist nur möglich auf dem Grunde extremen existentiellen *Einsatzes* des Entwerfenden selbst" (author's italics).

30. *Sein und Zeit* (GA2), p. 12. "Die Frage der Existenz ist immer nur durch das Existieren selbst ins Reine zu bringen. Das *hierbei* führende Verständnis seiner selbst nennen wir das *existenzielle*" (author's italics).

31. *Metaphysische Anfangsgründe der Logik* (GA26), p. 177. "Der existenzielle Einsatz der Fundamentalontologie führt mit sich den Schein eines extrem individualistischen, radikalen Atheismus."

32. Citing Plato, *Theaetetus,* 155e4 ff.

33. *Metaphysische Anfangsgründe der Logik* (GA26), p. 183. "πρώτη οὐσία, dieses Seiende, so wie es existiert, das Daß-sein, und die δευτέρα οὐσία, das Was-sein, das Wesen."

ing the temporal significance of οὐσία, that it is always present, not as eternal, ἀεί, but present in every 'now', so that it is as presentness (παρουσία).

Again, Heidegger is pointing to *die Kehre,* as transcendence metaphysically conceived. This is because in metaphysics the oscillation of transcendence is between *that*-being and *what*-being, first and second being, where that-being names first and what-being names second being. In *that*-being what is named is being-as-a-whole, which he named in *Vom Wesen der Wahrheit* as "being in general" and "beings in general".[34]

The oscillation between singular, being in general, and plural, beings in general, is here not accidental, but precisely the mark of the turn in its very turning about. In transcending (metaphysically understood) the turn covers up the beings I am among and hides them as being-as-a-whole, the persistent presence of pure presence. This pure presence, as we shall shortly see, is named as God, but God metaphysically understood (and so not the God of faith). This covering up is the same when transcendence is figured metaphysically and when it is understood through the very turn itself, that is in the overcoming of metaphysics, with one important difference. Through the overturning aspect of the turn, the unity of being-as-a-whole is replaced by the governing unity of being itself: my-self in being. In 1930 when Heidegger wrote this piece, however, he had not fully worked out the difference between the turn and the sayings of the turn, but this relatedness to language, or sayings, is at work here in this linguistic instability of this singular and plural in the text of sections 5, 6, and 7 of the lecture *Vom Wesen der Wahrheit.*

## TRANSCENDENCE AS DIVINE

How did transcendence first come to be understood as a way of determining the divine? In the lectures I have discussed, immediately before Heidegger carries out the distinction between first and second being as between πρώτη φιλοσοφία and θεολογία, and in connection with the temporal significance of οὐσία, he says:

---

34. Cf. *Vom Wesen der Wahrheit* (*Wegmarken* [GA9]), p. 193. The German term *das Seiende* has a double sense that in English the word being has great difficulty in rendering. It carries the resonance of both *this* being *here,* and the whole of whatever is extant in being. Heidegger usually clarifies the latter by describing the whole as *das Seiende überhaupt* or *das Seiende im Ganzen.*

Beings is the always present, in constant presentness. *Duration* and *presentness* possess a temporal feature, in a sense that is at first problematic. (Here we refer to the earlier mentioned expressions in Thomas [Aquinas]: intuitus praesens, omne praesentialiter subjectum, esse Dei as actus purus, where in principle the same conception of being occurs).[35]

Metaphysically the proper temporal significance of transcendence as the projecting of myself into the future from out of beings, the futural directedness of myself as the occurring of the being of beings, is covered up and concealed, above all, from my-self. I experience this concealment as presence to self, but most of all as what is the most constantly present of presence. The philosophical consequence of the working out of this concealment of constant presence becomes understood as the being of God, in consequence of the way in which metaphysics thinks. Just as God is the most beingful of any particular being, so God is the most time-persistent of any given experience of time.

However, it is clear even from the little Heidegger has already said that for him this notion of constant presence is not determined out of any notion of eternity (ἀεί) (remembering that in the lecture *Der Begriff der Zeit* he had ruled out any philosophical access to the eternal). If this is so, then implicitly he is arguing that constant presence is the (metaphysically) concealed temporal aspect of the transcendence of *Dasein*.[36] In this sense, *actus purus* is a masked determination of the being of *Dasein*, not of God. This can only be known once it is granted that God cannot be reached metaphysically: Heidegger's atheism brings this to light. The God who can no longer be reached metaphysically is *that* God who in metaphysics had also been declared dead by Nietzsche's madman. It is precisely for this reason, therefore, that the correct determination and significance of the temporality of transcendence will appear as a radical atheism. It is individual because *Dasein* as an embodied, worlded being has recovered its ownedness. I have become my-self for the first time. In *die Kehre* God and being are set apart, so that *Dasein* transcends into the future and nothing, for its own sake, not the sake of the divine.

---

35. *Metaphysische Anfangsgründe der Logik* (GA26), p. 184. "Seiendes ist das immer Anwesende—in ständiger Anwesenheit. *Beständigkeit* und *Anwesenheit* besitzen Zeitcharakter in einem zunächst problematischen Sinne. (Vergleichen wir damit die früher erwähnten Wendungen bei Thomas: intuitus praesens, omne praesentialiter subjectum, esse Dei als actus purus, so zeigt sich im Prinzip derselbe Seinsbegriff)" (author's italics).

36. *Der Begriff der Zeit* (GA64), p. 5.

Heidegger explicitly connects transcendence as a name for God with Christianity: "the Transcendent (also inadequately called 'transcendence') is the God of Christianity", but he immediately proceeds to argue that not only this, but also what comes after Christianity is what occurs when "this 'transcendence' is denied and replaced with 'the people' itself".[37] This successor understanding of Christianity "is only *apparently* unchristian; for it is *essentially* in agreement with that way of thinking that is called 'liberalism'".[38] As such it renders transcendence as an idea or value or meaning, something "which is to be realized through 'culture'".[39] The full significance of this will become clearer in relation to Nietzsche in chapter 7. What succeeds the worldview of Christianity does not necessarily go beyond it (despite its robust cosmopolitan claims), but rather reproduces its own worldview as a cultural form. This means that Heidegger's atheism will extend even beyond the question of God to all those questions of the failure adequately to describe the being of beings in favor of value, idea, or even culture. Paradoxically, even the study of culture or cultures, so often motivated by an atheistic affirmation of the whole variety of views, every possible standpoint, is simply another form of securing beings-as-a-whole, the metaphysical God, even though that God is now declared to be dead. Even corpses must rest somewhere.

Beings as a whole, *das Seiende im Ganzen,* names what Aristotle knew as τὸ θεῖον because it names the concealment of the significance of time in the metaphysical structure of transcendence, which occurs in *die Kehre* and reappears in being able to speak of *die Kehre.*

Where is God as far as *die Kehre* is concerned? The radical, individualistic atheism which Heidegger names has nothing to do with God, *so little* in fact that it does not speak of God at all. It speaks only of the no-longer-saying that God is either transcendent cause or ground. In consequence, in the 1949 lecture *Die Kehre,* the appearance of a reference to God toward the end of the text almost comes as a surprise. Heidegger begins by outlining again the structure of transcendence, that the human essence in *das Ereignis*

---

37. *Beiträge zur Philosophie* (GA65), p. 24. "Das Transzendente (genau auch 'die Transzendenz' genannt) ist der Gott des Christentums. Diese 'Transzendenz' wird geleugnet und das 'Volk' selbst . . . angesetzt."

38. *Beiträge zur Philosophie* (GA65), p. 24f. "Diese gegenchristliche 'Weltanschauung' . . . ist nur *scheinbar* unchristlich; denn sie kommt im *Wesentlichen* dennoch überein mit jener Denkart, die den 'Liberalismus' kennzeichnet" (author's italics).

39. *Beiträge zur Philosophie* (GA65), p. 25. "Solches . . . was aber durch 'Kultur' sich verwirklichen soll."

corresponds with its-owned, so that man and woman, so-corresponding in the safeguarding element of the world as mortal, turn out toward divinity.[40] This difficult language struggles to indicate that God is not given in a transcendent projection, but rather, transcendence and coming into one's own (ownedly) oscillating, vibrating—makes possible on the basis of transcendence (but not *as* transcendence) a reaching out toward . . . that will yield what, in other places, Heidegger calls hints of divinity, but not the divine itself.[41] He concludes in the next sentence:

> Otherwise not; for God is, if God is, a being, stands as a being in *das Seyn* and its essence, that itself events itself out of the worlding of world.[42]

What does "otherwise not" mean here? The passage refers to an oscillating, a vibrating of transcending *Dasein* reaching out *as* the worlding of world which is the giving of the being of beings in being. In *das Ereignis, Dasein,* as overcoming the metaphysically given God, becomes for the first time capable of experiencing itself and taking itself for itself in the availability it has for divinity. What this means in full we will explore in later chapters. Suffice it to say here that this does not mean that *Dasein* was not available for divinity before, but rather, in this being-available it can also be fully-self-disclosing. In the worlding of world God is and can only be (in factical life), given in being, which itself, in being-given to *Dasein* is given as any other being: only in the being of beings can God be known, and only in finitude. In the finitude of the being of beings there is always not-ness, nothing, as the mark of a finite being. In the giving of divinity *a* being is disclosed to itself divinely, which itself is just subject to that not-ness which I have already shown is elsewhere named as ruinance, and which, by virtue of its being-character, is open to the fading and decay of meaning.

Simultaneously, therefore, *Dasein* is open to God in coming to its own as self-owned, in the atheism that gives *Dasein* to be an entity for itself, and is open to the losing of that knowing of divinity that actually can be given in being.

---

40. Cf. *Die Kehre* (*Bremer und Freiburger Vorträge* [GA79]), p. 76.

41. Cf. for instance Heidegger's 1941 cycle of poems *Winke* reproduced in *Aus der Erfahrung des Denkens* (GA13), p. 23 ff.

42. *Die Kehre* (*Bremer und Freiburger Vorträge* [GA79]), p. 76. "Anders nicht; denn auch der Gott ist, wenn er ist, ein Seiender, steht als Seiender im Seyn und dessen Wesen, das sich aus Welten von Welt ereignet."

In the English translation of this lecture the translator William Lovitt indicates in a footnote that "'the god' of whom Heidegger speaks is not the god of the metaphysical-theological tradition of Christendom. Heidegger characteristically thinks of a dimension of the divine that the divinities make manifest—as among the Greeks, or of the Hebrew prophets, or in the preaching of Jesus".[43] Lovitt's words refer to a sentence from the *Nachwort* added to the published text lecture *Das Ding*,[44] which we will meet with again, and so he speaks with good warrant. I want to go further still. Although Heidegger does not say so, there is absolutely no incompatibility of this sentence either with a full understanding of Jesus as the divine son of the Father, nor as the divine informing me in words and sacramental life. Indeed, quite the reverse: the very phenomenology of ruinance suggests that in order to overcome the inevitable decay and not-ness inherent in all encounter with beings, the faithful believer would have to return to the record of preaching, return to the sacraments again and again, always purifying his or her appropriation of them in a continuing recovery and destructuring of their meaning back to its roots in order to be faithful to this availability to the divine.

It is no accident that Heidegger raises the question of God from within consideration of *die Kehre* itself. The question really asks: is God given *in* transcendence, or is God derived *from out of* transcendence, as ground? This is no different from asking whether I must wait for the God to reveal God's self, or whether I could derive God from creation. Is the default of divinity absence (*Ab*wesenheit), as Heidegger claimed it was, or is it derived out of presence (*An*wesenheit)? What is the relation of divinity to creation? Such a question never once denies that creation could also be given by God—it does not even ask a question concerning origins. Far from abolishing the possibility of God, *die Kehre* is that which makes my authentic, ownmost being-with God possible at all.

## NIETZSCHE AND THE TURN

In the foreword to Richardson's book, Heidegger makes the serious claim that "the reversal is in play within the matter itself. Neither did I invent it,

43. Lovitt, W., *The Turning* (1977), p. 47.
44. Cf. *Nachwort* to *Das Ding* (*Vorträge und Aufsätze* [GA7]), p. 177.

nor does it affect merely my thought".[45] Heidegger's claim here is that he did not create or invent *die Kehre*, it is not a feature of his thought, nor indeed *only* his thought. If this is the case, then surely he discovered it already at work somewhere else. Where?

The word *das Ereignis* and compounds of the verb *kehren* begin to appear together in Heidegger's published work in the second of the *Nietzsche* series of lectures, given in 1937 and published in 1961 as *Die Ewige Wiederkehr des Gleichen*.[46] Taken together they provide the key to Heidegger's analysis of Nietzsche's work *Also Sprach Zarathustra*. In these lectures Heidegger finds repeated sayings of the eternal recurrence. At the center of the sayings is the passage referring to the riddle of the doorway, with the two avenues leading off into the past and the future. Above the gateway is the inscription 'eye-blink' (*Augenblick*, which could also be translated as moment). Zarathustra presents the riddle to a dwarf, by asking whether the two lines contradict each other eternally? The dwarf solves the riddle disdainfully—he can hardly be bothered to talk of it. The use of the word talk here also echos Heidegger's inquiry into idle talk in *Sein und Zeit*.[47] The lecture continues:

"Everything straight deceives, murmured the dwarf contemptuously. All truth is curved; time itself is a circle".[48]

---

45. *Heidegger: Through Phenomenology to Thought*, p. xviii. "Die Kehre spielt im Sachverhalt selbst. Sie ist weder von mir erfunden, noch betrifft sie nur mein Denken."

46. *Die ewige Wiederkehr des Gleichen* (*Nietzsche* [GA6.1]), p. 255 ff.

47. The German word for talk with regard to the dwarf is *die Rede*. Cf. *Prolegomena zur Geschichte des Zeitbegriffs* (GA20), p. 376. "Als Rede hat das Gerede die Seinstendenz des Entdeckens; die alltägliche Ausgelegtheit lebt in diesem Sinne im Gerede." Cf. *Sein und Zeit* (GA2), §35. Idle talk represents an average understanding of the way things are. Consequently (p. 169): "Gossip is not based so much upon hearsay. It feeds upon superficial reading. The average understanding of the reader will *never be able* to decide what has been drawn from originary sources with a struggle and how much is just gossip. The average understanding, moreover, will not want any such disstinction, and does not need it, because, of course, it understands everything" (author's italics). ("Das Nach-reden gründet hier nicht so sehr in einem Hörensagen. Es speist sich aus dem An-gelesenen. Das durchschnittliche Verständnis des Lesers wird *nie* entscheiden *können*, was ursprünglich geschöpft und errungen und was nachgeredet ist. Noch mehr, durch-schnittliches Verständnis wird ein solches Unterscheiden gar nicht wollen, seiner nicht bedürfen, weil es ja alles versteht.")

48. *Die ewige Wiederkehr des Gleichen* (*Nietzsche* [GA6.1]), p. 294. "'Alles Gerade lügt, murmelte verächtlich der Zwerg. Alle Wahrheit ist krumm, die Zeit selber ist ein Kreis.'"

The dwarf's solution to the riddle is that time circles in on itself. The two avenues meet in eternity: the overcoming of contradiction—speaking-against—is the sameness of everything. Heidegger adds "truth itself—beings proceeding in truth—is curved . . . time's circling in itself, and hence the ever-recurring same for all beings in time, is the way in which beings as a whole is. It is in the manner of an eternal return. In this way the dwarf solves the riddle".[49] In this sense, the doorway is both anywhere on the two (really only one and the same) avenues and at all points on the avenue simultaneously. The moment which the doorway is, is constantly present and constant presence. It *is* only as the 'now'. Later, Heidegger gives an alternative solution to the riddle, a solution I intend to examine in chapter 7.[50]

For Heidegger, *die Kehre* and the overcoming of metaphysics had already been understood and carried out by Nietzsche: neither did I invent (*die Kehre*), nor does it affect merely my thought. Nietzsche is the inversion (*Umkehr*) of Plato that turns metaphysics in and back on itself and shows it to be a ring, a *Wiederkehr*. In the *Beiträge* Heidegger plays with how, in the turn out of metaphysics, this becomes a *Wider-kehre*, a turn-against that turns out of the eternal recurrence, into the new beginning.[51]

In chapter 3 I noted Heidegger's remarks that every hitherto philosophy (and this means philosopher) attempted to undertake philosophy as ontology, and yet none had succeeded. He amplified this by reference, first to his lectures on ancient philosophy, and then on the history of philosophy from Aquinas to Kant. Why, therefore, does Nietzsche stand in a special relation to the turn? Nietzsche (and Hegel, though differently) indicates that metaphysics has a beginning by bringing the possibilities which lie in metaphysics to a close, because beginnings only appear in their endings. Although, as Heidegger notes, metaphysics may continue to dominate thinking for centuries, nevertheless Nietzsche, in proclaiming the death of God, brings to a close the inherent possibilities in metaphysics. This is because, if with Parmenides and Heraclitus, and Plato and Aristotle, a beginning is opened

---

49. *Die ewige Wiederkehr des Gleichen* (*Nietzsche* [GA6.1]), p. 294. "Die Wahrheit selbst—das Seiende, wie es in Wahrheit verläuft—ist krumm. Das in-sich-Kreisen der Zeit und damit das Immerwiederkehren des Gleichen alles Seienden in der Zeit, ist die *Art, wie* das Seiende im Ganzen ist. Es ist in der Weise der ewigen Wiederkehr. So hat der Zwerg das Rätsel erraten."
50. See pp. 242–247 below.
51. *Beiträge zur Philosophie* (GA65), p. 407. "Kehre ist Wider-kehre." (Turning is turning-against.)

up through which the being of beings, the being of *Dasein*, is worked out through a being other than *Dasein* itself, the gods and God, nevertheless Nietzsche brings this to a close (it should be remembered Hegel also, though in a different way, proclaims the death of God).[52] In the same way that (for Heidegger) Aristotle and Plato base their working out of the science of being on the originary meaning of being understood by the Greeks and therefore point in two ways at once, both in the originary voice of being in what they say and their metaphysical determination of it, so also Nietzsche points in two ways, in the pointing toward a fundamental ontology in the (nevertheless metaphysically constructed) figure of Zarathustra, and in the metaphysics from out of which Zarathustra is construed, personified in the dwarf.

It is a puzzle in itself why throughout the *Nietzsche* lectures there is a constant oscillation between describing Nietzsche's doctrine of the eternal return as either *Wieder*kehr *des Gleichen* or *Wieder*kunft *des Gleichen*. As far as I know Heidegger never explains the instability thematically. He does, however, bring it to the fore in the very elaboration of this riddle, which I have now proposed is simultaneously the riddle of *die Kehre*. A little later in these lectures Heidegger says:

What does all this say about the right way to think the thought of eternal recurrence (*Wiederkehr*)? It says something essential: that which is to come (*künftig*) is precisely a matter for decision, since the ring is not closed in some remote infinity but possesses its unbroken closure in the moment, as the center of the striving; what recurs (*wiederkehrt*)—if it is to recur—is decided by the moment and by the force with which the moment can cope with whatever in it is repelled by such striving. That is what is peculiar to, and hardest to bear in, the doctrine of eternal return (*Wiederkunft*)—to wit, that eternity is in the moment, that the moment is not the fleeting 'now', not an instant of time whizzing by a spectator, but the collision of future and past. Here the moment comes to itself. It determines how everything recurs. Now, the most difficult matter is the most tremendous matter to be grasped, and the tremendous remains a sealed door to little men. Yet the little men too are; as beings they too recur forever. They cannot be put out of action; they pertain to that side

52. Hegel, G.W. F., *Vorlesungen über die Philosophie der Religion* (1995), III, p. 249. "'Gott selbst ist tot'." (God's very self is dead.)

of things that is dark and repulsive. If being as a whole is to be thought, the little men too wait upon their 'Yes'. That realization makes Zarathustra shudder.[53]

For Heidegger, the doctrine is based on the originary experience of time, it proposes no 'now's. It is possible to see the interplay of *Wiederkehr* and *Wiederkunft*, translated only slightly differently here as eternal recurrence and eternal return, but really the directedness in which I am turned when the moment constitutes its ordering of me to the whole of time—whether, with Zarathustra, I am turned out to the future, or whether, with the dwarf, I am produced and reproduced by the past. Here it becomes clear what the slight difference and instability of the interrelatedness of these two terms is: the instability is the temporal horizon of *die Kehre* at work—it is working through how something comes to me and is understood. Either I am turned toward the future, toward the moment of decision, the moment (which elsewhere Heidegger relates to the term *Ereignis*)[54] toward which I turn, which means *I* turn, and rather, I am *turned* into myself, I am called to myself: I become that being for whom its being becomes a concern for itself—*Dasein*. Otherwise, I remain in the past (which means determined *by* the past, and so out *of* the past), so that even my future is for me determined out of what has passed and gone by.

---

53. *Die ewige Wiederkehr des Gleichen* (*Nietzsche* [GA6.1]), p. 312. "Was ist mit all dem für das rechte Denken des Gedankens der ewigen Wiederkehr gesagt? Dieses Wesentliche: was künftig wird, ist gerade Sache der Entscheidung, der Ring schließt sich nicht irgendwo im Unendlichen, sondern der Ring hat seinen ungebrochenen Zusammenschluß im Augenblick als der Mitte des Widerstreits; was wiederkehrt—wenn es wiederkehrt— darüber entscheiden der Augenblick und die Kraft der Bewältigung dessen, was in ihm an Widerstrebendem sich stößt. Das ist das Schwerste und Eigentliche an der Lehre von der ewigen Wiederkunft, daß die Ewigkeit im Augenblick ist, daß der Augenblick nicht das flüchtige Jetzt ist, nicht der für einen Zuschauer nur vorbeihuschende Moment, sondern der Zusammenstoß von Zukunft und Vergangenheit. In ihm kommt der Augenblick zu sich selbst. Er bestimmt, wie alles wiederkehrt. Aber das Schwerste ist das Größte, was begriffen werden muß, es bleibt für die Kleinen verschlossen. Allein auch die Kleinen sind, und als Seiende kehren auch sie immer wieder, sie sind nicht zu beseitigen, sie gehören auf die Seite jenes Widrigen und Schwarzen. Soll das Seiende im Ganzen gedacht sein, dann muß auch zu ihm noch ja gesagt werden. Dies macht Zarathustra schaudern."

54. Cf. *Identität und Differenz* (GA11), p. 24. "Das Wort Ereignis ist der gewachsenen Sprache entnommen. Er-eignen heißt ursprünglich: er-äugen, d.h. er-blicken, im Blicken zu sich rufen, an eignen." This sentence was omitted from the English text edited by Joan Stambaugh. In a private letter to me, Professor Stambaugh has indicated that this was an error.

I am left in idle talk and chatter, which is also a plunging into nothing and grounded in nothing. In *Sein und Zeit* Heidegger had been at pains to point out that to refer to idle talk in itself is not a judgment of disparagement.[55] Rather: "Idle talk is the possibility of understanding everything without formerly making the thing one's own".[56] This instability is *temporal*, ordered to what is to come, *künftig*, or what turns back on itself, *wiederkehrt*. The instability between *Wieder*kehr and *Wieder*kunft is Heidegger's very struggle to bring *die Kehre* to light as a temporal phenomenon.

This is the very instability of speaking and reading themselves. It is for this reason that the very point where Heidegger most questions Richardson, the language he uses alludes continually to speaking. Similarly, Löwith's failure to rise adequately to the speaking of the turn in Heidegger *is still speaking of the same turn* because neither did Heidegger invent it nor does it affect merely *his* thought—it is the very originary structure of being and time itself, *Dasein*. *Die Kehre* is the instability, the differentiating, splitting ambiguity of thinking and speaking. In 1928 Heidegger noted the spatiality of language and then proceeded to speak of *Dasein* stretched out and occurring in time because the spatial marks of language are deceptive: I can insert myself into the thinking of another, without ever having moved a muscle.[57] I color the place I am *already* in differently, in a corresponding coloring to that which I strive to move myself to understand. Simultaneously, I can contradict another either by disagreement or *by failing to hear and read adequately what is here to be read and heard*, which never moves me *toward* that reading and hearing adequately, but *still determines my understanding* out of my failing sufficiently to be moved. I can simply mishear what was there to be heard. If I act on what I misheard, I am still determined out of what was said, but in the manner of its mishearing, so that both what was said and what gave it to be misheard are at work for me in the action. It is still a determination of what was there to be heard, even if a false one.

The underlying thought that governs what is at issue here is what Heidegger called being-with. The two contrary movements are temporalities masking

---

55. *Sein und Zeit* (GA2), p. 167. "Der Ausdruck 'Gerede' soll hier nicht in einer herabziehenden Bedeutung gebraucht werden."

56. *Sein und Zeit* (GA2), p. 169. "Das Gerede ist die Möglichkeit, alles zu verstehen ohne vorgängige Zueignung der Sache."

57. *Metaphysische Anfangsgründe der Logik* (GA26), p. 174. "Alle Sprachen (sind) primär durch Raumbedeutungen bestimmt."

spatialities and spatialities masking temporalities. "Where are you?" can ask: how far have you got (in time)? To be somewhere, in time or in space, means the *how* of my being, the way in which the moment is received and enacted.

## TRUTH AND THE TURN

Earlier I suggested that the 1937 lecture course *Grundfragen der Philosophie* plays a critical part in any unfolding of the turn. Here Heidegger carries out the *Kehre* from the essence of truth to the truth of essence that was first communicated, though insufficiently carried out, in the lecture *Vom Wesen der Wahrheit*. This is corroborated by Heidegger himself in the foreword to *Through Phenomenology to Thought* when he adds the cryptic comment to his assertion that the first time his published work appeared in the *Humanismusbrief* was in 1947 but "that the matter thought in the term 'reversal' was already at work in my thinking ten years prior to 1947".[58] I have already indicated how *die Kehre* is at work from the *Nietzsche* lectures, beginning in 1937, and from the *Beiträge* of 1936–38, but in the *Grundfragen* lecture course Heidegger actually carries out a description of this move from the essence of truth to the truth of essence:

> The question of the *essence of truth* is *at once and in itself* the question of the truth of essence. The question of truth—asked as a basic question—turns itself in itself against itself. This *turn*, which we have run up against, is an intimation of the fact that we are entering the compass of a pure philosophical question . . . only one thing is clear: if all philosophical thought must more unavoidably move in this turn the more it thinks originally, i.e., the more it approaches what in philosophy is from the first and always thought and reflected upon, then the turn must belong essentially to *that* on which philosophy alone reflects (*das Seyn* as *Ereignis*).[59]

---

58. Richardson, W. J., *Heidegger: Through Phenomenology to Thought* (1963), p. xvii. "Daß der unter dem Namen 'Kehre' gedachte Sachverhalt mein Denken schon ein Jahrzehnt vor 1947 bewegte."

59. *Grundfragen der Philosophie* (GA45), p. 47. "Die Frage nach dem *Wesen der Wahrheit* ist *zugleich und in sich* die Frage nach der *Wahrheit des Wesens*. Die Wahrheitsfrage—als Grundfrage gefragt—kehrt sich in sich selbst gegen sich selbst. Diese *Kehre*, auf die wir da gestoßen sind, ist das Anzeichen dafür, daß wir in den Umkreis einer echten philosophischen Frage kommen . . . nur das Eine ist deutlich: Wenn alles philosophische

In the 1937 lecture course *die Kehre* also arises as an issue concerned with how beings are to be thought, which means it points toward how being is to be thought as such, and this thinking has entirely to do with Heidegger's understanding of subjectivity and the overcoming of the subject-object distinction. What these lectures indicate is that *die Kehre* is also the turn-out of historiography (*Historie*) into history (*Geschichte*) and so belongs to the elaboration of the history of being, as what brings it to light.

Why is *die Kehre* present alongside the key moments of Heidegger's thinking? Because *die Kehre* always opens up the horizon of thought against the horizon of metaphysics. This is the meaning of Heidegger's comment that in 1927 thinking was not able to complete certain tasks "with the help of the language of metaphysics"—not that *Sein und Zeit* was still a *form* of the language of metaphysics, but rather *for Heidegger* metaphysics itself was as yet insufficiently thought through to allow thinking to carry through the fundamental tasks allotted to it. In this sense Heidegger's attitude to metaphysics may indeed be understood as constantly undergoing change, but perhaps better as a working through of perspective (metaphysics as worked through from the *perspective* of language, of truth, and so forth) rather than a change in fundamental position.

Different inquiries—into language, thinking, truth, beings, being, time, and so forth—arise and fall into the background depending on the matter at hand, what is under discussion. This means nothing more than that I am brought into proximity with different undertakings in thought along the way. It does not mean that, for instance, in the inquiry into language, an understanding of time is not also at work, although never named as such. Heidegger repeatedly says that, in any given inquiry, what is *not* spoken can be heard more resoundingly than what is said. In one sense, *die Kehre* is (because it turns me toward what being is, what gives me to-be, and so turns me away from beings-as-a-whole, the extantness of what is at hand) that very disposition and attunement to hear what is not said in what is spoken, because what is turned away *from* remains as governing and directing in some sense.

Can I confirm that this is what Heidegger himself intended? In the appendix to the 1937 lecture course which contains his preparatory sketches for the course, at that stage entitled *Die Wahrheitsfrage*, he notes: "Here

---

Denken um so unausweichlicher in dieser Kehre sich bewegen muß, je ursprünglicher es denkt, d.h. je näher es dem kommt, was in der Philosophie zuerst und immer gedacht und bedacht wird, dann muß die Kehre wesentlich zu dem gehören, worauf allein die Philosophie sich besinnt. (Das Seyn als Ereignis)" (author's italics).

*Da-sein* cannot even be mentioned, because it would immediately be interpreted as an object and the determination of the essence of truth would be denigrated into a mere 'new' theory".[60]

There is a further hint from Petzet's reported conversation which I have not yet investigated. Heidegger is reported as employing the phrase "the (for me) essential word *Kehre*".[61] What is essential about the word *Kehre?* The 1937 lecture course asks about the essence of truth. It does so by inquiring into the ground of truth as the "correctness of a representation", the correspondence theory of truth. This is carried out as an inquiry into how the Greeks founded truth, which means how they founded *das Wesen,* essence. Hence the inquiry into the essence of truth turns into an inquiry into the truth of essence. In asking how truth can come about as correctness it emerges that for Heidegger, the correctness of a representation (mental act) arises because of a prior understanding of truth held by the Greeks as unconcealment, ἀ-λήθεια. Truth turns out to be "for the Greeks . . . a, indeed *the* character of beings as such".[62] For the Greeks the grasping of the essence of a being is not the correctness of a representation, but an *er-sehen,* productive seeing: "Truth as correctness (ὁμοίωσις) has its ground in truth as unconcealedness (ἀλήθεια), the *coming-forth* and being in view in advance, of the essence of beings, which in the positing of truth as correctness of utterance is productively-seen and claimed as its ground, truth as ἀλήθεια".[63]

*Die Kehre* names how beings are understood in their original belonging to truth, which means that it names a more original experience of beings and so being itself. *Die Kehre* names this, however, precisely in how it comes to light, in what begins as an inquiry into the ground of metaphysics—of how truth as it has been received (the correctness of a representation) comes

60. *Grundfragen der Philosophie* (GA45), p. 193. "Das *Da-sein* kann aber hier nicht einmal genannt werden, weil es sogleich gegenständlich gedeutet würde und die Bestimmung des Wesens der Wahrheit nur zu einer 'neuen' Theorie herabgesetzt werden könnte."

61. In the passage from Petzet, H. W., *Auf einen Stern zugehen* (1983), p. 98, quoted earlier. "eines für mich wesentlichen Wortes 'Kehre'."

62. *Grundfragen der Philosophie* (GA45), p. 97. "Für die Griechen . . . ein—ja *der* Charakter des Seienden als solchen" (author's italics).

63. *Grundfragen der Philosophie* (GA45), p. 97f. "Die Wahrheit als Richtigkeit (ὁμοίωσις) hat ihren Grund in der Wahrheit als Unverborgenheit (ἀλήθεια), als dem *Hervorkommen* und schon im Blick Stehen der Seiendheit (des Wesens) des Seienden. Was in der Ansetzung der Wahrheit als Richtigkeit der Aussage als deren Grund ersehen und in Anspruch genommen ist, die Wahrheit als ἀλήθεια" (author's italics).

about. It names it as what brings the inquiry into the essentiality (*Wesung*) of essence (*Wesen*). In other words *die Kehre*, and what essence is, belong together; the one brings the other to light.

This inquiry is also the step out of the subject-object distinction, which for Heidegger arises because beings become objects given to subjects in acts of consciousness. The conceiving of truth as the correctness of a representation makes it possible for this to come about, because in *this* understanding, truth is always more an act of judging reason, than a character—indeed *the* character—of beings themselves. He cites Aquinas: "veritas *principaliter* in intellectu", which he translates as "truth has its place, above all and originally, in judging reason".[64] This is why Heidegger says that in understanding truth: "*Nietzsche* is unwittingly in perfect agreement with *Thomas Aquinas*"[65]— moreover this is in the context of the outlining of a particular interpretation of Aristotle undertaken by Aquinas. This is entirely consistent with Heidegger's later argument throughout the *Nietzsche* lectures, that nihilism arises precisely because what beings are is determined by the will, in judgment or calculating reason. As the overcoming of the subject-object distinction, *die Kehre* names how beings are thought of at all, and opens the possibility of thinking them in a new beginning, and even un-willing-ly.[66] There is a concretion in this that most commentators overlook. Heidegger says that in *die Kehre*, how things are known *undergoes a change*—out of the subject-object distinction into the new beginning.

## THE NEW BEGINNING

The new beginning that Heidegger names is simultaneously the self-questioning of *Dasein* as *Dasein*'s originary occurring out of the being of beings, and *Dasein*'s coming to know that it does this in the face of the whole history of being, by bringing that history out of its concealment. This

---

64. *Grundfragen der Philosophie* (GA45), p. 102. "Die Wahrheit hat in erster Linie und ursprünglich ihren Ort im urteilenden Verstand."

65. *Grundfragen der Philosophie* (GA45), p. 102. "*Nietzsche* . . . geht . . . ohne es zu wissen, vollkommen einig mit *Thomas von Aquin*."

66. Cf. especially in this respect, *Gelassenheit*, p. 30. [GELEHRTE] "Nicht-wollen bedeutet einmal noch ein Wollen, so, zwar, daß darin ein Nein waltet, und sei es sogar im Sinne eines Nein, das sich auf das Wollen selbst richtet und ihm absagt. Nicht-Wollen heißt demnach, willentlich dem Wollen absagen."

is the placing together of the method of atheism with its history. The new beginning emerges precisely because the whole of metaphysics has become visible in its being brought to a close by Nietzsche, while at the same time it emerges as my own self-questioning. The new beginning could not occur without reference to the former history of philosophy, the history of being itself, and yet this new beginning is utterly mine, it is my self-possession in a new way. Above all the new beginning arises out of the methodological atheism of phenomenology and is, strictly speaking, atheistic, in that it stands in readiness for the god but does not and cannot decide in advance how the god enters the realm of being. That there can be a new beginning is, strictly speaking, what makes Heidegger's atheism possible, and not the other way round, although without this atheism the new beginning would not come to light.

And yet, the new beginning is nothing other than the knowing of knowing, not as attributed to the gods and God, but as entirely mine. What is it to know that I know, which means to know that it is *I* as most myself who knows what is to be known. This selfly knowing is my coming to myself, being that being for whom being is an issue, *Dasein.* It is a beginning because I must constantly destructure what I know to its roots to remain with it in its essence. But why is it a new beginning? Because it can only come about *now,* in consequence of the death of God—its possibility is given by something beyond me, a possibility given not by God, but by the discovery that the default of God is not pure presence, either the unchanging first mover or the eternal return of the same, but absence, which is part of the same change or turn or reversal that makes it possible to think the being of beings. Heidegger comments: "Both the reflection on the first beginning and the founding of its end, an end equal to it and to its greatness, belong together in *die Kehre*".[67]

This inquiry is not historiographical (in the sense of *Historie*), that is to say it does not simply trace an artificial history of the concept or idea of truth, but is *geschichtlich,* guided by the destiny of being itself. The distinction Heidegger makes between *Historie* and *Geschichte* is fully treated in section 6 of the introduction to *Sein und Zeit* but is repeated elsewhere, for instance in the 1946 lecture *Der Spruch des Anaximander,* and specifically in

---

67. *Grundfragen der Philosophie* (GA45), p. 126. "Beides, Besinnung auf den ersten Anfang und Gründung seines ihm und seiner Größe gemäßen Endes, gehört in der *Kehre* zusammen."

relation to truth both in the 1937 lectures *Grundfragen der Philosophie*, as well as in a lecture series given in 1931–32 and published as *Vom Wesen der Wahrheit*.[68] In each case, the historiographical, *Historie*, is *un*historical (*ungeschichtlich*) because it does not take account of the unfolding history of being. For Heidegger the historiographical is that form of inquiry which simply takes for granted that it can inquire into the past as an unproblematic self-evidence. The historical, on the other hand, is that kind of inquiry which, understanding history as the history of being, puts me *as the questioner* into question and inquires into the past as an inquiry into being itself and so simultaneously into the being that I am. In this sense, being itself makes such an inquiry possible.

Why is this important? Because Heidegger, in elaborating the complexity of *die Kehre*, seeks to stress that the ordinary passage of time, that passage to which Richardson made appeal for the clarity of his analysis of Heidegger's central problematic, contains within it a trap. Time in *die Kehre* is always only understood within the moment, which means *this* moment from which past and future lead off together and away from each other. *Die Kehre* brings the priority of the moment to light and so destroys the very basis on which historiography is built. The fatefulness of the moment must give way to an originary understanding of time, so that I can be turned out toward a genuine future for myself or disclose my enslavement to endless re-enactments of the past.

## THE MEANING OF THE TWO HEIDEGGERS

The turn as it has been carried out in the literature is characterized by an imprecision, an instability, that is itself read into Heidegger's work. I have shown that what Heidegger meant by *die Kehre* could not be the same thing as Richardson's reversal and yet belongs together with it. I have also shown that *die Kehre*, the saying of *die Wendung*, the turn has a connection with all the key moments of Heidegger's work—the elaboration of *Dasein, das Sein, das Ereignis*, language, truth, time, technology, and so on. I am now in a position to say what should be heard in the phrase:

---

68. *Sein und Zeit* (GA2), pp. 19–23; *Der Spruch des Anaximander* in *Holzwege* (GA5), p. 322; *Grundfragen der Philosophie* (GA45), §24, Wiederholung, 1 and 2; *Vom Wesen der Wahrheit (Zu Platons Höhlengleichnis und Theätet)* (GA34), §2.

But (the thought of) Heidegger I becomes possible only if it is contained in Heidegger II.

Richardson reads Heidegger as 'the turning is a thought'. He seeks the thought (object) of this reversal. Heidegger's answer is that thought is the turning. There are two resonances here. This phrase says *thought itself* is the turning—to think at all is to turn—and it says the turning is *thought out* (explicated), to which Richardson must correspond, by speaking *the same as* Heidegger of what is to be said and heard (read). Heidegger's whole work is the thinking out of this turn that is (not even his own) thought, but emerges in thinking at the end of metaphysics, when it ceases to think subjectively. Thinking as such turns. To meet Heidegger's challenge is to overcome all idle talk (*Gerede*) so that it brings to an end the "groundless, endless prattle about the 'reversal'".[69] But *die Kehre* is not the turn, but the saying of the turning. *Die Kehre* is nothing other than the saying of *das Ereignis*, the eyeblink, or moment. Heidegger claimed that his thinking was the continued attempt to think more originally or primordially within the horizon that also opened up in the work *Sein und Zeit*. Finally what is meant by Heidegger's phrase can be glimpsed. For what is more primordial, more original, provides the basis for all else that is said. These statements, one of 1937, the other of 1963, confirm this to be the case. Heidegger II is more original, which means *closer to the origin as being more returned from out of the future* than Heidegger I, so that Heidegger II explains how Heidegger I came about. Heidegger says he is to be read in reverse, back through himself, in order to understand his engagement in thinking.

Why has the turn not been heard in this resonance in the literature? Why is it consistently associated with Heidegger's biography or voluntarism or quietism or whatever? How are Heidegger's cryptic references to the tasks "allotted" to thinking to be heard? Most particularly how is what I quoted much earlier from the foreword that "The reversal (*Kehre*) is in play within the matter itself. Neither did I invent it, nor does it affect merely my thought".[70] What does he mean here?

The *Wiederkehr* is a *Wider-Kehr*, a turn-against, as the reversal of Plato that completes and turns-in-back-on-itself and so becomes *ewig-*, ever, and a

69. *Heidegger: Through Phenomenology to Thought* (1963), p. xix. "des Boden- und endlosen Geredes über die 'Kehre'."
70. See p. 118, note 45, above.

circle; the hermeneutic circle itself, which can either be read from within or from without. If *die Kehre* is experienced from without, in spectating, it remains in the subject-object distinction as an object posited by a subject, hence why *die Kehre* read from within is both the same as and nothing whatsoever to do with the turn in nearly all the secondary literature. They belong together, but they are not the same. They are differentiated *proximally* in the place or vantage point from where they are experienced, but the proximation *produces* the difference. Heidegger's reading of Nietzsche's riddle of eternal return is that it is ambiguous, literally double-meaninged, in the persons of the dwarf and Zarathustra. Heidegger was aware of this when he replies to Richardson, which is why his foreword is ironic and ambiguous. He is poking fun at Richardson's reading of his work. The dwarf can never attain in speaking the stature of Zarathustra, as the one who has something to say.

Heidegger cannot inquire into the man and the thinker; this question would be of no interest to him. Heidegger inquires into *what is given to be thought.* But what could *give* to be thought? This question is at the absolute intersection of how I read Heidegger. If Heidegger gives what is to be thought, then the answer is easy: I read Heidegger. He becomes only one among so many theorists whose doctrines, thoughts, are to be read and pondered, rejected or accepted in the endless prattle and idle talk of discourse. Heidegger gives himself as anything between a technician, fraud, or master of thinking (all of these things are said of him, as if they explained, or made in any sense more accessible, what is to be thought).

About halfway through the lecture course *Grundfragen der Philosophie* Heidegger makes this remarkable observation:

> Scientific-cognition needs and creates distance (*Abstand*) from its object (*Gegenstand*), which is why a subsequent technical-practical canceling-out of distance becomes necessary. Conversely (*umgekehrt*) essence-cognition creates a belongingness to being.[71]

All thought is thought of something. The something that is given in the matter for thinking is beings. In this passage *umgekehrt* is not accidental; it speaks of *die Kehre.* To know *a* being essentially means to be "*that* being to

---

71. *Grundfragen der Philosophie* (GA45), p. 87. "Wissenschaftliches Erkennen schafft und braucht den Abstand zum Gegenstand, weshalb hier dann immer die nachträgliche technisch-praktische Wiederaufhebung des Abstandes nötig wird. Das Wesenswissen umgekehrt schafft gerade die Zugehörigkeit zum Sein."

whose ontological constitution the understanding of being belongs, the *Dasein*".[72] This means to think within the ontological difference. In the *Nietzsche* lectures Heidegger says that nihilism never even comes close to thinking of things being at all. The return to the origin means that what is to be thought becomes in a sense thought for the first time.

In the literature as it arises in consequence of Löwith and Richardson, the turn is used as a biographical marker to explain how particular terms come to the fore and how others fall back or even disappear. A feature of this turn is the endless investigation into periods of Heidegger's life which fall over into and inform his work, as if being human were no other than the crudest of materialisms. This arises precisely because of the desire to construct a narrative of Heidegger's work, to establish a corpus from which key doctrines and thoughts may be extracted, in short, to allow anyone to be Heideggerian, or, alternatively anti-Heideggerian and so to find a place in the business of interpreting Heidegger.

Heidegger himself decried such a possibility, which means he resisted the construction of a narrative perspective from which to judge his work. *Die Kehre,* in articulating proximity and placedness, either leads me to think the same as another in being-with them and from out of the same experience. You cannot tell me an answer to a question; you can speak only of how you found it yourself, which is a pointing along the way and a leading, but not a (logical, doctrinal) sharing of something which was already true in advance of us. This is the very reason why the 1937 lectures begin with a critique of the correspondence theory of truth: the correspondence sought is not one that can be given merely in language.[73] Language brings me to truth by articulating proximity but *is* not truth itself. Propositions in and of themselves are not true as such, apart from what they speak of.

In Heidegger's disgust at Löwith's terrible abuse of the word *Kehre,* Petzet reports Heidegger as saying that he was unsurprised that Löwith is taken as a serious witness because of the fact that Löwith had made so public his long-standing association with Heidegger. He was relying on common

---

72. Cf. *Grundprobleme der Phänomenologie* (GA24), p. 322. "das Seiende zunächst verstehen, zu dessen Seinsverfassung das Seinsverständnis gehört, das Dasein" (author's italics).

73. *Grundfragen der Philosophie* (GA45), §§4–9. Truth is normally understood as correctness. Heidegger notes (p. 16): "Wahrheit ist Richtigkeit, oder in der noch geläufigeren Fassung: Wahrheit ist die Übereinstimmung der Erkenntnis (des Vorstellens—Denkens—Urteilens—Aussagens) mit dem Gegenstand".

reports of his proximity to his teacher for the authority of his attack. Heidegger adds that for fully nine years Löwith took courses and seminars "and almost every other day in Marburg dashed into our house in order to squeeze something out of me" so that now he "can report on some things and thereby *appear* to many uninformed people to be in the know".[74]

What is Heidegger saying here? Is he not suggesting that Löwith's appropriation and objectification of him is in fact a form of false transcendence? To transcend is to reach forward for something and so be determined out of it. To reach out toward something also risks that it will be reduced to nothing other than an object. Löwith dashes in and out of Heidegger's house for years and so gives the appearance of being in the know, of delivering what is to be known. However, this is only the *appearance* of proximity; in reality he never comes close to Heidegger, for this squeezing something out does not attain to what it is that Heidegger also speaks, but rather is a seizing and grasping for its own sake. Löwith is never open to hear of what Heidegger hears. Consequently no one who approaches Löwith (and his reports), believing him to be in the know, will find anything but objectifications of Heidegger in him.

Why did Heidegger believe there could be no Heideggerian philosophy? because the task allotted to thinking is to think of a thing. Every *Dasein* must accomplish this for itself. Immediately after the 1937 passage cited above, he says:

> Essence-cognition, if it should come to be shared, must be accomplished anew by the one who takes it up. To speak precisely, it cannot be shared in the passing on of the meaning of a proposition, whose content is simply grasped without its basis and achievement being accomplished again.[75]

---

74. Petzet, H. W., *Auf einen Stern zugehen* (1983), p. 98. "Und in Marburg fast jeden zweiten Tag ins Haus zu uns rannte, um mich auszuquetschen, einiges berichten kann und beim Heer der heutigen Ahnungslosen den *Anschein* des Eingeweihten erwecken kann" (author's italics).

75. *Grundfragen der Philosophie* (GA45), p. 87. "Die Wesenserkenntnis muß daher—soll sie zur Mit-teilung kommen—von dem, der sie aufnehmen soll, selbst wieder neu vollzogen werden. Genauer gesagt, sie kann nicht mitgeteilt werden im Sinne der Weitergabe eines Satzes, dessen Gehalt einfach erfaßt wird, ohne daß die Gründung und Gewinnung nachvollzogen ist. "

Heidegger does not believe that the turn is his invention. The turning is given in Western thought *now*, in consequence of a negative thought about God, that God is no longer ground or highest being. Together with this is the disappearance of things in the calculative thinking which Heidegger characterizes as the *Ge-stell*, in which things claim me in thinking at the very point at which they are becoming most unthought.[76] What does it mean to argue that what is at issue in the turn concerns what it is to hear what speaks in Heidegger's work? Simply that Heidegger inquired into the matter for thinking—the thinking of thinking, or thinking of what thinking thinks *of*, νοήσεως νόησις, which Aristotle had displaced as proper not to human, but divine, being.

---

76. This is important for Heidegger in attempting to think through how God and the divine are to be thought, in the light of his post-Second World War analysis of technology, especially in the essay *Die Frage nach der Technik* (*Vorträge und Aufsätze* [GA7])

# Chapter Five

# The Death of God as Event

## The Connection between Heidegger's Atheism and Nietzsche's Death of God

*Dasein* is not a thing, in the sense of an object. If Heidegger stresses in the meaning of the word *Dasein* the there that being unfolds, then (in German at least) this is because the primary meaning of *Dasein* is existence. Not existence with the heavy, pregnant tone so often heard by English ears in the word Being, but existence as simply being available, being on hand to myself. *Dasein* is the happening of things, their there: *Dasein* worlds. *Dasein* does not, however *will* the worlding of world, but rather, as Heidegger says, it worlds for me. The essence of *Dasein* is to be, or being.

In the last chapter I demonstrated that Heidegger discusses the turn in relation to *das Ereignis,* the event. I want now to examine the origins of the term *Ereignis* and show how it is developed in Heidegger's thought in relation to his exploration of the concern I have already identified in chapter 2 that he discovered in Nietzsche: the death of God. In particular, I want to ask: does the belonging together of *die Kehre* and *das Ereignis* exhaust everything? Is there something left over? Might perhaps the unsaid that is left be of the utmost importance, an unsaid that troubles and embarrasses the reading of Heidegger from the very beginning—the embarrassment touched on in *Der Begriff der Zeit* to which only faith has access? That else is said as God—but if it is said, it brings with it an attendant danger. If I say God, what—who—do you hear? Do you hear 'God' or the one who attempts to speak of God (me) or of what God has to speak?

*Die Kehre* was worked out in 1930 critically in relation to the question of truth, although it turned out to have resonances in every other area of Heidegger's work. Through *die Kehre* Heidegger believed himself to have recovered an understanding of truth as ἀ-λήθεια, unconcealment. In order to understand *das Ereignis*, it is important to see how it relates to truth. Preparatory to this, it is necessary to investigate how truth lost its relation to concealment and came to be understood through the idea of the good (ἰδέα τοῦ ἀγαθοῦ). This preparatory investigation will reveal a number of important consequences, both for Heidegger's understanding of being and for how theology articulates who God is.

For Heidegger, understanding truth to be founded on a look, the appearance of a thing, is the basis for just that understanding of truth that covered over the primordial relation of truth to concealment and unconcealment, so that the truth of what was unconcealed in its extantness came to the fore and dominated all subsequent thinking. This covering over is not arbitrary, but rather is the event of the unfolding of the history of being itself. Heidegger worked through this argument primarily in relation to Nietzsche, but first through Plato, and in particular the allegory of the cave from Plato's *Republic*.[1] The working-out of this question is indicated by a number of extant interconnected texts spanning twelve years. In 1940 Heidegger wrote *Platons Lehre von der Wahrheit* (which he was unable to publish until 1942), a short interpretation of the allegory, together with some comments on Plato's connection with Nietzsche. What he wrote was based mainly on lectures given in Freiburg in 1931–32 on Plato's *Republic* and *Thaeatetus*. Central to both texts is an explication of the ἰδέα τοῦ ἀγαθοῦ, which Heidegger also investigates in lectures on Leibniz in 1928[2] and again on Nietzsche in 1940,[3] again both in relation to Plato's *Republic* but in these two latter cases not explicitly in relation to the allegory. At the beginning of the exposition of the allegory, Heidegger asked of the breaking-free out of the cave and into the daylight: "What events itself in these movements? Through what are these events possible?"[4] The use of the term event, *das Ereignis*, is not accidental. For Heidegger, something about being itself is unfolded through Plato's description of emerging from the cave into the daylight. For Heidegger, Plato is unfolding a fundamental understanding of being, so fundamental, in fact, that it lays the basis for the whole of metaphysics.

---

1. Cf. Plato, *Republic*, VII (514a2–517a7).
2. *Metaphysische Anfangsgründe der Logik* (GA26).
3. *Der europäische Nihilismus* (*Nietzsche* [GA6.2]).
4. *Platons Lehre von der Wahrheit* (*Wegmarken* [GA9]), p. 216. "Was ereignet sich in diesen Übergängen? Wodurch werden diese Ereignisse möglich?"

Two questions come to the fore: first, how did the look come to be the basis of truth as adequation and estimation of the correspondence between the thing and its intellection; and second, how did τὸ ἀγαθόν come to be a name for God? These are really the same question, namely, how did the ἰδέα τοῦ ἀγαθοῦ become connected with valuation in such a way that Nietzsche's devaluation of the uppermost values and the revaluation of all values becomes a way of understanding that **God is dead**? The underlying question in all of this is how did Heidegger connect Nietzsche's proclamation of the death of God with his own atheism? The answer to some extent lies within Heidegger's reading of the parallel between Aristotle's reading of Plato and his own reading of Nietzsche: that just as Aristotle drew out the ontological implications of Plato's work and brought them into a thematic confrontation with his own laying out of the science of being, so Heidegger resolved what Nietzsche understood figuratively, especially in the person of Zarathustra, in a thematic way.

In understanding how Heidegger explains the ἰδέα τοῦ ἀγαθοῦ I want to ask about four matters: first, how τὸ ἀγαθόν connects with truth and the allegory of the cave; second, how does it connect with willing and movement or change (δύναμις); third, how does it come to be thought as (first) cause and as a name for God; and finally, how does it become connected with value? There is a progression here, for the working-out of the first and second question will lay the basis for answers to the third and the fourth.

## PLATO'S ALLEGORY OF THE CAVE

In the allegory of the cave, Heidegger shows how the face or look of a thing is connected with an understanding of truth. He says that the idea is the appearance of a thing: "The appearance of a matter the Greeks named εἶδος or ἰδέα. Initially εἶδος had a resonance of what we mean if we say: the matter has a face, it can let itself be seen, it stands".[5] In a later period he says "If Plato named what constitutes the genuine element of beings, ἰδέα, the face of beings and that which is viewed by us; if still earlier, Heraclitus named what constituted the genuine element in beings, λόγος, the locution

---

5. *Einführung in die Metaphysik* (GA40), p. 46. "Das Aussehen einer Sache nennen die Griechen εἶδος oder ἰδέα. Im εἶδος schwingt anfänglich mit, was auch wir meinen, wenn wir sagen: die Sache hat ein Gesicht, sie kann sich sehen lassen, sie steht."

of beings to which we co-respond in hearing—then these both serve us notice that thinking is a hearing and a seeing".[6] For Heidegger, the connection of seeing with thinking and seeing as what *en*-visages as the giving of a face comes to light in the thinking of the Greeks, through a change where the original connection between thinking, seeing, and hearing first disappears in favor of something new. It is Plato's re-ordering of the connection between thinking and seeing that Heidegger understands to be the decisive moment for the outset of metaphysics as such.[7]

The lecture *Vom Wesen der Wahrheit* had stressed the meaning of truth as *un*concealment, where an original relation to concealment is recovered.[8] This reads the Greek word for truth, ἀλήθεια, with a stress on the privative ἀ- as ἀ-λήθεια, so that instead of a brute word, truth, the Greeks heard a movement from the hiddenness and forgottenness of concealment (λήθη) to *un*concealment.[9] In Heidegger's explication of the allegory he demon-

---

6. *Der Satz vom Grund* (GA10), p. 69f. "Wenn Platon das, was am Seienden das Eigentliche ausmacht, ἰδέα nennt, das Gesicht des Seienden und das von uns Gesichtete, wenn früher noch Heraklit das, was am Seienden das Eigentliche ausmacht, λόγος nennt, den Spruch des Seienden, dem wir im Hören entsprechen, dann gibt uns dieses beides Kunde davon, daß das Denken ein Hören und ein Sehen ist."

7. Heidegger later questioned whether the origin of the connection between seeing and thinking actually originated with Plato or even with the Greeks at any time (cf. *Zur Sache des Denkens* [GA14], p. 78). This does not, however, significantly alter the thrust of the argument, which is that the Greeks in general, and Plato in particular, took this connection as self-evident.

8. *Vom Wesen der Wahrheit* (*Wegmarken* [GA9]), esp. pp. 192–200.

9. In *Das Ende der Philosophie und die Aufgabe des Denkens* (*Zur Sache des Denkens* [GA14]), a lecture given in 1964, Heidegger appears to cast doubt on his reading of the relationship that he earlier traced between truth as ἀλήθεια, ὀρθότης and "der Lichtung von Anwesenheit", the clearing of presence (p. 78). Stambaugh noted in her translation (p. 70, footnote 6) that "this statement has profound implications for Heidegger's book *Platons Lehre von der Wahrheit*". Heidegger is attempting to answer his critics, who (from what he says) used older texts, Homer amongst them, to defend the connection between ἀλήθεια and ὀρθότης as truth. While Heidegger appears to concede that the particulars of his speculative philology may be open to debate, he does not concede the major point, arguing (p. 77f.): "The natural concept of truth does not mean unconcealment, neither in the philosophy of the Greeks. It is often and correctly pointed out that already with Homer the word ἀληθὲς is always only used in the *verba dicendi*, in statement and thus in the sense of correctness and reliability, not in the sense of unconcealment. However, this reference means only that neither the poets nor everyday language usage, not even philosophy, see themselves confronted with the task of aksing in what way truth, that is the correctness of statements, is granted only in the element of the clearing of presence". ("Der natürliche Begriff von Wahrheit meint nicht Unverborgenheit, auch nicht in der Philosophie der

strates how the transformation of truth comes as the founding moment of metaphysics. The allegory is ostensibly about education (παιδεία). For someone to come out of an accustomed home, the cave, he or she must attain certain steps of ascent to the open region of the light. Such an ascent "forms" in an educational process. The ascent moves through steps: of the shadow of the copy; the copy; the reflection of beings; to the being itself, in which the being shows itself at differing levels of unconcealment, ἀληθὲς. There is therefore a movement from concealment to unconcealment where the unconcealed, the extant, is the true. Education therefore frees human beings in a turning towards the unconcealed, which takes over as the mark of the true, which is the way out of chains and into the open air, in which a being is seen in its light. In this way truth loses its connection with concealment, so that unconcealment alone has a connection with truth. Truth as unconcealment is now thought solely as presence and permanence and loses its connection with emerging and becoming. Heidegger's analysis of the allegory shows what has been overlooked and concealed in that loss.

In Heidegger's interpretation παιδεία is connected with ἀληθὲς, however, as an inner wresting and change of the person that is characterized in the allegory as a fight for life and death. The fight means that wresting unconcealment from concealment is a re-orientation, as a turning-toward

---

Griechen. Man weist öfter und mit Recht darauf hin, daß schon bei Homer das Wort ἀληθὲς immer nur von der verba dicendi, vom Aussagen und deshalb im Sinne der Richtigkeit und Verläßlichkeit gebraucht werde, nicht im Sinne von Unverborgenheit. Allein dieser Hinweis bedeutet zunächst nur, daß weder die Dichter noch der alltägliche Sprachgebrauch, daß nicht einmal die Philosophie sich vor die Aufgabe gestellt sehen zu fragen, inwiefern die Wahrheit, d.h. die Richtigkeit der Aussage nur im Element der Lichtung von Anwesenheit gewährt bleibt.") The question of the accuracy of some of Heidegger's philological assumptions, particularly with regard to etymologies, has often been raised and is a complex one, which is not central to my concerns here (though as a genuine question it must not be overlooked or ignored, neither in terms of accuracy, nor in what it really asks *about*). Given that Heidegger insists that his basic insight remains, namely that the way truth is in relation to concealment and unconcealment is what provides for any understanding of truth as correctness and presence and so makes it possible and that Heidegger regards this as a philosophical issue, then he is entirely justified in arguing that Plato is the reference point for the foundation of metaphysics concretized and made philosophical an understanding which already lay at work in everyday language. This rather strengthens the argument, for it does not make Plato responsible, in the sense of culpable, for the change (in that Heidegger is often wrongly interpreted as blaming metaphysics for something which went terribly wrong), but rather draws attention to the fact that what Plato brought to light was already going on within thinking itself.

the unconcealed and away from the baseness of the hidden. Παιδεία, which Pöggeler translates exclusively as *Bildung*, has the twin resonance in German of education or culture and picturing or representing.[10] Heidegger warns that the word cannot be directly translated: it carries within it a connection with freedom, truth, and wresting to unconcealment as an interior action, connections which he attempts to bring to light in his reading of the allegory.[11]

## TRUTH AND UNCONCEALMENT

My concern is not principally with these aspects of the *Allegory*, but rather with how Heidegger understands truth to be transformed by what Plato says. The *Allegory* is conditioned by the conflict between unconcealment and concealment where unconcealment masters as the true. Unconcealment is therefore understood as a bringing into the light through various steps, but as a concern with the whatness of any being that appears: "Indeed, unconcealment is named in its various steps, but it is to be thought only as how it makes what appears accessible in its appearance (εἶδος) and what shows itself visible (ἰδέα)".[12] Thus the essence of truth comes to be thought in terms of the idea. The unconcealed as the true is the seen, which means that the being of any thing is in fact the *idea* of it. If παιδεία as a self-wresting-in-ascent to beings becomes the conditioning moment of truth, then the one who sees measures the correctness of the seen (i.e., relates to what a thing is) by means of the steps of education. Truth becomes the correctness (ὀρθότης) of the perception of the idea and likeness to the representation (ὁμοίωσις). Truth is no longer offered in unconcealment by a being itself, but rather the one who sees measures the correctness of what is seen (in its being already present, already unconcealed), in terms of what has been learned (from elsewhere): truth in its turn becomes an interior measuring out, a way of being directed toward *X*, of human conduct toward things. This has a transformative effect on knowing:

---

10. Pöggeler, O., *Der Denkweg Martin Heideggers* (1963), p. 101.

11. *Platons Lehre von der Wahrheit* (*Wegmarken* [GA9]), p. 217.

12. *Platons Lehre von der Wahrheit* (*Wegmarken* [GA9]), p. 225. "Die Unverborgenheit wird zwar in ihren verschiedenen Stufen genannt, aber sie wird nur daraufhin bedacht, wie sie das Erscheinende in seinem Aussehen (εἶδος) zugänglich und dieses Sichzeigende (ἰδέα) sichtbar macht."

Thus the unconcealed is grasped antecedently and by itself as that which is apprehended in apprehending the ἰδέα, as that which is known (γιγνωσκόμενον) in the act of knowing (γιγνώσκειν). Only in this change do νοεῖν and νοῦς (perception) preserve, according to Plato, their essential relation to the 'idea'. Settling into this self-orientation on the ideas determines the essence of perception and in what follows from it, the essence of 'reason'.[13]

Heidegger explains that truth as the look, the εἶδος as ἰδέα, is the basis of a separation of the self from beings, which Heidegger says is understood as θεωρεῖν, pure contemplation, which becomes for Aristotle the means to highest truth, σοφία. Θεωρεῖν already names a connection with seeing, which produces distance.[14] Such a distance prepares the ground for the later development of the subject-object distinction. How does it prepare the ground? Or rather, Heidegger says that Plato asks "What makes the thing seen and the act of seeing what they are in their relation? What spans the gap between them? What yoke (ζυγόν) holds the two together?"[15] In the allegory, the sun supplies the yoke, but as a figure for an idea. Not any idea, but the idea of ideas itself, the ἰδέα τοῦ ἀγαθοῦ, which we now translate as the idea of the good. Moreover, the allegory of the cave arises specifically after Plato has drawn attention to the connection between the sun as the making possible the visibility of all things and divinity; similarly the connection between σοφία and θεωρεῖν is itself divinity.[16]

Here, Heidegger issues an important warning. In no sense is the ἰδέα τοῦ ἀγαθοῦ to be understood in any moral or ethical sense. Twice in the

---

13. *Platons Lehre von der Wahrheit* (*Wegmarken* [GA9]), p. 225f. "So wird das Unverborgene zum vorans und einzig begriffen als das im Vernehmen der ἰδέα Vernommene, als das im Erkennen (γιγνώσκειν) Erkannte (γιγνωσκόμενον). Das νοεῖν und der νοῦς (die Vernehmung) erhalten erst in dieser Wendung bei Platon den Wesensbezug auf die 'Idee'. Die Einrichtung in dieses Sichrichten auf die Ideen bestimmt das Wesen der Vernehmung und in der Folge dann das Wesen der 'Vernunft'."

14. *Vom Wesen der Wahrheit* (GA34), p. 105. "Wir wissen: Platon faßt, wie die Griechen überhaupt, eigentliches Erkennen als ein Sehen, θεωρεῖν (zusammengesetzt aus θέα Blick und ὁρᾶν)."

15. *Platons Lehre von der Wahrheit* (*Wegmarken* [GA9]), p 226. "Wodurch sind das Gesehene und das Sehen, was sie in ihrem Verhältnis sind? Worin besteht die Bogenspannung zwischen beiden? Welches Joch (ζυγόν) hält beide zusammen?" Cf. *Vom Wesen der Wahrheit* (GA34), p. 111f.

16. Cf. Plato, *Republic*, VI, xix (508a, 508b).

1931 lectures he tells his students to "pay closest attention" to this matter.[17] Similarly in 1940 he argues that "we say the good and think the Christian, moral 'good', which, in so thinking, will obscure what is really meant".[18]

How is it that for Heidegger ἰδέα τοῦ ἀγαθοῦ is the yoke that holds together the seen and the seeable? Heidegger explains the coming to the fore of what comes to be known as the idea of the good in the following way. If the seeable is disclosed through the *idea*, then "every ἰδέα, the appearance of something, provides a look at what each being is. Thought in a Greek way the ideas make something suitable to appear as what it is and thus be present in its constancy. The ideas are the being (*Seiende*) of each being (*Seiende*)".[19] Heidegger argues that Plato thinks the original meaning of τὸ ἀγαθόν is the suitable, or the making-suitable, what makes beings fit to be beings.[20] This making suitable, insofar as any being is in fact an idea, is the making suitable of ideas in general, the idea of ideas: "The essence of every idea certainly consists in the making possible and making suitable of the appearing which grants a look of its outward appearance. Therefore the idea of ideas is the purely making-suitable, τὸ ἀγαθόν".[21] The yoke that ties the seeable to seeing is, in the mythic language of the allegory, the sun, and in Plato's explanation of it, the idea of

17. *Vom Wesen der Wahrheit* (GA34), p. 99f. "—beachten Sie das—. . . Nochmals sei eingeschärft: wir müssen uns von vornherein von jeder sentimentalen Vorstellung dieser Idee des Guten freihalten, aber ebenso auch von allen Perspektiven, Auffassungen und Bestimmungen, wie sie die christliche Moral und deren säkularisierte Abarten (oder sonst irgendeine Ethik) darbieten, wo das Gute als Gegensatz zum Bösen und das Böse als das Sündige gefaßt wird."

18. *Der europäische Nihilismus* (*Nietzsche* [GA6.2]), p. 225. "Wir sagen das 'Gute' und denken christlich-moralisch 'gut'."

19. *Platons Lehre von der Wahrheit* (*Wegmarken* [GA9]), p. 227f. "Jede ἰδέα, das Aussehen von etwas, gibt die Sicht auf das, was je ein Seiendes ist. Die 'Ideen' machen daher, griechisch gedacht, dazu tauglich, daß etwas in dem, was es ist, erscheinen und so in seinem Beständigen anwesen kann. Die Ideen sind das Seiende jedes Seienden."

20. *Der europäische Nihilismus* (*Nietzsche* [GA6.2]), p. 227, 228. "Das Taugliche," as "das Tauglichmachende"; cf. *Platons Lehre von der Wahrheit* (*Wegmarken* [GA9]) p. 227. "Τὸ ἀγαθόν bedeutet, griechisch gedacht, das, was zu etwas taugt und zu etwas tauglich macht."

21. *Platons Lehre von der Wahrheit* (*Wegmarken* [GA9]), p. 228. "Das Wesen jeder Idee liegt schon in einem Ermöglichen und Tauglichmachen zum Scheinen, das eine Sicht des Aussehens gewährt. Daher ist die Idee der Ideen das Tauglichmachende schlechthin, τὸ ἀγαθόν."

ideas. This yoke, which holds together, is, however, a making possible of the distancing that sets them apart.

Heidegger wants to show how, as the idea of ideas, τὸ ἀγαθόν comes to be thought as δύναμις and willing. In his earlier remarks about τὸ ἀγαθόν, Heidegger traced its relation to transcendence. As the making-suitable of all beings, τὸ ἀγαθόν is in a sense being itself, but being as constant presence, the always-extantness of everything that is extant. It is what lies beyond the changeableness of all given beings as the most stable, making their change-ableness possible. Here, immediately, the origin and ontological root and necessity of Aristotle's first mover become obvious, both as what remains unchanged in the soul and in the cosmos overall. Heidegger cites Plato: "Thus it is said of ἀγαθόν, ἔστι ἐπέκεινα τῆς οὐσίας πρεσβείᾳ καὶ δυνάμει. 'The good is above and beyond even being in worth and power; that is to say, in βασιλεία, dominion'—not merely above and beyond unconcealment".[22] Of this transcendence Heidegger says: "One must consider [it] the most original, insofar as the ideas are already transcendent with regard to changeable beings".[23] This primordiality of transcendence has two aspects. First, it is the οὗ ἕνεκα which Heidegger translates as "*das Umwillen*"[24] and which translates directly from the Greek as "for the sake of," or the "purposive" (that which is of service in effecting an object),[25] employed by both Aristotle and Plato:

... the purposive, that by which something is, or is not, in this or that way. The ἰδέα τοῦ ἀγαθοῦ, which lies beyond beings and the realm of ideas, is the purposive—which means it is the proper determination by

---

22. *Der europäische Nihilismus* (*Nietzsche* [GA6.2]), p. 225. "Daher wird vom ἀγαθόν gesagt: ἔστι ἐπέκεινα τῆς οὐσίας πρεσβείᾳ καὶ δυνάμει. 'Das Gute ist noch an Würde und Vermögen, d.h. an βασιλεία, an Herrschaft, hinaus sogar über das Sein'—nicht nur über die Unverborgenheit." Cf. *Metaphysische Anfangsgründe der Logik* (GA26), pp. 237, 284.

23. *Metaphysische Anfangsgründe der Logik* (GA26), p. 237. "Die man, sofern schon die Ideen transzendent sind gegenüber dem wechselnden Seienden, als die ursprüng-lichste in Anspruch nehmen muß."

24. *Metaphysische Anfangsgründe der Logik* (GA26), p. 237. Heidegger, to my knowl-edge, never explicitly discusses how οὗ ἕνεκα comes to mean 'final cause', but it will be entirely clear from this discussion how this interpretation came to be decisive.

25. Lest we assume Heidegger is artificially generating meanings, this is exactly the definition given in the *Oxford English Dictionary*.

which it transcends the whole of ideas and at the same time organizes them in their totality; the purposive as ἐπέκεινα exceeds the ideas. A purposiveness is, however, only possible where there is a willing.[26]

Following Heidegger's citation of Plato, and in the same way, τὸ ἀγαθόν as the 'beyond every power' is therefore the making-powerful, the power for power as the power for seeing.[27] He notes: "*What* this empowering is and *how* it occurs, that is up to today not answered, not only not answered, but not even in Plato's original sense asked. In the meantime it has become almost a triviality: every being is a good".[28] It is only through asking the question with regard to being that any of this can come to light. Beings are already and always present and so permanent. Τὸ ἀγαθόν, as a name for being, and which makes possible any beings, is therefore thought as the earlier, the prior to (and so ultimately, though not with Plato, the *a priori*). There is an ambiguity here, for Heidegger points out that Aristotle had noted that being is prior by nature (πρότερον φύσει), but not prior by knowledge (πρότερον γνώσει). As prior by nature it provides the possibility for subsequent knowledge, but as prior, it is a temporal determination: "'Earlier than' is obviously still a temporal determination: no earlier without time. Earlier than every possible 'earlier than' indeed is time! Thus if being is the πρότερον, the a priori, then it stands in a primordial connection with time".[29] Transcendence as the reaching forward for what is already there,

26. *Metaphysische Anfangsgründe der Logik* (GA26), pp. 237, 238. "... das, worum-willen etwas ist bzw. nicht ist, so bzw. anders ist. Die ἰδέα τοῦ ἀγαθοῦ, die noch über das Seiende und das Reich der Ideen hinausliegt, ist das Umwillen—das besagt: sie ist die eigentliche Bestimmung, die die Gesamtheit der Ideen transzendiert und sie daher zugleich in ihrer Ganzheit organisiert; das Umwillen als ἐπέκεινα überragt die Ideen ..."
"Ein Umwillen ist aber wesensmäßig nur da möglich, wo es einen Willen gibt."
27. *Vom Wesen der Wahrheit* (GA34), p. 101. "Damit etwas Sichtbares im gewöhnlichen Sinne gesehen werde, ist notwendig erstens eine δύναμις τοῦ ὁρᾶν, das Vermögen, mit den Augen zu sehen, und zweitens δύναμις τοῦ ὁρᾶσθαι, das Vermögen und die Ermöglichung des Gesehenwerdens."
28. *Vom Wesen der Wahrheit* (GA34), p. 111. "*Was* diese Ermächtigung sei und *wie* sie geschieht, das ist bis heute nicht beantwortet; nicht nur nicht beantwortet, sondern nicht einmal mehr im ursprünglichen Platonschen Sinne gefragt. Inzwischen ist es fast eine Trivialität geworden: omne ens sei ein bonum" (author's italics).
29. *Metaphysische Anfangsgründe der Logik* (GA26), p. 146. "'Früher als' das ist doch offenbar eine Zeitbestimmung: Kein Früher ohne Zeit. Früher als jedes mögliche 'Früher als' ist aber die Zeit! Mithin: wenn Sein πρότερον, a priori ist, dann steht es in einem ursprünglichen Zusammenhang mit Zeit." If there is any doubt that the Heidegger of

for what is earlier in its supersensual form as the being of the ἰδέα, translates the immediacy of permanent presence, the governing of the immediacy of the moment, into the ἀεί, the eternity of being.

## THE PURPOSIVE

What is the connection here between δύναμις and movement or change? Δύναμις, as Heidegger noted in his lectures on Aristotle, has the sense in Greek of potency, but as the unifying power for every action.[30] It retains its connection with Plato's understanding of transcendence as the highest and deepest.[31] Heidegger therefore emphasizes that as highest idea it *occurs*.[32] The verb *geschehen* (occurs) is one which Heidegger consistently uses to express theoretical distance. As highest and deepest idea it provides for an entirely different articulation of relation, separation, and distance, which has the following result: "The idea, and indeed the highest idea is what empowers all objectivity and all subjectivity, [as] what they are, in that it is the yoke spanning subject and object, under which yoke they become subject and object in general; for the subject *is* only what relates itself toward an object".[33] Movement here becomes mechanized as the theorization of possible space, *that* space laid out and which will come to be defined as the subject-object relationship: Newtonian space.

---

1928 is thinking the ἰδέα τοῦ ἀγαθοῦ in the same way as twelve years later in 1940, compare these passages with those in the *Nietzsche* lectures on this same matter (*Nietzsche* [GA6.2], esp. p. 227).

30. *Aristoteles Metaphysik* Θ *1–3* (GA33), p. 4. Heidegger points out in *Der europäische Nihilismus* (*Nietzsche* [GA6.2], p. 228) that Aristotle did not think being as the ἰδέα τοῦ ἀγαθοῦ, but "griechischer als Platon das Sein (denkt) als ἐντελέχεια", which is why he returns to the thought of the divine in a different way to Plato, as τὸ θεῖον.

31. In the Latin sense of *altus* and Greek βαθύς, both of which can simultaneously mean high and deep.

32. *Vom Wesen der Wahrheit* (GA34), p. 99. "Die höchste Idee ist also diese Ermächtigende, die Ermächtigung für das *Sein,* daß es sich solches *gibt,* und in eins damit die Ermächtigung der *Unverborgenheit,* daß solche als solche *geschieht*" (author's italics).

33. *Vom Wesen der Wahrheit* (GA34), p. 111. "Die Idee, und gar die höchste Idee, ist . . . was alle Objektivität und alle Subjektivität . . . ermächtigt, was sie sind, indem es das Joch zwischen Subjekt und Objekt spannt, unter welchem Joch sie überhaupt erst Subjekt und Objekt werden; denn Subjekt *ist* nur solches, was auf ein Objekt sich bezieht" (author's italics).

As the making-suitable, purposive, and potential, i.e., as highest and deepest, so the ἰδέα τοῦ ἀγαθοῦ as the idea of ideas comes to mean αἰτία, "cause." It is not difficult to see the connection, except that Heidegger points out that for both Plato and Aristotle there is an ambiguity left over. Citing Plato again, he notes that the idea of the good is "πάντων ὀρθῶν τε καὶ καλῶν αἰτία": "the cause of everything correct as well as of everything beautiful (i.e., the empowerment of essence)".[34] The ambiguity is contained in the determination of truth not solely as the correct but simultaneously as the unhidden. The same ambiguity is exhibited by Aristotle, who is forced to resolve it by noting: "In fact the false and the true are not in things themselves . . . but in the intellect".[35] It is in this ambiguity that the whole of metaphysics becomes concerned both with God and with the death of God. Throughout his explications of the ἰδέα τοῦ ἀγαθοῦ, Heidegger is at pains to stress that its meaning is not fully determined, either in Plato, or in its reworking (as τὸ θεῖον) in Aristotle. These two thinkers laid a foundation which was not fully clarified or determined, but was worked out by those who followed them in the Western tradition so that ambiguities which they left unclarified were resolved in particular directions over an extended period.

It should now be clear how the ἰδέα τοῦ ἀγαθοῦ becomes a name for God. Heidegger says:

Plato says that thinking goes μετ᾿ ἐκεῖνα, 'over' the former, that which is only experienced as shadowy and copied, out εἰς ταῦτα, 'away to' the latter, namely to the 'ideas.' They are the supersensuous, sighted in the nonsensuous glance. They are the being of beings which cannot be grasped with the tools of the body. And in the realm of the supersensuous the highest is that idea which as the idea of all ideas remains the cause of the permanence and appearing of all beings. Because this 'idea' is in such a way the first cause for everything, it is also 'the idea' which is called 'the Good'. This highest and primary first cause is called τὸ θεῖον, the divine, by Plato and correspondingly also by Aristotle. Since the exposition of being as ἰδέα, thinking about the being of

<hr/>

34. *Platons Lehre von der Wahrheit* (*Wegmarken* [GA9]), p. 231. "'Von allem Richtigen sowohl als auch von allem Schönen die Ursache' (d.h. die Ermöglichung des Wesens)."

35. *Platons Lehre von der Wahrheit* (*Wegmarken* [GA9]), p. 232. Citing Aristotle, *Metaphysics*, V, IV (1027b25ff.). "οὐ γάρ ἐστι τὸ ψεῦδος καὶ τὸ ἀληθὲς ἐν τοῖς πράγμασί . . . ἀλλ᾿ ἐν διανοίᾳ" Aquinas will rely entirely on this interpretation for his own exposition of truth (Cf. *Quaestiones Disputatae: de Veritate* q. 1, a. 1).

beings has become metaphysical, and metaphysics has become theological. Theology means here the exposition of the 'first cause' of beings as God and the misplacing of being into this first cause, which contains being in itself and discharges it from itself because it is the being in beings.[36]

The very ambiguity I have named, however, provides for what, as a name for God, also comes to mean value, or valuation. The ambiguity says that simultaneously being is the permanence of presence and is truth as correctness— a mental act. The ambiguity is subsequently resolved by arguing that the mental act which sustains the ideas and holds them in correctness is not an act in the human mind, but that of the mind of God. Heidegger quotes Aquinas as an exemplar: "Truth is properly met with in the human or divine intellect".[37] He notes that here truth is no longer understood as ἀλήθεια, but ὁμοίωσις. The consequences of the ambiguity are fulfilled, however, in Nietzsche. Heidegger notes Nietzsche's adequation of truth with error, adding "Nietzsche's concept of truth is an example of the last reflection of the uttermost consequences of that change in truth from unconcealment to the correctness of the look".[38] He points out the extent to which Nietzsche, as one who seeks the inversion of Plato's thinking, is faithful to what Plato understood, namely that there is no substance or intrinsicality to values,

---

36. *Platons Lehre von der Wahrheit* (*Wegmarken* [GA9]), p. 235f. "(Platon sagt): Das Denken geht μετ' ἐκεῖνα, 'über' jenes, was nur schattenhaft und abbildmäßig erfahren wird, hinaus εἰς ταῦτα, 'hin zu' diesen, nämlich den 'Ideen'. Sie sind das im nichtsinnlichen Blicken erblickte Übersinnliche, das mit den Werkzeugen des Leibes unbegreifliche Sein des Seienden. Und das Höchste im Bereich des Übersinnlichen ist jene Idee, die als Idee aller Ideen die Ursache für den Bestand und das Erscheinen alles Seienden bleibt. Weil diese 'Idee' in solcher Weise für alles die Ursache ist, deshalb ist sie auch 'die Idee', die 'das Gute' heißt. Diese höchste und erste Ursache wird von Platon und entsprechend von Aristoteles τὸ θεῖον, das Göttliche genannt. Seit der Auslegung des Seins als ἰδέα ist das Denken auf das Sein des Seienden metaphysisch, und die Metaphysik ist theologisch. Theologie bedeutet hier die Auslegung der 'Ursache' des Seienden als Gott und die Verlegung des Seins in diese Ursache, die das Sein in sich enthält und aus sich entläßt, weil sie das Seiende des Seienden ist."

37. *Platons Lehre von der Wahrheit* (*Wegmarken* [GA9]), p. 233, citing *Quaestiones Disputatae: de Veritate*, q. 1, a. 4, resp. "Veritas proprie invenitur in intellectu humano vel divino."

38. *Platons Lehre von der Wahrheit* (*Wegmarken* [GA9]), p. 233. "Nietzsches Begriff der Wahrheit zeigt den letzten Widerschein der äußersten Folge jenes Wandels der Wahrheit aus der Unverborgenheit des Seienden zur Richtigkeit des Blickens."

but rather as the latest representation of the meaning of the ideas, valuation is entirely a mental act.

Heidegger argues that because the ἰδέα τοῦ ἀγαθοῦ as δύναμις is the making-suitable and making-possible, then it is understood by Nietzsche as *Bedingung*, which would most normally be translated into English as "condition" but has the added resonance in German of en-thing-ment. As condition, it allows a thing to be a thing at all. Simultaneously "the 'ideas' are installed in 'God's' thought and ultimately in *perceptio*. The ἰδέα, then, is itself something placed in a sequence relative to which it is distinguished as πρότερον. The sequence is determined as the *differentiation* of being and beings".[39] If, however, God is dead, or rather the priority of God's perception ceases to act as the guarantor for every perception, whose look now guarantees the being of beings? In consequence:

> Being (idea) becomes a condition over which the one representing, the subject, has disposal and must have disposal if objects are going to be able to stand over against him. Being is conceived as a system of necessary conditions with which the subject, precisely with regard to the being as the objective, must reckon in advance on the basis of his relations with beings. Conditions with which one must necessarily reckon—how could one not eventually call them 'values', 'the' values, and account for them as values?[40]

If it is possible to see here how *Dasein* becomes thought as subject and subjectivity, it is also clear how thinking God through τὸ ἀγαθόν means that God is determined metaphysically. Such a thinking through, however, is an *Ereignis*, an event that occurs in consequence of the kind of proximity

---

39. *Der europäische Nihilismus* (*Nietzsche* [GA6.2]), p. 227 (Author's italics). "Die 'Ideen' werden im Denken 'Gottes' untergebracht und schließlich in der perceptio. Die ἰδέα ist dann selbst etwas, das in eine Ordnung gestellt und aus ihr her als πρότερον ausgezeichnet wird. Diese Ordnung bestimmt sich als die *Unterscheidung* von Sein und Seiendem."

40. *Der europäische Nihilismus* (*Nietzsche* [GA6.2]), p. 230. "Das Sein (Idee) wird zur Bedingung, über die der Vor-stellende, das Subjekt, verfügt und verfügen muß, wenn ihm Gegenstände sollen entgegenstehen können. Das Sein wird als System von notwendigen Bedingungen begriffen, mit denen das Subjekt, und zwar im Hinblick auf das Seiende als das Gegenständige, auf Grund seines Verhältnisses zum Seienden im vorhinein rechnen muß. *Bedingungen*, mit denen notwendig *gerechnet* werden muß—wie soll man sie nicht eines Tages 'Werte', 'die' Werte nennen und als Werte verrechnen?"

and distance articulated through the subject-object distinction and truth as *adaequatio intellectus et rei.* The look comes to be understood as the basis for nihilism as such. For Heidegger, Nietzsche's metaphysics turn on an understanding of valuation. The subject *e*-valuates, estimates, takes a measure of beings. Valuative thinking turns on the aim of an intended view (ἰδέα): "To esteem something, to hold it worthwhile, also means to be *directed* toward it. Such direction *toward* has already assumed an 'aim'. Thus the essence of value has an inner relation to the essence of aims".⁴¹

## TRUTH AND NIHILISM

How does it become possible, as something that events-itself, that the original understanding of the essence of truth (as ἀλήθεια) can be experienced again? Ἀλήθεια belonged to unconcealment and concealment, until the unconcealed (the extant as totally present) took over and dominated with respect to truth. Concealment does not, however, disappear, but rather continues to operate in a hidden way, almost as the concealment of concealment, as a hidden meaninglessness of nothing. It reappears in the *nihil* of nihilism. For Heidegger, it reappears above all in Nietzsche's articulation of it.

The nothing also reappears as a "movement",⁴² an analysis in which Heidegger was clearly influenced by Ernst Jünger.⁴³ It is not that the nothing was never discussed in metaphysics before nihilism, either as μὴ ὄν (Plato) or *nihil* (Augustine) or *daz Nîts* (Eckhart) or *die Verneinung* (Hegel). Rather the nothing comes to the fore in nihilism and dominates, so determining the outcome for thought itself. The thought of nothing which nihilism appears

---

41. *Der europäische Nihilismus* (*Nietzsche* [GA6.2]), p. 48. "Etwas schätzen, d.h. für wert halten, heißt zugleich: sich darnach *richten*. Dieses sich Richten '*nach*' hat in sich schon ein '*Ziel*' genommen. Deshalb steht das Wesen des Wertes im *inneren* Zusammenhang mit dem **Wesen des Ziels.**"

42. Heidegger rej ᵌatedly refers to nihilism as a "Bewegung", not just a moment of metaphysics inaugurated by Nietzsche. See for instance *Der europäische Nihilismus* (*Nietzsche* [GA6.2]), pp. 35, 74; and *Zur Seinsfrage* (*Wegmarken* [GA9]) pp. 386, 391–393, 395. The Second World War and what follows it in *das Gestell* is understood as part of the movement of nihilism.

43. A debt Heidegger fully acknowledged, in his many references to Jünger's political writings, especially *Die totale Mobilmachung* (1930) and *Der Arbeiter* (1932). Indeed, it was only at Heidegger's insistence that Jünger retained *Der Arbeiter* in his published collected *Werke.*

to think about is nothing at its most abstract and subjective.[44] Nihilism brings the nothing to the fore for the first time (and so makes it historical) as the devaluation of the highest values and subsequent revaluation of all values. Nihilism, however, in its articulation of nothing, as the pure *presence* of nothing (concealment appearing as its opposite; *this* is nihilism!), a movement of metaphysics, can still only think about beings, a thinking in which it seeks only to negate. The negation of beings does not, however, destroy beings or cause them to cease to be. The act of negation is a purely mental, abstract, *subjective* process. Negation therefore retreats into *de-valuation* and *re-valuation*, a mental, subjective movement which affects beings (things) as such not at all and so alters only the estimation of and relation to them. This means the way *I* think of them, the 'how' of thinking.

Heidegger concludes: "Perhaps the essence of nihilism lies in this: that it consists in not taking seriously the question of the nothing".[45] Thus nihilism's being defined by the will to power and the attempt to think valuatively of things (which means to give meaning to them at all, *Be-Ding-ung*) solely in terms of the essence of being human, conceals being as such (because it never even discusses beings but only the human *valuations* of beings undertaken by the human subject). This nihilistic conception of the nothing cannot get beyond subjectivity and abstraction because it deals only with the (human) subject and not with beings in their being.

## Detour: The Many Heideggers and the One

I have already indicated in a preliminary way that the meaning Heidegger ascribed to *das Ereignis* is fully developed through a reading of Nietzsche's proclamation of the event of nihilism par excellence, the death of God. In a summary of a seminar on the 1962 lecture *Zeit und Sein*, Heidegger comments almost as an aside that "the relations and contexts constituting the essential structure of Ereignis were worked out between 1936 and 1938".[46] Heidegger's

---

44. *Der europäische Nihilismus* (*Nietzsche* [GA6.2]), p. 52 ff. In particular: "The nothing of negation or no-saying is a mere mental construct, the most abstract of abstractions."

45. *Der europäische Nihilismus* (*Nietzsche* [GA6.2]), p 53. "Vielleicht liegt das Wesen des Nihilismus darin, daß man *nicht* ernst macht mit der Frage nach dem Nichts."

46. *Zur Sache des Denkens* (GA14), p. 46. "Die den Wesensbau des Ereignisses ausmachenden Bezüge und Zusammenhänge sind zwischen 1936 und 1938 ausgearbeitet worden."

lectures on *Nietzsche* began in 1936, and the first lecture series was delivered in the winter semester of 1936–37 with the title *Der Wille zur Macht als Kunst.*

*Das Ereignis* is presumed to be a creation of Heidegger's later work, not even at work in *Sein und Zeit,* but which comes to the fore in *Beiträge zur Philosophie,* which was subtitled *Vom Ereignis,* written in the years between 1936 and 1938 but never either completed or published in his lifetime. The comment I have cited from *Zur Sache des Denkens* appears to confirm that this is the place above all where the full meaning of *das Ereignis* was worked through. On the other hand, John van Buren has shown that *das Ereignis* appears, not only in 1936, in the midst of the elaboration of central topics like ontotheology and the *Nietzsche* lectures, but rather already in 1919, in the so-called *Kriegsnotsemester.* Section 15 of the published text of this lecture course is entitled *Process and Structure of Lived Experience: Process and Event.*[47]

In drawing attention to this use of *das Ereignis,* van Buren has shown that one of the most important terms in the "later" Heidegger is already at work in his earliest extant lecture course. How he handles this question is therefore critical for making sense of how Heidegger's earliest work connects with what he says later. In analyzing van Buren's handling of the matter, I intend to show that his inability adequately to approach what Heidegger has to say of *das Ereignis* actually reproduces just that critique of subjectivity that Heidegger seeks to overcome. Why is this important here? Because in my demonstrating van Buren's failure adequately to *approach* Heidegger, it demonstrates how proximity and distance have been articulated in much of the secondary literature concerning Heidegger's work and how proximity and distance belong fundamentally to interpreting and knowing. Similarly, if the metaphysics of subjectivity belongs to nihilism and this grounds all knowing and interpretation on taking a look, then the failure adequately to overcome subjectivity means that the one knowing and interpreting remains firmly within the compass of nihilism. More starkly still, if van Buren fails to overcome subjectivity, which means if he fails to overcome himself (posited through subjectivity) in order to approach Heidegger, then in interpreting Heidegger, he interprets him in terms of (van Buren) himself, instead of interpreting himself in terms of Heidegger. What is placed in question here, therefore, is what is concerned in approaching *anything at all:* interpretation, as such.

---

47. *Zur Bestimmung der Philosophie* (GA56/57), p. 73ff. *Vorgang und Erlebnisstrukturen: Vorgang und Ereignis.*

To fail adequately to hear what Heidegger has to say is to fail adequately to hear what Heidegger speaks *of.* This is the same failure that was encountered with Karl Löwith, explicitly brought to light by Heidegger. Löwith failed adequately to approach what Heidegger spoke of, which meant that, despite appearing authoritative, he had fundamentally misappropriated Heidegger's understanding of being. Is this because Heidegger is unique and occupies such a central position in Western metaphysics? Surely not, but rather, Löwith and van Buren approach Heidegger already taking for granted that they understand what they will find in him, and because of what they take as self-evident (that they already know of what he speaks) they are left only with themselves.

With this in view, how does van Buren present the earlier use of *das Ereignis* he uncovered in Heidegger? How does he open up what at first sight offers an extraordinary moment of unity of the so-called later with the early Heidegger? He says "there never was a single Heidegger, *mens auctoris,* topic, Heidegger's philosophy, since these are pluralized and differentiated into Heideggers, *topoi,* and thoughtpaths".[48] There is only *die Sache,* which "can be translated as matter, topic, issue, problem, question, point of dispute . . . the sameness of the *Sache,* which contains difference in itself".[49] Van Buren performs a simple objectification: moving, he claims, from *die Sache* to *das Selbe,* reminding his reader of a line from the 1957 publication of *Identität und Differenz* which says (to quote in full): "But the same is not the identical. In the identical, difference disappears. In the same, difference appears, and appears all the more pressingly, the more resolutely thinking is concerned with the same matter in the same way".[50] Van Buren concludes "I argue that the word *Sache* is a kind of family name, an empty 'formal indication',[51] for the different Heideggers housed and trying to get along together in the family quarrel of his collected edition".[52] Van Buren is of course at play, for he is taking the slogan of the phenomenologists, which means the slogan of

---

48. van Buren, J., *The Young Heidegger* (1994), p. 28.
49. van Buren, J., *The Young Heidegger* (1994), p. 28.
50. Cf. *Identität und Differenz* (GA11), p. 35. "Allein das Selbe ist nicht das Gleiche. Im Gleichen verschwindet die Verschiedenheit. Im Selben erscheint die Verschiedenheit. Sie erscheint um so bedrängender, je entschiedener ein Denken von derselben Sache auf dieselbe Weise angegangen wird."
51. This is a reference to van Buren's interest in Heidegger's designation of *die Formale Anzeige.* See van Buren, J., "The Ethics of Formale Anzeige" (1995).
52. van Buren, J., *The Young Heidegger* (1994), p. 28f.

Husserl and his "phenomenological child"[53] Heidegger (against the neo-Kantians), *zu den Sachen selbst!—to the things themselves!*—and reading it against Heidegger, turning *him* into the formal indication of something which has no *selbst*, no inner substance, no final essence, something which has sameness, but no identity; no person Heidegger, just Heideggers bound up in their respective texts.

There is a sleight of hand at work here, for van Buren has shifted from *die Sache*, the matter and topic, to *eine Ursache*, a causal ground on which the quarrel might take place. For a matter to stand as "an empty 'formal indication' for the different Heideggers" is nothing other than his judging there to be an inner unity, which as empty or formal is nothing other than the reappearance of precisely *that* empty, formal, ideal, vantage point from which the many Heideggers may be posited as one, so much understood as *an* ideal, that these Heideggers possess no self-subsistence, no intrinsic unity. Van Buren's reading of *die Sache* is nothing other than Heidegger's reading of the subject in its connection with εἶδος, the look. Heidegger's destructuring of metaphysics in *die Kehre* already not only foresaw but also included a destructuring of just *that* position taken up by van Buren. The vantage point that van Buren takes up is best understood as the vantage point of nihilism, of constituting things simply by a look. For van Buren, this look deprives Heidegger of his very self, because it is something conferred on him by an onlooker (in this case, van Buren). It is for this reason that van Buren's description of Heidegger's self is posited as a merely formal indication, the name Heidegger, tying together 102 planned volumes of the *Gesamtausgabe*.

What if it were the other way about? What if the many Heideggers assemble into one 'temporally differentiated' Heidegger given by being,[54] who, *as* differentiated, has his own unity, just that unity into which I would have to bring myself into proximity to know? Surely it is *this* bringing of myself into proximity, this *sameness* that is not identity, this sameness that gives difference (the matter named by van Buren from *Identität und Differenz*), temporality itself (*Dasein*), and therefore not a sameness which is something I externally *apply* to Heidegger, which to understand, I have to get up close to, to place myself within? For if it were not so, then *die Ursache*

---

53. This was the name given to Heidegger by Frau Husserl. Cf. Jaspers, K., *Philosophische Autobiographie* (1977), p. 92.

54. This is van Buren's very claim, that he had discovered a primordial shift in Heidegger in 1916 from the analysis of being to the temporally differentiated giving of being.

154 — Heidegger's Atheism

which van Buren posits is nothing other than the repetition of the metaphysics of subjectivity, which shatters Heidegger into Heideggers and is the
only place from which he (or I) might have taken up a position to see this
shattering taking place.

The sleight of hand in van Buren's citation of *Identität und Differenz* is
most at work when he neglects to say that in this matter of the same, and its
not being the merely identical, Heidegger is explicitly in conversation with
Hegel. The sentence in *Identität und Differenz* immediately before (and so hidden from view) that which van Buren cites says "if, therefore, we attempt a
thinking conversation with Hegel, then we must speak with him not only
about the same matter, but of the same matter in the same way".[55] Why is this
important? Because the matter and the same *belong*, which is to say they unfold
in a place so that "insofar, however, as Hegel's thinking belongs in an epoch of
history (this does not at all mean to the past), we attempt to think of being in
the same way as Hegel, that is, historically".[56] What is the place of the unfolding? *I* am the place of the unfolding, which is why this "epoch of history" does
not have to do with the past. *I* am present—to myself, in knowing Hegel.

There is a humorous note here, for this matter is none other than that
articulated by Heraclitus's question: can someone jump in the same river
twice? Cratylus's now well-worn answer is of course, "You cannot even jump
in the same river!"[57] The question, here concerning Hegel (but also generally), is how I interpret, and in so interpreting, where that takes me in relation
to what it is that I interpret. If I really ask about what Hegel asks, then I ask
about the same thing. The thing sames in itself and differentiates in me and
in Hegel, which means that, in its saming and differentiating, I am moved
close up to, and far away from, Hegel. When I think the same thought in the
same way as Hegel thought about the same thing, Hegel and I are at one with
one another. The same 'sames' us but does not make us identical.

Van Buren, on the contrary, invites me to interpret *die Sache* as *eine
Ursache*, a cause which stands under every *Sache*, allowing each to be understood and so unfold the many Heideggers in time as their point of unity. But

---

55. *Identität und Differenz* (GA11), p. 35. "Wenn wir also ein denkendes Gespräch
mit Hegel versuchen, dann müssen wir mit ihm nicht nur von derselben Sache, sondern
von derselben Sache in derselben Weise sprechen."
56. *Identität und Differenz* (GA11), p. 35. "Insofern nun aber Hegel's Denken in eine
Epoche der Geschichte gehört (dies meint beileibe nicht zum Vergangenen), versuchen
wir, das von Hegel gedachte Sein auf dieselbe Weise, d.h. geschichtlich zu denken"
57. Cf. Aristotle, *Metaphysics*, IV, v (1010a13).

for me, to find that thinking *belongs* historically is to find that it is *die Sachen selbst* (the matters themselves) which unfold *me* historically. I am not the vantage point; *die Sachen* vantage me.

What is at issue here is how I come to what is *there* to be known. Let me cut away for a moment the question of the real, of whether there is anything really to be known, anything really beyond me, and conflate every*thing* to ask what lies under even this question: is God other than me? For if the world is not beyond me, but just an ideal realm, how otherwise could God be there? It would be hard to underestimate the importance of this question. Traditionally metaphysics has sought the inner unity of "God, world, and Humanity"[58]: an external world, an internal subjectivity, and something that somewhere is their holding together. I want to show how for Heidegger in this question of *das Ereignis* there is no external world, there is no internal me, so God is not that one who holds the two together (precisely the role in Plato of the ἰδέα τοῦ ἀγαθοῦ, and so how τὸ ἀγαθόν came in metaphysics to be a name for God). I am inextricably concerned with world and bound up with it. How, therefore, after Heidegger's atheism does God enter *this world that I am* (because it worlds me)? How does this world that *I* am not collapse into solipsism, which is to say how am I given by a world (rather than giving a world)? Heidegger struggled for an answer in elaborating the meaning of *das Ereignis* where I do not give the world to be, but rather, it worlds for me.

## THE ORIGIN OF *DAS EREIGNIS*

What has this to do with *das Ereignis*, in 1919 or in 1936 or at any other time? Van Buren shows that in the *Kriegsnotsemester* an understanding of the term *das Ereignis* is at work. What he does not show is how the word *das Ereignis* belongs together with itself, which means no more than remains the same from 1919 to its reappearance in 1936, or from before even then to later still, so that it neither fragments along with and into the many Heideggers he has met nor splinters in a multitude of events.

58. This is Kant's question from §21 of the *Opus Postumum*, which Heidegger had argued in a 1936 lecture course had been taken up by Schelling for discussion in the treatise *Über das Wesen der menschlichen Freiheit*. For an extended discussion of this in relation to Kant, Schelling and Fichte, see *Schellings Abhandlung* (GA42), p. 78ff. "Rückbesinnung auf die Arbeit am 'System'"

What does Heidegger say of *das Ereignis* in 1919? In section 13 of the *Kriegsnotsemester,* Heidegger considers that "already in the opening of the question 'Is there . . . ?' something is given".[59] To ask this question, to pursue nothing other or less than the idea of a pre-theoretical founding-science, means: "we stand on the methodical crossroads, which decides the life or death of philosophy in general, at an abyss: either in nothing, which means absolute thingliness (*Sachlichkeit*), or where the leap into an *other world* succeeds, or more exactly, into the world at all".[60]

Van Buren characterizes this as Heidegger's unfolding of the worlding of the world for "nonobjectifiable personal experience, which is the 'genesis' of all knowing".[61] Indeed Heidegger confirms that there must be "no more thinking back to teleological method, ideally-given, materially-given, total psychological context, object-field . . .",[62] but just that thinking not only in which 'there is something' but also which (in the giving of something) places me on not *a* but *the* "methodological crossroads which decides the life or death of philosophy in general".[63]

In these opening sections of the second part of the 1919 *Kriegsnotsemester* Heidegger moves from a consideration of the 'there is' to 'I comport myself'. In 'there is something' to which I comport myself, my 'I' carries through the experience in which Heidegger says it worlds for me. Moreover, this is specifically not a theoretical experience but a lived experience. In the lived experience of the world I come across things which I do not build up in layers of objectliness as this thing with properties and intersecting surfaces, colors, shapes and so forth, but rather, I come across something and in my coming across it I see it all in one go. It is given to me as the thing that it is. This is the structure of lived experience. All of this is carried out in an environment or better, a surrounding world. Using the example of a lectern,

59. *Zur Bestimmung der Philosophie* (GA56/57), p. 63. "Gibt es etwas?" He replies: "Schon in dem Frageansatz 'Gibt es . . . ?' gibt es etwas."

60. *Zur Bestimmung der Philosophie* (GA56/57), p. 63. "Wir stehen an der methodischen Wegkreuzung, die über Leben oder Tod der Philosophie überhaupt entscheidet, an einem Abgrund: entweder ins Nichts, d.h. der absoluten Sachlichkeit, oder es gelingt der Sprung in eine *andere Welt,* oder genauer: überhaupt erst in die Welt" (author's italics).

61. van Buren, J., *The Young Heidegger* (1994), p. 253.

62. *Zur Bestimmung der Philosophie* (GA56/57), p. 63. "Nicht mehr zurückdenken an teleologische Methode, Idealgebung, Materialgebung, psychischen Gesamtzusammenhang, Sachbereich . . ."

63. *Zur Bestimmung der Philosophie* (GA56/57), p. 63. "Methodische Wegkreuzung, die über Leben oder Tod der Philosophie überhaupt entscheidet."

Heidegger concludes, "in the lived experience of seeing the lectern something gives itself *to me* out of an immediate surrounding world . . . it signifies
to me everywhere and always, it is world-like, 'it worlds'".[64]

There is, however, a sense in which the question 'is there something?'
occurs as the Something in General. The Something in General does not
world; indeed in the Something in General the world-like is wiped off. The
sense of the Something in General leads to a ceasing of my 'I' swinging
along . . . or resonating with particular things. Heidegger says of this same situation: "It lies in the sense of the Something in General, that in the securing of
it as such I am not swinging-with it, but this swinging-with, this delivering-
over-with of mine is undone. The objectly, the object-being as such does not
touch *me*. The I, as what is secured is an *I* no longer".[65] This sense of the
Something in General belongs, not to a lived experience, but to what Heidegger calls a de-lived, or mortified, experience.

In what does this distinction consist? In lived experience where it
worlds for me, in seeing the lectern I go out of myself, so that along with my
full 'I' it resonates or swings along with me, and my experience of the lectern
is a lived experience uniquely or only for *me*. It is an *Ereignis*, with the full
play of *Er-eignen*, what I en-own, literally make my own. Not only, therefore,
does it world for me, but *es ereignet sich*, which means I and the lectern are
given together; my 'I' comes into its own in its owning of the lectern. I could
not have the 'I' that I am except that it is given also by the lectern (in so far
as I comport myself to the lectern).

In mortified experience nothing *ereignet sich*, but only *geschieht*, occurs,
from the verb *geschehen*, to happen, such that there is no *Ereignis*, event, but
only *ein Geschehnis*, an occurrence. How is this? In securing something as an
object the 'I' of lived-experience must disappear such that it becomes
removed from 'me' into an objective 'occurring' that simply goes past me as
a process. It is de-lived in my taking up a purely theoretical comportment to
it. It is not mine, though I can know it theoretically:

64. *Zur Bestimmung der Philosophie* (GA56/57), p. 72. "In dem Erlebnis des
Kathedersehens gibt sich *mir* etwas aus einer unmittelbaren Umwelt . . . bedeutet es mir
überall und immer, es ist alles welthaft, 'es weltet'" (author's italics).
65. *Zur Bestimmung der Philosophie* (GA56/57), p. 73. "Es liegt im Sinne des Etwas
überhaupt, daß *ich nicht* in der Fest-stellung seiner als solchen mitschwinge, sondern
dieses Mitschwingen, dieses Mitherausgehen meiner ist unterbunden. Das Gegenstand,
das Objektsein als solches berührt *mich* nicht. Das Ich, das fest-stellt, bin *ich* gar nicht
mehr" (author's italics).

As an experience, determining that something is the case is only a rudiment of experiencing, a de-experiencing. The objectifying, as cognition, is de-hinged and as such re-moved from authentic lived-experience. The objectified occurring, occurring as objectifying, knowing, we identify as *pro-cess*, it simply goes past, before my knowing I, and has only the relation to it of the being-known, this paled-out I-relatedness is reduced to a minimum of lived-experience. It is the essence of a thing and a thing-context, to give itself only and directly in cognition, that is in theoretical comportment and to give itself for the theoretical I. In the theoretical comportment I am addressed to something, but *I* do not live (as historical I) out toward this or that world-like.[66]

Heidegger speaks of the theoretical I that is in consequence posited in theoretical knowing which replaces the true I-relatedness of the I to the thing given. He says the I is re-moved from what it knows so that the pro-cess can take place and pass me by.

What Heidegger unfolds is the crossroads he has identified as being the life or death of philosophy. In lived experience where 'it worlds for me' and so *es ereignet sich* such that my 'I' is fully present and, so to say, comes to its own in a particular, vivid experience. Here I receive no object, but in the lived experience where I myself en-own it, "its essence eventuates itself".[67] That which I might formally have understood as *eine Sache*, an object which occurs to me in a process, now comes to me in a whole new way—an *Ereignis*. In *Ent-lebnis*, the opposite, mortified experience, a purely theoretical object occurs in a process which also produces a purely theoretical, dehistoricized 'I', an 'I' from which all I-content, I-relatedness has been denatured: a *Geschehnis*, an occurrence. This is nothing other than the transcendental 'I', the subject. These two

66. *Zur Bestimmung der Philosophie* (GA56/57), p. 73f. "Das Feststellen als Erlebnis ist nur noch ein Rudiment von Erleben; es ist ein Ent-leben. Das Gegenständliche, das Erkannte, ist als solches ent-fernt, aus dem eigentlichen Erleben herausgehoben. Das objektivierte Geschehen, das Geschehen als gegenständliches, erkanntes, bezeichnen wir als *Vor-gang*; es geht schlicht vorbei, vor meinem erkennenden Ich, hat zu diesem nur den Bezug des Erkanntseins, diese abgeblaßte, auf ein Minimum von Erleben reduzierte Ichbezogenheit. Es ist das Wesen von Sache und Sachzusammenhang, sich nur und gerade im Erkennen, d.h. im theoretischen Verhalten zu geben und zu geben für das theoretische Ich. Im theoretischen Verhalten bin ich gerichtet auf etwas, aber *ich* lebe nicht (als historisches Ich) auf dieses oder jenes Welthafte zu" (author's italics).

67. *Zur Bestimmung der Philosophie* (GA56/57), p. 75. "Es er-eignet sich seinem Wesen nach."

ways, *das Ereignis* and *der Vorgang,* event and process, are contrasted in terms of their temporality. In *Ereignis* my 'I' is fully historicized, for I can only own the historical moment in its being 'there', its 'belonging', its 'proper place' (which English translators of Heidegger's later uses of these words will render with words like 'propriation'). In *der Vorgang* what is presented is what passes me by, quite simply 'time', with its former and later and endless series of nows. Theoretical cognition, which produces a theoretical 'I', also produces a theoretical time-horizon. This has an important consequence, which I demonstrate later in connection with analogy. If my 'I' is given to me (in fact, returns to me) in coming about 'together with' this or that thing in lived experience, then if this or that thing is given to me theoretically, the 'I' that gave it is also a theoretical 'I', an 'I' which might be said already to have occurred somewhere else: a dissociated, displaced 'I', a prior I.

Heidegger contrasts these ways, not just temporally, but also in their structure as movements. In theoretical cognition, what he describes is an intentional relation between the 'I' and the thing intended, which depends upon the separation, *Ent-fernung* of the I from the thing intended. In *Ereignis,* the opposite occurs, as my 'I' only comes to itself, comes into its own when it discovers itself as already ecstatically in the world-like, where it worlds for me. Far from being a moving-away, all distance collapses in the event. Moreover in 1919, Heidegger says that there is here no inner and outer,[68] which he will later describe as characteristics of the subject-object distinction, for instance in the 1927 lecture course *Die Grundprobleme der Phänomenologie,* but rather *das Ereignis* as the coming about of the I is *also* the disclosing of essence. He concludes:

> Lived-experience does not go past before me in the manner of a thing which I posit, as object, but I myself e-vent it to me and it e-vents itself from out of its essence.[69]

The verb posit is already an allusion to the structure of intentional theories of cognition, as one of the compounds of the verb posit, to place, and at the same time to conceive.

---

68. *Zur Bestimmung der Philosophie* (GA56/57), p. 75.

69. *Zur Bestimmung der Philosophie* (GA56/57), p. 75. "Das Er-leben geht nicht vor mir vorbei, wie eine Sache, die ich hinstelle, als Objekt, sondern ich selbst er-eigne es mir, und es er-eignet sich seinem Wesen nach."

What Heidegger presents is an entirely different mediation of distance and proximity to that of the look which gives an idea of a thing or reproduces its value. The thing and I are one: all distance is collapsed. To be me at the moment of seeing the lectern is to be me-seeing-the-lectern. 'This-lectern-seeing', when I see it, is part of who I 'then' (when seeing it) am. 'How' I see it, the mood in which I-and-it are disclosed will also be part of who 'I' (then) am. This 'how', in a sense, is part of my involvement in its being (for me).

Immediately a question is raised, not by Heidegger, but by van Buren's reading of him. For was not the promise that what would tie all the Heideggers together from at least 1916 to 1976 (beyond then) would be the persisting, ever-present *Sache selbst?* Yet already here in 1919 *die Sache* has begun to disappear, or rather what in one (theoretical) way produces *eine Sache* is in another way, a *new* way, an event, which in its eventfulness yields its essence, not as a thing, *eine Sache*, but as *das Ereignis*. Moreover these two ways proceed from a cross-roads, on which stands the life or death of philosophy in general. Here already the persistence of the same, the persistence of persistence itself, presence, is dissolved into the becoming and falling-away of genuine lived events.

## Circularity: *Das Ereignis* in 1919 and Later

The elaboration of the two differing experiences of time represented by lived and mortified experience comes about specifically in the early Heidegger's critique of the methodology of the sciences. The temporal hori-zon of "theoretical comportment" is exemplified by an astronomer carrying out an astrophysical analysis of the phenomenon of a sunrise.[70] When van Buren describes what Heidegger is doing as an elaboration of the genesis of all knowing, he is in danger of presenting Heidegger as simply providing an alternative, underlying moment which explains the character of theoretical comportment. Heidegger is, however, moving in the opposite direction. The very coming about of theoretical knowledge in its fullness as a process with its intentional structure actually provides the possibility and lays the basis for the new way of *das Ereignis*. For Heidegger is already aware that the process of theoretical comportment or cognition has come about at a par-ticular time and is itself historically located. The fact that it itself is pursuing that kind of knowledge from which the genuine, historical 'I' has been de-

---

70. Cf. *Zur Bestimmung der Philosophie* (GA56/57), p. 74.

lived and re-moved is one of the very features of its historical locatedness. Later, he will call this kind of separation from and occlusion of the thing a mark of the epoch of nihilism. Here (in 1919) he shows how the whole phenomenological analysis is dependent not on what underpins or grounds, but rather on the temporal, historical, and spatial locatedness of the 'I'.

Why does all this place me at *the* crossroads, and why does my standing here have something to do with deciding the life or death of philosophy in general? In 1919 Heidegger is compelled to break off, for, he concludes, "the character of *Ereignis* is not yet fully determined here".[71] To gain an answer, it is necessary to connect what Heidegger has said in 1919 with the working-out of the full meaning of *das Ereignis* in the mid-1930s. The basis for connecting the two has already been raised as the circularity of meaning and interpretation, both with regard to the hermeneutics of destruction and facticity in chapter 2, and in the first solution to the riddle of the doorway in chapter 4. The basis is circularity itself.

Section 18 of the *Kriegsnotsemester* is entitled "The Circular Disposition of the Theory of Cognition."[72] Heidegger notes that: "Circularity is itself a theoretical and *theoretically produced* difficulty".[73] He provides a reminder that circularity is an index of the genuineness of philosophical problems; indeed, it is the structure of theoretical difficulty as such, a point repeated in *Sein und Zeit.* Here he notes that for something to be interpretable, that which interprets it must already have understood what it is in fact interpreting.[74] Can the circle be avoided? Heidegger replies: "The deciding issue is not how to get out of the circle but how to enter it in the right way. This circle of understanding is not an orbit in which any kind of random knowledge moves, but is the expression of the existential *fore-structure* of *Dasein* itself".[75] Immediately we can see the connection between the temporal structure of *Dasein* which I considered at the end of chapter 3 and this question of the circle. In order fully

---

71. *Zur Bestimmung der Philosophie* (GA56/57), p. 75. "Ereignischarakter hiermit noch nicht voll bestimmt."

72. *Die Zirkelhaftigkeit der Erkenntnistheorie.*

73. *Zur Bestimmung der Philosophie* (GA56/57), p. 95 "Die Zirkelhaftigkeit ist eine theoretische und *theoretisch gemachte* Schwierigkeit" (author's italics).

74. *Sein und Zeit* (GA2), esp. p. 152. "Alle Auslegung, die Verständnis beistellen soll, muß schon das Auszulegende verstanden haben."

75. *Sein und Zeit* (GA2), p. 153. "Das Entscheidende ist nicht, aus dem Zirkel heraus-, sondern in ihn nach der rechten Weise hineinzukommen. Dieser Zirkel des Verstehens ist nicht ein Kreis, in dem sich eine beliebige Erkenntnisart bewegt, sondern er ist der Ausdruck der existentialen *Vor-struktur* des Daseins selbst" (author's italics).

to make sense of this, however, it is necessary to see that the circle is also concerned with language and truth. The fore-structure of *Dasein* is really none other than speaking as its very temporalizing; as I have already noted, the two are the same, though they can be understood from different aspects. Circularity asks: How do things come to be known in language? If I interpret something *as* something, is it because the interpreting (this name, this idea) is already known to me so that the thing-named is the same as the thing-to-be-known (i.e., is a thing known by being subsumed under a category)? Or in coming across any given thing, do I have to reach forward for *just that experience of it* which also shakes the name to its very roots and puts it into question in its very naming, which brings *me* to the fore (and so into the question) as a one-naming? This is the essential structure of Heidegger's atheism: is God already known to me as what grounds me, and so lies at the basis of everything I know, as Heidegger suggests is the case with Plato, Aristotle, Aquinas, Descartes, and the whole tradition of metaphysics; or am I groundless in just that way that, as ungrounded, everything I know comes to me anew, in a properly (authentically) original way?

Heidegger's question, 'how do I properly enter the circle?' is also just that question raised by the riddle of the doorway put to the dwarf by Zarathustra. The dwarf, you will recall, solves the riddle disdainfully.[76] That is his way ('how') of entering the circle: from a distance. The question of circularity has also arisen in connection with *die Kehre* and the working out of the meaning of the essence of essence in 1937.[77] Here the concern is explicitly with truth, particularly with asking why the correspondence theory of truth has anything to do with the essence of truth.

It is immediately possible to see, from the perspective of circularity, what is at issue. If interpretation decides in advance what any thing (being) might be (which means if the ontological difference is not a question, but is

76. See p. 118 above.
77. Cf. for instance, the 1937 lecture course *Grundfragen der Philosophie* (GA45), p. 47. "All this is full of riddles: The question of the *essence of truth* is at the same time and in itself the question of *the truth of essence*. The question of truth—asked as a basic question—turns itself in itself against itself. This *turn* which we have run up against, is thereby an indication, that we have come into the compass of a genuine philosophical question" (author's italics). ("Rätselhaft ist dies alles: Die Frage nach dem *Wesen der Wahrheit* ist *zugleich und in sich* die Frage nach der *Wahrheit des Wesens*. Die Wahrheitsfrage—als Grundfrage gefragt—kehrt sich in sich selbst gegen sich selbst. Diese *Kehre*, auf die wir da gestoßen sind, ist das Anzeichen dafür, daß wir in den Umkreis einer echten philosophischen Frage kommen.")

decided, secured, certain), then truth will simply be the correspondence of any given thing with my pre-knowledge (mental knowledge or representation) of it. Truth becomes correctness, or as Heidegger later argues: "A basic trait of every metaphysical definition of the essence of truth is expressed in the principle that conceives truth as agreement of knowledge with beings: truth is the adequation of the intellect to the thing".[78] This is a change in the nature of truth. Here Heidegger is discussing how Descartes's position is foreshadowed by and connected to Protagoras's principle πάντων χρημάτων μέτρον ἐστὶν ἄνθρωπος.[79] If humanity is understood as the basis of truth, then what gives man to be (being) in advance of itself becomes covered over. This in itself becomes the grounding of all metaphysics, which is also the founding of nihilism.

What is at issue is proximity: if *I* am the measure, that is what measures and ascribes value (truth) to any given thing, then I am distanced from the thing. I have to take up an aim toward it in order for it to correspond to what I already might know it to be. This is exactly the position of the dwarf: he takes up a standpoint from which to see the doorway. The whole of its meaning is disclosed to him, but from a distance, so that his orientation toward it is disdainful and dismissive. The orientation is governed by a look that could only be given in distance. Correspondence does, therefore, explain the comportment of the dwarf, but its ability to do so does not make it an originary explanation. Circularity can, to some extent, tie *das Ereignis* of 1919 together with *das Ereignis* of 1936 and beyond.

## THE DEATH OF GOD

There is however a further determination of *das Ereignis* that appears with Heidegger's reading of Nietzsche that was absent from the work of 1919. Heidegger's 1961 published text of his lectures on Nietzsche opens the first lecture series with a quotation from Nietzsche's *Der Antichrist:* "Well-nigh two

---

78. *Der europäische Nihilismus* (*Nietzsche* [GA6.2]), p. 169. "Ein Grundzug aller metaphysischen Wesenbestimmung der Wahrheit kommt in dem Satz zum Ausdruck, der die Wahrheit als Übereinstimmung der Erkenntnis mit dem Seienden begreift: veritas est adaequatio intellectus rei."

79. Cf. Plato, *Thaeatetus,* 152a. Normally translated as "man is the measure of all things", but see Heidegger's extended discussion of the fragment in *Der europäische Nihilismus* (*Nietzsche* [GA6.2]), pp. 131–141.

thousand years and not a single new God!"⁸⁰ This might almost be the guiding thought of Heidegger's reading of Nietzsche. Certainly he returns to this thought more than once in order to unravel how it is that Nietzsche is the fulfillment or completion of Western metaphysics.

In a lecture course planned for the winter semester of 1944–45 but interrupted because of the needs of war, a second confrontation with 'wartime emergencies', Heidegger calls this "the *one* word that should indicate to us Nietzsche's basic-experience and basic-determination".⁸¹ This word begins and ends the *Nietzsche* lecture courses. It is therefore important to understand what this *word* says, for elsewhere the 'word of Nietzsche' has nothing to do with the creation of a god but rather God's death.⁸² Nietzsche's word is: God is dead. Moreover, Heidegger asserts (elsewhere and repeatedly) that Nietzsche's basic experience and determination are nothing other than nihilism. In the lecture course *Die ewige Wiederkehr des Gleichen* he says:

> Nietzsche's whole philosophy is rooted and resonates in the experience of the very fact of nihilism ... with the unfolding of Nietzsche's philosophy there grows at the same time the depth of his insight into the essence and power of nihilism and the need and necessity of its overcoming increases.⁸³

It is worth noting here the circularity indicated by this text—for the very growing depth of the insight into the power and essence of nihilism is the same movement as the increasing of the need and the necessity of its overcoming. Moreover, all of this is a becoming aware, a coming to the self. The verb resonates, *schwingt*, characterizing the swinging along of the 'I' in the resonating of *das Ereignis* in the example of the lived experience at the table in the *Kriegsnotsemester* of 1919. In this text there is an 'I' most clearly coming to itself as an overcoming.

---

80. *Nietzsche* (GA6), I, p. 11. "Zwei Jahrtausende beinahe und nicht ein einziger neuer Gott!"
81. *Nietzsches Metaphysik* (GA50), p. 107. "Das *eine* Wort, das uns Nietzsches Grunderfahrung und Grundstimmung andeuten soll" (author's italics).
82. Cf. *Nietzsche's Wort 'Gott ist Tot'* (*Holzwege* [GA7]), pp. 209–267.
83. *Die ewige Wiederkehr des Gleichen* (*Nietzsche* [GA6.1]), p. 435. "In der Erfahrung der Tatsache des Nihilismus wurzelt und schwingt die ganze Philosophie Nietzsches ... mit der Entfaltung von Nietzsches Philosophie wächst zugleich die Tiefe der Einsicht in das Wesen und die Macht des Nihilismus, steigert sich die Not und Notwendigkeit seiner Überwindung."

Are there *two* words of Nietzsche? Are Nietzsche's basic experience and determination that there are no new gods, or is it the philosophy of nihilism? In Heidegger's Nietzsche lectures the phrase basic-determination means two things. Each is simultaneously a determination of *das Seiende im Ganzen,* beings as a whole, first, as the will to power, and second, as the eternal return of the same.[84] Basic-determination therefore means those two determinations with which Nietzsche sought to clarify and make transparent the philosophy of nihilism. What then is the 'basic experience' of which these two are the basic determinations? In the 1937 lecture series *Der Wille zur Macht als Kunst,* Heidegger says:

> The word "God is dead" is not an atheistic doctrinal principle, but the formula for the basic experience of an event of Western history.[85]

Nietzsche's word is not, therefore, declaring that there is no God, the common interpretation of what atheism is. In other words, this declaration is in line with the meaning I indicated for 'atheism' throughout Heidegger's work. The word *das Ereignis* is used to describe nihilism itself, for Heidegger says, shortly after describing the 'need and necessity' of nihilism's overcoming:

> We can say, in seeking support from the word itself, that nihilism is an event, or a doctrine, which is a concern with the *nihil,* the nothing. Considered formally, the nothing is the negation of something, indeed of every something. *All* 'something' constitutes beings as a whole. The positing of the nothing is the negation of beings as a whole.[86]

This something has been named before: when the Something in General acted as the basis for and gave rise to the intentional structure of cognition as

---

84. *Die ewige Wiederkehr des Gleichen und der Wille zur Macht (Nietzsche* [GA6.2]), p. 15. "Die beiden Grundbestimmungen des Seienden im Ganzen—der Wille zur Macht und die ewige Wiederkehr des Gleichen."

85. *Der Wille zur Macht als Kunst (Nietzsche* [GA6.1]), p. 183. "Das Wort 'Gott ist tot' ist kein atheistischer Lehrsatz, sondern die Formel für die Grunderfahrung eines Ereignisses der abendländischen Geschichte."

86. *Die ewige Wiederkehr des Gleichen (Nietzsche* [GA6.1]), p. 435 f. "Nihilismus, so können wir in Anlehnung an das Wort sagen, ist ein Ereignis, bzw. eine Lehre, wo es sich um das nihil, das Nichts handelt. Das Nichts ist—formal genommen—die Verneinung von Etwas, und zwar von jeglichem Etwas. *Alles* Etwas macht das Seiende im Ganzen aus. Die Setzung des Nichts ist die Verneinung des Seienden im Ganzen" (author's italics).

contrasted with the new way of *Ereignis*. Nihilism is therefore to be understood as that event (*Ereignis*) which brings before me as a basic, or grounding experience that there are beings as a whole, the Something in General, and it brings me before it in the character of a nihilation, which is its *Ereignis*.

In chapter 3 I indicated that for Heidegger, beings as a whole function as the name for God as thought by metaphysics. For an answer which clarifies the question *exactly* as it is posed here it is necessary to turn to a lecture course given in the summer semester of 1936, the year preceding this statement. Keeping firmly in view that *das Seiende im Ganzen* is solely a determination of metaphysics as *Seiendheit*, being-ness, rather than being itself, here Heidegger says in his 1936 lectures on Schelling:

> Every philosophy as metaphysics is theology in the original and essential sense that the conceiving (λόγος) of beings as a whole asks about the ground (i.e., the first-cause) of being (*Seyn*), and this ground is named as θεός, God. Indeed, Nietzsche's philosophy, for instance, in which an essential saying states 'God is dead' is in accord with this saying 'Theology'.[87]

For Heidegger, theology, especially as we have met it in Aristotle (and also where it can be found in Plato), hitherto belongs firmly within the realm of metaphysics; hence his elaboration in these lectures of the term ontotheology, a term he will repeat in key texts until the end.[88] He even goes so far as to name what is normally understood by the word theology as "theiology", a term that is later taken up by Jean-Luc Marion.[89]

---

87. *Schellings Abhandlung* (GA42), p. 87. "Jede Philosophie als Metaphysik ist Theologie in dem ursprünglichen und wesentlichen Sinne, daß das Begreifen (λόγος) des Seienden im Ganzen nach dem Grunde (d.h. der Ur-sache) des Seyns fragt und dieser Grund θεός, Gott, genannt wird. Auch Nietzsches Philosophie z. B., darin ein wesentlicher Satz lautet 'Gott ist todt', ist eben gemäß diesem Satz 'Theologie'."

88. Cf.: the 1942/43 seminar published in *Hegels Begriff der Erfahrung* (*Holzwege* [GA5]); the 1949 *Einleitung* to the 1929 lecture on the nothing entitled *Was ist Metaphysik?* (*Wegmarken* [GA9]); in 1957 in *Identität und Differenz* (GA11); and in 1962 in *Kants These über das Sein* (*Wegmarken* [GA9]).

89. In *Hegels Begriff der Erfahrung* (*Holzwege* [GA5]), p. 195. "Die erste Philosophie ist als Ontologie zugleich die Theologie des wahrhaft Seienden. Genauer wäre sie die Theiologie zu nennen. Die Wissenschaft des Seienden als solchen ist in sich onto-theologisch." Jean-Luc Marion appropriated the term in his work *Dieu sans l'être* (1982), p. 96.

How can this be understood? For Heidegger the metaphysical position concerning God is that being and God are the same: *Deus est suum esse*. Ontotheology says no more than this. What does it mean for God and being to be the same? Heidegger says that God as being is the thought of beings as a whole, construed as what gives being to beings, what is most being-ful about them. Heidegger draws the distinction between metaphysics construing being in this way, which is being-ness, the being-ness of beings, and so remains *a* being rather than being itself (which is not *a* being). In the whole history of metaphysics, beings as a whole is for Heidegger always thought as God. Metaphysics has traditionally made a distinction between questions of an ontological order, in which beings as such are considered, and the theological order of questioning, which considers beings as a whole, or in general, a questioning directly related to the being of God. In the widest sense, Heidegger says, "philosophy is *ontotheology*. The more originally it is both in one, the more authentically is it philosophy".[90] You will note that for Heidegger, all that is under consideration is beings, either as a whole or in particular. So even when this topic is treated in relation to God, nothing more is actually being said about God than that God is beings as a whole. This is an inquiry solely determined by what is found in the world and allows for nothing outside it. It *already* is solely factical or, as more contemporary commentators have styled it, immanent. So far from Heidegger being the champion of a nihilism that disbars anything beyond the purely phenomenal, the purely factical, the immanent, Heidegger's accusation is that metaphysics is already this facticity, immanence, and nihilism.

While the distinct term ontotheology seems to make its appearance first in a lecture series on Hegel's *Phänomenologie des Geistes* in 1930 and then again in much greater detail in 1936 (in relation to Kant in particular), Heidegger claims that he had worked out the perspective it names much earlier and that the whole of the 1929 lecture *Was ist Metaphysik?* was written with this perspective in view.[91] Indeed in the opening sections of the so-called *Kantbuch* (developed from a lecture series given in 1927–28) Heidegger takes

---

90. *Schellings Abhandlung* (GA42), p. 88. "Philosophie ist *Ontotheologie*. Je ursprünglicher sie beides in einem ist, um so eigentlicher ist sie Philosophie" (author's italics).

91. *Einleitung* zu *Was ist Metaphysik?* (*Wegmarken* [GA9]), pp. 208–210. This introduction was first added to the fifth edition in 1949. That Heidegger's claim is correct is substantiated in his discussion of Aristotle's terms πρώτη φιλοσοφία and θεολογία in the 1928 lectures on Leibniz (see p. 119 above). For the earliest use of the term of which I am aware, see the text of his 1930s lectures, *Hegels Phänomenologie des Geistes* (GA32), §10.

Baumgarten's 1743 distinction: "To metaphysics is referred ontology, cosmology, psychology, and natural theology".[92] *Metaphysica Generalis* refers to ontology, or beings in their generality (*ens commune*), and *Metaphysica Specialis* is "theology (the object of which is the *summum ens*), cosmology, and psychology". Metaphysics as taken over by Kant is then summarized as that which has for its object "beings in general and the highest being".[93]

It is worth noting that there is a circular movement carried through in the working out of *das Ereignis*. In metaphysics God is conceived as the ground of beings as a whole, as what underpins and causes them as their founding possibility. For Heidegger's interpretation of Nietzsche, "nihilism is the event of the dwindling away of the weight out of all weighty things, the fact of the absence of gravity".[94] *Das Ereignis* in nihilism is the death of God, in which the ground becomes groundless and weightless; it floats off. This has the effect of depriving things of their weight. Nihilism is therefore also the experience of the coming about of ground or basis as something other than God. What could this be? For Heidegger, the "weightiest" of thoughts and the hardest is the eternal recurrence of the same.[95] How does Heidegger understand the relation of eternal recurrence of the same to beings as a whole and in general? The eternal recurrence of the same is the securing of all things as the permanentizing of presence, being secured in terms of becoming. God as the ground of all things is the *inverse* of this, the securing of all things, everything that becomes, in consequence of what most *is*, God. Becoming is secured in terms of being. Here, therefore, is the explanation why for Heidegger, Nietzsche's nihilism is a movement that is a "countermovement".[96] Nietzsche is in this sense the countermovement to the Greek privileging of the unmovedness of being over becoming, but this

---

92. *Kant und das Problem der Metaphysik* (GA3), pp. 3–6. "Ad metaphysicam referuntur ontologia, cosmologia, psychologia et theologia naturalis." The lectures are published as *Kants Kritik der Reinen Vernunft* (GA25).

93. *Kant und das Problem der Metaphysik* (GA3), §1, esp. p. 9. " . . . da sie das Seiende im allgemeinen und das höchste Seiende zum Gegenstand hat."

94. *Die ewige Wiederkehr des Gleichen* (*Nietzsche* [GA6.1]), p. 421. "Der Nihilismus ist das Ereignis des Schwindens aller Gewichte aus allen Dingen, die Tatsache des Fehlens des Schwergewichtes."

95. *Die ewige Wiederkehr des Gleichen* (*Nietzsche* [GA6.1]), p. 323. "Das größte Schwergewicht."

96. *Die ewige Wiederkehr des Gleichen* (*Nietzsche* [GA6.1]), p. 433 f. "Gegenbewegung."

countermovement still secures extantness over concealment, albeit extantness no longer conceived as immovability but as total movement. Extantness,
presence as such, continues to hold sway.

## THE MORAL GOD

Which God is it that is pronounced dead? Heidegger says: "the God who is
seen in terms of 'morality', and only this one is meant, in so far as Nietzsche
says 'God is dead'".[97] Here, therefore, is the very coming to the fore of that
interpretation of the Good as moral good which he had warned his students
against with regard to reading Plato. It would be possible to overlook what
work the participle *seen* is doing here. It refers to nothing other than the
intentional relation, the very relation named by Plato as an εἶδός. How does
one see God? I do not *see* God, but in intentionality I take up a view, a seeing
in relation to things. When *I* take up a view, I see the dead God, for it is *I*,
*now*, who in the countermovement of nihilism, under-stand, e-valuate, give
life to things in the intentional relationship.

What has this to do with morality? Morality is the fitting of the is to the
ought. The is of the world is fitted, made true, to the realm of God when God
as beings as a whole is the underpinning of all things. Morality is one of the
aspects (literally, faces) of the securing of the becoming of things in terms of
being as beings as a whole: God. In the inversion of this in the countermovement of nihilism, everything is a creation of value, of the subject's creative
production of the meaning, the value of objects. The full impact of this is
described in Heidegger's 1940 lecture course *Der europäische Nihilismus.* Here
he comments: "Nietzsche mostly understands the moral as the system of valuation in which a transcendent world is posited as the desired standard of
measure. Nietzsche consistently understands the moral metaphysically, that
is with a view to the fact that in it something is decided about the whole of
beings".[98] The proclamation of the death of God is none other than that

---

97. *Die ewige Wiederkehr des Gleichen* (*Nietzsche* [GA6.1]), p. 320. "Der 'moralisch'
gesehene Gott und nur dieser ist gemeint, wenn Nietzsche sagt: 'Gott ist tot'."
98. *Der europäische Nihilismus* (*Nietzsche* [GA6.2]), p. 118. "Unter Moral versteht
Nietzsche meist das System solcher Wertschätzungen, in denen eine übersinnliche Welt als
maßgebend und wünschbar gesetzt wird. Nietzsche begreift die 'Moral' stets 'metaphysisch', d.h. im Hinblick darauf, daß in ihr über das Ganze des Seienden entschieden wird."

event in which the uppermost values are devalued and where the thought of the moral ceases to have any meaning. The ideal-moral (the uppermost values) is replaced by the values posited by the subject in a revaluation.

The devaluation of the uppermost values is carried out for and as a revaluation. This revaluation occurs in the will to power. The revaluation as the will to power is nothing other than the subject securing things in terms of the intentional relationship of valuation, the *ratio* or reckoning of objects by subjects.

This experience which comes about as an event comes about in an experience of need and necessity. The word necessity in German is *Notwendigkeit*, a turn-toward-and-into-a-need, from *die Not*, "need," and the verb *wenden*, "to turn" or "to wend." Heidegger asks:

> What is this experience? What need is experienced in it, as a needful turn and thus necessity, of a revaluation and therewith a new valuation? It is that event in the history of Western humanity that Nietzsche designates with the name nihilism.[99]

Why does this experience come about as a need? The uttermost need arises from the experience of being God-less. To be God-less is to be deprived of a creator, which means the same as to need to create: "as (the) God-less (Zarathustra) experiences the outermost need, and therewith the innermost necessity, to create what is needed".[100] Zarathustra takes over from God the structure of the *ens creatum*. Again this has an intentional structure, for there is an outer experienced as outermost, and an inner, as innermost, in order to create. This is nothing other than the intentional structure of what in 1919 was called theoretical cognition.

To recapitulate: the word of Nietzsche, God is dead, is that *Ereignis* which is the *Ereignis* of nihilism itself, determined by both the will to power and the eternal return of the same, which comes about as the *Ereignis* of the demand

---

99. *Die ewige Wiederkehr des Gleichen* (*Nietzsche* [GA6.1]), p. 435. "Welches ist diese Erfahrung? Welche Not wird in ihr erfahren als dasjenige, was eine Wende und damit die Not-wendigkeit einer Umwertung und damit eine neue Wertsetzung ernötigt? Es ist jenes Ereignis in der Geschichte des abendländischen Menschen, das Nietzsche mit dem Namen 'Nihilismus' bezeichnet."

100. *Die ewige Wiederkehr des Gleichen* (*Nietzsche* [GA6.1]), p. 322. "Als dieser Gottlose erfährt (Zarathustra) die äußerste Not und damit die innerste Notwendigkeit, das Nötigste zu schaffen."

for a devaluation of the uppermost values and the revaluation of all values and is the negation of every something, which means the *Ereignis* of the negation of beings as a whole. This *Ereignis* brings to light the circular movement which is the completion or fulfillment of Western metaphysics. In these various events there are always two movements taking place. At the same time as the will to power, the eternal return of the same, the death of God, and the basic experience and determination of nihilism come about and are seen for what they are *for the first time* in Nietzsche's philosophy, so also are the need and possibility of the turn-out of nihilism. *This alone* is *das Ereignis* and allows the meaning of the riddle of the door to be unlocked when I come to consider how Heidegger interprets Nietzsche's *Zarathustra*. Why is any of this to do with the *word* that says 'well-nigh two thousand years and not a single new God!'?

The clarification of this question can be found in Heidegger's interrupted lecture course of 1944–45. These lectures were assigned the title *Einführung in die Philosophie*. In section 6, *God- and World-lessness of Modern Humanity*, Heidegger says first, that for Nietzsche, "this word says not only that, as Nietzsche has often before pronounced, 'God is dead', but that for two thousand years Europe has been unable to create a new God". He concludes: "For this is an essential thought of Nietzsche's, that the Gods have been created by humanity".[101] He adds: "God and the gods are a 'production' of humanity".[102] After raising the question of whether the createdness of God is anything religious and pointing out in passing that the Greeks had no religion because they are the ones who were and still are in the sight of the gods (which is nothing other than the inverse of the currently pertaining intentional relationship and so also the same thing), Heidegger concludes: "For Nietzsche not only are God and the gods productions of humanity, but all, whatever is, is a singular anthropomorphism".[103] Second, Heidegger says that "in itself humanity is '*the* creating'. 'Creativity' is the essence of humanity".[104]

101. *Nietzsches Metaphysik* (GA50), p. 107. "Dies Wort sagt nicht nur, daß, wie Nietzsche es zuvor oft ausgesprochen, 'Gott tot ist', sondern daß Europa seit zwei Jahrtausenden außerstande gewesen, einen neuen Gott zu schaffen. Denn dies ist ein wesentlicher Gedanke Nietzsches, daß die Götter von den Menschen 'geschaffen' werden."
102. *Nietzsches Metaphysik* (GA50), p. 108. "Der Gott und die Götter sind ein 'Erzeugnis' des Menschen."
103. *Nietzsches Metaphysik* (GA50), p. 107. "Für Nietzsche sind nicht nur der Gott und die Götter 'Erzeugnisse' des Menschen, sondern alles, was ist . . . alles, was ist, ist eine einzige Anthropomorphie."
104. *Nietzsches Metaphysik* (GA50), p. 110. "In ihr ist der Mensch '*der* Schaffende'. 'Das Schöpferische' ist das Wesen des Menschen" (author's italics).

Humanity, as the creating, produces the all, whatever is. Humanity *as* creating is the self-positing subject through which all objects are determined in their objectivity. Heidegger intends a meaning of misplacedness that this self-positing conveys and tells us:

> In that man makes his essence autonomous, he rises into the willing of himself. With this up-rising (*Auf-stand*) of humanity into the will as the willing of himself all things at once and only now become objects (*Gegen-stände*). Man in his uprising and the world as object belong together. Man stands in rebellion in the world rendered as an object. Rebellious man permits the world to be only as an object.[105]

The essence of this activity of modern humanity in this creativity is the subject-object distinction. The creativity of humanity is to render the world into objects, things that are experienced under the conditions of objectification. As I demonstrated in the discussion of the character of time at the end of chapter 3, Heidegger understands this on the basis not only of the understanding of being, but also of time, as the way in which each 'now' is analogous in its character to beings or things.

This is a productive process, an *in-tention*. It involves separation, for to take up a position means to separate the self from the thing towards which one directs something like an intention, in order that the intention can be taken up. In this separation the self is also posited as a projection. This is exactly the sense of the Latin verb *intendere*. To intend in an *intentio* is to stretch out, to produce a distance in order to direct one's attention, to take an aim. *Intentio* comes to mean to stretch out a distance between two things in a mental act. Here it means the rising up (*Auf-stand*) of something (the subject) against which something else might stand: the object (*Gegenstand*). Stretch, which belonged to the character of time in the succession of 'nows', also belongs to the Cartesian character of space as extension.

---

105. *Nietzsches Metaphysik* (GA50), p. 111. "Indem der Mensch sein Wesen auf sich selbst stellt, steht er auf in das Wollen seiner selbst. Mit diesem Aufstand des Menschen in den Willen als das Wollen seiner selbst werden alle Dinge zugleich und erst zum Gegenstand. Der Mensch im Aufstand und die Welt als Gegenstand gehören zusammen. In der Welt als Gegenstand steht der Mensch im Aufstand. Der aufständische Mensch läßt nur die Welt als Gegenstand zu."

## THE IMPLICIT ATHEISM OF SUBJECTIVITY

What has this got to do with God and the gods, and with Heidegger's athe-ism? Recall that this section is entitled *God- and World-lessness of Modern Humanity*. The key term here is *-lessness:* to posit the self out of itself as sub-ject is to be deprived of God (and the gods) and world. To be deprived of God and the gods and world is also to be deprived, to deliver over into los-ing, just that 'I' which can come into a genuine, originary belonging with God and the gods and world. The question which I shall endeavor to answer in what follows later is just what such a belonging might consist in. What I indicated here in the whole of the reading of Nietzsche is nothing other than the unfolding of a de-living, contrasted against a lived experience, the *Er-eignis* that actually brings all of this to light, the methodological crossroads of the life and death of philosophy of 1919, read as an elaboration of Nietzsche's doctrine of the will to power. Subjectivity, as the triumph of nihilism and the end of metaphysics, is a *negative* atheism which banishes the possibility of a genuine belonging to world, the world in which God might appear. It is atheism without being known as such. Heidegger's atheism, in bringing this implicit atheism to light, renders it, as explicit, into an openness to God without forestalling God.

In what way does this *God- and World-lessness* which is also an *I-lessness* and which is the most extreme carrying out of the subject-object distinction manifest itself? "The current concealed inner essence of objectification is technology".[106] Technology is itself the objectification of the sciences.

It is time to draw some conclusions from this reading of *das Ereignis*. I indicated what arises out of the period 1936–1945 (and in particular 1937–1940) in the working-out of the essential structures of *das Ereignis*, as that event which nihilism itself is. I have, however, largely considered this from the perspective of Heidegger's elaboration of nihilism as *das Ereignis*. While not completely losing sight of the other horizon along which thought could proceed from the crossroads of 1919, it is clear that for Heidegger, the whole of the meaning of Nietzsche is brought to light in considering the death of God as *Ereignis*, event, and so out of which *there has already been* a turn.

---

106. *Nietzsches Metaphysik* (GA50), p. 111. "Das heute noch verborgene innerste Wesen der Vergegenständlichung . . . ist die Technik."

Several times in this chapter I indicated a tension between the two words *das Ereignis* and *das Geschehnis,* event and occurrence. The first, I suggested, is always connected with lived experience and with the 'authentic' owned experience of being, the collapse of all distance between me and the thing (so much so that the thing 'things' me), that understanding of being which Heidegger often writes not as *das Sein* but as *das Seyn.* The second is its opposite, having always to do with *Ent-lebnis,* the distance named in θεωρεῖν, of truth as correspondence, as the setting out of distance from which a nihilistic look might be aimed.

Does Heidegger ever consider the death of God as *ein Geschehnis,* an occurrence, in contrast to *das Ereignis,* the event, which would be necessary in order to claim that for Heidegger the crossroads of 1919 is the same thing as the crisis that Heidegger repeatedly says is present in the work of Nietzsche? If he does, then it would be possible to show that in *das Ereignis* the death of God is brought consciously to light, whereas in *das Geschehnis* the death of God is still present but at work in a concealed way, governing what is known but also covering it up. This is exactly where metaphysics holds sway, and so where the meaning of *das Ereignis* has not been brought to light or where I have not realized what *das Ereignis* is (where I am still constituted subjectivally, which means when I understand myself to be a subject). In showing this, a further point can be made, one on which much of this interpretation depends. When Heidegger elaborates a term, almost invariably that term becomes a kind of shorthand, the presence in subsequent places of the thinking through that went into the coining of the term at earlier stages. Meanings become sedimented so that these terms become markers for the presence of one way of thinking through the questions Heidegger encountered when thinking them through later, in different ways.

In 1943 Heidegger gave a summary lecture of his reading of Nietzsche which was later published as *Nietzsches Wort 'Gott ist Tot'.* Here Heidegger discusses again what it means to think through the proclamation of the death of God. He has already pointed out that in the work *Die fröhliche Wissenschaft,* Nietzsche's madman has indicated that it is 'we, we ourselves who have killed God'. Heidegger explains:

> . . . what is intended in the occurrence that God is killed. Killing means, through human action, the doing-away with the suprasensory world in itself. The killing means that process in which any being as such does not simply come to nothing, but does indeed become something else in its being. But above all in this process man himself becomes something

else. He becomes that which does away with the being in itself. The human uprising into subjectivity renders beings objects. The objective, however, is that which is brought to stand through conceptual-representing. The doing-away with beings, which is the killing of God, is carried out in the securing-as-coming-to-a-stand through which man secures the material, bodily, spiritual, and intellectual stocks, for the sake however of his own security, a willing of dominion over beings as possible objectivity, in order to do justice ('correspond') to the being of beings, to the will to power.[107]

There are two important terms to notice here: process and *das Geschehnis*, occurrence. This is once again a description of mortified experience, but as what takes place when the death of God remains as a mere process and occurrence that passes me by. The ever-intensification of the will to power and the eternal return as humanity's overarching dominion over all things is understood as an anthropomorphism and above all manifested in technology. To those who argue that Heidegger's critique of technology is a purely post-war phenomenon, intimately linked to a so-called quietism that arises from his reaction to the defeat of Germany in 1945 and his supposed postwar 'secret' Nazism, I merely point out that this passage demonstrates without doubt that the entire perspective of his critique of technology was worked out by 1943 at the very latest.[108]

---

107. *Nietzsches Wort 'Gott ist Tot'* (*Holzwege* [GA5]), p. 262. "Was in dem Geschehnis, daß Gott getötet wird, gemeint ist. Das Töten meint die Beseitigung der an sich seienden übersinnlichen Welt durch den Menschen. Das Töten meint den Vorgang, in dem das Seiende als solches nicht schlechthin zunichte, wohl aber in seinem Sein anders wird. In diesem Vorgang wird aber auch und vor allem der Mensch anders. Er wird zu dem, der das Seiende im Sinne des an sich Seienden beseitigt. Der menschliche Aufstand in die Subjektivität macht das Seiende zum Gegenstand. Das Gegenständliche aber ist das durch das Vorstellen zum Stehen Gebrachte. Die Beseitigung des an sich Seienden, das Töten des Gottes, vollzieht sich in der Bestandsicherung, durch die sich der Mensch die stofflichen, leiblichen, seelischen und geistigen Bestände sichert, dies aber um seiner eigenen Sicherheit willen die die Herrschaft über das Seiende als das mögliche Gegenständliche will, um dem Sein des Seienden, dem Willen zur Macht zu entsprechen."

108. If, on the other hand, a more plausible view were taken, that Heidegger's analysis of technology arises out of his reading of Jünger from the early 1930s, and he found full confrontation for it in his interpretation of Nietzsche, then it would be necessary to understand that his critique of technology is worked out through the crucible of his political engagement almost from the very beginning and at least from the date of his resignation of the rectorate of the University of Freiburg in 1934.

Heidegger understands Nietzsche's self-understanding of his philosophy as the inversion of Platonism as the whole history of metaphysics:

> [Nietzsche's] inversion does not do away with the grounding platonic position, but in that it appears to do away with it, it actually entrenches it. But the essential point remains, in that Nietzsche's metaphysical thinking goes back into the commencement, the circle closes . . . metaphysics is at an end.
>
> . . . however, in that Nietzsche's grounding position is the end of Western metaphysics, it can be the counterposition for the other beginning only if the latter adopts a *questioning* stance over against the initial beginning.[109]

*Das Ereignis* is *that* event which is possible at the closing of the circle of metaphysics, that circle which began with Plato and closes with Nietzsche, which means they speak of the same. When the circle closes, it hardens into a ring.

The path Heidegger traverses is that of questioning. In questioning the path unfolds. In questioning Heidegger delineated in a preliminary way the structure of the event, *das Ereignis*. In so doing he discovered he also had to take account of what thinking had thought metaphysically. He thereby discovered the event as the death of God and that this event had already been announced by Nietzsche. What remained but to make it his own, to appropriate it? Such an appropriation meant to think through for himself the meaning of the philosophy of Nietzsche, to inscribe himself into the Nietzschean thought of nihilism and so to make it his own, as the only way that the event could be en-owned to himself. Heidegger swings along with Nietzsche. In doing so, Heidegger throws open the whole question of what it is to know or interpret, at all. The question is thrown open both by throwing into question how metaphysics lost sight of a fundamental way of being in

---

109. *Die ewige Wiederkehr des Gleichen* (*Nietzsche* [GA6.1]), pp. 469, 470. "Die Umkehrung beseitigt die Platonische Grundstellung nicht, sondern verfestigt sie gerade durch den Anschein, als sei sie beseitigt. Das Wesentliche aber bleibt: Indem Nietzsches metaphysisches Denken in den Anfang zurückgeht, schließt sich der Kreis . . . die Metaphysik . . . ist am Ende.
"... Da aber die Grundstellung Nietzsches in der abendländischen Metaphysik deren Ende ist, kann sie für den anderen Anfang nur dann die Gegenstellung sein, wenn dieser sich dem ersten Anfang *fragend* gegenüberstellt" (author's italics)

nearness, proximity, as the articulation of distance and closeness, and it is thrown open by re-articulating what proximity, belonging-to, might mean.

If the event, authentically experienced, which means the event present to itself and as an atheism, always carries within it the trace of the death of God (the metaphysical God), how can the God of faith live within the atheism of the event? It is this question which it will be necessary to keep always in view in what follows.

Chapter Six

# Heidegger's Critique of Theology

## HEIDEGGER'S ANTI-CHRISTIAN POLEMIC

In January 1919 Heidegger wrote to Engelbert Krebs renouncing his formal links to the Catholic Church.[1] A section of the letter reads:

> I believe that I have experienced too deeply—more so, perhaps than those officially charged with its investigation—what values the Catholic Middle Ages bear within themselves, and we are still very far from a truthful evaluation. My investigations into the phenomenology of religion . . . will make great use of the Middle Ages.[2]

At the outset, Heidegger saw himself as being in dialogue with the medieval meditation on being, a meditation he names as Catholic (and therefore Christian) in character. To what extent did he remain in that dialogue? Inasmuch as I have dealt with Heidegger's philosophical atheism in earlier chapters, nevertheless Heidegger's sustained anti-Christian polemic, especially in the period immediately prior to the Second World War, is also a question. Surely this polemic is indicative of an aggressive, personally held atheism, and does not *this* atheism disqualify any

---

1. Krebs, a Catholic priest, theologian, and philosopher, was a personal friend of Heidegger and had presided at his marriage to Elfride Petri in 1917.
2. Quoted in Casper, B., "Martin Heidegger und die Theologische Fakultät Freiburg 1909–1923" (1980), p. 541. "Ich glaube zu stark—vielleicht mehr als seine offiziellen Bearbeiter—empfunden zu haben, was das katholische Mittelalter an Werten in sich trägt u. von einer wahrhaften Auswertung sind wir noch weit entfernt. Meine religionsphänomenologischen Untersuchungen . . . (werden) das m. A. stark heranziehen."

concern Heidegger might have with Christian theology, in that it places him outside or beyond any real concern for the God of whom theologians speak? If Heidegger has by the time of his later work become an atheist, does this not decide in advance what he will have to say of God, so that his claims to the openness of the question of being foreclose any question of God?

In Heidegger's lecture courses from this period there are frequent sharp-tongued asides, exemplified in his comment that "a 'Christian philosophy' is a round square and a misunderstanding".[3] Five years later the comment is extended: "Square and circle are at least compatible in that they are both geometrical figures, while Christian faith and philosophy remain fundamentally different".[4] However, it is not faith and philosophy that are in opposition, but *Christian* faith and any attempt at a *Christian* philosophy. Heidegger's anti-Christian polemic sets into a new light three terms: faith, philosophy, and theology. I considered in chapters 1 and 2 questions concerning philosophy and theology; how is faith differentiated from these other two? This question lies at the heart of Heidegger's reading of the medieval authors.

Heidegger's critique of Christianity always relies on a distinction between faith and metaphysics. The question 'what is metaphysics?' leads to the question which overcomes metaphysics, the most original, the widest, deepest, and most self-displacingly-self-questioning question of Leibniz: "Why are there beings rather than nothing?"[5] Heidegger argued: "Anyone for whom the Bible is divine revelation and truth already has the answer to the question 'why is there anything at all and not rather nothing?' before

3. *Einführung in die Metaphysik* (GA40), p. 6. "Eine 'christliche Philosophie' ist ein hölzernes Eisen und ein Mißverständnis." It is, however, only the sharpness of voice that is new: the reference to round square appears in 1927 in the lecture *Phänomenologie und Theologie* (*Wegmarken* [GA9]), p. 66. This is the same lecture in which Heidegger makes it clear that, for him, faith is in the crucified Christ (p. 54). This is a clear example of how, so often in his writing, Heidegger hints at earlier moments in his work which inform what he is later trying to say.

4. *Der europäische Nihilismus* (*Nietzsche* [GA6.2]), p. 132. "Viereck und Kreis kommen noch darin überein, daß sie räumliche Gebilde sind, während christlicher Glaube und Philosophie abgründig verschieden bleiben."

5. Cf. *Einführung in die Metaphysik* (GA40), pp. 2–3. "Warum ist überhaupt Seiendes und nicht vielmehr Nichts?" This question (which concludes the lecture *Was ist Metaphysik?*) is investigated thoroughly in the 1935 lecture series *Einführung in die Metaphysik* (GA40) and forms the basis of Heidegger's last official lecture series at Freiburg in 1956, published as *Der Satz vom Grund* (GA10).

even asking the question, insofar as everything that is not itself God, is created through him. God himself 'is' as the increate creator".[6] This is again a
discussion of the *ens creatum*, but now considered from a different aspect.
Therefore Heidegger says that to posit God as increate creator is to disclose
God's essence: to decide what God *is*. Does this therefore mean that faith
and those who are faithful are closed off from asking the question of being?
No, because faith in the Bible as divine revelation and truth (which means
here truth as *doctrina*) is not faith as Heidegger understood it:

> Anyone who stands in the soil of such faith . . . can only act 'as if' . . . but
> on the other hand that faith, if it does not remain constantly in the pos-
> sibility of unfaith, is no faith, but only a convenience and a set-up to
> hold fast to a commonly accepted doctrine. That is neither faith nor
> questioning, but an indifference which can busy itself with everything,
> perhaps with a great show of interest even with faith as in much the
> same way they do with questioning.[7]

Faith defined as dogmatic teaching or biblical revelation as doctrinal truth is
the commonest, cheapest form of metaphysics. To illustrate his point,
Heidegger cites Nietzsche's taunt that "Christianity is Platonism for the
masses".[8] What is at issue is neither revelation nor even the Bible, but that
understanding of the Bible which renders it into a set of true propositions.
Biblical revelation is understood from within a correspondence theory of
truth: truth as the universally (because propositionally) true, independent
of it being true for me, my own. This is not relativism—it asks to what

---

6. *Einführung in die Metaphysik* (GA40), p. 5. "Wem z. B. die Bibel göttliche Offenbarung und Wahrheit ist, der hat vor allem Fragen der Frage 'Warum ist überhaupt
Seiendes und nicht vielmehr Nichts?' schon die Antwort: Das Seiende, soweit es nicht Gott
selbst ist, ist durch diesen geschaffen. Gott selbst 'ist' als der ungeschaffene Schöpfer."
   7. *Einführung in die Metaphysik* (GA40), p. 5. "Wer auf dem Boden solchen
Glaubens steht . . . kann nur so tun, als ob . . . aber andererseits ist jener Glaube, wenn
er sich nicht ständig der Möglichkeit des Unglaubens aussetzt, auch kein Glauben, sondern eine Bequemlichkeit und eine Verabredung mit sich, künftig an der Lehre als einem
irgendwie Überkommenen festzuhalten. Das ist dann weder Glauben noch Fragen, sondern Gleichgültigkeit, die sich nunmehr mit allem, vielleicht sogar sehr interessiert,
beschäftigen kann, mit dem Glauben ebenso wie mit dem Fragen."
   8. *Einführung in die Metaphysik* (GA40), p. 80. "Christentum ist Platonismus fürs
Volk", quoting the 1885 *Vorrede* to *Jenseits von Gut und Böse* (*Friedrich Nietzsche* [1999],
V), p. 11.

extent biblical revelation can be enowned to me: how do I receive it, and in receiving it, who do I become?

In contrast, Heidegger continues, faith, as determined to unfaith, is "a thinking and questioning working through of the Christian experiencing of the world, i.e., of faith. That is then theology", which cannot decide the question of being even before it has been asked, and which is therefore not a part of metaphysics.[9] Theology as *this* science of faith and the question of being may (but need not) occur together. The one neither abolishes the other, nor do they stand in opposition.[10]

Why and in what way is theology (normally understood) metaphysics? I have already considered how Aristotle and Plato use the term θεολογία and how for Aristotle this is first philosophy. For Heidegger, the intensification of that view in the subsequent Christianization of God (as increate creator), considered philosophically, decides in advance any answer to the question of being. The question of being, however, is the only question for philosophy to open up. Heidegger excludes any suggestion that the words 'in the beginning God created heaven and earth' are an answer to that questioning which is the question of being. He concludes: "Quite aside from whether these words from the Bible are true or false for faith, they can supply no answer to our question because they are in no way related to it".[11] To faith such questions are foolishness (a biblical point he repeats in 1949 in the introduction added to the lecture *Was ist Metaphysik?*).[12] For Heidegger the

---

9. *Einführung in die Metaphysik* (GA40), p. 6. "Eine denkend fragende Durcharbeitung der christlich erfahrenen Welt, d.h. des Glaubens. Das ist dann Theologie."

10. It is worth noting how very differently John Caputo interprets these and other remarks that are made in the lecture course *Einführung in die Metaphysik* ("Heidegger and Theology" [1993], esp. pp. 276, 278f.). Caputo does not seem to acknowledge the difference between Christian faith and Heidegger's denomination of Christianity as Christian doctrine or dogma, *die Kirchenlehre*, which for him is an attempt at a system of metaphysics. Consequently Caputo interprets Heidegger's hostility as toward both. This is not to justify Heidegger's words or actions, but rather to attempt to make sense of what distinctions were operating in his work. See also John Macquarrie's remarks concerning these passages in *Heidegger and Christianity* (1994), esp. pp. 54ff.

11. *Einführung in die Metaphysik* (GA40), p. 6. "Ganz abgesehen davon, ob dieser Satz der Bibel für den Glauben wahr oder unwahr ist, er kann überhaupt keine Antwort auf unsere Frage darstellen, weil er auf diese Frage keinen Bezug hat."

12. *Einleitung zu: 'Was ist Metaphysik?'* (*Wegmarken* [GA9]), p. 379, quoting I Corinthians 1:20. "Has God not made foolish the wisdom of this world?" ("οὐκὶ ἐμώρανεν ὁ θεὸς τὴν σοφίαν τοῦ κόσμον.")

question clearly involves the origin of beings, which metaphysically is understood to be the problem of causes (as I have already indicated in relation to Plato and discuss in relation to Aristotle). The passages here examined in the 1935 *Einführung* lectures that deal with God, faith, and theology come directly after a consideration of what Heidegger calls the 'origin'. Metaphysics either thinks God as first cause or correspondingly as ground. For this reason the very raising of the question of being which pushes toward overcoming metaphysics displaces understanding God as ground because it involves a leap which reveals the real meaning of the word origin: "We call such a leap, which opens up its own source, the original-source or origin, the finding of one's own ground".[13] This leap, therefore, puts me in question, it is a coming to the self (as a self-questioning).

Metaphysics begins by positing God as first cause, ground, highest being. That which is grounded, which is not-God, are created things. To create, therefore, is to ground. Heidegger notes that for the medievals: "The being of beings consists in their being-created by God (*omne ens est ens creatum*)".[14] The death of God, however, supplants God-as-ground with self-grounding. This may alter the configuration to the metaphysical God of grounds, but it does not alter the configuration of ground as such. Ground is therefore established through the assertion of subjectivity, in which ground is understood through the certitude of being-human (*ens certum*),[15] and which Nietzsche represents in his doctrine of the eternal recurrence of the same:

As an ontology, even Nietzsche's metaphysics is at the same time theology, although it seems far removed from scholastic metaphysics. The ontology

---

13. *Einführung in die Metaphysik* (GA40), p. 5. "Einen solchen sich als Grund erspringenden Sprung nennen wir gemäß der echten Bedeutung des Wortes einen Ursprung: das Sich-den-Grund-er-springen."

14. *Der europäische Nihilismus* (*Nietzsche* [(GA6.2)]), p. 132. "Das Sein des Seienden besteht in seinem Geschaffensein durch Gott (omne ens est ens creatum)."

15. Cf. Descartes, R., *Meditationes de prima philosophia* (*Descartes*, VII, 1996), p. 27. (Second meditation) "To cogitate? Here I find: it is cogitation; this alone cannot be rent from me. I am, I exist, it is certain." ("Cogitare? Hîc invenio: cogitatio est; haec sola a me divelli nequit. Ego sum, ego existo, certum est.") See *Der europäische Nihilismus* (*Nietzsche* [(GA6.2)]), p. 166. "In the dominating realm of [the] subject, *ens* is no longer *ens creatum*, it is *ens certum, indubitandum, vere cogitatum, 'cogitatio'*." ("Im Herrschaftsbereich dieses subiectum ist das ens nicht mehr ens creatum, es ist ens certum: indubitandum: vere cogitatum: 'cogitatio'.") See also Heidegger's discussion of *ens certum* and Descartes in *Hegels Begriff der Erfahrung*, p. 147 f.

of beings as such thinks *essentia* as will to power. Such ontology thinks the *existentia* of beings as such and as a whole theologically as the eternal recurrence of the same. Such metaphysical theology is of course a negative theology of a peculiar kind. Its negativity is revealed in the expression 'God is dead.' This is an expression not of atheism, but of ontotheology, in just that metaphysics in which nihilism proper is fulfilled.[16]

Heidegger explicitly discounts that this is a genuine atheism, but rather, that the assertion that God is dead is in fact a theological assertion.

## THE 1951 ZURICH SEMINAR

It should be clear from what has preceded that for Heidegger the history of being can in a certain sense be construed as unfolding a history of God, though of God as thought metaphysically, and therefore not the God of faith. A critical juncture in this history is the way in which God is thought of in medieval metaphysics. At a seminar of the Old Bultmannians— Bultmann's former pupils—in Zurich in 1951, when Heidegger is asked "May being and God be posited as identical?",[17] he replies, referring specifically to Aquinas, "God and being is not identical . . . being and God are not identical, and I would never attempt to think the essence of God through being . . . if I were yet to write a theology—to which I sometimes feel inclined—then the word 'being' would not occur in it".[18] There is no syntactical error here,

---

16. *Die seinsgeschichtliche Bestimmung des Nihilismus* (*Nietzsche* [GA6.2]), p. 348 (a text composed in 1944–46 and published in 1961). "Auch Nietzsches Metaphysik ist als Ontologie, obzwar sie weit von der Schulmetaphysik entfernt zu sein scheint, zugleich Theologie. Die Ontologie des Seienden als solche denkt die essentia als den Willen zur Macht. Diese Ontologie denkt die existentia des Seienden als solchen im Ganzen theologisch als die ewige Wiederkehr des Gleichen. Diese metaphysische Theologie ist allerdings eine negative Theologie eigener Art. Ihre Negativität zeigt sich in dem Wort: Gott ist tot. Das ist nicht das Wort des Atheismus, sondern das Wort der Onto-Theologie derjenigen Metaphysik, in der sich der eigentliche Nihilismus vollendet."
17. *Seminare* (GA15), p. 436. "Dürfen Sein und Gott identisch gesetzt werden?" For the full text of the *Reply* see the appendix to this book, p. 291.
18. *Seminare* (GA15), p. 436. "Gott und Sein ist nicht identisch . . . Sein und Gott sind nicht identisch, und ich würde niemals versuchen, das Wesen Gottes durch das Sein zu denken . . . wenn ich noch eine Theologie schreiben würde, wozu es mich manchmal reizt, dann dürfte in ihr das Wort 'Sein' nicht vorkommen."

and the move from *is* to *are* is the very movement of Heidegger's thinking through the separation of being and God from their metaphysically posited togetherness.

Heidegger's brief reply in Zurich is one of the most enigmatic and complex of Heidegger's utterances and at the same time one of the few remarks he makes about the most central question of his relation to theology. The question really asks whether Heidegger is either still thinking through a province laid out by medieval thought and ancient cosmology or whether, exactly as in Löwith's accusation, Heidegger had supplanted God with being. As I have just demonstrated from Heidegger's interpretation of Nietzsche, Heidegger's criticism of nihilism is that it never attains to a genuine atheism precisely because it is the place where being, nihilistically occurring as subjectivity, supplants the place that God has come to occupy in philosophy: the metaphysical place of grounds. To ask the question of being in a genuine way, however, is already to have asked it atheistically, therefore, already to have separated the very being-together of God and being: neither God nor *Dasein* have a ground. The question of being, as Heidegger understands it, can only appear at all because it appears atheistically, as finite, the being of being-human which has nothing to do with God. The questioner's question, from the outset, has collapsed God back into being (both thought metaphysically) just even to see the question as a possible question. Or rather, Heidegger might say, the questioner has entirely failed to ask *any* question concerning being at all.

When the questioner names being, he asks about it within the province of metaphysics and ontotheology. When Heidegger says being, he says it as already in a questioning relation to the way it is thought in metaphysics, outside ontotheology, though taking ontotheology into account. Heidegger and his interlocutor say the same (word) and speak of different things. Heidegger knows this; the questioner does not. The riddle of the reply is precisely Heidegger's attempt to make the questioner ask a question about *him*self, not about a question for Heidegger. The riddle of the answer is a device, at once pedagogical—think again!—and disciplinary: think more thoughtfully! Think yourself into what *you* are asking! Heidegger's reply says that he is neither thinking through a province laid out by the medievals nor supplanting God with being, but thinking through what laid out the Middle Ages as a province for thought and what goes on laying out thinking. Indeed, Heidegger explicitly conceives what follows the thinking of the Middle Ages as remaining within the province laid out for it, in stark contrast to his own view.

In the *Einführung* lectures (to which I referred earlier) he says that "the Christian Middle Ages translated themselves into modern philosophy, which moves within the conceptual world of the Middle Ages",[19] this despite the fact that they are supposed to have been long overcome. Heidegger's atheism is precisely the genuine overcoming of the Middle Ages, not by exceeding them, but by inquiring into the originary ground of what made them and modern philosophy possible, the being of being-human. If we are to consider his reply in Zurich in 1951, we must consider it in this light.

In the reply, Heidegger speaks of the essence of God while wishing to exclude from the discussion of this essence the word *being*, by which he means the being of Dasein. Heidegger is saying here nothing other than that hitherto all theology has been ontotheology, that God and being are the same—metaphysics—and that he, Heidegger, would not speak of the essence of God in the terms of the being of *Dasein*. For Heidegger to undertake theology would be to say (before even beginning to undertake a theology) that the essence of God and God's existence are not the same when considered philosophically by *Dasein*. This does not disbar the word *being* from theological discourse, but sets it in its proper place. In this sense the separating of the thought of the essence of God from any proofs or discussion of the philosophical structure of God's existence is the same thing as the overcoming of metaphysics.

At the beginning of the reply, Heidegger says:

> I am asked this question almost every fortnight, because it (understandably) disconcerts theologians, and because it relates to the Europeanization of history, which already began in the Middle Ages, through Aristotle's and Plato's penetration into theology, specifically the New Testament. This is a process whose immensity cannot be overestimated.[20]

---

19. *Einführung in die Metaphysik* (GA40), p. 11. "Das christliche Mittelalter . . . setzte sich über in die neuzeitliche Philosophie, die sich in der Begriffswelt des Mittelalters bewegt."

20. *Seminare* (GA15), p. 436. "Diese Frage wird mir fast alle vierzehn Tage gestellt, weil sie die Theologen (begreiflicherweise) beunruhigt, und weil sie zusammenhängt mit der Europäisierung der Geschichte, die schon im Mittelalter beginnt, nämlich dadurch, daß Aristoteles und Plato in die Theologie eingedrungen sind, respektive in das Neue Testament. Das ist ein Prozeß, den man sich gar nicht ungeheuer genug vorstellen kann."

It is clear from this alone that in the question of theology, and most specifically faith, it is only Christian theology that is at issue. The believing referred to here is Christian believing. The question therefore concerns the way in which the Greek conception of God, at the very inception of metaphysics in Plato and Aristotle, is driven into Christian thinking (above all by the medievals) and turned into the key for interpreting the New Testament.

What Heidegger brings to the fore is the way in which the Greek ontology, which privileges the movable over the immovable as a way of understanding God, becomes a way to articulate the God of faith. This very process, in the Christianization of Europe, is how the whole of Europe also becomes dominated by the thinking of the Greeks, although only because the θεολογία of Plato and Aristotle is conflated into the reflection on faith in the Christian God, even when the theologies of faith and philosophy are named apart.[21]

There is in the reply a deliberate play on the words believing and thinking. Heidegger begins by saying that faith and the thinking of being have no need of each other.[22] The next sentences begin in turn, first, "I think . . ." and next, "I believe . . ." In what follows it becomes clear that thinking points away from determining the essence of God because thinking as such is thinking the thinking of *Dasein*. Thinking, in its very structure, has nothing to do with God's appearing—God does not appear through my thinking about thinking. This is again to direct reference to Aristotle's understanding of the divine as a "thinking on thinking".[23]

Thinking here is concerned with self-thinking (αὐτὸν ἄρα νοεῖ), which at the same time for Aristotle is most divine (θειότατον), without change (οὐ μεταβάλλει), and without place (ἄτοπον). As I have already demonstrated, for Heidegger the Aristotelian understanding of being displaces the being of being human to the being of being-divine, precisely by displacing the fundamental working out of being (through place, τόπος) and time (through change, κίνησις) to the immovability of being, which is divine. Heidegger, atheistically, simply refuses to refer this thinking about thinking to divinity. Through methodological atheism, Heidegger unfolds

---

21. Aquinas, *Summa Theologiae*, Ia, q. 1, a. 1, resp. ad 2 (see p. 11 above).
22. What happens when faith is explained solely in terms of metaphysics and is therefore determined by and out of the unfolding of the history of being, is explained in greater depth by Heidegger in his *Die Metaphysik als Geschichte des Seins* (*Nietzsche* [GA6.2]), pp. 399–458.
23. Aristotle, *Metaphysics*, XII, XII (1074b35). "νοήσεως νόησις".

this displacement to return *Dasein*'s thinking of itself to its originary structures. Thinking is therefore not something proper to the divine but to the being of *Dasein:* it is a self-concern, though in the broadest sense.

In his mention of Luther in relation to the separation of thinking and believing in the reply, Heidegger points again to Aristotle: it is specifically the early Luther's radical critique of the presence of Aristotelian metaphysics that had drawn Heidegger to Luther in the first place. The whole of the reply is, in a sense, the recapitulation of Heidegger's Marburg period, when he most closely engaged with theology, represented in many cases by those present in Zurich when he makes this reply, and which culminated in the 1927 lecture *Phänomenologie und Theologie.* Once again, the early and later Heidegger are shown to tie each other together in their concerns.

What of the next sentence, beginning 'I believe'? Heidegger's contrast of thinking and believing separates the Aristotelian and Platonic understanding of divinity from the New Testament understanding of the God revealed in Christ (and, given Heidegger's concerns at Marburg, above all with the early Pauline texts). Believing points toward that place where God appears within the dimension of being, which Heidegger further qualifies by adding, "insofar as [the experience and manifestness of God] meet with humanity".[24] The implication would be that, for Christian believing, this *insofar* refers to the man Jesus and the faith of the early church (exemplified in the preaching of Paul), the very things Heidegger indicates, along with a mention of prophetic Judaism and the Greek experience of the divine in the *Nachwort* to the 1949 lecture *Das Ding* (itself a reply to a question), which we have met in chapter 4.[25]

Faith determines *Dasein* with regard to God. Thinking is self-disclosed atheistically, discovering itself not to be a divine activity, but something proper to *Dasein*. Its historical meaning in the history of being is precisely disclosed through methodological atheism. Thinking yields its own history as a coming to itself in both appropriating and pointing toward the overcoming of metaphysics. In this sense thinking thinks only *Dasein*, the event (and here event is meant in the full sense of the last chapter) of thought. Believing points toward the *what the event discloses* of God's revelation, when the event concerns the revelation of God: in this case, to God's appearing in the realm of being, insofar as the experience and manifestness of God meet

24. *Seminare* (GA15), p. 437. "Sofern [die Erfahrung Gottes und seiner Offenbarkeit] dem Menschen begegnet."
25. *Nachwort* to *Das Ding* (*Vorträge und Aufsätze* [GA7]), p. 177. See p. 117 above.

with humanity. Thinking cannot determine in advance the God who will be met, who might appear, insofar as God's experience and manifestness do, in the realm of being. In this sense, God appears only within the ontological difference, the being of beings, the being of *Dasein*.

Faith, considered from the point of view of the Christian New Testament, is the character of the disclosure of God's appearing.[26] The man Jesus is known as the Christ through faith, not philosophically, let alone scientifically.[27] Faith is the mode of disclosure of God in the being of beings: it says nothing about the being of beings as such (which is the concern of thinking), but is intrinsic to the possibilities made available by the being of beings. In this sense Heidegger says "faith has no need of the thinking of being".[28] So the separation of faith and thinking precisely opens up an atheism toward attempting to explain God metaphysically. Thinking opens up a space in which theology as reflection on faith can clarify and correct its reflection. Above all, this space is not foundational, which means it does not determine the outcome of *what* is to be thought, only a *how* as a reflection on experience, on a content given for thought itself to reflect on.

In the Zurich reply, Heidegger adds: "I have asked an old Jesuit friend of mine to show me the place in Thomas Aquinas where he says what *'esse'* specifically means and what the proposition means that says *'Deus est suum esse'*. I have to this day received no answer".[29] In the text to which he refers, Aquinas responds: "Therefore God is his own existence, and not merely his own essence".[30] Aquinas believes this is something that must be demonstrated, namely that the existence and essence of God are the same. It is clear therefore that Heidegger regards Aquinas's position as determined in consequence of metaphysics and therefore ontotheology.

---

26. Faith, in this sense, is not proper to the meaning of the appearing of the gods in Greek thinking, above all in Greek mythology. For Heidegger's full discussion of this see *Parmenides* (GA54), pp. 161–168.

27. Cf. Matthew 16:13–16. The reply to the question "who do men say I am" and "who do you say I am" is a disclosure of faith. Peter's reply: "You are the Christ" in its structure is an event for Peter's being, an *Ereignis*, but it is at the same time a disclosure strictly in virtue of Peter's faith.

28. *Seminare* (GA15), p. 437. "Der Glaube hat das Denken des Seins nicht nötig."

29. *Seminare* (GA15), p. 436. "Ich habe einen mir wohlgesinnten Jesuiten gebeten, mir die Stellen bei Thomas von Aquin zu zeigen, wo gesagt sei, was 'esse' eigentlich bedeute und der Satz besage: Deus est suum esse. Ich habe bis heute noch keine Antwort."

30. *Summa Theologiae*, Ia, q. 3, a. 4, resp. "Est igitur Deus suum esse, et non solum sua essentia."

What is the character of this determination? I have indicated how Heidegger articulates a number of the Scholastic determinations of *esse*, being, and *ens*, beings, and *ens commune*, being as a whole (*das Seiende im Ganzen*). There is, however, a further determination requiring explication, *esse commune*. In the passage I have cited from the Zurich reply there is a hint that Heidegger is well aware that Aquinas wished to avoid subsuming God under the category of *ens commune* while still wishing to think of God as *summum ens* and that this problem is as much a problem for faith as it is for metaphysics, when he says "I believe that being can never be thought as the ground and essence of God".[31] Heidegger is only too aware that Aquinas insists that God alone knows God in God's self, and that human being knows God only in God's effects. Heidegger remains faithful to that insight, while disentangling it from its metaphysical manifestation. Construed as an understanding that arises out of faith, it is, for Heidegger, without difficulty. Construed philosophically, it is impossible. It is, however, an insight of faith, especially in Aquinas.

## Return to the Question of Analogy

In Heidegger's Zurich reply we have, however, only a hint of his understanding of Aquinas. What happens in his discussion of the province of thought laid out in the Middle Ages is made more explicit in the 1931 lecture course on division Θ of Aristotle's *Metaphysics*. Here Heidegger makes explicit the problem of analogy in its formulation and shows both how Aquinas resolves a question concerning being and how this resolution results in an impasse and an indeterminacy. He says:

> In the Middle Ages, the *analogia entis* which nowadays has sunk again to the level of a catchword, played a role, not as a question of being, but as a welcomed means of formulating a religious conviction in philosophical terms. The God of Christian belief, although the creator and preserver of the world, is altogether different and separate from it; but he is being (*Seiende*) in the highest sense, the *summum ens;* creatures infinitely different from him are nevertheless also being (*seiend*),

---

31. *Seminare* (GA15), p. 436. "Ich glaube, daß das Sein niemals als Grund und Wesen von Gott gedacht werden kann."

*ens finitum.* How can *ens infinitum* and *ens finitum* both be named *ens*, both be thought in the same concept, 'being'? Does the *ens* hold good only *aequivoce* or *univoce*, or even *analogice?* They rescued themselves from this dilemma with the help of analogy, which is not a solution but a formula.[32]

Here in 1931 Heidegger carries out a distinction between the question of being and the God of Christian faith in exactly the same way as he later does in Zurich. The appeal to analogy in some sense safeguards faith as such in that the appeal to analogy is not truly a statement of metaphysics; it is merely playing a role. The appeal to analogy both represents and, as this representation, also forestalls, determining the God of faith metaphysically, in which a purely univocal understanding of being, *ens commune*— beings in general—would otherwise subsume and determine the essence of God.

How (for Heidegger at least) might Aquinas have achieved this? Which means: how does analogy stand with *esse?* For Aquinas, the answer is by an appeal not to *ens* but *esse commune.* Aquinas indicates in the *Summa* that there are numerous ways that one thing can be like another and lists them. Similitude to God, however, is of a different order to similitude between things, and is similitude specifically and only in virtue of a thing's being. This kind of similitude is "only according to some sort of analogy, as existence is common to all. In this way all created beings are like God as the first and universal principle of all being".[33] In this sense beings are in virtue of being-caused, and not beings but being-caused is in virtue of the being of God. *Esse commune* is therefore, when understood in relation to God, understood

32. *Aristoteles, Metaphysik* Θ *1–3* (GA33), p. 46. "Im Mittelalter hat die analogia entis—die heute wieder als Schlagwort verkauft wird—eine Rolle gespielt, aber nicht als Seinsfrage, sondern als ein willkommenes Mittel dazu, eine Glaubensüberzeugung mit philosophischen Ausdrücken zu formulieren. Der Gott des christlichen Glaubens, obzwar Schöpfer und Erhalter der Welt, ist schlechthin von dieser verschieden und getrennt; er ist aber das im höchsten Sinne Seiende, das summum ens; seiend sind aber auch die von ihm unendlich verschiedenen Geschöpfe, das ens finitum. Wie kann ens infinitum und ens finitum beides ens genannt, beides im selben Begriff 'Sein' begriffen werden? Gilt das ens nur aequivoce oder univoce, oder eben analogice? Man hat sich aus der Schwierigkeit gerettet mit Hilfe der Analogie, die keine Lösung ist, sondern eine Formel."

33. *Summa Theologiae,* Ia, q. 4, a. 3, resp. "Secundum aliqualem analogiam, sicut ipsum esse est commune omnibus. Et hoc modo illa quae sunt a Deo, assimilantur ei inquantum sunt entia, ut primo et universali principio totius esse."

as *esse analogice*. In relation to things it is not their logical unity (*ens commune*) but their common being-caused. This is in fact the *ens creatum* at work. In his *Commentary on the Divine Names* (of pseudo-Dionysius) Aquinas makes a number of distinctions concerning *esse commune*. In the first place, *esse commune* is not a merely mental or logical construct; it really inheres in things.[34] Secondly, created beings depend on *esse commune*, but God does not; rather the reverse: *esse commune* depends on God. In this sense beings are not grounded in God, but beings are grounded in being-caused, which is in consequence of God, thereby protecting God from strict dependency on beings and separating beings from a univocal dependence on God. Rudi te Velde notes:

> *esse commune* coincides with created being. The *commune* is added in order to distinguish the being that all beings have in common from the divine being that is self-subsistent and therefore radically distinct from all other things. The reason for making this distinction is to exclude the pantheistic error which might arise from the thesis that God is 'being' without any addition.[35]

Finally, although things participate in *esse commune*, God does not participate in *esse commune* but rather the reverse, *esse commune* is that way in which created things participate in God. Fran O'Rourke's extensive investigation into *esse commune* and its dependence as a formulation on Dionysius concludes: "It would appear evident that . . . *ipsum esse commune* is identical with St. Thomas' notion of *actus essendi*, the intimate act of existing which is at the heart of every reality".[36]

---

34. John Caputo, in treating this subject, appears to confuse the logical concept of *ens commune* with *esse commune*. (Caputo, J., *Heidegger and Aquinas* [1982]) He says on p. 141: "*Esse commune* is a universal constructed by the mind in the light of actual beings.") Fran O'Rourke shows decisively from a multiplicity of Aquinas's texts that this is not the case (O'Rourke, F., *Pseudo-Dionysius and the Metaphysics of Aquinas* [1992], p. 144 f.): "It exists primarily within the multiplicity, not as an abstract unity but as a concrete perfection realized differently in the individual members of the many . . . *esse inhaerens.*"
35. te Velde, R., *Participation and Substantiality in Thomas Aquinas* (1995), p. 188 f. Te Velde supplies an extended discussion of the problematic term *esse commune* in chapter 10.
36. O'Rourke, F., *Pseudo-Dionysius and the Metaphysics of Aquinas* (1992), p. 143 f. His whole discussion may be found in chapter 6, "Dionysian Elements in Aquinas' Notion of Being."

Earlier in the 1931 *Aristotle* lectures Heidegger had argued that analogy as a formula is also a stringent aporia, which is no answer to the being-question, but actually the mark of its not being asked at all, and that it represents the "impasse in which ancient philosophy, and along with it all subsequent philosophy right up to today, is enmeshed".[37] In this sense it is both a figure for metaphysics as a history and a figure of Christianity's lack of need of metaphysics for faith. It is also a figure for the way that both the ancient ontology and its developments are incapable of asking about the being of being-human, because they displace this question into a question concerning the being of God. Precisely because of this displacement, the question itself becomes an impasse, because the quite proper refusal of the rendering-transparent of the divine essence (the assertion that God is known properly only to God's self, and so cannot be interrogated transparently by us) becomes the condition under which *any* question about being may be asked (because God alone is true being). Analogy therefore becomes a way of interrogating the being of God with respect to asking questions about created being. Questions asked analogically are, therefore, fraught with limitation. They can never attain the openness of questioning myself.

For Heidegger, however, the being to whom the question of being properly belongs is not one to which no answer must be returned, God, but *Dasein*, the being for whom the question of being properly is an issue. Why can we return no answer to the question about the being of God? Because, as we shall see in later chapters, strictly speaking God is not a being, so even the possibility of God's self-inquiry is nonsensical, something the medievals understood intuitively, though as an issue of faith rather than philosophically. The question of being therefore becomes an impasse precisely because of the way the ancient theology gets taken up into the Christian articulation of *esse*. As an impasse, however, analogy allows a matter of faith to be articulated in philosophical terms.

Is this the same as saying that with the notion of analogy Aquinas frees God from being, *esse?* To some extent at least, this question asks about the sense in which Aquinas's and Aristotle's understanding of analogy are the same. Heidegger pointed out elsewhere that the inquiry into causes is primarily guided, not by metaphysics, but by faith, because faith dictates that

---

37. *Aristoteles, Metaphysik* Θ *1–3* (GA33), p. 46. "(Die) Ausweglosigkeit, in der das antike Philosophieren und damit alles nachfolgende bis heute eingemauert ist."

God as *causa prima* is also creator of the world.[38] In this sense, even the question of causes is one guided by faith, not metaphysics. He concludes: "Thus *prima philosophia* is knowledge of the highest cause, of God as the creator—a train of thought which was completely alien to Aristotle in this form".[39]

How then should Heidegger's reading of Aquinas be understood? For Heidegger, Aquinas's understanding of God is determined out of the historical unfolding of metaphysics but is not finally determined by metaphysics. If Heidegger demands to be shown what *esse* actually means in Aquinas, he is being ironical, because for Heidegger *esse commune* and *esse analogice* (he refers to it as *analogia entis*) are already indeterminate at the point where Aquinas receives them and applies them as a solution to the problem of being in medieval metaphysics.[40] The indeterminacy is not in the counterposition of God as *ipsum esse subsistens* and *ens infinitum* with *ens finitum* but that any analogical relationship between beings and God is already indeterminate. *Esse* is indeterminate in advance of Aquinas, and Aquinas relies on this indeterminacy for the sake of faith. The irony is still more emphasized in Heidegger's reply in Zurich as a question to a Jesuit to explicate a Dominican's thinking, as this understanding of Aquinas is achieved through the incontrovertibly metaphysical position of the Jesuit Suárez.[41] Heidegger's suggestion is that what comes after Aquinas is decisive for modern metaphysics, not

38. Cf. *Die Grundbegriffe der Metaphysik* (GA29/30), p. 71f. "Something is known in the highest sense whenever I go back to its *ultimate cause*, to the *causa prima*. This is, however, according to what is said through faith, God as creator of the world" (author's italics). ("Im höchsten Sinne ist etwas erkannt, wenn ich auf die *letzte Ursache* zurückgehe, auf die causa prima. Diese aber ist, wie durch den Glauben gesagt wird, Gott als Schöpfer der Welt.")

39. *Die Grundbegriffe der Metaphysik* (GA29/30), p. 72. "Also ist die prima philosophia Erkenntnis der höchsten Ursache, Gottes als des Schöpfers—ein Gedankengang, der Aristoteles in dieser Form vollkommen fernlag."

40. *Analogia entis* has the feeling always of having been Aquinas's own words. It cannot be found in Aquinas: von Balthasar attributes it exclusively to the early twentieth-century German theologian Erich Przywara and says it has no history prior to him. Cf. von Balthasar, *Karl Barth: Darstellung und Deutung seiner Theologie*, chapter 4; Przywara, E. *Analogia Entis* (1962).

41. One might make the accusation here that I am simply reading too much into the text. That I am not, however, is indicated by Heidegger's own comparison of Aquinas and Suárez in the 1929 lecture course *Die Grundbegriffe der Metaphysik* (GA29/30). Here (p. 77f.) he says "for the development of modern metaphysics ... Aquinas, and medieval

Aquinas himself. As we have already seen Heidegger point out, Aristotle's νοῦς "has not the slightest thing to do with the God of Thomas".[42]

Of greater interest should be why Aquinas appeals to the metaphysical conception of being, *esse,* in the first place. What understanding of being led the medievals to want to chain being to God? The answer (which I can no more than sketch out here) has entirely to do with the intellection (*intelligere,* νοεῖν) of being. This is somewhat clearer if the dispute between Caputo and O'Rourke is recalled concerning the meaning of *esse commune.* While Caputo argued *esse commune* was purely an intellection, O'Rourke demonstrated that while it can be an intellection, it also must and does refer to the reality of beings; it is an *esse inhaerens.* For Dionysius, the relation between knowing and God is clearly explicated in chapter 7 of *De Divinis Nominibus.* The question is how God is to be approached. Dionysius stresses that God is not known in God's nature. God is not one of the things that are, God cannot be understood, words cannot contain God, and no name can lay hold of God. In this sense God 'is' beyond being. Dionysius adds: "the most divine knowledge of God, that which comes through unknowing, is achieved in a union far beyond mind, when the mind turns away from all things, even from itself".[43] I do not want to underestimate the force of Dionysius's notion of "beyond being" (ὑπὲρ πάντα τὰ ὄντα, ὑπερουσίος). O'Rourke interprets Dionysius's use of the term non-being (οὐκ ὄντων) in a way guided by Maximus: "The interpretation of non-being as referring to God and to formless matter is generally espoused by Dionysius' commentators and would appear to be correct".[44] This is confusing. When applied to God, non-being can be a figure for beyond-being, but not in the sense of non-being as formless matter. This is confirmed in

---

philosophy in the sense of High Scholasticism, are important only to a lesser extent . . . direct influence was exercised by the Spanish Jesuit Franz Suárez." ("Für die Entwicklung der neuzeitlichen Metaphysik . . . (kommt) nur zum geringen Teil *Thomas* und die mittelalterliche Philosophie im Sinne der Hochscholastik in Betracht. Unmittelbaren Einfluß . . . hat . . . der spanische Jesuit *Franz Suárez* [ausgeübt].")

42. *Logik* (GA21), p. 123. "Der νοῦς . . . [hat] mit dem Gott des Thomas nicht das mindeste zu tun."

43. Pseudo-Dionysius, *Corpus Dionysiacum* (1990), I, 198, II 12–13. "Καὶ ἔστιν αὖθις ἡ Θειοτάτη τοῦ Θεοῦ γνῶσις, ἡ δι᾽ ἀγνωσίας γινωσκομένη κατὰ τὴν ὑπὲρ νοῦν ἕνωσιν, ὁτά ὁ νοῦς, τῶν ὄντων πάντων ἀποστάς, ἔπειτα καὶ ἑαυτὸν ἀφεὶς . . ."

44. O'Rourke, F., *Pseudo-Dionysius and the Metaphysics of Aquinas* (1992), p. 82.

the *Mystica Theologia* when he says that God (as cause) "falls neither within the predicate of non-being nor of being".[45] God is unknowable because God does not exist; God exceeds existence.

Aquinas concurs with this insofar as what is at issue is finite knowledge of God. He considers the objection that God is nonexistent and beyond existence, "as Dionysius says".[46] He replies that God exists as "above all that exists"[47] and is in this sense alone non-existent. Hence it follows not that God cannot be known, but that God exceeds every kind of knowledge. Still more important, to know and to be are the same: "everything is knowable according as it is actual".[48] God is comprehendible absolutely, but only in proportion to any particular finite being's capacity to know. God therefore as infinite alone knows God's self. God alone is omniscient so that no creature can have the knowledge God has of God's self. The assertion that God is *ipsum esse* is in part a defense of the (metaphysical) attributes of *summum ens* and *causa omnium*. Dionysius, in contrast, seeks only to show that God is the cause of all that is. In this sense, Dionysius's position, like Aquinas's, is also in consequence of the language of metaphysics, though through appeal to τὸ ἀγαθόν, rather than *summum ens*.

O'Rourke notes "whereas for Dionysius it is a hindrance to our discovery of God that human knowledge is oriented towards finite beings, this for Aquinas is the very foundation of our natural disclosure of God. Through the notion of being, and via its analogous value, our certitude of his existence is existentially grounded".[49] Aquinas, unlike Dionysius, makes no appeal to un-knowing, as leading to un-being. Nevertheless, each is using the language of metaphysics for the sake of faith, though construed slightly differently.

What is Heidegger's understanding of the grounding of finite predications infinitely in and of God? To answer this question it is necessary to turn to his consideration of Aristotle's discussion of δύναμις in the *Metaphysics,*

---

45. Pseudo-Dionysius, *Corpus Dionysiacum* (1990), II, 150. "οὐδέ τι τῶν οὐκ ὄντων, οὐδέ τι τῶν ὄντων ἐστίν."
46. *Summa Theologiae,* Ia, q. 12, a. 1 ad 3. "Sed Deus non est existens, sed supra existentia, ut dicit Dionysius."
47. *Summa Theologiae,* Ia, q. 12, a. 1 resp. ad 3. "Deus non sic dicitur non existens, quasi nullo modo sit existens: sed quia est supra omne existens, inquantum est suum esse."
48. *Summa Theologiae,* Ia, q. 12, a. 1. resp. "Cum unumquodque sit cognoscibile secundum quod est in actu."
49. O'Rourke, F., *Pseudo-Dionysius and the Metaphysics of Aquinas* (1992), p. 56.

where he analyzes "the inner essential togetherness of withdrawal and not-ness to the essence of force".[50] This he names as finitude. He adds:

> Where there are force and power, there is finitude. Hence God is not powerful and 'all-powerfulness' (omnipotence) is, properly thought, a concept that dissolves like all its companions into thin air and the unthinkable. Or otherwise, if God is powerful, God is finite and in any case something other than that which is thought in the common representation of God who can do anything and so is belittled to an ordinary essence.[51]

Here, as we have met it before, is the answer to the question whether God and being can ever be the same or thought in any kind of equation for Heidegger. Being itself is finite. To think God in terms of being is to impose limit and finitude on God. Heidegger had said earlier in the same lecture course that "Meister Eckhart . . . says God 'is' not at all because 'being' is a finite predicate and absolutely cannot be said of God".[52]

Heidegger's critique of theology can best be understood as a destructuring of the attempt to establish the existence of God as first cause. As I have already indicated, metaphysically, God is variously the cause or ground of beings. Heidegger uses for the metaphysical figure of God as first cause Spinoza's and Suárez's phrase *causa sui*.[53] In *Zur Sache des Denkens* he understands this phrase as "that theological moment of metaphysics, which consists in the fact that the *summum ens* as *causa sui* accomplishes the grounding

50. *Aristoteles, Metaphysik* Θ *1–3* (GA33), p. 158. "Die innere Wesenszugehörigkeit des Entzugs und der Nichtigkeit zum Wesen der Kraft."

51. *Aristoteles, Metaphysik* Θ *1–3* (GA33), p. 158. "Wo Kraft und Macht, da Endlichkeit. Daher ist Gott nicht mächtig und 'Allmacht' ist, recht gedacht, ein Begriff, der wie alle seine Genossen sich in Dunst auflöst und nicht zu denken ist. Oder aber, wenn der Gott mächtig ist, dann ist er endlich und jedenfalls etwas anderes als das, was die gemeine Vorstellung von Gott denkt, der alles kann und so zu einem Allerweltswesen herabgewürdigt wird."

52. *Aristoteles, Metaphysik* Θ *1–3* (GA33), p. 46. "Meister Eckhart sagt: Gott 'ist' überhaupt nicht, weil 'Sein' ein endliches Prädikat ist und von Gott gar nicht gesagt werden kann." Heidegger notes this is the thinking of the early Eckhart.

53. Cf. Descartes, R., *Meditationes de prima philosophia* (*Descartes*, VII, 1996), p. 49. (Third meditation). In *Zur Sache des Denkens* (GA14, p. 36) Heidegger actually attributes the phrase *causa sui* to the 24 *Metaphysical Theses* of Leibniz which he lists at the end of *Die Metaphysik als Geschichte des Seins* (*Nietzsche* [GA6.2]), p. 454.

of all beings as such".⁵⁴ Elsewhere he describes *causa sui* as the metaphysical representation of the being of beings. Being as such (*das Sein*) is concealed in favor of the beingness (*Seiendheit*) of beings (*die Seiende*) conceded solely as God.⁵⁵ Here the ontological difference is again concealed, because it is made to refer to God and not to the being of being-human, *Dasein*. For Heidegger, being can never ground individual beings. Indeed, the being of beings, the ontological difference, is understood variously as an abyss and as the inner finitude of beings. Being itself is, in its belonging together with the nothing, finite and finitude.⁵⁶

It would be the crudest error to conceive Aquinas's elaboration of ontological difference as between God (as an infinite being-in-general) and finite beings. This is in contradistinction to the strictly metaphysical positions of Descartes, Leibniz, etc., where the ontological difference is posited in exactly this way. As I indicated, it is precisely to prevent this error that Aquinas employs the term *esse commune,* though it relies on an impasse. The ontological difference in Aquinas must be understood as that difference represented by the distinction between *esse commune,* being in general, and any given *ens,* or individual being. On this basis, does Heidegger understand Aquinas to have evaded metaphysics? No, because *esse commune* as far as the being of individual finite beings is concerned operates rather as a mark of the impasse of analogy through beingness (*Seiendheit*) and so is enmeshed in the language of God as *ens creatum.* Is Aquinas's position strictly metaphysical? Not really.

Whereas it can be argued that Dionysius and Aquinas used the *language* of metaphysics to work out an understanding of God which in fact depended on faith, with those who followed Aquinas the question of the nature of God comes to be worked out solely as metaphysics. Aquinas continues to maintain that nothing can be said (known) concerning the essence of God in itself: God and God's essence are known only in a very limited sense through God's effects (i.e., in creation). This means that insofar as Aquinas inquires into God through an inquiry into being, *esse,* being is still

54. *Zur Sache des Denkens* (GA14), p. 36. "Das theologische Moment der Metaphysik [ist] gemeint, dies also, daß das summum ens als causa sui die Begründung alles Seienden als solchen leistet."

55. *Identität und Differenz* (GA11), p. 51.

56. In this sense being and its belonging together with the nothing do not constitute an ever vaster totality than being alone. Being in its belonging together with the nothing is what makes finitude possible.

understood as creation or created being. It is only later positions (those for instance undertaken in Suárez's and Cajetan's reading of Aquinas) that produced 'Thomism' as a metaphysics.

## GOD AS *A* BEING

Metaphysics, precisely because it attempts to determine the essence of God and exhaust it, produces God as 'a' being, even if highest and best. If Descartes had attempted to found the subject on God, Nietzsche's critique of Descartes is that he lacked the radicality to admit that the self-founding thought of the *cogito* is in no sense dependent on God, but that the subject is self-founding. Heidegger interprets Nietzsche's understanding of Descartes by saying: "Behind Nietzsche's sharpest rejection of the Cartesian *cogito* stands an *even more rigorous commitment* to the subjectivity posited by Descartes".[57]

Heidegger is at pains to show how, even if Nietzsche's own philosophical position is only possible in consequence of Descartes's, nevertheless, because "Nietzsche refers the *ego cogito* back to an *ego volo* and interprets the *velle* as willing in the sense of will to power"[58] he founds the whole of beings on the subjectivity of the human subject. Now human being and not God plays the metaphysical role of the *ens creatum*. God, functioning no longer metaphysically, as the creator of beings, can and must simultaneously appear as one other being among the many, and as dead.

## THE PEDAGOGICAL ROLE OF HEIDEGGER'S POLEMIC

I have shown that what Heidegger calls variously theology, theiology, systematic theology, dogmatics, church doctrine, or Christian philosophy he means to be understood as determined by nothing other than metaphysics, ontotheology. The sustained anti-Christian polemic is nothing other than a shorthand for his own claim for the end of metaphysics, the

---

57. *Die europäische Nihilismus* (*Nietzsche* [GA6.2]), p. 174. "Hinter Nietzsches schärfster Ablehnung des Descartesschen cogito [steht] die *noch* strengere *Bindung* an die von Descartes gesetzte Subjektivität" (author's italics).

58. *Die europäische Nihilismus* (*Nietzsche* [GA6.2]), p. 181f. "Nietzsche führt das ego cogito auf ein ego volo zurück und legt das velle aus als Wollen im Sinne des Willens zur Macht."

end of God as *Deus positivus,* that being whose being it is necessarily to be because it is that which is most beingful about any particular being, *causa sui,* ground, or beingness (*Seiendheit*). And all of this philosophical research is in consequence of Nietzsche's madman's frolicking proclamation: God is dead.

There is important confirmation of this view in the difference in tone between two of Heidegger's consecutive lecture courses. The lectures later published as *Einführung in die Metaphysik* from the summer semester of 1935 contain perhaps Heidegger's sharpest remarks about the absurdity of a Christian philosophy.[59] This sharpness must, however, be compared with his remarks in a lecture course from the following semester, given in the winter of 1935–36. Here he remarks that

> the following is the usual picture of Descartes and his philosophy: during the Middle Ages philosophy stood—if it stood independently at all—under the exclusive domination of theology and gradually degenerated into a mere analysis of concepts and elucidations of traditional opinions and propositions. It petrified into an academic knowledge which no longer concerned humanity and was unable to illuminate reality as a whole. Then Descartes appeared and liberated philosophy from this disgraceful position.[60]

He reiterates the same point he made in 1935 about the way in which Christianity's predominance in the West thinks the universe as created. He shows how the connection between faith and its use of philosophical formulations becomes philosophical formulation as such: "The metaphysical doctrine of God becomes a theology; but a *theologia rationalis;* the doctrine of the world becomes a cosmology, but a *cosmologia rationalis;* the doctrine concerning

---

59. See, for example, notes 6–11 at the beginning of this chapter for the places where this critique is advanced.

60. *Die Frage nach dem Ding* (GA41), p. 76. "Das übliche Bild von Descartes und seiner Philosophie ist folgendes: Im Mittelalter stand die Philosophie—wenn sie überhaupt für sich bestand—unter der ausschließlichen Herrschaft der Theologie und verfiel allmählich der bloßen Begriffszergliederung und Erörterung überlieferter Meinungen und Sätze; sie erstarrte in ein Schulwissen, das den Menschen nichts mehr anging und außerstande war, die Wirklichkeit im Ganzen zu durchleuchten. Da erschien Descartes und befreite die Philosophie aus dieser unwürdigen Lage."

humanity becomes psychology, but a *psychologia rationalis*".[61] Heidegger describes the same movement in the lecture course of summer 1935, of how an understanding belonging to faith ossifies into a metaphysical position, but this time by tracing Newton's codification of Galileo's observations concerning the movement of bodies. He concludes that Newton's first law, on which so much modern science is based, is formulated not in terms of experience of some thing or object, but on the basis of something which cannot exist.[62] He says:

> How about this law? It speaks of a body, *corpus quod a viribus impressis non cogitur,* a body which is left to itself. Where do we find it? There is no such body. There is also no experiment which could ever bring such a body to direct perception. But modern science, in contrast to the merely dialectical poetical conception of medieval scholasticism, is supposed to be based on experience . . . this law speaks of a thing which does not exist.[63]

The issue here is not only Heidegger's argument concerning Newton but the pedagogical voice he employs. Whereas in the previous course he castigates the consequences of a medieval cosmology, here he is concerned to demonstrate its superiority over a supposed scientific worldview which cannot even adduce the evidence of experience to its defense. The point is therefore

---

61. *Die Frage nach dem Ding* (GA41), p. 85. "Wird die metaphysische Lehre von dem Gott eine Theologie, aber eine theologia rationalis, wird die Lehre von der Welt Kosmologie, aber eine cosmologia rationalis, wird die Lehre vom Menschen Psychologie, aber eine psychologia rationalis."

62. Newton's first law states that "Every body perseveres in its state of being at rest or of moving uniformly straight forward, except insofar as it is compelled to change its state by forces imprseed." "Corpus omne persevare in statu suo quiescendi vel movendi uniformiter in directum, nisi quatenus illud a viribus impressis cogitur suum mutare" (Newton, I, *Principia Mathematica,* [1972 (1726)], p. 54.

63. *Die Frage nach dem Ding* (GA41), p. 69. "Wie steht es mit diesem Grundsatz? Er spricht von einem Körper, corpus quod a viribus impressis non cogitur, einem sich selbst überlassenden Körper. Wo finden wir ihn? Einen solchen Körper gibt es nicht. Es gibt auch kein Experiment, das jemals einen solchen Körper in die anschauliche Vorstellung bringen könnte. Nun soll doch die neuzeitliche Wissenschaft im Unterschied zu den bloß dialektischen Begriffsdichtungen der mittelalterlichen Scholastik und Wissenschaft auf Erfahrung gründen . . . er spricht von einem Ding, das es nicht gibt."

reinforced that what he says is intended to provoke a reorientation to the questions he raises; it cannot simply be taken at face value as his opinion.

The separation of the thought of God from the question of being, a separation that comes about in the making-questionable of metaphysics that is also its overcoming, makes possible the ontic science of faith, which for Heidegger is that understanding of theology which is opposed to theiology. What is the proper relation between philosophy and faith? Heidegger developed this relation in his 1927 lecture *Phänomenologie und Theologie:* here he argues that the object of theology as a positive science is not God as such, but rather the "object of theology is the relation between God in general to humanity in general and the other way about".[64] Such a theology is only possible in consequence of the question of being. Faith itself is defined as rebirth. Heidegger adds that the Christian experience of rebirth is that pre-Christian existence is overcome in faith, which means it is ontologically included within faith-full existence. He concludes: "All theological concepts necessarily harbor *that* understanding of being that is constitutive of human *Dasein* as such, insofar as it exists in general".[65] Philosophy is that inquiry into human existence into which faith later enters and which, through faith, it is sublated, which means that faith receives and preserves *Dasein* in the new creation.[66] Heidegger's reference to new creation alludes to the letters of St. Paul.[67] The proper concern of philosophy is always the existence of *Dasein;* in this sense God's 'existence' is always known only through the existence of believing *Dasein.*

This is less shocking than it sounds. That God might not exist, but possess essence, is an open question for at least some medieval theologians. Eckhart, for instance, strongly implies that God does not exist, because God is pure intellect, which has no place and no time.[68] While this position is only possible in one sense on the basis of Aristotle's ontology and theology, nevertheless

---

64. *Phänomenologie und Theologie* (*Wegmarken* [GA9]), p. 59. "[Der] Gegenstand der Theologie ist die Beziehung Gottes überhaupt zum Menschen überhaupt und umgekehrt."

65. *Phänomenologie und Theologie* (*Wegmarken* [GA9]), p. 63. "Alle theologischen Begriffe bergen notwendig *das* Seinsverständnis in sich, das das menschliche Dasein als solches von sich aus hat, sofern es überhaupt existiert" (author's italics).

66. Cf. *Phänomenologie und Theologie* (*Wegmarken* [GA9]), p. 63.

67. Cf. 2 Corinthians 5:17. "Therefore, if any one is in Christ, he is a new creation." ("ὥστε εἴ τις ἐν Χριστῷ, καινὴ κτίσις.")

68. Cf. Eckhart, *Werke* (1993), *Quaestiones Parisiensis,* II; German Sermons, 9; Latin Sermons, 29.

something remarkable is also being said here, that existence is proper, strictly speaking, only to human being. If Heidegger has sometimes been criticized for an immanentism that disallows transcendence, in fact he is saying as much as Eckhart says here, at least as far as existence is concerned.

Could it be that for Heidegger, God, of whose essence he might be moved to speak, does not exist? In saying God does not exist, the contested meaning for Heidegger is not the word God, but the word existence, so that what is named as God is only questionable when brought into the realm of existence. Heidegger actually says as much in 1949, in the introduction to the lecture *Was ist Metaphysik?:* "Human beings alone exist. Rocks are, but they do not exist. Trees are, but they do not exist. Horses are, but they do not exist. Angels are, but they do not exist. God is, but does not exist".[69]

## Aristotle's Understanding of Analogy

In order to understand why Heidegger is able to interpret Aquinas's position as one more determined out of faith than metaphysics, it is necessary to ask in what way did analogy become the name of an impasse that also allows Aquinas to say *Deus est suum esse* without rendering God as *a* being? To answer this question requires a fuller investigation of how Heidegger understood the origins of Aristotle's use of the term ἀναλογία.[70]

In chapter 2 I considered Heidegger's discussion of analogy in *Sein und Zeit* as a fundamental part of how the understanding of being is worked out metaphysically. The discussion of analogy arises out of Heidegger's consideration of the Greek understanding of how speaking and being belong together. He refers frequently to the dictum of Parmenides, "for the same is for knowing (thinking) as is for being", throughout his work.[71] Heidegger

---

69. *Einleitung zu: 'Was ist Metaphysik'* (*Wegmarken* GA9), p. 374f. "Der Mensch allein existiert. Der Fels ist, aber er existiert nicht. Der Baum ist, aber er existiert nicht. Das Pferd ist, aber es existiert nicht. Der Engel ist, aber er existiert nicht. Gott ist, aber er existiert nicht."

70. Cf. Aristotle, *Metaphysics,* V, ix (1018a12 f.).

71. Fragment III (Coxon, A. *The Fragments of Parmenides* [1986], p. 4). "τὸ γὰρ αὐτὸ νοεῖν ἐστίν τε καὶ εἶναι." The dictum, which Heidegger names in *Sein und Zeit* as Parmenides' 'ontological thesis' (and which he translates and re-translates with a variety of different emphases throughout his work) formed the basis for Heidegger's last seminar in 1973 at Zähringen (*Seminare* [GA15], p. 401ff.). It is worth noting that in *Sein*

unfolds the speaking (knowing) of being by investigating the meaning of the Greek term λόγος.

Heidegger's consideration of the question of analogy is undertaken in detail in the 1931 lectures on Aristotle I have mentioned. Here he considers that λόγος is understood by the Greeks as a kind of producing in speaking. Heidegger considers Aristotle's dictum from the *Metaphysics:* "being is said in many ways".[72] This he describes as a recurrent formula (the same word he used of analogy with regard to Aquinas), but which names a task, that of understanding how the many is said according to the one. He proceeds to show how for Aristotle the one (ἕν) and the many (πολλά) belong together. He notes "*The ὄν is so little deprived of unity through the* πολλαχῶς *that, to the contrary, it could absolutely never be what it is without the* ἕν. Indeed, ὄν and ἕν are different conceptually, but in their essence they are the same, that is, they belong together".[73]

Heidegger comments that this belonging together is never considered either before Aristotle or after him, until his own work, *Sein und Zeit,* although these unasked questions are of central concern to Aristotle. For Aristotle, the saying of the many of the one results in analogy, in the giving of a primary meaning which hinges and secures all subsequent meanings as a sustaining and guiding meaning. The sustaining and fundamental meaning to which all other meanings are led back is οὐσία.[74] How οὐσία, translated as "substance," can be the sustaining and fundamental meaning remains obscure, an impasse. Heidegger's interpretation of this saying is that to speak of *a* being is to speak of it in the being of its being.

---

*und Zeit* Heidegger connects the working out of Parmenides' dictum explicitly with Aquinas, in which he connects Aquinas's understanding of the soul with the analytic of *Dasein.* Cf. *Sein und Zeit* [GA2], p. 14: this "soul" has nothing to do, he says "with the vicious subjectivizing of the totality of beings". ("Die Seele . . . hat offensichtlich nichts gemein mit einer schlechthin Subjektivierung des Alls des Seienden.") From what has been said above, it is clear this totality of beings, viciously subjectivized, is nothing other than the metaphysical conception of God. Once again, Heidegger is keen to draw a sharp distinction between Aquinas and the metaphysics of subjectivity.

72. Aristotle, *Metaphysics,* VI, II (1026a33). "τὸ ὂν λέγεται πολλαχῶς."

73. *Aristoteles, Metaphysik Θ 1–3* (GA33), p. 29. "*Das ὄν geht durch das* πολλαχῶς *sowenig der Einheit verlustig, daß es vielmehr gar nie ohne das* ἕν *sein kann, was es ist.* Zwar sind das ὄν und ἕν dem Begriffe nach verschieden, dem Wesen nach aber dasselbe, d.h. sie gehören zusammen" (author's italics).

74. Aristotle, *Metaphysics,* IX, I (1045b25). Περὶ μὲν οὖν τοῦ πρώτως ὄντος καὶ πρὸς ὃ πᾶσαι αἱ ἄλλαι κατηγορίαι τοῦ ὄντος ἀναφέρονται εἴρηται, περὶ τῆς οὐσίας.

In the course of the lectures Heidegger shows the inner relationship of force, δύναμις, to λόγος, as the determination of λόγος to εἶδος and ποίησις. To speak of a being brings it to light in a particular way, *as* what it is. This speaking, λόγος, is that speaking-to-oneself that occurs in the laying out and producing of a thing, a being, that selects its *this* way and not *that* way, hence a deciding-in-producing that includes within itself the other ways of speaking in their concealment, i.e., as the unsaid in any given being, because the same being could be said in different ways.

There is always in speaking a deciding, a selecting, which means an excising of every other possibility in favor of the one which is realized in its being spoken. Speaking is therefore in itself a way of dividedness, in the sense in which one might cut a distinction. It is therefore at the same time an imposing of finitude in the sense of the producing-perceiving of a thing by giving and defining its limits (τό πέρας) in giving it its 'how' as the *this*-thing that it is declared to be, rather than the *that*-things it could have been. By this means its finitude is brought to light and spoken.

Λόγος also belongs to being ensouled, ἔμψυχον, which means it belongs to human being, so that speaking of a being in its being always discloses that there is a one who speaks—even if only to himself or herself. Λόγος is not only the 'how' of making a being present, but also the 'how' of making a soul present *at the very same time as* the coming about and making present of a thing. Speaking is in this sense comportment, the 'how', the mood, of how I and a thing come about, drawn out of the hiddenness of the future. Heidegger argues this is exactly Aquinas's notion of ensoulment, where the soul is "a being which is of a kind to come together with all beings"[75] which, he argues, is exactly how Aquinas establishes the priority of *Dasein*, even though not thematically. It is also fundamentally in accord with Heidegger's description of the relation of time to knowing, discussed at the end of chapter 3.

In Heidegger's 1931 investigation of λόγος he simultaneously investigated its connection with ἀρχή, the origin or originary, in order to show how the horizon of time is also at work in all speaking. For Heidegger, ἀρχή belongs to λόγος not as its origin (what lies behind, and so causes it) but its end (what I am trying to get to, what lies ahead of me). Ἀρχή is then a projection,

---

75. *Sein und Zeit* (GA2), p. 14, quoting Aquinas *Quaestiones Disputatae: de Veritate*, q. 1, a. 1, resp. "Ens quod natum est convenire cum omne ente." This is itself a reference to Aristotle (*de Anima*, III, VIII [431b21]).

the striving after (transcending toward) the thing in its being-produced, the ὀρεκτόν, or "projection of what is to be produced there, [the] making known of the outward appearance".[76] How, therefore, did ἀρχή as the projected-toward (and so what is named and known) come to be understood as originating, and so come to be an αἰτία, cause, and specifically one of the causes discussed by Aristotle? It is not possible here to do anything more than sketch Heidegger's argument in the briefest terms. The ἀρχή of λόγος is οὐσία, which comes to be named as substance. But οὐσία thought in this way does not mean substance at all, but the here-brought-forward-produced-and-known. What occurs in consequence of speaking (even as a 'speaking to myself') is something which is wrested here from what lay ahead of me. Not presence, but presencing, as that which is a bringing into presence, into being.

Heidegger does not make this explicit in 1931, but later shows with respect to Aristotle's understanding of φύσις, that in the two meanings of οὐσία, becoming present and being present, being present takes over and dominates so that being present becomes that which always already underlies as what in any being was ready to become present even before it begins to present itself. This is the very privileging of the immovable (the always-already)[77] over the movable or changeable. The effect of this privileging is that the being in question's appearing is already determined in advance of itself; it can only come about in *this* way, rather than any other, in order for it to be known as the being it is not yet—or rather, it is only not-yet for me and already present somewhere else (for Plato, in the suprasensory realm). This understanding of οὐσία is later developed as ὑποκείμενον and *substantia,* the under-lying (*sub-stans*), and therefore the ground of a being in its presence. Thus grounding becomes being-caused. Substance as such then becomes the being-caused of all and any given being.[78] All of this is in consequence of *speaking,* as the speaking to myself that Heidegger says all knowing is.

---

76. *Aristoteles, Metaphysik* Θ *1–3* (GA33), p. 151. "Der Entwurf dessen, was da hergestellt werden soll, das Kundmachen des Aussehens."

77. For a discussion of how this is grounded in the Greek language as such, and how Heidegger interprets this in his discussion of *das Gewesen* in relation to temporality, see Sheehan, T., "Das Gewesen" (1996–97), pp 1–31.

78. Cf. *Vom Wesen und Begriff der* φύσις, *Aristoteles Physik B, 1* (*Wegmarken* [GA9]), pp. 239–301, esp. p. 272. "Beingness indeed becomes conceived as stability, but one-sidedly in favor of the always-already-underlying. Thus the other moment of the essence of οὐσία is omitted: *presencing*" (author's italics). ("Wird die Seiendheit zwar als Ständigkeit begriffen, aber einseitig in der Richtung des Zum-voraus-stets-zugrunde-Liegenden. Daher fällt das andere Wesensmoment der οὐσία aus: die *Anwesung.*")

For Heidegger, Western thinking names the relation to being of beings in a reversal, where the being-present of things takes over and masters its 'how' of becoming-present in λόγος, where the I-speaking that produces disappears in favor of the already-present of any given being in itself. This reversal determines an outcome for human being and also for God. In this reversal the 'I' that speaks-in-producing disappears in favor of something else and so loses its determination to λόγος; yet it retains the trace of its origin, understood no longer as the Greek experience of λόγος, but rather as relation.[79] This reversal is, in a sense, *die Kehre* in its origin, but it functions in Aristotle through the name of analogy.

How is this? Heidegger does not make it entirely explicit in the lectures from 1931, but it is clear, especially in his critique of the way the divine operates in the Aristotelian ontology which he discusses in his lectures on Plato's Sophist of 1924, that it was his thinking of God that entirely governed this critique. If 'I' am no longer the being that has, and hold myself in λόγος (setting aside for now Heidegger's question: in what way does λόγος have me and hold me in itself?),[80] then I am no longer that being who comes across and speaks of the being of beings, but rather I discover beings as already founded, as already being-present (already having been spoken, but with the meaning of this already-spoken having been covered up to be thought of as origin, and having-been-caused). The worlding of world (in that it worlds for me) is not something I any longer produce and bring-forth in speaking, but rather something into which I enter as something already there, already other than me, and so from where I am already displaced, what might be called an external world. It no longer worlds for me, but rather, it worlds, irrespective of me—it worlds, already without me. It worlds, not for me, but in consequence of some(one) else. It appears as already-having-been-spoken and as other.

To discover this reality as already *there* in advance conceals the meaning of my there-being (*Dasein*) in favor of understanding myself as that one who has to account for the origin of what I find (because I am displaced from its origination), *these* beings in their already *being-present*. Such a thinking retains within it the trace of the being of beings and their being-known, precisely because in being already spoken, which means now originated and caused, an originary soul who is other than me is implied, an originator, a prime-mover, or a first cause.

---

79. Cf. *Einführung in die Metaphysik* (GA40), p. 95.
80. *Brief über den 'Humanismus'* (*Wegmarken* [GA9]), p. 348.

Moreover, I am transformed from one who reaches into the future in order to speak (even to myself) of beings and brings them here in order to know them in what they are now in their being. I am transformed into one who must reach into the past for the origin and primary cause of everything that is, as something extraneous to me. To push this still further, as Leibniz did, it does not matter which world I am in, because this world did not world for me; it is not originately, originally, *mine.*

If I do not discover myself as that being who brings forth and gives these beings to be discovered in their being (futurally), then (because being is the same as being-known) there must be some other 'I' for whom this has already occurred. Such a one must be that I who precedes every other I and explains the origin of I-being as such, overall, the I-being of the God of metaphysics. This is the basis for Heidegger's claim that in metaphysics transcendence understood as the freedom of *Dasein* disappeared in favor of the already-transcendent, God. God, thought in metaphysics, is therefore the trace of my 'I', its universalization, but now separated from me, in a separation whose occurrence is utterly concealed and forgotten. Again, for this reason, the God of metaphysics (no more than human transcendence, an anthropomorphism) can never be the God of faith. Only an atheism toward this metaphysical God could clear the way for who the God might really be. Heidegger's atheism therefore unravels the question of analogy to transform the meaning not only of *Dasein,* but also of God.

The God of metaphysics is in consequence that being who precedes, founds, universalizes, and omnitemporalizes every possible being and time that my 'I' might ever be, *Ens,* but only as *ens infinitum,* God, as given in metaphysics, but nothing other than a projected and transcendent 'I', myself, reflected back as wholly alien to me, myself, in the reflecting back that belongs to the very originary structure of time which Heidegger had laid out in *Sein und Zeit* and in his lectures of 1927, but concealed from me because the meaning of being is concealed and forgotten.

Nihilism proclaims this 'I' to be dead and so open to question. The divine 'I' that is this reflection becomes questionable in and as nihilism. The tragic character of nihilism is its disdain for the question, because this questionable I strives for certainty and in its striving manifests its drive for certainty as a constant self-empowering, through the will to power. Constant self-empowering is not, however, the exercise of the will to power but its consequence: I am utterly driven now by what willing is, the will to power that wills that I should seek to recover myself, as my own exercise of will. I do not will, I am determined out of willing, which is a drive, not a free transcending. However, this tragic struggle has another consequence: as the meaning of 'I' becomes questionable in nihilism, which means as I enter the question, so God as the universal 'I' is no longer the transcendent (the end of transcending), but dead, in favor of something else transcending. What that something else might be appears as a phantom, a shadow disclosed in moods of negation and darkness, and yet as phantom it has the possibility of appearing, which means becoming disclosed all over again. It appears, first as shadow, then as the being that it is.

Heidegger understands transcendence as a speaking of the being of beings. The speaking of the being of beings means different things in the history of being. Thought by Aristotle and Plato the speaking of the being of beings means transcendence: "Transcendence, finally . . . is that highest being itself which can then also be called 'being'".[81] Transcendence here, therefore, means beings-in-general, thought as God; beings determined out of prior, or causal, being, universality sought in a higher (μετα-, über-, trans-) sphere. This is another way of understanding that for Heidegger, perceiving and knowing as striving-toward, or the ὀρεκτὸν described earlier, are all what it means to transcend. In other words, knowing, speaking, and transcending are all different ways of understanding the same thing, the human being (*Dasein*) in its being (*das Sein*). It is for this reason that human freedom is transcending into nothing.[82]

If God is dead, then *Dasein*,—egoity—'I' find myself as that being which transcends in order to be and which transcends into nothing, the mark of my finitude and the finitude of being. This means that I discover my questionableness, but that this is a self-questioning, a discovering of my groundlessness, and that my being-questioned brings me before myself *as myself* for the first time, a new beginning. Questioning is in this sense no different from transcending, which means that knowing and speaking (even to myself) are reconnected as two aspects of the same thing, my 'I'. All of this is also part of the conversation that *Dasein* is with the whole history of being, of philosophy itself. This is a conversation of the human being with

---

81. *Zur Seinsfrage* (*Wegmarken* GA9), p. 397. "Transzendenz heißt schließlich . . . jenes höchste Seiende selbst, das dann auch 'das Sein' genannt wird."
82. See the discussion of this undertaken in 1929 in *Vom Wesen des Grundes* (*Wegmarken* [GA9]).

himself, the speaking to oneself which for Heidegger characterizes λόγος or what he elsewhere calls the worlding of world.[83]

When, for Heidegger, transcendence ceases to mean highest being and comes to mean the finitude of being as transcending into nothing, then what nothing is comes to be heard for the first time. When I come into the question, I can ask aloud: who now is God? This question is above all mine, a question in consequence of my becoming *Dasein*, not as an object, but as self-existing. It can, in this sense, be a question which, as wholly mine, subsequently concerns me with faith.

Heidegger's destructuring of this God is simply to insist that God is no *ens*, no object. Heidegger's interpretation of movement and change in Greek thinking, in Plato, and especially in Aristotle's discussion of δύναμις and κίνησις, and Nietzsche's countermovement is that the bringing of *any* God to language objectifies—it reasons, renders, reckons, or e-valuates—God as *that* uppermost value which (in such a rendering) calls forth the devaluation of the uppermost values and the revaluation. The very bringing of the object 'God' to life in language brings such a God about as already stillborn.

## HEIDEGGER'S GOD

Heidegger says in the small work we considered in chapter 3, *Der Feldweg*, that in the unspoken in speech is God only God.[84] It would be easy to miss the import of the word *only*. Here the shift is from *primum ens*, first being, to *Gott erst Gott*, God only God. This shift takes place in a discussion of the "one-fold" or "simple".[85] Here we discover that for Heidegger God is one and simple, a claim entirely compatible with medieval thought. Heidegger is speaking of God's essence here, without reference to God's supposed existence (as object). For Heidegger, any experience of God first comes about when no longer *ens*, no longer hitched to the being of being-human. As no longer hitched, God can appear for God's self-sake, not out of who and what I am.

---

83. Cf. for instance, the 1949 lectures *Das Ding* and *Die Kehre* (*Bremer und Freiburger Vorträge* [GA79]), pp. 19, 74. In both cases worlding of world relates to the being of God and to *das Geviert*.

84. See p. 83 above.

85. *Der Feldweg* (*Aus der Erfahrung des Denkens* [GA13]), p. 39. "Das Einfache."

Such divinity, Heidegger says, only "hints"[86] in consequence of the destructuring of metaphysics. Such hinting is lost in speech, which objectifies. One of the ways Heidegger attempted to illustrate this was by appeal to *die Göttlichen* as one dimension of the fourfold of earth and heaven, mortals and *die Göttlichen*. *Die Göttlichen* is that part of the fourfold which is discussed in the 1949 lecture *Das Ding*, among other places. Here the most extraordinary things happen—not least where the jug 'jugs'. In the *Nachwort* to the the lecture (already mentioned earlier and in chapter 4), Heidegger says "the default of God and *des Göttlichen* is absence. But absence is not nothing; rather it is precisely the presence, which must first be appropriated, of the hidden fullness and wealth of what has been and what, thus gathered, is presencing, of the divine in the world of the Greeks, in prophetic Judaism, in the preaching of Jesus".[87] What else does this mean except that for Heidegger, God can no longer be thought as pure presence, in order to be heard in the moving of God's historical unfolding? God is known to the Greeks, to the Christian centuries that have gone before, now less surely. This can be understood, but not through metaphysical seizing of God as a determination of presence, but in the very events of the disclosure themselves, our dwelling with the history of the West, our own history, and the history of (other peoples') abiding with the divine.

Heidegger says repeatedly that metaphysics is *Anwesenheit*, presence. So this absence which is not nothing is that which comes after the completion of metaphysics, *in contrast* to the presence, the *Deus positivus*, of metaphysics. The fourfold is described as earth and heaven, mortals and *die Göttlichen*.

How is *die Göttlichen* to be translated? First it must be established what *die Göttlichen* is not. Despite all the attempts to say so, it is not gods, or divinities—I have already indicated how for Heidegger, God belongs in the province of the Simple, or onefold. For Heidegger says (in a clear allusion to the *Beiträge*) "*Die Göttlichen* are the hinting messengers of godhead. Out of

---

86. Cf. *Beiträge zu Philosophie* (GA65), §§253–254, esp. p. 408f. "In the turn the hints of the last God play as onset and staying-away of the arrival and flight of gods and their places of mastery." ("In der Kehre spielen die Winke des letzten Gottes als Anfall und Ausbleib der Ankunft und Flucht der Götter und ihrer Herrschaftsstätte.")

87. *Brief an einen jungen Studenten* from the *Nachwort* to *Das Ding* (*Vorträge und Aufsätze* [GA7]), p. 177. "Der Fehl Gottes und des Göttlichen ist Abwesenheit. Allein Abwesenheit ist nicht nichts, sondern sie ist die gerade erst anzuzeigende Anwesenheit der verborgenen Fülle des Gewesenen und so versammelt Wesenden, des Göttlichen im Griechentum, im Prophetisch-Jüdischen, in der Predigt Jesu." See pp. 117, 188 above.

the hidden sway of *die Göttlichen* God emerges into what God is, which removes God from any comparison with beings that are present".[88] What else could this say, but that God is not a being—does not exist—but could have essence? *Die Göttlichen* are then not God, nor a substitute for God, nor a plurality—gods. But their proximation to the emergence of God and gods, as what gives the emergence in its coming about, and their non-objectivity, non-object*ness* means they belong to God, but are not God. I advance this (admittedly rather clumsy) translation: *die Göttlichen* are simply the divinities or perhaps godlylies, or even sacralizings: that aspect of beings in their being in which God might "*sich ereigne[n]*", bring God forth in eventuation and reveal God's self.[89] Not God, nor gods, but what in the worlding of world (for me) hints at God, things which bring me close to God, which means things which move *me* in a divine way, along a path toward the divine. The recovery of an understanding of such a self-revealing is in consequence of the overcoming of metaphysics, which means of metaphysics having come to its full-end. *Die Göttlichen* are, therefore, in consequence of Nietzsche's word: God is dead.

Again it is important to understand that Heidegger is neither ruling out nor defining in advance what any given inquiry into the God of faith might be, for to do so would be to trespass into the ground of theology, which, as his comments in Zurich in 1951 indicate, he is only inclined to, but never actually does. This means that Heidegger only carries out what in *Sein und Zeit* is also named the structural analytic of *Dasein, and nothing else* throughout his work.

Heidegger's critique of theology is his unfolding of the structure of onto-theology: it is in this sense in consequence of his radical, individual atheism. Through successively investigating first Plato, and then Aristotle (via the tradition of receiving Aristotle through Aquinas's use of the term analogy) I have sought to indicate how for Heidegger the fundamental structure of transcendence does not yield a natural or philosophical knowledge of God, which then lays down the conditions in advance for the possible structure of a God to be given in or by a revelation. The question is not whether the good or being are adequate names for God or can be re-thought as adequate names, but rather what else these names were already doing before they

88. *Das Ding* (*Bremer und Freiburger Vorträge* [GA79]), p. 17. "Die Göttlichen sind die winkenden Boten der Gottheit. Aus dem verborgenen Walten dieser erscheint der Gott in sein Wesen, das ihn jedem Vergleich mit dem Anwesenden entzieht."
89. Recalling here the phrase of the 1951 Zurich seminar (see p. 188 above).

were taken up in metaphysics. What emerges in the unfolding of Heidegger's position is his continued pointing toward a task which he then refuses to take up or speak on.

Why should Heidegger refuse a theological voice? The question might better be put, what did Heidegger understand a theological voice to be, at the end of metaphysics, that led him to refuse to take it up? In the second section of a treatise written between 1946 and 1948 but not published until 1999 and entitled *Die Überwindung der Metaphysik,* under the title *Das Zeitalter der 'Theologien',* Heidegger makes it clear that, at the end of metaphysics, theologies emerge, things which have no responsibility toward God at all, but reduce God to the kind of commodity that technology routinely manipulates. Theology thereby becomes diabology, which "admits and unleashes the unconditional non-essence of God into the truth of beings".[90] Unconditional non-essence is almost impossible to translate in this context, having the additional sense of an absolutely dreadful state of affairs. The clear inference is that theology, while claiming to speak of God, simply juggles names and concepts and ceases to touch anything that might really be of God. Heidegger notes that the full consequences of this are yet to be realized: moreover consequences that will be felt not just by theologians, but in every area where the truth of beings is at issue. To refuse such a voice is therefore precisely the refusal of metaphysics for the sake of God. Heidegger's atheism can therefore be understood exactly as pointing toward God in the face of other articulations of God which hide who God is.

In order to understand this pointing-toward more fully I want to conclude my investigation of Heidegger's work by returning to Heidegger's Nietzsche interpretation, in order to understand fully what for Heidegger had occurred in Nietzsche's proclamation of the death of God. For Heidegger, the question becomes structured as follows: if the essence of God is not disclosed as a consequence of human transcending, what is? Heidegger's Nietzsche interpretation is the very act of the triumph of subjectivity in the unfolding of the doctrines of the will to power and the eternal recurrence of the same. These doctrines are, however, critiques of the coming about of the subject. Such a coming about of the subjectivity of the subject is simultaneously a coming about in an overcoming: a kind of death of the subject. The death of God, in this sense, unleashes a movement that is its own

---

90. *Metaphysik und Nihilismus* (GA67), p. 155. ". . . das unbedingte Unwesen Gottes in die Wahrheit des Seienden ein- und losläßt.

overcoming: the death of the death of God, which is a roundabout way of saying that the need to proclaim the death of God at its end ceases to have the potency and urgency it possessed in its emerging. Its proclamation gives way to something else. It is precisely this that Heidegger was pointing toward: the possibility for an entirely renewed and original (in the sense of latest, closest to the source, the origin) eventuation of God. To understand this, it is necessary to investigate who Heidegger understood Nietzsche's Zarathustra to be.

Heidegger's critique of theology is only preparatory to something else: the eclipse of that kind of theology which itself eclipses faith. In what follows I want to look at Heidegger's Zarathustra interpretation in order to understand what Heidegger's atheism means, and then, in the chapter following that, to look at how one theologian in particular has interpreted Heidegger's later work. This allows me to draw the conclusions that will open up the question of what Heidegger's atheism really is.

Chapter Seven

# Zarathustra and the Death of God

## HEIDEGGER'S *SELF-ASSERTION*

In Nietzsche, Heidegger found the highest possible figuration of the methodological atheism he had argued through the analytic of *Dasein*. As a figuration it could be taken in two ways: either for its own sake, in the implicit atheism of modern philosophy, which simply declares God to be dead and endlessly reproduces forms of subjectivity or as a freeing from and overcoming of subjectivity, thereby allowing both who 'I' am, and who God might be, to appear. In this chapter I want to consider how this 'I' appears in Nietzsche and how Heidegger related it to his own thinking, most of all in the questionableness that *Dasein* is.

Much of the investigation of Heidegger's atheism so far has intended to bring to the fore Heidegger's account of the temporal analytic of *Dasein* in relation to the unfolding of metaphysics. At the center of this is *Dasein*'s questionableness, the bringing of *Dasein* to light as the being whose own, proper concern is the being of beings. This self-questioning is simultaneously the overcoming of subjectivity, as the overcoming of the subject-object distinction. This brings to the fore *Dasein*'s embodiment, and in it the destructuring of those limits which constitute the subject as such.

It should now be clear that, for Heidegger, there is no prior substance as something which subsequently enters a world which is extended by time and space, to the subject; rather I 'am' as time, which gives me to world (it worlds for me). These questions of time and interpretation, together with Heidegger's analysis of technology and the unfolding of his understanding of nihilism, have been worked out above all in his lectures on Nietzsche between 1936 and 1941 (with smaller lectures and discussions continuing until after the end of the war). Heidegger argued that his

Nietzsche lectures in particular were intended for "all who could hear", that they "heard that this was a confrontation with National Socialism".[1] His confrontation with Nietzsche, however, extended in significance even beyond this. In chapter 1 I indicated how in *Das Rektorat 1933/34* Heidegger says he worked out the meaning of the phrase *God is dead* through his reading of Nietzsche's understanding of the will to power and devaluation of the uppermost values. Here Heidegger indicates the significance Ernst Jünger's text *Der Arbeiter* had for his politics.[2] This work, together with its forerunner *Die totale Mobilmachung*, represented "an essential understanding of Nietzsche's metaphysics . . . insofar as the destiny and present of the West is seen and foreseen within the horizon of this metaphysics".[3] The consequences of Jünger's delineation of the figure of the worker are "the universal rule of the will to power in planetary destiny. Today everything is a part of this reality, whether it is called communism or fascism or world democracy".[4]

It is of great significance that in these two (rare) places where Heidegger comments on his own political engagement (both published only posthumously, on his explicit instruction) the commentary also concerns his interpretation of his own thought. The *Spiegel* interview was given in 1966, though published only after Heidegger's death in 1976; *Das Rektorat 1933/34* was written shortly after the cessation of hostilities in 1945 but published only in 1983. In each case, however, the commentary specifically concerns Nietzsche's word: God is dead. This declaration is significant not only for Heidegger's work, but also for understanding the extent to which he supported or opposed the Nazi regime.

There has been much historical investigation of Heidegger's claims in these statements, but what has to some extent been overlooked is Heidegger's use of the term *Selbstbehauptung* (self-assertion), which appears in both texts.[5] *Selbstbehauptung* is a very strong term in German, meaning more

---

1. *Spiegel-Gespräch* (*Reden* [GA16]), p. 664. "Alle, die hören konnten . . . eine Auseinandersetzung mit dem Nationalsozialismus war."

2. See *Das Rektorat*, p. 25.

3. *Das Rektorat*, p. 24. "Ein wesentliches Verständnis der Metaphysik Nietzsches . . . insofern im Horizont dieser Metaphysik die Geschichte und Gegenwart des Abendlandes gesehen und vorausgesehen wird."

4. *Das Rektorat*, p. 25. "Die universale Herrschaft des Willens zur Macht innerhalb der planetarisch gesehenen Geschichte. In dieser Wirklichkeit steht heute Alles, mag es Kommunismus heißen oder Faschismus oder Weltdemokratie."

5. See chapter 1.

than simple assertiveness: it indicates forcefulness, even aggression. The term comes from the title of the *Rektoratsrede,* the inaugural address given in 1933 on the occasion of Heidegger's accession to the rectorate of Freiburg University, shortly after Hitler's own accession to power and coinciding with his decision to take membership of the Nazi Party. In both texts Heidegger suggests that *Selbstbehauptung* was the basis of his opposition to the Nazi Party's view of the university. In *Das Rektorat 1933/34* what *Selbstbehauptung* means for Heidegger becomes of central concern. He asks the reader to consider what kind of talk (*Rede*) the *Rektoratsrede* might be: is it condemned to be interpreted idly, in interpretations that miss the point of the critique it represents, which would be a "flight into idle talk"[6] (directly recalling the section on idle talk in *Sein und Zeit*)? The very phrasing of the question demonstrates that even in 1945, after the defeat of Nazism and of war, the text of the *Rektoratsrede* is still alive for Heidegger.

Heidegger describes criticisms of the *Rektoratsrede* made by Wacker, a ministerial official at the inaugural banquet of his rectorate, suggesting that they were immediately communicated to Ernst Krieck, the leading Nazi educational theoretician, with the clear implication that these criticisms either initiated or certainly fueled Krieck's feud with Heidegger and therefore the regime's suspicion of him.[7] These criticisms show both how *Selbstbehauptung* as a term was misunderstood in its meaning and only too well understood as his own criticism of the regime from the start.[8] The nature of the criticism is more fully explained in the *Spiegel* interview, where Heidegger says that the term indicated his personal refusal of the rhetoric and thinking of Nazi

---

6. *Das Rektorat,* p. 30. "Flucht ins Gerede."
7. Krieck's full significance, and his hostility to Heidegger is discussed in full in Safranski, R., *Ein Meister aus Deutschland* (1994), pp. 267–269, 281, 315f.
8. It is perhaps important to note that what is at issue in interpreting the meaning of the complex term *Selbstbehauptung* is not whether these claims are 'true' in the historiographical sense that Hugo Ott has required they be substantiated, but rather to ask what was at issue for Heidegger in penning this text. My suggestion is that the very reason the significance of this word has been overlooked is because substantiation has been sought in the matter of Krieck's (together with other Party apparatchiks) and Heidegger's exchanges with the regime, rather than trying to investigate the significance of Heidegger's claims for his own thought. To be fair, Ott has always been careful to point out that his concerns are not philosophical, but historical. While wishing to exercise considerable reserve in conceding the finality of such firm categorial distinctions, I would only too willingly accept that his method is intended to demonstrate rather different things to those I have at hand here.

218 — Heidegger's Atheism

political science in that "at the same time, *Selbstbehauptung* was to have set itself the positive task of winning back a new meaning, in the face of the merely technical organization of the university, through reflection on the tradition of Western and European thinking".[9] Heidegger understands *Selbstbehauptung* specifically in the context of nihilism, the death of God, and the work of the poet Hölderlin:

> What is essential is that we are in the midst of the fulfillment of nihilism, that God is 'dead', and every time-space for the godhead is buried. The surmounting of nihilism nevertheless announces itself in German poetic thinking and song. The Germans, admittedly, still have the least understanding of this poetry, inasmuch as they strive to adapt themselves to the standards of the nihilism that surrounds them and thus to misjudge the essence of a destinal self-assertion.[10]

*Selbstbehauptung,* not only on an individual scale but also in the extended form of a people coming to itself, has the potential to surmount nihilism: it is, in other words, a critique of nihilism.[11] If *Selbstbehauptung* is an implied criticism of nihilism even in 1933, then the clear implication we are meant to draw is that Heidegger saw the nihilistic danger represented by the Nazi regime from the outset. Heidegger's assumption of the rectorate was, therefore, an act of self-assertion, his own coming to himself (which by implication represented opposition to at least some of the tendencies represented

---

9. *Spiegel-Gespräch (Reden* [GA16]), *Nur noch ein Gott kann uns retten,* p. 198. "Die Selbstbehauptung sollte sich zugleich positiv die Aufgabe stellen, gegenüber der nur technischen Organisation der Universität einen neuen Sinn zurückgewinnen aus der Besinnung auf die Überlieferung des abendländisch-europäischen Denkens."

10. *Das Rektorat,* p. 39 (see p. 38, note 94, above). "Das Wesentliche ist, daß wir mitten in der Vollendung des Nihilismus stehen, daß Gott 'todt' ist und jeder Zeit-Raum für die Gottheit verschüttet. Daß sich gleichwohl die Verwindung des Nihilismus ankündigt im dichtenden Denken und Singen des Deutschen, welches Dichten freilich die Deutschen noch am wenigsten vernahmen, weil sie darauf trachten, sich nach den Maßstäben des sie umgebenden Nihilismus einzurichten und das Wesen einer geschichtlichen Selbstbehauptung zu verkennen."

11. As Gregory Bruce Smith has noted "for nations, and the nation, not autonomous individuals, always remains the unit of analysis for Heidegger" (Smith, G. B., *Nietzsche, Heidegger, and the Transition to Postmodernity* [1996], p. 185). There is not the space here for a thorough analysis of Heidegger's political understanding; however, what is at issue could be summed up by saying that the self, as always worlded, is always in and of a πόλις, so therefore, in a modern sense, politicized, or implicated politically.

in Nazism), a language he uses right up until 1966 (and even, in a way, after his death).[12] It is entirely consistent with the task he sets for phenomenology as early as the 1925 lecture course *Prolegomena zur Geschichte des Zeitbegriffs* where what is at issue is *the self-understanding of phenomenology*, which I have laid out in more general terms in earlier chapters.[13]

Does this make Heidegger's philosophy a Nazi philosophy? Heidegger is at pains to stress that his own *Selbstbehauptung* in acceding to the rectorate was made within the context of the situation at the time.[14] The naïveté and detachment of Heidegger's political judgment are thrown into sharp relief in several places in the *Spiegel* interview. On one occasion the interviewer asks Heidegger "So you saw a connection between the particular situation of the German university and the political situation in general?" to which Heidegger replied: "Of course I followed the political situation between January and March 1933 . . . but at the time my work was concerned with an extensive interpretation of pre-socratic thinking". At a time when all of Germany was being transformed by a violent political force, Heidegger was much more captivated by the πολέμος in Heraclitus.

Heidegger's self-assertion did not make his philosophy a Nazi philosophy, but it made of the philosopher Heidegger a Nazi, even if one concedes he (at least to some extent) undertook from the outset a critique of the Nazi regime. *Selbstbehauptung* is not, therefore, a political term, still less a Nazi one, but rather lies at the heart of Heidegger's thinking through his confrontation with

---

12. No matter how true this may be, at least in Heidegger's mind, and while it may confirm the view that Heidegger sought to influence the regime in particular directions, it does not explain, for example, his enthusiastic speeches in support of Hitler, reported in the Nazi press. Had he gained the influence he sought, to what extent, for instance would he have had to concede in matters of policy the biologism of the regime (irrespective of the extent to which he appears not privately to have subscribed to it himself)? While questions like this have no simple or final answer (they were different in 1933 and 1934 when he had to face them, compared to 1945), they must surely be kept in view in examining these aspects of his work. In this sense, Safranski's nuanced and intelligent treatment of the question of Heidegger's anti-Semitism or otherwise is particularly helpful. (Cf. *Ein Meister aus Deutschland* [1994], pp. 287–292.)

13. Cf. *Prolegomena zur Geschichte des Zeitbegriffs* (GA20), p. 108. The title of §8, b, is *"Selbstverständnis der Phänomenologie"*.

14. *Spiegel-Gespräch* (*Reden* [GA16]), p. 653. "Sie sahen also einen Zusammenhang zwischen der Lage der deutschen Universität und der politischen Situation in Deutschland überhaupt?" Heidegger: "Ich verfolgte die politischen Vorgänge freilich zwischen Januar und März 1933 . . . Aber meine Arbeit galt einer umfangreicheren Auslegung des vorsokratischen Denkens."

Nietzsche, nihilism, and the death of God. Self-assertion is that worlding of world where I come to myself. *Selbstbehauptung* has, therefore, a more fundamental connection with Heidegger's atheism. Coming to myself is in this sense not a self-discovery of the subject (that 'finding myself' beloved of popular fiction), rather it is the character of a relation, of a comporting: coming to myself secures me precisely not as an *ens certum*, a certain thing. Rather, I 'am' always in question because I am delivered over to the worlding of world, and I come to myself in and from out of the worlding of world. It worlds *for* me, and, strictly speaking, it worlds *me*. This coming to self can, and may indeed have to have, violent, sharp moments of self-possession against the prevailing trends, moments where the self is put into extreme danger and risk. I am tempted to ask, as an aside, how Heidegger measures up to what he implies. How do any of us measure up in these kinds of situations?

For Heidegger, *Selbstbehauptung* means not the triumph of the subject, but just that ecstasis of the self, self-transcending, which means the self occurs in exceeding itself and then returns to itself, described through the originary understanding of time and in *die Kehre*. If Heidegger's assumption of the Freiburg rectorate was hasty, opportunistic, ill-considered, naïve, and even latterly the grossest embarrassment for Heidegger (as is suggested by his correspondence with Karl Jaspers),[15] in contrast his subsequent confrontation with Nietzsche represented a deepened reflection on what he later called "the movement of nihilism",[16] and the "basic questions of thinking that indirectly also concern social and political questions".[17] This reflection, carried out through the Nietzsche lectures, enabled Heidegger to work out to the fullest extent the meaning of Nietzsche's declaration that God is dead.

## HEIDEGGER AND NIETZSCHE

It was not until 1961 that most of Heidegger's *Nietzsche* lectures were published. The published lectures were those delivered between 1936 and 1941, together with one essay prepared between 1945 and 1946.[18] At the center of

---

15. Cf. Heidegger/Jaspers *Briefwechsel 1926–1963* (1992), esp. letters 144 and 145.

16. *Zur Seinsfrage* (*Wegmarken* [GA9]), p. 386. "Die Bewegung des Nihilismus."

17. *Spiegel-Gespräch* (*Reden* [GA16]), p. 656. "Grundfragen des Denkens, die mittelbar auch die nationalen und sozialen Fragen betreffen."

18. Only later did other lectures and essays appear. See, for instance, volumes 50 and 67 of the *Gesamtausgabe*.

these lectures lies Heidegger's interpretation of Nietzsche's figure Zarathustra. For Heidegger, Nietzsche's Zarathustra speaks in consequence of the death of God. Zarathustra is only in consequence of this event. For Heidegger, Zarathustra, in speaking of the death of God, speaks of the death of the willed and willing God by asserting the triumph of the subject's will to power. This death shows how God lives (and dies) in willing, and so, who only being willed as dead, can again occur outside any willing. This death of God, therefore, opens a renewed way to God: just that God, who, to address (and so save) us, must be declared dead. In proclaiming God as dead, Zarathustra proclaims *der Übermensch*, the overman.[19] Zarathustra is the teacher of overman. Overman is *only* in consequence of the death of God. Over-man (recalling *über-*, μετα-, the *trans* of transcendens) is the finite appearance of my 'I' in virtue of the death of infinite (moral) transcendence, being in general, or the death of God thought metaphysically. Zarathustra says (with a direct reference to the Greeks, to Ὠκεανός): "Once we said God, when we looked over distant seas, but I have taught you to say: over-man".[20] Zarathustra teaches that overman has come about in virtue of God as the no-longer-transcendent but dead. When transcendence ceases to be universalized and understood as God and is simply *Dasein* as transcending, then *Dasein* transcending discovers itself to be overman.

Zarathustra speaks only of the death of God, revealing that the transcendence that humans have taken to be God in fact both conceals who God is and at the same time conceals what it means to be human. In consequence of what Zarathustra has to say, human being is a way of being that re-opens what it is to know myself. The real meaning of the self re-appears because I have come to myself through a difficult, deathly, and anxious struggle: *Selbst-behauptung*. Because this re-appearance occurs in consequence of the proclamation of the death of God, it is also concerned with who God is. God is intimately involved in this self-giving because the 'God' that previously concealed the self is now dead *in virtue of something that has*

---

19. There is simply no support for translating *der Übermensch* as 'superman'. Walter Kaufmann has demonstrated that the term overman originated in English with the American author Emerson's coinage of the term Over-soul, in a passage which Nietzsche refers to explicitly in *Die Götzen-Dämmerung* under the title *Emerson* (cf. translator's introduction to *The Gay Science*, p. 7 ff., esp. p. 11).

20. Nietzsche, F., *Also sprach Zarathustra* (*Friedrich Nietzsche* [1999], IV), p. 109. "Einst sagte man Gott, wenn man auf ferne Meere blickte; nun aber lehrte ich euch sagen: Übermensch."

*happened in a worlded and historical sense.* For Heidegger, the history of metaphysics (which is also the history of being as forgotten and concealed) unfolded the proclamation that God is dead. This, as a knowing of myself, is simultaneously the end of the God of metaphysics and a renewed possibility of experiencing God.

However, this is *Heidegger's* Nietzsche interpretation, which means that it is only possible because of the question of being. It occurs not only when God is dead, but also when the subject (*ens certum*) is overcome in questioning. As far as God is concerned, this constant questioning recalls Heidegger's claim that faith must remain constantly in the possibility of unfaith, to be faith.[21] To understand this, it is necessary to understand better how Heidegger arrived at his interpretation of who Nietzsche's Zarathustra is.

In a 1953 lecture to the Bremen Club entitled *Wer ist Nietzsches Zarathustra?* Heidegger summed up his interpretation of Zarathustra in the Nietzsche lectures as the figure whose task it is to communicate the doctrine of the eternal recurrence of the same and who therefore has a particular task in explaining the meaning of time.[22] Zarathustra's importance has been considered in relation to interpretation itself in chapter 4. I want to illustrate the connection between interpretation and the death of God and how this connection is concerned with the doctrine of eternal recurrence. At the outset of the lecture Heidegger says that in *Also Sprach Zarathustra* there is a word to be thought toward in the manner of a struggle, a contested seeking, and this 'word' is in a relation with the text, but it is not the text, though the text makes for a thinking toward the word. The text seeks a speaker, for it is not enough to cite the text, but rather 'who' cites the text is also in question. Those who come close to Nietzsche come in various ways, and the very 'how', the manner of this coming and going, will be what differentiates who they are and of whom and what they speak. This is the very *manner* of either passing by or seeking to hear what Nietzsche also heard and so struggled to bring to speech. So if one were to ask the question 'who am I to Nietzsche?' the answer never yields a general 'I', a presumed neutral or universal reader, but in reality turns to face the questioner and lends the question an imperative note. 'Who am I in this?' acts like a mirror into which a light is shone: I can either be dazzled by the reflected light or struggle

---

21. See p. 181 f. above.
22. *Wer ist Nietzsches Zarathustra?* (*Vorträge und Aufsätze* [GA7]).

to discern the features which the light at first obscures: the struggling itself will bring me before myself. The struggle for self-disclosure is therefore the very entering into the question of being.

Heidegger's critique of subjectivity is central to his interpretation of who Zarathustra is. However, there is a question that arises in the manner of Heidegger's procedure, particularly when what is sought is the interpretation of a figure, be it Nietzsche or Zarathustra. Surely, an account of intersubjectivity, the meaning of the other, as it is laid out by Buber or Lévinas, would better serve Heidegger's purpose than an attempt to overcome subjectivity overall. The answer to this is twofold. In the first instance (which might hold with regard to interpreting Nietzsche), in a 1928 lecture course and with Buber clearly in mind, Heidegger argued that *Dasein* is already an I-you relation even before the question of intersubjectivity arises, which is why intersubjectivity can never explain what *Dasein* already is, because the explanation itself already presupposes intersubjectivity. He adds:

> Togetherness thus cannot be explained by the I-you relation and on its basis, but rather conversely: this I-you relation presupposes for its inner possibility that *Dasein* (not only the *Dasein* functioning as I but also as you) is defined as togetherness; indeed even more than that: even the self-comprehension of an I and the concept of I-ness arise only on the basis of togetherness, but not as I-you relation.
>
> It is equally wrong to allow togetherness to arise from an I-torso as it is to think that the I-you relation is the basis from which *Dasein* as such can be defined.[23]

The torso is headless: it cannot speak. Speaking is of the essence of what I am, and that I can speak already includes you before you have come into

---

23. *Einleitung in die Philosophie* (GA27), p. 145f. "Das Miteinander ist also nicht durch die Ich-Du-Beziehung und aus ihr zu erklären, sondern umgekehrt: Diese Ich-Du-Beziehung setzt für ihre innere Möglichkeit voraus, daß je schon das Dasein, sowohl das als Ich fungierende als auch das Du, als Miteinandersein bestimmt ist, ja noch mehr: Sogar die Selbsterfassung eines Ich und der Begriff von Ichheit erwächst erst auf dem Grunde des Miteinander, aber nicht als Ich-Du-Beziehung.
"Es ist gleich irrig, das Miteinander erst von einem Ichrumpf aus entstehen zu lassen, wie zu meinen, die Ich-Du-Beziehung sei die Basis, um von ihr aus das Dasein als solches zu bestimmen." Cf. also *Metaphysische Anfangsgründe der Logik* (GA26), p. 186f.

view. The presupposed neutrality of *Dasein* is always broken, always *includes* separatedness just in existing, which is why, he notes at the same time (and almost incidentally), that *Dasein* 'is' always sexed.[24] Sexedness is integral to the differentiation of my 'I'. In the second case (which I want to consider in greater detail), Zarathustra is a figure, albeit of a special kind, but as a figure who figures something, he is not in the least any kind of subject: indeed, his very figurativeness is already the possibility of overthrowing subjectivity. Zarathustra is (better yet, has) no *Dasein*.

What is posed by the question of intersubjectivity (which I will treat only in passing) is the mysteriousness of the other: the claim on me to exceed myself that the other represents. To be called to exceed myself is to be pulled out of myself, to transcend myself so that in the ecstatic event I can be turned back to see the very thing from which I have been pulled. This is another way of thinking through *die Kehre*. This turning back is textured and shaped by the thing that first pulled me forth, so that, in being-together with what pulls, it disappears from view in the turning back because the turning back is given by the thing toward which I am first pulled.[25] This means no more than when confronted by another, in order to be most myself, I am forced to ask in the most open way: who are you? However, just this asking presupposes the relation-character of the very possibility of asking at all (because I always ask about some*thing*). It is the relational character of asking (language as such) that makes possible the question, or in other words, that brings the question to light *as* a question. It is this that is posed for Heidegger by the figure of Zarathustra. Zarathustra is the mysteriousness of what is most not mine in the mode of replying. The mystery answers back.

---

24. *Einleitung in die Philosophie* (GA27), p. 146. "In its essence the being which we really are, the human, is a neuter. We call this being: the *Dasein*. But it belongs to the essence of this neuter, that it, insofar as it indeed factically exists, has broken its neutrality; that is, that *Dasein* as factical is either male or female, it is sexed essentially." ("In seinem Wesen ist das Seiende, das wir je sind, der Mensch, ein Neutrum. Wir nennen dieses Seiende: das Dasein. Aber zum Wesen dieses Neutrums gehört es, daß es, sofern es je faktisch existiert, notwendig seine Neutralität gebrochen hat, d.h. das Dasein ist als faktisches je entweder männlich oder weiblich, es ist Geschlechtwesen.")

25. Put abstractly like this, it might be hard to see what is being said. If I am pulled toward something, I assume it or attain it: in the turning back, it disappears, either because it now has become 'for me' in a way or it is now just behind me and so no longer visible in itself. This latter explanation works only if it is clearly understood that in some sense I have become one with what I am pulled toward—as again, in the example of the lectern.

In Zarathustra, however, that mysteriousness is revealed as *not* a mystery of God. Zarathustra is precisely a prophet who is not Jesus, nor a herald of the Christian God (Nietzsche's very intention in taking up the name Zarathustra, from Zoroaster). Zarathustra's name is not arbitrary: it implicitly contradicts (literally, speaks against) the names of God which have become false in the subsumption of the God of faith by the God of metaphysics (*summum bonum, summum ens*).

For Heidegger, such an interpretation is possible, however, only on the basis of the question of being. Was there never such a radical questioning before, such that the very 'I' that I am is experienced precisely as questionable? Did not, for example, the 'I' of the subject first come into view as a self-questioning through Descartes's method of doubt? As I have already indicated with regard to Descartes, Heidegger remarks that in the coming-about of the subject the only thing that is not put into question is the 'I'.[26]

It is this very critique of subjectivity that for Heidegger discloses metaphysics as a history of being and brings it into view for the first time as questionable, not as a God-question but put into *the* questioning and questionable, the being-question. The question has a history, its unfolding over time, but in its history it is concealed. When the question re-appears from its concealment, it puts that whole history of concealment into question with it. Heidegger notes, therefore, that the question comes about "in a conversation with the whole history of philosophy".[27] This conversation is my interrogation of this history, and by interrogating my having been thought (and this means produced) by this history. I am, in consequence of how 'am' (being) has unfolded in the West, in the whole history of philosophy. This historical unfolding throws first God and then the subjectivity of the subject into question, so much so that in the declaring of God to be dead, a further question also unfolds as historical: a *being*-question, not a *God*-question: who now is God?

This is the formal meaning of Heidegger's radical, individual atheism: a renewed openness toward who God might be, that yields no answer, only a question which endlessly sharpens itself, because it throws everything that went before into relief. To ask about God requires a renewal which throws the whole of philosophy into question, because philosophy in the

---

26. Cf. chapter 2, from *Die Grundbegriffe der Metaphysik* (GA29/30), p. 30.
27. *Identität und Differenz* (GA11), p. 47. "In einem Gespräch mit dem Ganzen der Geschichte der Philosophie."

unfolding of its very history has objectified and trivialized God and must be destroyed back to its roots to renew that of which it speaks. *Now* I am surrounded by the cultural detritus of two thousand years and more of thinking about who God is, which means what I know of God is mediated by this history, in which an original experience of the divine has been covered over and obscured, because it was never mine, I never en-owned it. Even where it is present, for instance, as it might be in someone else's faith, it is not yet mine.

Heidegger suggests that what is put in question by Zarathustra is the emptiness of everything up until this hour. What is required beyond this hour that has so far remained empty? Heidegger says that the phrase "'for everyone' means for every human being as a human being, for every given individual insofar as he or she becomes in his or her essence a matter worthy of thought for him or herself".[28]

There is an essence to be attained and so not yet thought. Are not essences those things into which I inquire when I ask "what is . . ." (τὶ τὸ ὄν)? Heidegger adds, concerning Zarathustra or rather concerning Nietzsche and most of all concerning essences, that in the essence being thought here "Nietzsche is not Zarathustra, but the questioner who seeks to create in thought Zarathustra's essence".[29] Does Nietzsche (in order to think through who Zarathustra is *as* what he has to say) project Zarathustra as one who is simply a literary figure, a conceit? Rather Heidegger interprets Nietzsche as having to rise to the occasion that Zarathustra *is*. If I am that which is thought (which means that I am produced, I come from somewhere, who my 'I' can ever be is already laid out as one among a particular range of possibilities), then to attain to an essence is to think how I am thought, in short to enter into a conversation with myself, which is simultaneously an entering into conversation with the world that worlded me: my surrounding world or environment. In a figurative sense, Zarathustra is the stuff of that speaking to myself which in chapter 6 was discussed under the name of λόγος. Heidegger therefore asks how far Nietzsche is a creature of Zarathustra.

---

28. *Wer ist Nietzsches Zarathustra?* (*Vorträge und Aufsätze* [GA7]), p. 97. "'Für Alle' dies meint: für jeden Menschen als Menschen, für jeden jeweils und sofern er sich in seinem Wesen denkwürdig wird."

29. *Wer ist Nietzsches Zarathustra?* (*Vorträge und Aufsätze* [GA7]), p. 103. "Ist Nietzsche nicht Zarathustra, sondern der Fragende, der Zarathustras Wesen zu erdenken versucht."

## HEIDEGGER'S INTERPRETATION OF ZARATHUSTRA

Why is there need for the figure of Zarathustra, rather than, as for others who have analyzed it, a cohesive, rational, narrative of the history of nihilism? Michael Gillespie's account in *Nihilism before Nietzsche* of a nihilism that stands apart from Nietzsche fails to understand the extent to which the doctrine of the eternal return must first be expounded in figures like that of Zarathustra or in aphorisms before it can be told as a history: it is not *inherently* narratable.[30] The narrative, the history, is a forgotten one: nihilism is in consequence of the forgetfulness that interpretation is (raising again the question of ruinance discussed in chapter 4). What Gillespie's form of account cannot do is explain why the history was forgotten, but only account for *how* it became concealed.[31] How could he account for its concealment *in* its concealment, since his narrative is its very coming back to light? Heidegger's approach to Nietzsche means that there is a sense in which Gillespie can bring it to light again because of Nietzsche's figuration of its concealment, which both hides and discloses it simultaneously. Put more sharply, Gillespie's argument is always indebted to Nietzsche's.

Heidegger, citing fragment 726 of the *Großoktav* edition of the notes appended to *Also sprach Zarathustra* points out in a discussion of the development of the doctrine during the "Zarathustra-time"[32] that the consequence of the doctrine is

'Didn't you know? In each action you do, the history of everything that has happened is repeated and condensed' (n. 726).

While at first blush the doctrine of return introduces an immense, paralyzing indifference into all beings and in human behavior, in truth

---

30. See p. 33f. above.

31. This rather reads Gillespie's argument against himself. He contends that Nietzsche misunderstood the origins of nihilism, a misunderstanding which resulted in his declaration that God is dead. Whilst I accept many of Gillespie's arguments and conclusions, I remain unconvinced by Gillespie's argument that Nietzsche fails to describe the essence of nihilism in its unfolding; rather the reverse: Nietzsche's brilliance is that he presents not simply an historical insight, but the essence of what can also be explained as a history in figures—as, for instance of a madman, or of Zarathustra. In short, Nietzsche, unlike Gillespie, has understood that what history *is*, is brought to light by nothing, strictly speaking, historical.

32. *Die Aufzeichnungen aus der Zarathustrazeit (1883/84)*, Division 20 of the 1937 lecture course *Die ewige Wiederkehr des Gleichen* (*Nietzsche* [GA6.1]), pp. 405–410.

the thought of thoughts gives the highest keenness and decisiveness to beings in every moment. [33]

In Nietzsche, figuration itself as a form of the event (*Ereignis*) is the eventfulness of what I know, how I am textured in a particular way without even being aware of the way in which all that has gone before has made of me the texture or form that I am. It is only possible for me to attain the moment (and so reveal the moment in its being) because of everything that has already made me what I am. The narrative, as the enunciative unfolding of a genealogy, is simply the commentary on what I already am. I am still that thing, this moment is still in its moment what it is for me, even without the enunciation (which means before I have understood that the meaning of what I am has been concealed from me). In order to reveal it for what it is, I have to come to myself, which means, un-conceal, dis-close, the hiddenness of the moment. Put another way, Zarathustra's speaking reveals to me what I am, only if I am prepared to hear it. To be prepared means to attain to the essence that I am by placing myself into question, which means asking 'who?' of myself. Who am I in this moment? Who is Zarathustra (for Heidegger or Nietzsche or me)?

To ask 'who?' is already to ask differently to asking 'what is?' It is to be distant from the province of the quiddity of substances, of the 'whatness' of essences. It is the reverse of the question concerning the lectern.[34] In asking about the lectern I discovered that I and the lectern were given together: this giving together made it possible to know *what* the lectern is at all. Now, in asking about any*thing* I simultaneously try to come to know what kind of I is given in my already knowing anything at all. The lectern essences me. When I become questionable, what comes to be questioned is the who of essence rather than the what. So to ask 'who?' is already to have understood that essence has undergone a change or (at the risk of over-using the language of Heidegger himself), to ask anew the question of the essence of essence. The

33. *Die ewige Wiederkehr des Gleichen* (*Nietzsche* [GA6.1]), p. 408 f. "'–Weißt du nicht? In jeder Handlung, die du tust, ist alles Geschehens Geschichte wiederholt und abgekürzt' (note 726).

"Während dem nächsten Anschein nach durch die Wiederkunftslehre in alles Seiende und in das menschliche Verhalten eine maßlose und völlige Gleichgültigkeit kommt, bringt in Wahrheit der Gedanke der Gedanken in das Seiende für jeden Augenblick die höchste Schärfe und Entscheidungskraft."

34. See chapter 5, p. 156 ff. above.

essence to which Nietzsche is striving, which Zarathustra *is* when attained, is an essence yet to come, yet still an essence. To ask in this way is to ask in what way I come from out of the future.

In his work on Nietzsche, Gilles Deleuze comments:

> According to Nietzsche the question 'who?' means this: what are the forces which take hold of a given thing, what is the will that possesses it? Which one is expressed, manifested, and even hidden in it? We are led to essence only by the question: which one? For essence is merely the sense and value of the thing; essence is determined by the forces with affinity for the thing and by the will with affinity for these forces. Moreover, when we ask the question 'what is it?' we not only fall into the worst metaphysics but in fact we merely ask the question 'which one?' in a blind, unconscious, and confused way.[35]

Heidegger's asking who Zarathustra is has the same force. It asks 'who?' as 'which one?': which of the ones among you? His inscription of himself into the place Nietzsche unfolds is in play: which is to say, Heidegger's own consideration of essence arises out of something with which Nietzsche is also concerned, both the same as and (in a simultaneity) utterly differing from it. Essence as the what-is question (τὶ τὸ ὄν) of the Greeks has a history. Through Plato and Aristotle it came to be thought as substance, ὑποκείμενον, the underpinning, the prior, the weight and gravity of all things *in opposition* to the thinking of essence as what is to become, what is attained, as the sense and value of a thing. Heidegger's Nietzsche lectures discussed essence by discussing the sense and value of a thing, as the transformation of the meaning of substance so that for Nietzsche it is no longer thought as what lies under, *sub*-stans (being determined as prior presence), but what over-comes (in consequence of the death of God, the devaluation of the uppermost

---

35. Deleuze, G., *Nietzsche et la philosophie* (1962), p. 87. "La question : 'Qui ?', selon Nietzsche, signifie ceci: une chose étant considérée, quelles sont les forces qui s'en emparent, quelle est la volonté qui la possède ? Qui s'exprime, se manifeste, et même se cache en elle? Nous ne sommes conduits à l'essence que par la question: Qui? Car l' essence est seulement le sens et la valeur de la chose; l'essence est déterminée par les forces en affinité avec la chose et par la volonté en affinité avec ces forces. Bien plus: quand nous posons la question: 'Qu' est-ce que?' nous ne tombons pas seulement dans la pire métaphysique, en fait nous ne faisons que poser la question: Qui?, mais d'une manière maladroite, aveugle, inconsciente et confuse."

values, and the revaluation of all values) *as* will, specifically will to power, being determined as becoming. So to ask 'who?' is a questioning *as* already taking into account the whole history of metaphysics.

Zarathustra is that one whose essence is to attain to his essence. Zarathustra's being is secured as becoming. The speaking of Zarathustra, therefore, is a mode of the speaking of being, the taking up of a voice. How might Zarathustra be a figure of the voice of being? I indicated how Zarathustra's voice can be understood as belonging to λόγος. Being and λόγος belong together. At one point Heidegger says that λόγος comes to be as speaking because "unconcealing of the concealed into unconcealment is the very presencing of what is present. We call this the being of beings".[36] The being of beings (the ontological difference) is, however, always also to be understood as transcendence.[37] What then is transcendence? Transcendence here would be understood as the speaking of the being of beings. But the speaking of the being of beings means different things in the history of being. Thought by Aristotle and Plato, the speaking of the being of beings as transcendence means "the relationship leading from a changeable being to a being in repose. Transcendence, finally . . . is *that highest being itself* which can then also be called 'being'".[38] Transcendence here, therefore, means being in general thought as God; beings determined out of prior, causal being: universality, sought in a higher sphere (τὸ ἀγαθόν, τὸ θεῖον). If God is dead, then it is not transcending that disappears, but God as the consequence of transcending. If human knowing is transcending, then something other than God is given in transcendence. It is in consequence of this that Zarathustra speaks. So is Zarathustra God? Or a replacement for God? This cannot be, for Zarathustra is finite. If Zarathustra is not God, then Zarathustra is the very mark of separation of the human being and God. Zarathustra is the very *figure* of radical, individualistic atheism.

---

36. *Logos* (*Vorträge und Aufsätze* [GA7]), p. 204. "Die Entbergung aber des Verborgenen in das Unverborgene ist das Anwesen selbst des Anwesenden. Wir nennen es das Sein des Seienden."

37. Heidegger repeatedly makes this point. Twice in the introduction to *Sein und Zeit* he describes being as the "transcendens" of medieval ontology (pp. 3, 38.). In *Zur Seinsfrage* (*Wegmarken* [GA9], p. 397), he notes that "die Transzendenz ist einmal die vom Seienden aus auf das *Sein* hinübergehende Beziehung zwischen beiden."

38. *Zur Seinsfrage* (*Wegmarken* [GA9]), p. 397. "Die vom veränderlichen Seienden zu einem ruhenden Seienden führende Beziehung. Transzendenz heißt schließlich . . . *(das) höchste Seiende selbst,* das dann auch 'das Sein' genannt wird" (author's italics).

## The Return of Transcendence

In chapter 3 I indicated that when, for Heidegger, transcendence ceases to mean highest being, it comes to mean the finitude of being as transcending into nothing. For this reason the nothing comes to be heard for the first time, however in the manner of a withdrawal. Transcendence, both in metaphysics and at the end of metaphysics, occurs as a 'how', a way of speaking. In Nietzsche's figurative style, the consequence of this is Zarathustra's horror at becoming who he is. Heidegger says: "Whoever has failed and continues to fail to apprehend from the start the horror that haunts all of Zarathustra's speeches, arrogant though they often sound and mere drunken posturings—will never be able to discover who Zarathustra is".[39] Horror here is being thought philosophically, translating the word *der Schrecken*, which may also be translated as dismay or even terror. Horror stands in opposition to wonder as a determination of anxiety (*Angst*), a central theme of *Sein und Zeit*. This is a historical opposition. Horror as the mode of speaking of Zarathustra stands in opposition to θαυμάζειν, awe and wonder, as Plato's and Aristotle's characterization of the beginning of philosophy.[40] If θαυμάζειν is the mode of beginning, horror and terror must be the mode of the end (of that beginning). If all of Zarathustra's speeches are characterized by horror, then Zarathustra is that one who speaks the end, and speaks it in the mode of horror.

How else does Heidegger articulate horror and anxiety? Heidegger begins the 1937 lecture course where he elaborates the meaning of *die Kehre* and the discussion of the essence of essence by speaking of the meaning of disposition in thinking, which elsewhere in relation to Nietzsche he describes as the 'how', the manner or mode of Zarathustra's speaking. He tells us:

> Two elements originally belong together and are as one in it: *terror* in the face of what is closest and most obtrusive, namely that beings are,

---

39. *Wer ist Nietzsches Zarathustra?* (*Vorträge und Aufsätze* [GA7]), p. 101. "Wer diesen Schrecken nicht aus allen oft anmaßend klingenden und oft nur rauschhaft sich gebärdenden Reden zuvor vernommen hat und stets vernimmt, wird nie wissen können, wer Zarathustra ist."

40. Plato, *Theaetetus*, 155d. "μάλα γὰρ φιλοσόφου τοῦτο τὸ πάθος, τὸ θαυμάζειν. οὐ γὰρ ἄλλη ἀρχὴ φολοσοφίας ἢ αὕτη." ("For the feeling of wonder shows that you are a philosopher, since wonder is the only beginning of philosophy.")

and *awe* in the face of what is remotest, namely that in beings, and before each being, being essences.[41]

Their belonging together is also metaphysics.

A point in the consideration of horror comes about in the *Einleitung* to the 1949 fifth edition of the lecture *Was ist Metaphysik?* Heidegger, in considering again the question of *die Angst*, associates it with the consideration of horror by saying:

> If the oblivion of being . . . should be real, would there not be occasion enough for a thinker who recalls being to experience a genuine horror? What more can his thinking do than endure in dread this fateful withdrawal while first of all facing up to the oblivion of being?[42]

What exactly does this say? The beginning of philosophy is wonder. Wonder is an ecstatic relation; it draws forward toward what is wondered at: it brings one up close to what is wondered at. Horror is, however, the relation of shrinking back, of struggling for distance to what is too close, too immediate to be borne. Wonder is the condition of production, what Heidegger calls cognitive *Er-sehen*, cognitive production of the thing. Horror is the condition of receipt, of being-produced, of cognitive abandonment of the thing for the sake of anything else that is other than the thing—the nothing. The thinker who recalls being will hear Zarathustra's mode of speaking in horror and as horror.

Horror and dread are, however, not my modes of being but the conditioning moods of the prevailing epoch. They are the tone in which Zarathustra speaks *back*. This receives repeated confirmation throughout Heidegger's work, from the publication of *Sein und Zeit* itself to the very end. In the lecture *Wer ist Nietzsches Zarathustra?* Heidegger says that Zarathustra's

---

41. *Grundfragen der Philosophie* (GA45), p. 2. "In ihr sind ursprünglich einig und zusammengehörig: das *Erschrecken* vor diesem Nächsten und Aufdringlichsten, daß Seiendes ist, und zugleich die *Scheu* vor dem Fernsten, daß im Seienden und vor jedem Seienden das Seyn west" (author's italics).

42. *Einleitung zu 'Was ist Metaphysik?'* (*Wegmarken* [GA9]), p. 371. "Wäre, wenn es mit der Seinsvergessenheit so stünde, nicht Veranlassung genug, daß ein Denken, das an das Sein denkt, in den Schrecken gerät, demgemäß es nichts anderes vermag, als dieses Geschick des Seins in der Angst auszuhalten, um erst das Denken an die Seinsvergessenheit zum Austrag zu bringen?"

'who' is decisive. Zarathustra as "the form of a teacher . . . who teaches the overman, involves us, involves Europe, involves the earth as a whole—not merely today but tomorrow. That is so, no matter whether we affirm or reject this thinking, whether we neglect it or ape it in false tones".[43] Heidegger occasionally asserts that in his work he invents nothing but speaks out of what already is taking place. The manner of speaking is a comportment *to* something. As early as *Sein und Zeit*, comportment belongs to λόγος as a determination of it as what brings something to be seen.[44] Affirmation, neglect, aping, falsehood, to which might be added concealment, forgottenness, cynicism, dread, horror, and so on are all relations, comportments toward something, modes of disclosure and cognition. They are the modes of disclosure of phenomena, as modes of speaking being and being spoken.

How is it that Europe is involved here? The prevailing epoch conditions the tone of the speaking of Zarathustra because these are the tones of the surrounding world. This surrounding world in its appearing, as it appears, is the overcoming of the barriers and limits which constitute the subject, barriers of an inner and outer world, of myself as substance, and so revealing me to be stretched out over time, the gap between my being as an entity and being itself. It is how Zarathustra brings speech itself to the fore, as not only its content but at the same time its tone, or 'how', and the fact that Zarathustra as a figure is most decisively not a subject, either imagined or real, that indicate that the inner and outer of the difference between the world and my-self is shown. In *Wer ist Nietzsches Zarathustra?* Heidegger says:

> In the piece "On the Great Longing" Zarathustra speaks with his soul. According to Plato's teaching, which became definitive for Western metaphysics, the essence of thinking is to be found in the soul's speaking with itself. It is the λόγος, ὃν αὐτὴ πρὸς αὐτὴν ἡ ψυχὴ διεζέρχεται

---

43. *Wer ist Nietzsches Zarathustra?* (*Vorträge und Aufsätze* [GA7]), p. 102f. "Die Gestalt eines Lehrers . . . der den Über-Menschen lehrt, geht uns, geht Europa, geht die ganze Erde an, nicht nur heute noch, sondern erst morgen. Das ist so, ganz unabhängig davon, ob wir dieses Denken bejahen oder bekämpfen, ob man es übergeht oder in falschen Tönen nachmacht."

44. *Sein und Zeit* (GA2), p. 34. "And finally, because λόγος as λεγόμενον can also signify that which, as something to which one addresses oneself, becomes visible in its relation to something in its 'relatedness', λόγος acquires the signification of *relation* and *relationship*" (author's italics). ("Und weil schließlich λόγος qua λεγόμενον auch bedeuten kann: das als etwas Angesprochene, was in seiner Beziehung zu etwas sichtbar geworden ist, in seiner 'Bezogenheit', erhält λόγος die Bedeutung von *Beziehung* und *Verhältnis*.")

234 — Heidegger's Atheism

περὶ ὧν ἄν σκοπῇ: the telling self-assembling which the soul itself undergoes on the way to itself, within the scope of whatever is showing itself.[45]

What Zarathustra places into question is speaking itself. Zarathustra, in speaking to himself as a speaking to his soul, can never speak *privily* to himself, for this speaking is received, open to everyone and yet no one has yet attained his saying. Speaking, as I have already argued, implies being in a world, being worlded.[46] Heidegger, in dialogue with Nietzsche, heeds (and hears) the speaking of Zarathustra and so himself is able to speak of what Nietzsche and Zarathustra have to say.

## THE DESTINY OF THE WEST

Europe is involved, therefore, because Europe is the surrounding world which is disclosed in the tone of Zarathustra's speech. In Heidegger's *Festschrift* piece for Ernst Jünger's sixtieth birthday he mentions again that human being exists as a turning toward and away in being. Repeating the structure of transcending of *die Kehre* Heidegger says:

> The human-essence depends on the fact that it lasts and dwells either in the turning-toward or turning-from.[47]

Heidegger adds that in speaking of the human-essence one says too little of being, leaving out the extent to which the human-essence determines

---

45. *Wer ist Nietzsches Zarathustra?* (*Vorträge und Aufsätze* [GA7]), p. 104f. "In dem Stück 'Von der großen Sehnsucht' spricht Zarathustra mit seiner Seele. Nach der Lehre Platons, die für die abendländische Metaphysik maßgebend wurde, beruht im Selbstgespräch der Seele mit sich selbst das Wesen des Denkens . . . Es ist der λόγος, ὄν αὐτὴ πρὸς αὐτὴν ἡ ψυχὴ διεξέρχεται περὶ ὧν ἄν σκοπῇ: das sagende Sichsammeln, das die Seele selbst auf dem Weg zu sich selbst durchgeht, im Umkreis dessen, was je erblickt (Theaetetus 189e; cf. Sophist 263e)."

46. On one occasion Heidegger uses a most entertaining illustration of this. He cites the example of a snail, noting that when the snail retreats into its shell, this is not a retreat from the world, but rather a different way of being in the world (Cf. *Prolegomena zur Geschichte des Zeitbegriffs* [GA20], p. 224).

47. *Zur Seinsfrage* (*Wegmarken* GA9), p. 407. "Das Menschenwesen beruht vielmehr darauf, daß es jeweils so oder so in der Zuwendung und Abwendung währt und wohnt."

being: too little is said of humanity if in saying 'being', "we . . . set humans apart and then only bring that which has thus been set apart into relationship with being".[48] Being and being human constitute relationship *as such*, which from the perspective of being human is disclosed in comportment. All relationship as turning (in transcending, so that transcending and comporting are the same thing) is disclosed in λόγος, in a mode of disclosure, as a speaking. So comportment is a speaking and being also 'speaks'.

Horror, as Zarathustra's mode of speaking, is, because it is the mode of withdrawal, the mode of nihilism. In the Jünger *Festschrift* Heidegger speaks cryptically about the movement of nihilism, a phrase which I have already considered.[49] He does this in the context of speaking of Jünger's 1932 essay *Der Arbeiter*, which, he says, gives an account of what Nietzsche describes as "active nihilism": "The action of the work consists in the fact that it makes the 'total work character' of all reality visible from the figure of the worker".[50] He adds: "Thus nihilism, which at first is only European, appears in its planetary tendency".[51] That Heidegger links the Nazi regime to nihilism itself becomes clear when he speaks of how he undertook in 1939 and 1940 "to think on a planetary scale" (one of *Der Arbeiter*'s central themes), through an attempt to work through, with a number of others, the meaning of the text of *Der Arbeiter*.[52] He adds that the attempt to study this text was initially watched and finally forbidden. He concludes:

For it belongs to the essence of the will to power that reality, which it powers-up and produces is not allowed to appear as that reality which it itself essences.[53]

---

48. *Zur Seinsfrage* (*Wegmarken* GA9), p. 407. "Wir . . . [setzen] den Menschen für sich und [bringen] das so Gesetzte dann erst noch in eine Beziehung zum 'Sein'."

49. *Zur Seinsfrage* (*Wegmarken* GA9), p. 386. "The movement of Nihilism." See p. 220 above.

50. *Zur Seinsfrage* (*Wegmarken* GA9), p. 389. "'Aktiven Nihilismus' . . . die Aktion des Werkes bestand . . . darin, daß es den 'totalen Arbeitscharakter' alles Wirklichen aus der Gestalt des Arbeiters sichtbar macht."

51. *Zur Seinsfrage* (*Wegmarken* GA9), p. 389. "So erscheint der anfänglich nur europäische Nihilismus in seiner planetarischen Tendenz."

52. *Zur Seinsfrage* (*Wegmarken* GA9), p. 390. "Planetarisch zu denken."

53. *Zur Seinsfrage* (*Wegmarken* GA9), p. 390. "Denn es gehört zum Wesen des Willens zur Macht, das Wirkliche, das er be-mächtigt, nicht in der Wirklichkeit erscheinen zu lassen, als welche er selber west."

The powers of Nazism are understood in the will to power, that moment which enforces itself powerfully as something appearing other than it really is. In what follows Heidegger offers some insight into his personal view of the situation before and after Nazism. He asserts "the movement of nihilism has become more manifest in its planetary, all-corroding, many-faceted irresistibleness".[54] He adds: "The two world wars neither checked the movement of nihilism nor diverted it from its course".[55] These passages say nothing directly about Heidegger's engagement with Nazism and his continued membership in the Nazi Party right up to 1945. Indeed, here Heidegger confirms his refusal to acknowledge the particularity of Nazism, because he sees the whole movement of nihilism as something inaugurated before the First World War (and still continuing). In this shocking move Heidegger places *our* political engagements also under scrutiny as in themselves also a comportment to nihilism, because the movement of nihilism, which takes many forms (only one of which is Nazism), is what constitutes this epoch. The still-continuing movement of nihilism is the condition under which I am also questioned when I seek to question Heidegger.

## HEIDEGGER'S POLITICAL ENGAGEMENT

It is in connection with these matters that Heidegger raises the question of his own political engagement and how he understood it. I do not propose to resolve this issue but note that if I am to make a demand on Heidegger, for instance that he explain himself, I must also face that same demand. This is in effect Heidegger's riposte to a certain way of reading his work. This reading, without ever putting itself into question, presumes to question Heidegger in a search that says (in advance) Heidegger was just that kind of philosopher whose politics and thought must belong together, and so if I (whoever 'I' might be here) can simply indicate the connection, if I can isolate the passages which indicate the connection between the two, then my search is over, my thesis vindicated, and another Nazi is condemned, this without paying much attention to just what a 'Nazi' might be—which means 'who'—and

---

54. *Zur Seinsfrage* (*Wegmarken* GA9), p. 392. "Die Bewegung des Nihilismus [ist] in ihrer planetarischen und alles anzehrenden, vielgestaltigen Unaufhaltsamkeit offenkundiger geworden."

55. *Zur Seinsfrage* (*Wegmarken* GA9), p. 394f. "Die zwei Weltkriege haben die Bewegung des Nihilismus weder aufgehalten, noch aus ihrer Richtung abgelenkt."

never myself entering the search. In other words, 'I' remain just as that generalized and neutral *theoretically constructed* 'I' which pretends to universal knowledge and so to the right to speak for *us all*. Heidegger, whose *Selbstbehauptung* was to lead him into the Nazi Party, challenges me to reveal from what *Selbstbehauptung* I also question him. It is not enough to take for granted that the place from which I speak is not itself open to question.

Part of the difficulty of coming to terms with Heidegger's political engagement is that what is at issue is not as simple as it at first seems. Most commentators (particularly those who are most critical) want to identify what it is about Heidegger's thinking that either propels him in the direction of or rescues him from being a Nazi. This has led to the often journalistic approach exemplified by Tom Rockmore, who gives a chapter in one of his works the title *Revealing Concealed Nazism in Heidegger's Thinking.*[56] James Ward suggests that the "Heidegger Case" belongs on the periphery of his texts, because "I am convinced his political thinking transcends his political engagement".[57] What Ward points toward, although he does not adopt this particular way of articulating it, is that Heidegger's political engagement and his subsequent commentary or silence about that engagement were primarily his own attempts to bring himself into proximity with what he was thinking. What is at issue is whether I want to think 'Heidegger', the author of doctrines and systems whose entanglements may or may not revolt me (for whatever reason) or that I want to think *about* what Heidegger thought *about*. The question is one of proximity: proximity to Heidegger, to Europe (or the tradition of interpretation in which I stand and which is still constitutive for me not just as a tradition, but in terms of what I eat, how I behave and think, and so forth), to how I understand a planetary or (in a more contemporary voice) global situation.

Perhaps the most serious charge (if we are making charges) against Heidegger is that of his having no ethics, essentially the charge laid against him by Emmanuel Lévinas. From the perspective of Christian theological thinking, however, it is required that Heidegger have no ethics, for two reasons. First, if being is not either to be understood as *summum ens* or as *summum bonum*, if, in other words, being, or the good, and God are not the same, then the disclosure of being itself to itself (*Dasein*'s being as the place of the ontological difference) both need not and must not lay any foundation for ethics. Only abstractions from and objectifications of the ontological

56. Cf. Rockmore, T., *On Heidegger's Nazism and Philosophy* (1993).
57. Ward, J., *Heidegger's Political Thinking* (1995), p. xix.

difference will be ethical, but that resolute 'turning into' the question of being as such, the resolute questioning of every erection of moral norms, will itself take the form of what is articulated by Zarathustra as the *overcoming* of the moral as a self-grounding sphere, of the destroying of the moral back to its roots. Any attempt to construct a morality *on the basis of the being of beings alone* will produce a false God. Only God and the gods (who are not being) might offer, through revelation, or the appearing of the divine, something like an ethics. Why do I behave in a moral way apart from God? To ask this question is to ask it as if it were in a vacuum apart from every pattern of behavior, every manner and mannerism, every social and moral code into which I have entered (which means have entered into me, as things I learn and have learned), is to ask the question to be meaningful while denying it the very possibility of its meaning at all, history, and context.

Should the philosopher of being have himself been without blame in the sphere of the moral and political, which is simply to ask nothing other than why the faithful believer still sins and is in need of forgiveness. The mistake has been not to inquire into Heidegger's Nazism, but rather to assume that what he thought *of* is itself tainted by *how* he brought himself to think it. Was Heidegger a Nazi? Yes, and yet as a statement it says very little. Was Heidegger's thought infected with Nazism even before 1933, which is to ask only about Heidegger and not about being. Hans Sluga makes exactly this point in relation to Gottlob Frege's avowed anti-Semitism and its relation to his mathematics.[58] Was Heidegger so detached from what he thought *of* that the question has no meaning? Of course not, which is why there is a question. The question as it arises in connection both with what Heidegger thought *of* and his political engagement can only be understood as his articulation of nihilism.

Heidegger, citing Jünger, noted: "The area of completed nihilism forms the boundary between two eras. The line designating it is the critical line. By means of it is determined whether the movement of nihilism ends in negative nothingness or whether it is the transition to the realm of a 'new turning-toward on the part of being'".[59] If, however, nihilism is a normal state of affairs, then what comes to be at issue is *how* I relate myself to it, which

---

58. Sluga, H., *Heidegger's Crisis* (1993), p. 99f.
59. *Zur Seinsfrage* (*Wegmarken* GA9), p. 386. "Der Bezirk des vollendeten Nihilismus bildet die Grenze zwischen zwei Weltaltern. Die ihn bezeichnende Linie ist die kritische Linie. An ihr entscheidet sich, ob die Bewegung des Nihilismus im nichtigen Nichts verendet oder ob sie der Übergang in den Bereich einer 'neuen Zuwendung des

means *who* I might be with regard to the movement of nihilism. Heidegger confirms that what (following Jünger) he refers to as the figure (*die Gestalt*) of the worker is that form which, through the globalization of technical dominance of the earth, is the movement of nihilism. He concludes: "The metaphysical seeing of the form of the worker corresponds to the outline of the essential-form of Zarathustra within the metaphysics of the will to power".[60] What is important here is that Zarathustra can only speak now, when nihilism appears as global technical domination. Is Zarathustra the worker? Surely, Zarathustra is the one who reveals to the worker who he or she is. The worker works (the resonance here is of *die Wirklichkeit,* the real, as a work, a production, but with its additional senses of weft and texture) because God is dead.

## ZARATHUSTRA AND *DASEIN*

The metaphysical form of the worker is nihilistic. Its metaphysical figure is Zarathustra, who *is* the form of nihilism *as* the figure and form of the legitimized (and this means epochal) being of the essence of being-human. What does it then mean to attain to Zarathustra in the way Heidegger first describes Zarathustra's essence? Precisely this: to think through and experience the will to power. Put another way, this means, to be of one's age, to be of the times in the most extreme sense: to have seen into the essence of the age. It also means that who Zarathustra is will be determined out of what Zarathustra has to say. Heidegger rejects any reading of *Zarathustra* as a projection simply of Nietzsche's imagination. He says: "The solution frequently offered in the form of an observation, that Nietzsche's thinking had fatally turned over into poetry, is itself an abandonment of thoughtful questioning".[61]

---

Seins' ist." The reference to lines is to Jünger's use of the word line in the title of his address to Heidegger, "*Über die Linie*" ("Across the Line"). The original title of *Zur Seinsfrage* was *Über 'die Linie'*" ("On 'the Line'").

60. *Zur Seinsfrage* (*Wegmarken* GA9), p. 396. "Das metaphysische Sehen der Gestalt des Arbeiters entspricht dem Entwurf der Wesensgestalt des Zarathustra innerhalb der Metaphysik des Willens zur Macht."

61. *Zur Seinsfrage* (*Wegmarken* GA9), p. 396. "Die oft gegebene Auskunft, Nietzsches Denken sei fatalerweise ins Dichten geraten, ist selbst nur die Preisgabe des denkenden Fragens."

Heidegger explicitly discusses the relationship of Zarathustra to *Dasein* in the Jünger *Festschrift*. He concludes in the same passage as he discusses the figurative form of Zarathustra, "the essence (verbal) of humanity, the '*Dasein* in humanity' is nothing human".[62] From this he immediately proceeds to discuss the nature of transcendence in its relation to the ontological difference, the being of beings. Heidegger gives as a proof-text the citation of section 43 of *Kant und das Problem der Metaphysik*. The text (which he does not cite) reads:

> The *Dasein* in humanity determines the human as that being who, being (*seiend*) in the midst of beings comports itself to them as such and who, as this comporting to beings, is essentially differently determined in its own being from all other beings manifest in *Dasein*.[63]

I have already explored how the essence of Zarathustra is the character of relationship or comportment, and how Zarathustra relates to transcendence. Such comportment toward beings is in fact a comportment toward being itself. For Heidegger, therefore, Zarathustra is neither an imaginary figure nor the analytic of *Dasein*, but a retro-jection, the form of the *return* of the transcendence of *Dasein* in an epochal moment, the moment of nihilism. Zarathustra *is* in a sense the being of beings in reverse, not human *Dasein* in its speaking to being, but being in its speaking to *Dasein*, nothing human, something verbal, something which has the character of returning (the inverse of transcending in order, for instance, to know the lectern).

Heidegger repeatedly says throughout all the *Nietzsche* lectures that Zarathustra, the teacher of overman, is the teacher of the eternal return, which means the teacher of the meaning of *die Kehre*. As I indicated in chapter 3, however, *die Kehre* is *die Wendung* in its coming to speech.[64] Horror and anxiety belong to *die Wendung*. Heidegger says of horror and essence in the 1946 essay *Wozu Dichter?*:

---

62. *Zur Seinsfrage* (*Wegmarken* GA9), p. 397. "Aber das Wesen (verbal) des Menschen, 'das Dasein im Menschen' (vgl. *Kant und das Problem der Metaphysik*, 1. Aufl. 1929, §43) ist nichts Menschliches."

63. *Kant und das Problem der Metaphysik* (GA3), p. 234. "Das Dasein im Menschen bestimmt diesen als jenes Seiende, das, inmitten von Seiendem seiend, zu diesem als einem solchen sich verhält und als dieses Verhalten zu Seiendem wesenhaft anders in seinem eigenen Sein bestimmt wird denn alles übrige im Dasein offenbare Seiende."

64. Heidegger retains *die Wendung* as a name for *die Kehre* as late even as the 1955 Jünger *Festschrift* in order to echo Jünger's 1932 use of the "neuen Zuwendung des Seins", already quoted in *Zur Seinsfrage* (*Wegmarken* [GA9], p. 386).

Even horror, taken by itself as a ground for turning, is powerless as long as it does not turn itself with mortals. But there is a turn with mortals when these find the way to their own essence.[65]

Finding the way to (and this means attaining) his essence as a speaking is what Zarathustra is called to do. In this sense, Zarathustra speaks *die Wendung* as *die Kehre*. This speaking is in the mode of discovery, a shrinking back, and a turning away from.

In *Also sprach Zarathustra* the ring or circularity in its differing forms in the text is understood by Heidegger to be the figure of eternal return. He understands the ring to be disclosed as the eternal return both by Zarathustra's animals (the circling eagle around whose neck is coiled the serpent) and the two pathways leading out from the doorway above which is the title *Moment*. Early on I characterized Zarathustra as the form or figure of the will to power. Zarathustra is that one who speaks the will to power from out of the eternal recurrence. This speaking is in consequence of a movement.

At the very beginning of Nietzsche's text, Zarathustra goes under—the verb is *Untergehen* which means not simply to go down, but to sink, to decline, to come to an end, to disappear: "Thus began Zarathustra's going-under".[66] This *Untergang* opposes the *trans-scendens*. Zarathustra begins by moving to an end. Heidegger says, "For Zarathustra begins by going under. Zarathustra's commencement is his downgoing. Nietzsche thought no other essence for Zarathustra".[67] This discussion comes in the context of a lecture entitled *Third Communication of the Doctrine of Eternal Return*, a section entirely concerned with God and with Zarathustra as the "god-less one". So for Heidegger, Zarathustra is the one whose going-under, *de*-cline is in consequence of his godlessness and it is to communicate this godlessness in its character that the downgoing occurs. The communication of godlessness is

---

65. *Wozu Dichter?* (*Holzwege* [GA5]), p. 271. "[Weil] sogar der Schrecken, für sich als ein Grund der Wendung genommen, nichts vermag, solange es sich nicht mit den Sterblichen wendet. Mit den Sterblichen wendet es sich aber, wenn sie in ihr eigenes Wesen finden."

66. Nietzsche, F., *Also Sprach Zarathustra* (*Friedrich Nietzsche* [1999], IV), p. 12. "Also begann Zarathustra's Untergang."

67. *Die ewige Wiederkehr des Gleichen* (*Nietzsche* [GA6], I), p. 323. "Zarathustras Anfang ist sein Untergang, ein anderes Wesen Zarathustras hat Nietzsche niemals gedacht."

the devaluation of the uppermost values, the speaking out *of* and *as* the will to power. It is what Zarathustra has to say.

In Heidegger's 1940 lecture course *Der europäische Nihilismus* he comments: "Nietzsche mostly understands the moral as the system of those valuations in which a transcendent world is posited as the desired standard of measure. Nietzsche consistently understands the moral metaphysically, that is with a view to the fact that in it something is decided about the whole of beings".[68] The proclamation of the death of God is none other than that event in which the uppermost values are devalued and where the thought of morality ceases to have any meaning. The ideal-moral (the uppermost values) is replaced by the values posited by the subject in a revaluation.

The devaluation of the uppermost values is carried out for and as a revaluation. This revaluation occurs as the will to power. Zarathustra's going down is a revaluation and an *Umkehre*, a turn-about of the 'way' things are— the way they present themselves and are comported to. However, this devaluation is not an intellection, but as I have already argued in chapter 5, a basic experience. The supplanting of intellection by experience is precisely the mark of this turn-about, the inversion of Plato and the Greeks.

## THE SECOND SOLUTION TO THE RIDDLE OF THE DOORWAY

With these preliminary remarks in mind, it is now possible to make sense of the second solution to the riddle of the doorway, which the dwarf resolved disdainfully as his 'how' in chapter 4. Referring to the text of *Also sprach Zarathustra*, Heidegger says that in the allegory of the young shepherd into whose mouth the black snake has fastened itself, the black snake is nihilism. The shepherd must bite off the head of the snake in an eyeblink in order to release it from his mouth. Zarathustra is the shepherd or the doorway itself; *he* is the solution to the riddle. He also therefore experiences *from within* the eyeblink, the demand of the moment, the place where *Ereignis* takes place. In understanding this, it is possible to understand that the doctrine of eternal recurrence is the overcoming of nihilism, of metaphysics itself, in a turning toward what comes out of the future.

---

68. *Der europäische Nihilismus* (*Nietzsche* [GA6.2]), p. 118. "Unter Moral versteht Nietzsche meist das System solcher Wertschätzungen, in denen eine übersinnliche Welt als maßgebend und wünschbar gesetzt wird. Nietzsche begreift die 'Moral' stets 'metaphysisch', d.h. im Hinblick darauf, daß in ihr über das Ganze des Seienden entschieden wird."

To be on the threshhold, in the doorway, is to be where 'I' most am in my own time, where I attain the moment and make it my own: "This means: inserting oneself into the temporality of acting for oneself and deciding by looking ahead into what is coming to me and behind into what is given as endowment", which would be the originary experience of time.[69] If the snake is the meaninglessness of nihilism as such, biting into the snake however is the event (*das Ereignis*), the thought of the eternal recurrence, in the moment of its overcoming. This means that God (being in general) as thought metaphysically is the very ground of nihilism. The overcoming of nihilism, the seizing of the moment is in itself, then, a renewed being open to God.

When 'I' come to myself, when I can think the moment, I am faced with what lies on the two sides of the threshold: everything matters, all is alike; and nothing has meaning, all is alike. I can meditate on the endowment, what has already been given to me, and I can decide the task (for the future) that is mine. I can think and act. (The echo of what it means to be resolved in *Sein und Zeit* is intended here.) The possibility of likeness is raised for the first time and as a likeness that retains difference within it (the very sense of the likeness of the 'same' that van Buren overlooked in chapter 5).

The title of the twenty-third division of the Neske text is *The Doctrine of Return as the Overcoming of Nihilism*.[70] Zarathustra is the one whose task is to say the doctrine of the eternal recurrence. Because he is this, he also (for Heidegger) says *die Kehre*. The dwarf remains solely a spectator.[71]

Heidegger cites Zarathustra's early encounter with the saint (in the second chapter of *Zarathustra*) who has *as yet* heard nothing of the fact that God is dead. It is important to notice that this discovery takes place for Heidegger as a sexual difference, as one of the few places where Heidegger refers specifically to sexual difference as such. He notes in the same lecture that the God who is dead is (for Nietzsche) "The God of 'morality', the Christian God is dead—the 'Father' in whom we seek sanctuary . . . the 'paymaster' from whom we receive our virtues' reward, that God with

---

69. *Die ewige Wiederkehr des Gleichen* (*Nietzsche* [GA6.1]), p. 446. "Dies besagt: das Sichversetzen in die Zeitlichkeit des Selbsthandelns und Entscheidens aus dem Vorblick in das Aufgegebene und im Rückblick auf das Mitgegebene."

70. *Die ewige Wiederkehr des Gleichen* (*Nietzsche* [GA6.1]), p. 432. The section *Die Wiederkunftslehre als Überwindung des Nihilismus*.

71. Cf. *Die ewige Wiederkehr des Gleichen* (*Nietzsche* [GA6.1]), p. 311.

whom we 'do business.'" He adds: "Yet where is the mother who will take pay for loving her child?"[72]

The death of this particular sexual identity of God as a move from father to mother is itself the devaluation of the uppermost values and the revaluation of all values, the going-down as a reversal, a turning-over of the sexual hierarchy of the Greeks. Sexual difference, as a sameness that is also a difference, can for the first time appear and be understood anew.

Heidegger points out that the coming about of this body in Nietzsche's thinking is a body figured not biologically but in the will to power, that is, figured metaphysically, just indeed as it is sexually differentiated metaphysically, and for Nietzsche this means nihilistically, motherhood, as that which for the first time is also contained in the child.[73] He notes: "'Body' is the name for that form of the will to power, in which it is immediately accessible to the human being as a distinct 'subject', because it is always a distinct component of his/her condition".[74] It is this having of a body, however, which is both brought to light nihilistically and metaphysically, which allows for the possibility of thinking *Dasein* as embodied. Already in 1928 Heidegger had noted that in elaborating the facticity of *Dasein*, "*Dasein* harbors the inner possibility for the factical dispersion in bodiliness and therefore sexedness".[75] What is the difference between figuring the body metaphysically as opposed to understanding it in its essence?

Heidegger's point is that the reappearance of the body makes possible the overcoming of metaphysics, but is not yet this overcoming. Nowhere could this be clearer than in the appearance of Zarathustra himself, for

---

72. *Die ewige Wiederkehr des Gleichen* (*Nietzsche* [GA6.1]), p. 321. "Der 'moralische' Gott, der christliche Gott ist tot; der 'Vater', zu dem man sich rettet, die 'Persönlichkeit', mit der man verhandelt und sich ausspricht, der 'Richter', mit dem man rechtet, der 'Belohner', durch den man sich für seine Tugenden bezahlen läßt, jener Gott, mit dem man seine 'Geschäfte' macht . . . der 'moralisch' gesehene Gott und nur dieser ist gemeint, wenn Nietzsche sagt: 'Gott ist tot' . . . Wo aber läßt sich eine Mutter für ihre Liebe zum Kind bezahlen?"

73. Cf. Nietzsche, F., *Also sprach Zarathustra* (*Friedrich Nietzsche* [1999], IV), p. 123. "Daß euer Selbst in der Handlung sei, wie die Mutter im Kinde ist"

74. *Nietzsche* (GA50), p. 48. "'Leib' ist der Name für jene Gestalt des Willens zur Macht, in der dieser dem Menschen als dem ausgezeichneten 'Subjekt' unmittelbar zugänglich, weil stets zuständlich ist."

75. *Metaphysische Anfangsgründe der Logik* (GA26), p. 173. "Das Dasein überhaupt birgt die innere Möglichkeit für die faktische Zerstreuung in die Leiblichkeit und damit in die Geschlechtlichkeit."

Zarathustra has no body at all, but only *is* as a figure, who speaks metaphysically. The figuration (as I have noted with respect to the analysis of transcendence) is a reflection, a retrojection, a return of the projection of *Dasein;* it is not *Dasein* embodied as such. Zarathustra is the non-embodied form or figure who brings bodiliness to light philosophically.

Nietzsche's word, God is dead, brings to light the possibility of thinking through the sexedness, or as might now be said, gendering, of me, of my 'I'. Conversely, 'I' comes to be questionable as sexed or gendered. Sexedness enters into the questionability that *Dasein* is. It would be incorrect to say that there is a fully worked-through discussion of sexual and gender difference in Heidegger's reading of Nietzsche or even in Heidegger's work in general. What is clear, however, is that Heidegger envisages such a thinking-through on the basis of the possibilities opened by the death of God or by Heidegger's own atheism.

Heidegger believed *die Kehre* to be just that ambiguous moment both revealed and simultaneously concealed in the figurative form of Zarathustra, a figurative form who in coming about in the ontological difference between being and beings is nothing human, but only the speaking of speaking. Nietzsche, in bringing the completion of metaphysics about, also prepared for its overcoming. But Heidegger is *that one* who speaks of overcoming in consequence of what Zarathustra says to him. In this sense, Heidegger becomes Zarathustra, attains his essence as *that one* who speaks to Nietzsche. Heidegger's discovery of who Zarathustra is, is Heidegger's own *Selbstbehauptung.*

Here there is also a reversal in play: for Heidegger's attaining to who Zarathustra is takes place through the most profound meditation on interpretation, where speaking is shown to belong together with hearing, a theme recurrent in Heidegger.[76] This hearing is the hearing that withdraws to pay attention and remain obedient to the call of being. The one who continues to speak will speak in the manner that Zarathustra speaks, in a manner determined by horror. The hearing of horror, however, will usher in what Heidegger calls the new beginning. This, however, does not take place in isolation, but in a sphere which is planetary, in the context of the globalization

---

76. He alerts us to the importance of the way these two, hearing and seeing, belong together at the very beginning of his lectures on Plato's *Sophist* by reminding his audience that the opening section of Aristotle's *Metaphysics* begins with a consideration of the relation between hearing and seeing (Cf. *Platon: Sophistes* [GA19], p. 70f.).

of technology, in the arena which can also be figured as the political, but also as that place which is in play with itself and which I have to attain in order to speak and be spoken to, hear and be heard.

All of this is confirmed in *Überwindung der Metaphysik*, written between 1936 and 1946, exactly those years which coincide with the Nietzsche lectures and dealing entirely with their themes, yet never addressing directly the 'who' of Zarathustra, and where incidentally, there are again repeated references to Jünger's *Der Arbeiter*. The issue at hand is the overcoming of being (*das Sein*) that is *Er-eignis*.[77] Here the perspective outlined is of an overcoming of metaphysics that begins as a going-under. Heidegger warns: "Metaphysics as overcome does not vanish".[78] Rather what is at issue is the passing of metaphysics. What Heidegger is pointing toward is a renewed experience of time. To pass away in German is *vergehen*. The past is that which is *vergangen*. To find a way in is to find *der Eingang*. So Heidegger says that "in that metaphysics passes away, is it past . . . but metaphysics is past in the sense that it has entered into its ending".[79] Metaphysics, in confronting the possibility of its being overcome in the death of God, enters into the temporalizing passingness of time and opens up a renewed experience of time (as other than past, i.e., as futural) from a new origin, a new beginning. For Heidegger, Zarathustra is that one, who, in speaking in the horror of the ending of metaphysics, allows the origin of the new beginning to be heard.

Who then am I? In *Selbstbehauptung*, self-assertion, where the self comes to itself and so comes about as a being for itself in the ontological difference, *I* can become one who heeds the meaning of the death of God and so am re-opened to what it would mean to have faith. *Selbstbehauptung* as my unwilled coming to myself is the new beginning. To be an 'I' at all is to stand in the possibility of beginning again.

In *Selbstbehauptung*, I become one who might yet believe, not despite, or in the face of, or against nihilism, but in consequence of it, and this means, by being comported to it and turning into it—as one who turns into the essence of nihilism and experiences it from *within in order to believe*. In step-

---

77. *Überwindung der Metaphysik* in *Vorträge und Aufsätze* (GA7), p. 67. "Es ist das Ereignis, in dem das Sein selbst verwunden wird."

78. *Überwindung der Metaphysik* in *Vorträge und Aufsätze* (GA7), p. 68. "Die überwundene Metaphysik verschwindet nicht."

79. *Überwindung der Metaphysik* in *Vorträge und Aufsätze* (GA7), p. 67. "Indem die Metaphysik vergeht, *ist* sie vergangen . . . ist aber die Metaphysik zugleich vergangen in dem Sinne, daß sie in ihre Ver-endung eingegangen ist.

ping out of everydayness, out of the anonymity of *das Man* of *Sein und Zeit,* and into the demand of the moment, not because I will to, but called out in heeding what being has to say, I am torn between the fulfillment of metaphysics, of nihilism as a normal state of affairs and discovering myself as questionable and questioned, which means discovering myself at all. This *Selbstbehauptung,* which is nothing other than self-interpretation, reveals for me the extent to which nihilism is a normal state of affairs in the world in which I find myself, and reveals to me the extent to which this environment re-opens the question of who God is.

Chapter Eight

# Jean-Luc Marion and the Contemporary Theological Appropriation of Heidegger

## JEAN-LUC MARION'S READING OF HEIDEGGER

In the previous chapters I have endeavored to unfold how Heidegger's atheism opens up the place for the divine, the being of beings as the ontological difference, but refuses to think the essence of God. The site may remain empty, as in nihilism, or God may enter this place. For the one who seeks to believe, the question remains: entered how? Before coming to some conclusions of my own about what Heidegger's atheism means and how it might be understood, in this chapter I examine how one theologian has constructed a contemporary response to Heidegger's work as a response to what he says of being and how this theologian understands it. I want to show how this response fails, in important but nevertheless irretrievable ways, precisely because it has taken a conventional reading of Heidegger to be sufficient to explain what Heidegger has to say. There is not the space in this book to work out in full all the theological consequences of Heidegger's work. The task I set myself at the beginning was to raise Martin Heidegger's atheism as an issue, one which has consequences for contemporary theology. In conclusion, I want to do no more than indicate what the possibilities might be if Heidegger's atheism is understood and taken seriously by anyone who wishes to speak of God, even those who would deny that God is.

Jean-Luc Marion is the contemporary theologian who, perhaps more than any other, has attempted to engage with the work of Martin Heidegger, and to address with considerable seriousness the demands he believes Heidegger to be making on the work of theologians, particularly after Heidegger's description of theology as metaphysics. Although he has considered Heidegger's work in a number of places (notably in *L'Idole et la Distance*, published in 1977), his most important confrontation has been in *Dieu sans l'être*, published in 1982. In the preface to the English edition of this work, *God without Being*, Marion describes his project as a "confrontation between the philosophical prohibitions of nihilism and the demanding opening of Christian revelation".[1] He brackets the name of the metaphysical God as 'God' and replies by offering a theology of G⊗d, as the one who does not occupy the site proffered in Heidegger's ontological difference but attempts to transgress ontological difference altogether.

In the *Envoi* to *Dieu sans l'être* the question which emerges from the tension between the prohibitions of nihilism and the opening of Christian revelation is: "God, before all else, has to be . . . but does being relate, more than anything, to God? . . . and what if God did not have first to be, since he loved us first, when we were not?".[2] For Marion, this question takes place in the attempt to contrast the idol and the icon "in order to advance to being—the name of God that in theology is assumed to be the first, just as in philosophy God, as first being, supposedly invests being".[3] From the beginning, Marion names philosophy and theology as standing in different relations to the question of being.

Marion sketches out the initial impetus of the project of *Dieu sans l'être* in the terms of Heidegger's question of being. He opposes Heidegger's phenomenological path: for him, the gift is not *of* being (in either of the double sense in which Heidegger described it from the *Humanismusbrief*, the objective and subjective genitive) but stands in opposition to being, because God, who comes as gift (and so by implication is the one who gives being at all), does not fall within the domain of being. Immediately, therefore, the whole topic within which Marion is attempting to address Heidegger is that which the Scholastic tradition has understood to be the naming of God in univocal, equivocal, or analogical terms. More simply, he raises the questions, are God and being the same; is God subordinate to being or radically exteriorized to it; or is there some other relation?

---

1. Marion, J.-L., *God without Being* (1991), p. xix.
2. Marion, J.-L., *Dieu sans l'être* (1982), p. 11. "Dieu, avant toute autre chose, a à être . . . Mais l'être a-t-il rapport, plus que quoi que ce soit, à Dieu? . . . et si Dieu n'avait pas, d'abord à être, puisqu'il nous a aimé le premier, quand nous n'étions point?"
3. Marion, J.-L., *Dieu sans l'être* (1982), p. 11. "Pour . . . avancer jusques à l'être—nom supposé premier de Dieu en théologie, comme, en philosophie, Dieu investit censément comme étant premier l'être."

Marion wishes to move from a God who is the promise of what stands *sans l'être* (not just without being, but by implication *sans lettre*, without the text), as the transgression of the text, which in the *Hors-Texte* to his work he argues stems from the Eucharist where, because "love makes the body",[4] the Eucharistic mystery is one of charity.[5] Love, in consequence, precedes the event of corporeality, facticity, and being. For Marion, this movement transgresses Heidegger's thought because it overcomes his (atheistic) phenomenology with a theology of revelation. From the outset, therefore, Marion wants to show that revelation is more primordial, more original (closer to the origin, as closer to God), than a (Godless, atheistic) phenomenology.

Marion's resolution of Heidegger's analysis of being (and his fulfillment of this project) is to decide to free God from being altogether. This decision, as I show, inevitably leads him into conflict with St. Thomas Aquinas, because of the way in which he understands Aquinas's elaboration of *esse*, and precisely because of the extent to which he has failed to appreciate how the finitude of the ontological difference does not transgress God's infinitude, but is precisely what allows God to appear at all. This conflict is of an entirely different order to Heidegger's engagement with Aquinas. Marion's reading of Aquinas throws such important light on his reading of Heidegger and simultaneously illustrates the extent to which Heidegger is speaking out of the same tradition from which Aquinas also speaks, that it will be discussed more fully in the conclusion of this chapter.

## MARION'S ATHEISM

Marion identifies in Heidegger a move from the (atheistic) phenomenological analytic of *Dasein* accomplished "in fact *definitively*"[6] in his earlier work, to a second moment, that of the anteriority of *das Sein* over *Dasein:* "The later isolated anteriority of being is secured concretely by *Dasein* over itself; phenomenologically, the anteriority of being can be developed and justified

---

4. Marion, J.-L., *Dieu sans l'être* (1982), p. 12. "L'amour fait le corps."

5. Cf. Marion, J.-L., *Dieu sans l'être* (1982), p. 226. "Le mystère eucharistique de charité."

6. Marion, J.-L., *Dieu sans l'être* (1982), p. 66. "En fait *définitif*" (author's italics).

252 — Heidegger's Atheism

only by the anteriority of the analytic of *Dasein*".[7] The "appearance of an extremely individualistic, radical atheism",[8] which lays the basis for the analytic of *Dasein*, prepares for the possibility of the movement toward the isolation of being and makes possible the "double idolatry" of "theologically an instance anterior to 'God,' hence that point from which idolatry could dawn".[9] The move that Marion identifies is the "turn",[10] and this usage indicates the extent to which Marion reads Heidegger in the conventional framework initiated by Karl Löwith and developed by William Richardson, which was discussed in chapters 3 and 4.

Marion asserts that, prior to the turn, the analytic of *Dasein* is secured phenomenologically *over* being, in advance of it: subsequent to the turn, being takes priority. It is in this way that he reads Heidegger's comments concerning God at the end of the Bremen lecture *Die Kehre*: "also the God is—if (*wenn*) he is [Marion translates 'when he is']—a being, and stands as a being in being and its presence, which brings itself disclosingly out of the worlding of world".[11] The essential thought here is if. *If* has less of a sense of necessity, which is exactly the sense in which Heidegger intends it. Marion reads it as *when* in order to stress a necessary sense that Heidegger precisely does not intend.

Marion, having cited the phrase from the lecture *Die Kehre*, asks: "but is it self-evident that God should have to be, hence to be as a being (supreme, plural—however you like) in order to give himself as God? How is it that being finds itself admitted without question?".[12] It is the phrase from the

---

7. Marion, J.-L., *Dieu sans l'être* (1982), p. 66. "L'antériorité ultérieurement isolée du *Sein* se conquiert ici concrètement par le *Dasein* sur lui-même; phénoménologiquement l'antériorité de l'Être ne peut se déployer et se justifier que par l'antériorité de l'analytique du *Dasein*."

8. Marion, J.-L., *Dieu sans l'être* (1982), p. 67. "L'apparence d'un athéisme extrêmement individualiste et radical."

9. Marion, J.-L., *Dieu sans l'être* (1982), p. 67. "Une instance antérieure à 'Dieu', donc ce à partir de quoi l'idolâtrie pourrait poindre."

10. Marion, J.-L., *Dieu sans l'être* (1982), p. 66, "tournant."

11. *Die Kehre* (*Bremer und Freiburger Vorträge* [GA79]), p 76. "Denn auch der Gott ist, wenn er ist, ein Seiender, steht als Seiender im Seyn und dessen Wesen, das sich aus dem Welten von Welt ereignet." Marion in fact quotes the text from *Die Technik und die Kehre*, which is identical to the *Gesamtausgabe* text, with the exception that the latter writes *das Sein* as *das Seyn*.

12. Marion, J.-L., *Dieu sans l'être* (1982), p. 69. "Mais va-t-il de soi que Dieu ait à être, donc à être en tant qu'étant (suprême, pluriel, ou comme on voudra) pour se donner comme Dieu? D'où vient que l'Être se trouve admis sans question?"

lecture *Die Kehre* that leads him to the project of thinking God without being, which he describes as a critical demand, that he must attempt to think God outside the ontological difference. The only possible way of understanding what it is that Marion is concerned about is if Marion understands Heidegger's phrase as if it said: God is a being.

Marion fails to understand that the structure of the ontological difference that Heidegger proposes, *precisely because* it is atheistic, means that God, not being, *freely* deploys *if*. Being deploys only *Dasein: Dasein* as the site for God may remain empty, which means no more than any given human existence may never accede to thinking the divine. Heidegger's phrase here, however, is: "Whether God lives or remains dead".[13] This directly recalls the lecture *Nietzsches Wort 'Gott ist Tot'*: "The place . . . this site for God can remain empty".[14]

Marion's understanding of the turn in Heidegger means he thinks beings as subordinated to being, being has priority. When therefore, he finds in the later Heidegger the thought which he reads as God is a being, this must mean (for him), God, as *a* being is subordinated to being: being has priority over God. Marion has leaped out of the factical, temporal horizon that Heidegger insists is the very taking place of the ontological difference—what thinking itself *is*—in order to think: God is a being—eternally. The whole thrust of Heidegger's understanding of God and his methodological atheism is to betroth being alone to *Dasein*, so that God can have an anteriority to *Dasein*, but if God did have this anteriority, the question would remain, not how (philosophically), but: how does *Dasein* know? The question is about *Dasein*'s knowing, not about God's being. The mode of *Dasein*'s knowing with regard to God, at least for Christian theology, is faith, not phenomenology.

The implication is that Marion, in attempting to think about God's relation to being apart from the ontological difference, attempts to think being apart from factical beings, because God is not a factical being, but must exist somewhere. He reinstates the supersensuous and atemporal realm which Heidegger claims is installed with Plato and overcome by Nietzsche. Or, in another direction, he reproduces precisely the theology

---

13. *Die Kehre* (*Bremer und Freiburger Vorträge* [GA79]), p. 77. "Ob der Gott lebt oder tot bleibt."

14. *Nietzsches Wort 'Gott ist Tot'* (*Holzwege* [GA5]), p. 255. "Die Stelle . . . dieser Ort Gottes kann leer bleiben."

that Aristotle unfolds of a God disclosed within and as the final meaning of the cosmos. Marion never escapes the province for thinking about God laid out by Greek metaphysics.

In contrast, Heidegger shows that the whole province of thought laid out between Plato and Nietzsche is that of metaphysics. For Marion to make the claim to think God apart from the ontological difference, the being of *Dasein*, is for him to return to this province. If God is a being—eternally, then God is always consequent to whatever deploys beings which, in Marion's reading of Heidegger, is being as such. The logic of the atemporal, supersensory realm dictates, however, that God be prior to everything, including being, because God is the cause of all things. Causality and priority belong together metaphysically. Marion, assuming that Heidegger's atheism means that he has no place for God, inadvertently returns to the thinking of metaphysics in order to resolve the challenge he believes Heidegger poses to theology. To elude the challenge, Marion is forced to want to think God outside the onto-logical difference because otherwise (in his reading of Heidegger's turn—the reading inspired by Löwith and Richardson) the ontological difference *deploys God.* He says, conceding the whole of the province of phenomenology to Heidegger, "We admit therefore, without arguing or even explaining it here, the radical anteriority of ontological difference as that through and as which the *Geschick* of being deploys beings".[15]

## God is Not a Being

Marion never inquires into whether or not God is *a* being. The first page of the *Preface to the English Edition* says (of the French text) that "the whole book suffered from the inevitable and assumed equivocation of its title: was it insinuating that God 'without being' is not, or does not exist? Let me repeat now the answer I gave then: no, definitely not. God is, exists, and that is the least of things".[16] If the question of God's being or existence is not at issue, what is? He adds: "At issue here is not the possibility of God's attain-ing to being, but, quite the opposite, the possibility of being's attaining to

---

15. Marion, J.-L., *Dieu sans l'être* (1982), p. 52. "Nous admettrons donc, sans la dis-cuter ni même l'exposer ici, l'antériorité radicale de la différence ontologique comme ce par et comme quoi le *Geschick* de/comme l'Être déploie les étants."

16. *God without Being* (1991), p. xix.

God".[17] Does this therefore mean that Marion turns to face the question of being as Heidegger unfolds it? Quite the opposite. It is not being that is put into question by this phrase of Marion's. Marion takes the question of being as self-evident; it is, he says "outside discussion". What therefore is put into question by this phrase of Marion is—God.

This does not mean that for Marion the question of being is empty. It means that for Marion, what and how being 'is' is not in question. He has failed to understand that for Heidegger, to put being into question is to put *myself* into question. For Heidegger, strictly speaking, God is never in question. Everything I know about God is something *I* know, and therefore an issue for *Dasein*, even as (phenomenologically speaking) it is an issue about God. In other words, knowledge of God, knowledge that can belong to *Dasein*, can be *mine*, is knowledge that always also concerns my self-description. This says nothing about the content of what is known: it simply says that in the knowing of what is known, *Dasein* is also disclosed by the knowing. For this reason the word being would not be allowed to occur in any theology undertaken by Heidegger (recalling the 1951 Zurich seminar)—not because being has nothing to do with God, but because the content of faith is not decided by the question of being. Only *Dasein* is in question where being is concerned.

How does Marion understand being within the theological horizon within which he wishes to work? To answer this question, he quotes a passage of Heidegger from the Zurich seminar that was considered in chapter 6. The words of Heidegger he draws attention to are:

> Of being, there is nothing here of impact. I believe that being can never be thought as the ground and essence of God, but that nevertheless the experience and manifestness of God, insofar as they meet with humanity, eventuate in the dimension of being, which in no way signifies that being might be regarded as a possible predicate for God. On this point one would have to establish wholly new distinctions and delimitations.[18]

---

17. *God without Being* (1991), p. xix f.
18. *Seminare* (GA15), p. 437. (See also pages 183–190 above). Marion quotes the passage in full as a footnote on p. 93 of the French text. "Mit dem Sein ist hier nichts anzurichten. Ich glaube, daß das Sein niemals als Grund und Wesen von Gott gedacht werden kann, daß aber gleichwohl die Erfahrung Gottes und seiner Offenbarkeit (sofern sie dem Menschen begegnet) in der Dimension des Seins sich ereignet, was niemals besagt, das Sein könne als mögliches Prädikat für Gott gelten. Hier braucht es ganz neue Unterscheidungen und Abgrenzungen."

How does Marion read this passage? He says: "A single indication comes to us: the word being must not intervene in a theological discourse".[19] This passage does not say, however, that the word being must not intervene in theological discourse. It says: I (Heidegger) would never attempt to think the essence of God by means of (thinking the essence of) being. If this passage is read as Marion reads it, it contains a contradiction, for Heidegger, having said that the essence of God does not belong to being, immediately speaks of being in relation to the manifestness of God. Marion notes the distinction: "The caesura clearly appears: thought, here philosophy, concentrates on the open manifestness (*Offenbarkeit*) of being, theology is attached to the revelation (*Offenbarung*) of 'God' . . . they remain 'separated by an abyss'".[20] This passage, however, speaks not of the revelation (*Offenbarung*) of God, but of God's manifestness (*Offenbarkeit*). Is Heidegger crossing his own abyss? Is this the manifestation of a contradiction that suggests Heidegger wants to erase being from theology, and yet presumes to subordinate God to being? Is Heidegger undertaking a *thei*ology, which Marion says is not the concern of theology but "the possibility of a strictly philosophical science of the divine"?[21] Theiology is another name for ontotheology. For Heidegger, this comes to an end with the end of metaphysics. How could he want to undertake a theiology? How are these contradictions to be understood?

The key to this passage of Heidegger is the use of the words *sich ereignet* which Marion renders into French as *fulgure* and is rendered in the English translation as flashes. What does *sich* mean in this passage? It means: God's self flashes in the realm of being. This passage neither thinks God from out of being nor even God subordinate to being; it thinks the flashing *manifestation* of God's *self*-deploying in the realm of being. God enters the realm of being as *a being*. Then and only then does God become a being. The deployment of God here has nothing to do with the essence of God. Why does Marion refer to revelation (*Offenbarung*) and not manifestness (*Offenbarkeit*)? When Heidegger speaks of revelation in the *Nietzsche* lectures cited by Marion,

---

19. Marion, J.-L., *Dieu sans l'être* (1982), p. 95. "Une seule indication nous parvient: le mot *être* ne doit pas intervenir dans un discours théologique" (author's italics).

20. Marion, J.-L., *Dieu sans l'être* (1982), p. 94. "La césure paraît clairement: la pensée, ici la philosophie, se concentre sur la manifestation ouverte (*Offenbarkeit*) de l'Être, la théologie s'attache à la révélation (*Offenbarung*) de 'Dieu' . . . 'abyssalement distinctes'." Citing *Der europäische Nihilismus* (*Nietzsche* [GA6.2]), p. 132.

21. Marion, J.-L., *Dieu sans l'être* (1982), p. 96. "La possibilité d'une science strictement philosophique du divin."

he is referring (on the very same page) to "Church teaching . . . the doctrine of (church) doctors . . . ecclesiastical teaching",[22] truth, as it is thought by Christian metaphysics. *Offenbarung* means the discipline which the church teaches, the tradition of metaphysics, of *theio*logy, as opposed to the God who self-manifests, who flashes in being: Marion, in returning to thinking God from within the province of metaphysics, has returned to thinking the 'square circle' of a 'Christian' philosophy, and not God's manifestness. To think God through how God appears disbars theology from thinking along the lines of *die Kirchenlehre,* which prompts theology to have to think "wholly new distinctions and delimitations".[23] Theology itself is given a new direction, an essential task, by the thought of being. There are no contradictions in this passage of Heidegger.

To free God from being, to free 'God' from the quotation marks Marion places around the name, does not mean that God cannot enter the realm of being. It means never to think the essence of God in God's-self as 'God is a being'. Aquinas said nothing different in stressing that God's essence was known only to God. Consequently, for Heidegger, the understanding of the ontological difference through the event (*Ereignis*) already frees God from being: moreover, it never presumes to put God into question, only *Dasein.*

Heidegger, *quite the opposite* from Marion, never thinks that God is a being, because it is only metaphysics which attempted to think of God in terms of being. Only the *manifestness* of God is a being in the domain of being. The primary manifestness of God in Christian revelation is Christ. For Christian faith, the human being is called to manifest Christ in his or her life, which means to become an icon of Christ. In faith, therefore, and in consequence of Christ, *Dasein* is the potential horizon within which God might become visible. Put another way, through God's gracious self-gift, God calls me to be the horizon wherein that self-giving might be realized. Being deploys my *Dasein,* in which this self-giving might become manifest, or this place that is my *Dasein* might remain empty of God. This might be construed as a freedom: both the freedom of God's appearing and my own freedom with regard to God. Heidegger's atheism brings precisely this freedom to light, in all its manifestations.

---

22. *Der europäische Nihilismus* (*Nietzsche* [GA6.2]), p. 132. "Die Kirchenlehrer . . . die doctrina der doctores . . . (der) kirchlichen Lehre."

23. Cf. *Seminare* (GA15), p. 437. "Ganz neue Unterscheidungen und Abgrenzungen."

The way in which Heidegger unfolds the meaning of *das Ereignis* as the event of the manifesting of being makes it impossible to accept Marion's characterization of a "double idolatry"[24] represented by the work of the later Heidegger. If, however, for Marion, God is a being, then *as* a being, God belongs to and is deployed by being as such. If Marion attempts to think God is a being without reference to being, then being is occluded, forgotten from the path of his thought. Marion cannot, however, occlude being with a forgetfulness that has not yet come to light, in the way that it comes to light in Heidegger's understanding of metaphysics as the history of being, for Marion is in dialogue with Heidegger, which means that he is aware that the question of being has come to light *as a question.* Not to undertake metaphysics because it is the forgotten history of being, yet to need to 'forget' being because of the directive he is following, namely to think God without being, means that Marion must proceed in the direction of attempting to 'forget' being all over again.

In announcing the thought of G⊗d outside the ontological difference, something remains. Marion, quoting 1 John 4:8 says "God (is) agape".[25] Already the copulative reference to being arrives under an elision (is) far more fundamental than the crossing of G⊗d. For the elision of being here means that an identity is posited, but simultaneously denied. For Heidegger, when identity is posited as belonging to the movement of concealment and unconcealment, it is as *das Ereignis* in which being and beings play into each other, turn (the verb is *kehren*) toward each other. They bring each other to light. When identity is posited under an elision, the thought of one thing is elided into the thought of another. 'God-*love*' means: God is determined out of love (whatever love may mean). In *das Ereignis* what is posited is the mutual belonging together of two that are the same: in Marion's elision what is posited is the identity of two things that are different.

To think God is a being apart from the being of beings and worlding of world is to think the God of metaphysics: it is to think God in the terms of being-ness, infinitude, immovability, supremacy, highest value, atemporality (eternity), and so forth. Marion says, in his throwaway comment: supreme, plural, or how you like. To think God how you like is to think God as transcendence, because in any attempt (any how-you-like) to think the

---

24. Cf. *God without Being* (1991), p. xxi.
25. Marion, J.-L., *Dieu sans l'être* (1982), p. 73. "Dieu (est) *agapè*" (author's italics and parenthesis).

essence of God, God is the highest, the most. God is this because God is not *this* (in the sense of any particular) being or thing *here*, but something other than it, while yet also *a* being. This is to think God as what is most being-ful of *any* being, God is the defining possibility of *all beings*. That is to say, of *any* particular being, God is what is most being-ful about it. God is the exemplary existence of any particularly existent thing. God is the *transcendent aspect* (the cause of the extantness and what is most extant) of *this* being. For Heidegger, thought in a Greek sense, this means God is the good beyond being, the ἰδέα τοῦ ἀγαθοῦ του ὑπερούσιου. God confers being on beings. Such a view is simply to return to thinking God metaphysically, as highest being or highest good.

Marion quotes Heidegger's comment that "in Christian theology, we define God, the *summum ens qua summum bonum* as the highest value",[26] saying "This announcement is at least doubly stupefying",[27] first because, Marion argues, Heidegger attributes this notion to Christian theology and not to the *theiology* of ontotheology, and second because Heidegger accords the *summum ens* priority over the *summum bonum*. This, he argues, means that Heidegger opts "in favor of *ens* as the first of the divine names".[28] The stupefaction is surely with the reader. How can Marion not have understood that for Heidegger *Christian theo-logy* as Marion names it here means both the ontotheology and *theiology* of Scholasticism? What corpus of non-Christian philosophical documents does Marion hold in his possession that date from this time (saving Avicenna and the Arab schools, who are, nevertheless, *theo*logians, and who taught the medieval Christians almost all they knew of Aristotle)? Second, how can he have failed to notice that Heidegger reads τὸ ἀγαθόν as a figure of the forgetfulness of being, and that therefore in the history of metaphysics both *summum ens* and *summum bonum* as names of God never mean being and always mean being-ness? Why is it that Heidegger, the proponent of a radical individualistic atheism which is intended to eradicate from God the name of being, should nevertheless opt for being as God's first name? Surely, this is none other than to repeat, without

---

26. From *Nietzsches Wort 'Gott ist Tot'* (*Holzwege* [GA5]), p. 227. "In der christlichen Theologie bestimmt man Gott, das summum ens qua summum bonum, als den höchsten Wert."

27. Marion, J.-L., *Dieu sans l'être* (1982), p. 108. "Cet énoncé stupéfie à tout le moins doublement."

28. Marion, J.-L., *Dieu sans l'être* (1982), p. 108. "En faveur de l'*ens* comme nom divin premier."

questioning it, Löwith's charge that Heidegger substitutes being for God? How is it that Marion can have collapsed Heidegger into a metaphysical (Scholastic, Neo-Thomist—call it what you will) reading of Aquinas?

It is this move, identifying Heidegger with Aquinas, that leads Marion to the extraordinary position of identifying in St. Thomas an idolatry of the involvement of the *ens* with imagination, the place where human thinking may form a figure of the idol. Marion claims that he is forced to shrink from Aquinas's entrenched involvement with the term being (*esse*).

Marion's solution is to propose a game: to think God outside the onto-logical difference, to outwit being:[29]

> To distort one difference by another outwits (the) being (of being) by resulting in a being that no longer refers to being . . . and no doubt we would think immediately of biblical revelation to play this role, for 'to the wisdom that the Greeks seek' (hence to the always sought ὄν of Aristotle) it opposes the 'wisdom of God' . . . incontestably, biblical revelation is unaware of ontological difference, the science of being/beings as such, and hence of the question of being.[30]

What can this mean? First, Marion denies what Heidegger has been so careful to argue, that every experience of faith, and so biblical revelation also, has an originary basis in the structures of *Dasein*, precisely as its relation to the truth of being. Second, Marion wishes to think God as a being without reference to being or the world, or what is worlded and is the worlding of world, human *Dasein*. Marion attempts to think God without being or world, and detached from being-human. What human, from whom God would be so fully detached, could even know of this detachment? Is this not the unreal body, *corpus quod a viribus impressis non cogitur,* supposed by Newton, transposed to the being of God?[31] Such a God could not exist! By this means, Marion attempts to think of a God who does not exist, that is, to think God

---

29. Marion, J.-L., *Dieu sans l'être* (1982), p. 126. The verb in french is *déjouer*.

30. Marion, J.-L., *Dieu sans l'être* (1982), p. 127f. "Gauchir une différence par une autre déjoue l'Être (de l'étant) en faisant que l'étant ne renvoie plus à l'Être . . . et sans doute nous songerions aussitôt à là révélation biblique pour tenir ce rôle, car elle oppose à 'la sagesse que cherchent les Grecs' (donc à l'*on* toujours recherché d'Aristote) , la 'sagesse de Dieu' . . . Incontestablement, la révélation biblique ignore la différence ontologique, la science de l'Être/étant en tant que tel, et donc la question de l'Être."

31. Cf. Newton's first law, discussed on p. 201 above.

without the 'I', the very self that Heidegger's atheism has painstakingly brought to light and elaborated so carefully as a possibility in the thought of Nietzsche, the 'I' for whom God indeed exists, insofar as God's experience and manifestness meet with humanity, the 'I' that disappears in Aristotle's theology, and reappears, but only as a possibility, after Nietzsche's declaration that the moral, metaphysical God is dead.

## To Think the Essence of God

The whole force of Heidegger's argument, demonstrating how God first became entangled in metaphysics, is to show how the forgottenness of being, which is really the concealment of self-presence to the self, the 'I', produced a God who is in effect the form or figure the concealed 'I' assumes in order to manifest itself. The coming to the self that I have argued is the force of Heidegger's work does not mean, therefore, that the 'I' is erased from faith and thought concerning God—how could there be a thought without an 'I' to think it? How could I be faithful without myself? Rather, self-disclosure in self-questioning opens the site into which God may enter. God cannot be thought without the 'I', the overcoming of the forgottenness of the 'I' means that who God is can be thought at all—because the 'I' is no longer concealed; I, in knowing God, am also fully available to myself, I cannot objectify or anthropomorphize God to my own ends. This is a *Selbstbehauptung:* in having come to myself, I must confront the question of who God might really be.

According to Heidegger, to think the essence of God does not involve being, would not include any reference to it, because being and 'I' are delivered over to *each other,* which means make thinking and make each other *possible at all,* possible so that thought of something which is not the 'I', not mine, can become mine. To think God without being simply means, to accept in its fullness God's radical otherness from me. It does not mean God is without being, but rather, I am (at first, in the order of being) without God. Here, "without" is again being used in the same sense as I might say: I am without the city walls. According to Marion, being must be erased with the thought: God is a being. Yet being cannot be unthought, for it pertains to world, as beings pertain to world. If being cannot be erased then it is not being, but God, who must be erased with the thought: God is a being. This is exactly Marion's thought of God. God appears under an erasure. God is G⊠d. This is the essential identity which lies taken for granted, without discussion, throughout Marion's work *Dieu sans l'être,* and yet it appears on page after page. Moreover as a repetition of Heidegger's figure for the forgottenness of being in the 1955 Jünger *Festschrift*, later published as *Zur Seinsfrage*, where he writes being as be⨉ng,[32] Marion already indicates, without discussion, that the figuration of erasure (as a crossing-out) can apply either to being or to God. In applying to either, it already decides *for* the identity of both—before any explanation is given. There is a sense therefore, in which Marion, exactly as Löwith before him, reads himself into Heidegger's work even before he has begun seriously to engage with it. Marion's thought of the icon as an erasure of God as G⨉d is an attempt to think the essence of God under the terms of how he has understood (and how little he has understood) the question of being. Because his coming close to Heidegger nevertheless already takes for granted the thought: God is a being. It means Marion, irrespective of Heidegger, already thinks the essence of God as a concept. Marion's thought of God is no icon, it is (to use his own phrase) a conceptual idol.

## MARION AND AQUINAS

What, then, of Marion's confrontation with Aquinas? He has continued to ask: "Does speculative Christian theology as understood in its exemplars— and in this context I am of course thinking primarily of St. Thomas Aquinas—belong to metaphysics in the strict sense, or has it been a response to the specific conceptual demands of the Revelation which gave rise to it?"[33] With the publication of his *Dieu sans l'être* he made his now renowned attack on St. Thomas, suggesting that "the Thomist apprehension of G⨉d as *ipsum esse* is determined out of God as *ens* and so determined, in the order of rea-

---

32. *Zur Seinsfrage* (*Wegmarken* [GA9]), pp. 385–426. Heidegger comments (p. 385) that the change of title from *Über die Linie* to *Zur Seinsfrage* indicates "that the meditation on the essence of nihilism stems from a discussion locating being as be⨉ng". ("daß die Besinnung auf das Wesen des Nihilismus aus einer Erörterung des Seins als Se⨉n herstammt.") He proceeds to write *das Sein* as *das Se⨉n* from pp. 411–424.

33. Marion, J.-L., "Métaphysique et phénoménologie: Une relève pour la théologie" in *Bulletin de Littérature Ecclésiastique* (1993), p. 21f. "La théologie spéculative chrétienne, entendue dans ses figures exemplaires (et en ce lieu je songe évidemment d'abord à saint Thomas d'Aquin) appartient-elle à la métaphysique prise au sens strict, ou a-t-elle répondu aux exigences conceptuelles propres de la Révélation qui l'a provoquée?"

son *before* the doctrine of divine names, hence of analogy".[34] He concludes: "can one not hazard that, according to what Saint Thomas himself freely insinuates, the *ens*, related to 'God' as his first name, indeed could determine him as the ultimate—idol?".[35] This troublesome statement led him in the preface to the English edition, *God without Being,* to say (without much explanation) "even when he thinks God as *esse,* Saint Thomas nevertheless does not chain God either to being or to metaphysics".[36] This is less of a retraction than it seems—no medieval metaphysician would have chained God to being or metaphysics, which is not at all to say that he and she would not earnestly have sought to chain the being of things, and so metaphysics, to God. If *esse commune* is precisely that which in St. Thomas protects God from being chained to the finitude of creatures, it is also the figure of how creatures are formally dependent on God. In January 1995 Marion retracted his attack on St. Thomas altogether.[37] Has Marion arrived in his retraction at the same place from where Heidegger began? How did he achieve this retraction?

Whereas Marion can say "if the doctrine of Thomas Aquinas could assimilate itself to an ontotheology . . .", Heidegger could not.[38] For Heidegger there are not ontotheologies, only ontotheology, as the concealment of being which, while on the one hand determines God in a particular direction, is yet on the other also the name for the impasse of metaphysics and the name of the history of being itself, when understood as metaphysics. To speak of ontotheologies is to relativize thinking itself to thinkers, which means every thinker has his or her own ontotheology. Understanding ontotheology in this way does

---

34. Marion, J.-L., *Dieu sans l'être* (1982), p. 120. "L'appréhension thomiste de Dieu comme *ipsum esse,* donc sa dénomination à partir de l'*ens* intervient, dans l'ordre des raisons, *avant* que ne se constitue la doctrine des noms divins, donc de l'analogie" (author's italics).

35. Marion, J.-L., *Dieu sans l'être* (1982), p. 122. "Ne peut-on pas risquer que, selon ce que saint Thomas lui-même se laisse aller à insinuer, l'*ens* pourrait bien, rapporté à 'Dieu' comme son premier nom, en en fixer l'ultime—idole?"

36. Marion, J.-L., *God without Being* (1991), p. xxii.

37. Marion, J.-L., "Saint Thomas d'Aquin et l'onto-théo-logie" (1995), Cf. esp. p. 45. "Thomas Aquinas therefore absolutely challenges the first criterion of ontotheology in general: the inscription of 'God' in the field of metaphysics unified by being(s), indeed by an identical concept of being(s)." ("Thomas d'Aquin récuse donc absolument le premier critère d'une onto-théo-logie en général: l'inscription de 'Dieu' dans le champ métaphysique unifié par l'étant, voire par un même concept d'étant.")

38. Marion, J.-L., "Saint Thomas d'Aquin et l'onto-théo-logie" (1995), p. 33. "Si la doctrine de Thomas d'Aquin pouvait s'assimiler à une onto-théo-logie . . ."

264 — Heidegger's Atheism

not explain either ontotheology or thinking, and, moreover, as an attempt at an explanation is a masked return of the subject. The whole force of ontotheology is to explain, not only how the thinker thinks, but how the thinker *is thought*, how he and she comes into thinking. Any re-presentation of the subject, or any metaphysics, cannot possibly do this, because it would take for granted and so reinstall the transcendental conditions of the universality of a common way of thinking—reason—or it would explain the collapse of transcendental reason through the calculative difference between subjects, through valuation and the will to power—intersubjectivity.

For Heidegger the question concerning Aquinas is solely how what he says stands in relation to ontotheology. What is revealed here is a fundamentally different perspective from Marion's. Heidegger is concerned to illustrate how the God of faith becomes subordinated to metaphysics, while admitting that the subordination has not been decisive for faith, at least in the case of Aquinas, because Aquinas is making use of the language of metaphysics in order to present something which is really a concern of faith. Marion, however, is concerned to free God from metaphysics, because he has already accepted that metaphysics, and Aquinas's use of it in particular, is decisive *and fatal* for faith. Having in his own view so decisively freed Aquinas from metaphysics, he is unable to show how he genuinely relates to it, and so whether, and how Aquinas's understanding belongs to the history of being. This places Marion in an unfortunate position as one who still wishes to appeal to the history of being as a critique of nihilism. He is thereby incapacitated from showing how the God of revelation and the world to whom God is revealed belong together.

Marion's reading of Aquinas is such that he argues that the concept of analogy evades the force of *esse commune* and in fact works in the opposite direction to it. He concludes: "Analogy does not administer the tangential univocity of *esse commune*, but on the contrary opens the space where all univocity of being is exploded".[39] Despite earlier in the article having explained the Thomist revision of Dionysius's conception, in contrast to the understanding of Heidegger's position I laid out in chapter 6, he simply fails to show how *esse commune* and analogy work together precisely to provide the impasse which might free Aquinas's faith from his conceptuality.

---

39. Marion, J.-L., "Saint Thomas d'Aquin et l'onto-théo-logie" (1995), p. 44. "L'analogie ne gère pas l'univocité tangentielle de l'*esse commune*, mais ouvre au contraire l'espace où toute univocité d'être doit exploser."

Marion's stress on the separation of *esse commune* and *esse divinum* in Aquinas means that he is driven toward an assertion that *esse divinum* is construed in an exclusively negative sense and leads him to conclude his retraction by an appeal solely to God as luminous darkness—what better light can he shed for us on God? Marion's critics have remained skeptical as to the extent to which he has really understood Aquinas. Brian Shanley makes the pertinent point: "Marion's reading simply cannot be reconciled with Aquinas's position that certain terms can be predicated of God positively and substantially (though non-quidditatively) through analogy".[40] The question is not decided in the separation of *esse divinum* and *esse commune*. Heidegger's entire point is that in their being brought together *analogice* by Aquinas nothing is decided—even for metaphysics.

Marion, in failing to understand Heidegger adequately because of the frame within which he reads Heidegger, because he has never been sufficiently open to what Heidegger speaks of to speak the same, is simultaneously forced to condemn Aquinas in the same breath. His placing of them together, however, illustrates the extent to which they are already close to each other, which means the extent to which they are both engaging with the same things in the same way, although Marion's reaching of this conclusion is by a negative rather than positive route.

## HEIDEGGER AND THE QUESTIONS OF CONTEMPORARY THEOLOGY

What is at issue with this contemporary engagement with Heidegger's work? Its failure to address the significance of Heidegger's work for theology is the failure to understand Heidegger's refusal of a theological voice. Marion, in attempting to grapple with what is meant by being, never escapes a notion of being that remains resolutely metaphysical. If Heidegger approaches being at all, he does so by understanding that being and nothing are the same. Every attempt either to return to a scholastic understanding of *esse* or an understanding that God and being are the same will fail. The truth of being is not a propositional truth about being. Being 'trues' because it is the place which is *Dasein*'s being-worlded. At this stage in my argument I make no apologies for this dreadful piece of 'Heideggerizing'—I have been at pains to unfold what is intended here through seven chapters. Being is the

---

40. Shanley, B., "St. Thomas Aquinas, Onto-Theology and Marion" (1996), p. 623.

time-place from out of which God might be known (or not) and into which God might step (or refuse) to be known: in a Christian sense (though only for a believing Chrsitian), through the person of Jesus Christ.

In being, *Dasein* oscillates in reaching forward to know and returning to itself in its knowing. Part of the structure of this oscillating is the decay of the meaning of the known. For this reason there is never only *one* step into the moment, but rather the step is repeated and repeated and repeated, in *Dasein*'s constant self-disclosure of its future for itself. Without this self-disclosure, this ever-renewing return to openness, what *Dasein* has in knowing ossifies and decays: it passes away and remains in its traces only as objects and shards of ruined meaning. Mortified experience is part of what it is to be *Dasein*. One way to understand Heidegger's silence regarding theology is to suggest that he refused to objectify his faith into objects of knowledge—sentences and propositions which would be tussled over by those who followed. This troublesome refusal to theologize, which leaves open and undecided the questions which theology posed to Heidegger's thought, has been precisely that motor which has kept Heidegger's work forceful. Every subsequent generation of theologians has included an engagement with Heidegger or rather with what Heidegger's thinking engages. This engagement returns to his work again and again and again.

In a sense, being's refusal to be thematized has been what beckons theologians to re-engage with Heidegger. Being, therefore, has no meaning: rather, Heidegger thought all over again how meaning might be. The contemporary engagement of theology with Heidegger's work is to find its way back to the demand of the moment, at an ever-deepening level. The moment demands an encounter with God. The question of God can never be resolved finally. Final resolution, on the other hand, is what theology as metaphysics has always attempted. There is no final framework for faith except being itself: no set of principles, neither canons nor dogmas nor doctrines which will resolve every demand. Rather, I, as the demand that is ushered in by being, must learn theologically to reflect on faith, perhaps assisted through canons and dogma and the carefully sedimented memory of my forebears that goes under the protective title of tradition, but nevertheless resolutely, I must, in believing, face the question of myself that being opens up.

To understand better Heidegger's significance for theology, it is necessary to understand just what he thought theism meant at all. In the *Beiträge zur Philosophie*, the seventh division includes a section entitled *The Last*

*God.* This section opens with a chapter called simply *The Last.*[41] Here Heidegger says:

> The last God has its most unique singularity and stands outside that reckoning determination which the titles 'mono-theism', 'pan-theism', and 'atheism' intend. Monotheism and all kinds of theism have existed only for as long as the Judeo-Christian 'apologetic' which takes for granted the thinking of metaphysics. With the death of God all theisms collapse.[42]

For Heidegger, all theisms, including atheisms, are determinations of the same thing: metaphysics. The key term in this passage is *reckoning*. Throughout his work, Heidegger locates this word firmly within the province of two thinkers in particular. The first is Leibniz, the second, Nietzsche. For Leibniz, reckoning and other compounds of the verb "to reckon" translate in one way the Latin *ratio*, which is normally translated as reason. To reckon means to think, but to think in a particular way, to total-up, to count, to give account, to do accounting, to undertake that thinking which as mathesis certifies and produces certainty. Heidegger's reading of Nietzsche's use of reckon, *ratio*, also bears this meaning, but becomes still more weighty, for reckoning thinking is that thinking which values, e-valuates, produces value, which culminates in the devaluation of the uppermost values and revaluation of all values.[43]

Metaphysical thinking is that reckoning thinking which produces all theisms, including atheisms. Within this calculative thinking the Judeo-Christian apologetic is subsumed so that theology comes to be conceived as metaphysics. With Nietzsche's proclamation of the death of God, metaphysical thinking can be understood for the first time as that thinking which reckons God as an object, a being, an existence, a rendering reckoned by a subject, the manifestness of the God who appears not in the realm of being, insofar as it does, but in the subject-object distinction.

---

41. *Beiträge zur Philosophie* (GA65), §253. *"Das Letzte."*
42. *Beiträge zur Philosophie* (GA65), p. 411. "Der letzte Gott hat seine einzigste Einzigkeit und steht außerhalb jener verrechnenden Bestimmung, was die Titel 'Mono-theismus', 'Pan-theismus' und 'A-theismus' meinen. 'Monotheismus' und alle Arten des 'Theismus' gibt es erst seit der jüdisch-christlichen 'Apologetik', die die 'Metaphysik' zur denkerischen Voraussetzung hat. Mit dem Tod dieses Gottes fallen alle Theismen dahin."
43. Cf.: *Vom Wesen des Grundes*, 1929 (*Wegmarken* [GA9]); the lecture course given in 1955/56 as *Der Satz vom Grund* (GA10); *Der europäische Nihilismus* (Nietzsche [GA6.2]).

Such a God is dead, says Heidegger, and yet after paying due attention to the death of God, he goes on to speak of another God, *The Last God,* who defies all reckoning and determination. Heidegger indicates that *The Last* does not simply mean the (temporal) last, but more importantly the outermost, the most distant, the furthest away, the one, therefore, that makes the greatest demand and claim upon me if I am to bring myself into this God's proximity. It also means the latest (in the sense of Latin *novissimus*) and the most immediate. If Heidegger can say nothing of God, which means here, if he can say *the* nothing in connection with God, if he can contradict the medieval dictum *ex nihilo nihil fit*—out of nothing nothing comes—the highest reason of *Deus positivus,* and bring God into an approximation with nothing so that he can speak of the outermost of God—if he can do this and I can hear it, might I be approaching what Heidegger has to say of God? To bring God into relation with being and nothing is to return God to a relation with finitude, *my* finitude, not any finitude of God, which would be to overcome the dualism announced in the origins of nihilism traced by Gillespie and figured by Nietzsche. This is in reality no returning of God, for how could I return God to anything? It is rather, a way in which, in the very overcoming of nihilism, I might return myself to God. It is not God who must become more proximate, but me. Through my coming to know God's being God, insofar as I know it, I am more proximate to the God who appears.

In the anglophone reading and critique of Heidegger especially, and elsewhere, there has remained the lingering suspicion that Heidegger's talk of and silence about God is just that pretension to vastness that haunts the phantasmic enormity of the being-question. It is for this reason that the interlocutor of the Zurich seminar asked the seemingly tantalizing question which might loosely be paraphrased: so is your being really your God? It is for this reason above all that Heidegger's English translators have loved to translate *Das Sein* with a capital letter, Being. Something of this can be found, for instance, in Herbert Dreyfus's suggestion that the way to understand Heidegger's God is in the same manner as Nietzsche's idea of "politics in the grand style"[44] or Stanley Corngold's understanding of Heidegger's reading of Hölderlin that "Heidegger seems to claim that Being itself is present, for Hölderlin 'speaks the sacred'".[45] For these interpreters and many

44. Dreyfus, H., "Mixing Interpretation, Religion, and Politics: Heidegger's High Risk Thinking" (1992).
45. Corngold, S., *The Fate of the Self* (1986), p. 199

others, Being is just that looming, ectoplastic haunting that might otherwise be figured as the very substance of the stench of the decay of Nietzsche's God. I have, I hope, shown that being can never be this vastness, that the attempt to unfold the ontological difference is a firmly phenomenological account of finitude, and that freed from the metaphysical shackles of causality, Heidegger's atheism has a compelling claim to be open to the divine.

In this, might Heidegger be understood as pious, indeed with a lively piety more in touch with godliness than any dry love of a metaphysical being might yield? This, surely, is his unspoken claim. In unfolding the history of being while still speaking of God, does not Heidegger publish his piety, which means, does Heidegger's atheism not share with those who strive to engage with him an openness, even a silent pointing, to who the God might be?

Chapter Nine

# Conclusion

## HEIDEGGER'S UNDERSTANDING OF WHAT THEOLOGY IS

In 1970 Heidegger republished his 1927 lecture *Phänomenologie und Theologie* in a new edition, together with a foreword and an appendix, the latter dating from 1964. The clear indication was that this text is still a way in to how he understood the relationship between theology and philosophy. The foreword gives an indication of how his thought had proceeded since 1927, the date of the lecture. He points the reader toward three texts: *Nietzsches Wort 'Gott ist tot'*; the lecture series *Der europäische Nihilismus;* and the text *Die seinsgeschichtliche Bestimmung des Nihilismus,* all of which I have considered to some extent. As I have already suggested, the lecture attempts to understand what theology is by saying on the one hand "theology is not speculative knowledge of God"[1] and on the other:

> Theology, as at a conceptual self-interpretation of believing existence, that is, as historical knowledge, aims solely at that transparency of the Christian occurrence that is revealed in, and delimited by, belief itself.[2]

Theology in this sense is strictly a (scientific) reflection on the activity of faith, as a self-interpretation. The self at issue here is that self *Dasein* has in coming to itself. What underpins this view is Heidegger's

---

1. *Phänomenologie und Theologie* (*Wegmarken* [GA9]), p. 59. "Theologie ist nicht spekulative Gotteserkenntnis."
2. *Phänomenologie und Theologie* (*Wegmarken* [GA9]), p. 56. "Die Theologie zielt als begriffliche Selbstinterpretation der gläubigen Existenz, d.h. als historische Erkenntnis, einzig auf die in der Gläubigkeit offenbare und durch die Gläubigkeit selbst in ihren Grenzen umrissene Durchsichtigkeit des christlichen Geschehens."

272 — Heidegger's Atheism

interpretation of transcendence: God is not deduced from the structure of (*Dasein*'s) transcending, but rather *Dasein*'s experience of what is given in transcending (knowledge) is also *Dasein*'s self-disclosure. Such a disclosure means that, as worlded, *Dasein* discovers the kind of self it is and how as a self it is. That form of self-transcending which discloses God to the self, however, proceeds from out of the experience of faith, in special directions which give it a character which is a mode of that kind of transcendence in which (for instance) a lectern or any other thing is disclosed.

I must indicate here an important clarification. In *Phänomenologie und Theologie* Heidegger proposes that theology be thought of as an ontic science. It is not, however, the ontic science of God; rather, it is an ontic science whose object is faith, which is a mode of *Dasein*'s self-disclosure. The science of theology could never be the science of the *object* God, because God is not a being, a thing, or in any sense an object against which a subject could stand.

## ONTIC AND ONTOLOGICAL LOVE

It is the very non-objectness of God that makes theology a special science. Heidegger cites Luther's comment: "Faith is permitting ourselves to be seized by the things we do not see".[3] This statement of Luther's is parallelled in numerous places in the tradition of mystical writings. Compare, for example, the negative formulation of this same thought in St. Catherine of Siena's mystical work *Il Dialogo*. God speaks to her of the souls of those who are lost and no longer love or care for God, saying: "Do you want me to tell you why they suffer? You know that love always brings suffering if what a person has identified with is lost. These souls have identified in one way or another with the earth in their love, and so in fact have become earth themselves".[4] The suffering that is named here has the same structure as Heidegger's understanding of ruinance[5] and as Zarathustra's suffering at the

---

3. *Phänomenologie und Theologie* (*Wegmarken* [GA9]), p. 53. "Glaube ist das Sichgefangengeben in den Sachen, die wir nicht sehen."

4. Catherine of Siena, *Il dialogo* (1589), p. 169. "Vuoi tu ch'io ti dica, come essistâno in pena? Tu sai che l'amore sempre dà pena: perdêdo quella cosa cô cui essi sono con formati, et costoro hâno fatto cônformità per amore nella terra in diversi modi, et però terra sono divêntati."

5. See chapter 2.

end of the third section of *Also Sprach Zarathustra*.[6] Heidegger comments on Zarathustra's suffering: "These three, 'life—suffering—the circle' belong together, they are the same".[7] Life, he adds, is to be understood as a figure for the will to power, the circle as the eternal return of the same. He then asks, what about suffering? Replying to his own question he says that suffering must be understood as the *willed* concern for things within time: "All that suffers wills to live".[8] What he means is that suffering is a desire not to let go. Time is, however, as part of its timeliness, a distancing and letting-go. Suffering is that form of timeliness which is always a hankering-after, a misery toward what passes, because it eludes my grasp and forces distance upon me, against my will.

This can be better understood if Heidegger's sense of un-willing is recalled, un-willing as *Gelassenheit*, detachment.[9] To be seized by that which I do not see is always to be turned forward into the mystery of things: it is to be turned into the openness of transcending. This being turned into is exactly how Heidegger understands *Gelassenheit*. *Gelassenheit*, understood in this way, is that letting-be where I do not seize or grasp or seek to comprehend (literally, place my hand over) things so that I become them, but rather their appearing and emerging and passing by is without suffering and yet discloses me to myself. They do not 'make' me or produce me (as acts of will) any more than I make them or produce them (in willing, which would be the will to power). They disclose me in my coming across them, which also discloses them. We are co-disclosed, both in an identity and through difference. I am related to them in their coming hither and passing by— which means it is I also who come close to and am distanced from them. Things of this kind do not become ob-jects, against which I am also posited, as a subject.

What St. Catherine of Siena calls love here has the same ontological structure as Heidegger's explication of care. Using Heidegger's own terminology, care is the ontological basis for the ontic experience of love. Care is

---

6. Nietzsche, F., *Also Sprach Zarathustra* (*Friedrich Nietzsche* [1999], IV), p. 271. "Ich, Zarathustra, der Fürsprecher des Lebens, der Fürsprecher des Leidens, der Fürsprecher des Kreises—dich rufe ich, meinen abgründlichsten Gedanken."
7. *Wer ist Nietzsches Zarathustra* (*Vorträge und Aufsätze* [GA7]), p. 98. "Diese Drei: 'Leben—Leiden—Kreis' gehören zusammen, sind das Selbe."
8. *Wer ist Nietzsches Zarathustra* (*Vorträge und Aufsätze* [GA7]), p. 98. "Alles, was leidet, will leben."
9. See p. 126 above.

the basic structure of *Dasein*'s being. It makes possible any and all of *Dasein*'s being-related, or comportment-to.[10] Care was used in the English translation of *Being and Time* to translate *die Sorge*. This word means concern, almost worry, but could be taken for relatedness as such, the ineluctability of being betrothed to world in ecstasis, the instability of the disjuncture between ἔρως and φίλια. The term *betroth* here is not accidental, but supplies well the original relation to truth in temporality, knowing and speaking that is intended in *die Kehre* and in particular the lecture *Vom Wesen der Wahrheit*. Betrothal springs from the Old English *tréowsian*, the giving of a word for the sake of a truth.

Heidegger's later work confirms and extends this understanding with direct reference to love as a kind of betrothal of the meaning of a thing that has access to and that formally respects what the thing offers of itself to be open to being-betrothed. Betrothed does not mean related in its materiality, but rather, relating as to its meaning: however, its materiality does not 'exist' prior to its meaning (there is no *thing-in-itself* lying prior to its meaning), but rather its meaning is its materiality co-disclosed. Always at work is that understanding which was exemplified in the example from the 1919 *Kriegsnotsemester* of the lectern, to which I have made repeated reference. In any ecstatic being-toward, I become determined out of the thing toward which I transcend, in order to know it. There is a sense in which it also becomes me, which means, in my becoming myself in order to know it (this becoming is a temporal determination, it is my projecting into the future), it and I are at one. Heidegger illustrates this with regard to love in the *Humanismusbrief*:

Thinking is of being. The genitive speaks in a twofold way. Thinking is of being, insofar as thinking, belonging to being, is an event of being. Thinking is at the same time of being, insofar as thinking, belonging to being, hears being [the play is on *hören*, to hear, and *gehören*, to belong]. As that which, hearing, belongs to being, thinking is what by its essential origin it is. Thinking is—this says, being has fatefully embraced its essence. To embrace a thing or a person in its essence means to love it, to favor it. This favoring means, more originally thought, to give (it) essence.[11]

---

10. Cf. *Sein und Zeit* (GA2), §4, *Das Sein des Daseins als Sorge*, esp. p. 193. "Being-in-the-world is essentially care." ("Das In-der-Welt-Sein [ist] wesenhaft Sorge.")
11. *Brief über den 'Humanismus'* (*Wegmarken* [GA9]), p. 316. "Das Denken ist des Seins. Der Genitiv sagt ein Zweifaches. Das Denken ist des Seins, insofern das Denken vom Sein ereignet, dem Sein gehört. Das Denken ist zugleich Denken des Seins, insofern

The question of what I *turn toward* therefore becomes paramount. Every turning toward is an offering of embracing, a preparation for betrothal, an opening out toward whatever is there to be opened in to. *How* I must love in order to be ecstatic toward God is a matter entirely proper to faith and to the reflection on that faith which theology is: in Christian terms it belongs to reflection on the divine disclosure. The ontological structure of *loving* as such is not disclosed by God's revealing, but belongs to the unfolding of the question of being. If, therefore, care is the ontological structure that makes reflection on the ontic experience of love possible at all, then Heidegger and St. Catherine are, as far as he is concerned, speaking of *the same.*

This is the very reason why Heidegger is no 'Heideggerian': to think a matter essentially is to know it in what it has to give you, (to hear it) as it is, which is nothing other than to embrace and favor it, to be betrothed into it from out of it. In this sense, every attempt to suggest that Heidegger is simply nostalgic for some pristine state of philosophy or primordial Greek thinking or some such is flawed: equally, Heidegger did not believe himself ever to be evincing opinions or doctrines or ideas that were not themselves disclosive of some*thing.*[12] Heidegger is not nostalgic because he is always concerned with the moment and with how it is determined and understood. It may be shaped by the past and oriented toward the future (which is its openness) or it may be trapped by its having been shaped and so is distanced from what in the event is attempting to speak. The distance, however, does not come from nowhere, but in understanding the distance, the distance can be both attended to and overcome, and the original experience of what attempts to speak in the moment recovered. Simultaneously, therefore, what has gone before must be understood (as what gave distance) and surpassed (as what over-comes distance and becomes mine).

It is in this way that the thing, the phenomenon, betroths itself to me. How any thing (any being) is to be addressed (its call, the demand it makes on me) is always given together with how I am addressing it. To be estranged

---

das Denken, dem Sein gehörend, auf das Sein hört. Als das hörend dem Sein Gehörende ist das Denken, was es nach seiner Wesenherkunft ist. Das Denken ist—dies sagt: das Sein hat sich je geschicklich seines Wesens angenommen. Sich einer 'Sache' oder einer 'Person' in ihrem Wesen annehmen, das heißt: sie lieben: sie mögen. Dieses Mögen bedeutet, ursprünglicher gedacht: das Wesen schenken."

12. John Caputo, for instance, attempts to interpret Heidegger's thought as nostalgia. See, for example, Caputo, J., *Demythologizing Heidegger* (1993), p. 91, and the whole of chapter 5, "Heidegger's Revolution" (esp. pp. 115 ff.).

from something (to be distant from it), therefore, recalling the example of the lectern, means also in some way to be estranged from myself.

What then, is the connection between care and love? For Heidegger, the ontological structure of care would have to make possible the ontic, theological description of love, but the theological description could never be deduced from elaborating the ontological structure. The theological description would always have to belong to God's own disclosure of God. In this sense the ontological serves as a corrective to the ontic, drawing it back to the limits of what it might say, but not determining the content of what occurs within those limits.[13] Heidegger's own example of this corrective process is not love, but the relation between sin and guilt. Far from Heidegger's description of guilt in *Sein und Zeit* being a secularized theological concept which he has (atheistically) broken off into an existentialist romanticism,[14] he argues that any theological understanding of sin must have a basis in the fundamental structure of *Dasein*. He says in the lecture *Phänomenologie und Theologie:*

> Hence we can say that precisely because all basic theological concepts, considered in their full regional context, include a content that is existentially powerless, i.e., *ontically* sublated, they are *ontologically* determined by a content that is pre-Christian and that can thus be grasped purely rationally . . . so, for example, sin is manifest only in faith, and only the believer can factically exist as a sinner. But if sin, which is the counterphenomenon to faith as rebirth and hence a phenomenon of existence, is to be interpreted in theological concepts, then the *content* of the concept *itself* . . . calls for a return to the concept of guilt. But guilt is an original ontological determination of the existence of *Dasein*.[15]

---

13. See p. 66 above.

14. This is very much Löwith's view, as discussed in chapter 3. Others have followed suit, notably John Macquarrie. See, for example, Macquarrie's analysis of Heidegger's appeal to *die Schuld* in *Sein und Zeit* for his argument in *Heidegger and Christianity* (1994), pp. 37–38.

15. *Phänomenologie und Theologie* (*Wegmarken* [GA9]), p. 63f. "Hieraus ergibt sich: alle theologischen Grundbegriffe haben jeweils, nach ihrem vollen regionalen Zusammenhang genommen, in sich einen zwar existentiell ohnmächtigen, d.h. *ontisch* aufgehobenen, aber gerade deshalb sie *ontologisch* bestimmenden vorchristlichen und daher rein rational faßbaren Gehalt . . . so ist z. B. die Sünde nur im Glauben offenbar, und nur der Gläubige vermag faktisch als Sünder zu existieren. Soll aber die Sünde, die das Gegenphänomen zum Glauben als Widergeburt und sonach ein Existenzphänomen ist, theologisch-

This means, as far as my argument is concerned, that the theological reflection on love is grounded ontologically in care and in the essence of being, as sin is grounded in guilt. Without the ontological possibility of *Dasein* experiencing itself as guilty, there could be no redemptive understanding of sin. The theological elaboration of sin is always a redemptive elaboration; it carries within it the disclosure of the need of God. Sin without this is condemnation, which would also only be possible on the basis of ontological guilt, but from which there could be no redemption. Sin and love both belong ontically to theology and ontologically to the being of *Dasein*. The ontic reflection on the divine love has a basis in everyday life. Care, however, is the basis of *Dasein*'s being in the world, as how it knows things and has them in its purview.

Understood from the theological, ontic reflection indicated by St. Catherine, love is a mode of knowing. It is that mode of knowing things that is informed by and fulfilled in revelation. It is an authentic mode of the being of *Dasein*. All modes of the being of *Dasein* do not differ simply across themselves, but rather make possible what can be known in *Dasein*'s taking place or worlding. Dread, for instance, reveals the nothing. Care, as the ontological basis for theological love, is also its ruination: love points in a particular direction which care, understood in its phenomenological structures alone, does not. Care, therefore is timely, but love would necessarily have a slightly different time-structure. Care, as transcending toward, is also the return of transcendence: it returns things, beings, to *Dasein* in *Dasein*'s return to itself. In ruinance the return brings with it decay in the passing of time.

---

begrifflich ausgelegt werden, dann erfordert der *Gehalt* des Begriffes *selbst* . . . den Rückgang auf den Begriff der Schuld. Schuld aber ist eine ursprüngliche ontologische Existenzbestimmung des Daseins" (author's italics). That love might operate in the same way with respect to care is indicated in the note on p. 190 of *Sein und Zeit* (GA2): "It is no accident that the phenomena of anxiety and fear, which have never been distinguished in a thoroughgoing manner, have come within the purview of Christian theology ontically and even, although within very narrow limits, ontologically. This always happens whenever the anthropological problem of the being of man towards God has won priority and when phenomena like faith, sin, love, and repentance have led the formulation of questions". ("Es ist kein Zufall, daß die Phänomene von Angst und Furcht, die durchgängig ungeschieden bleiben, ontisch und auch, obzwar in sehr engen Grenzen, ontologisch in den Gesichtskreis der christlichen Theologie kamen. Das geschah immer dann, wenn das anthropologische Problem des Seins des Menschen zu Gott einen Vorrang gewann und Phänomene wie Glauben, Sünde, Liebe, Reue die Fragestellung leiteten.")

For Heidegger, care is the conditioning possibility of embracement, of embracing some*thing*. God, however, is not a *thing*, a being. If revelation shows that love is the basis of being turned toward God, then the kind of love which has no *thing* in its purview, no object to pursue, is that kind of embracement which *as betrothal* always produces not the experience of a thing, but renewed distance, renewed embracement. In contrast to care, therefore, love that discloses the divine, God's love, has no return. It is only open to the future. It has no ruinance of its own, or rather, every time love is objectified or produces a thing, a being, an object, a moment or 'now' of love, it ceases to be love and lapses into some other mode of *Dasein*.

Love of another person can indicate well what is meant here: it is the mysteriousness of the person toward whom I direct my love that maintains it in love. Love of another has its ruinations however, in jealousy, mistrust, indifference, callousness, carelessness, cruelty, violence, possessiveness, selfishness, and so on. Each of these is determined out of an initial possible love-relation, but all are ruinations, diminutions, or parodies of that relation. To return to divine love, therefore, theology *as* metaphysics is a form of ruination of a primordial reflection on the experience of God. To return to St. Catherine, if in love, false or otherwise, I become what I love—either the earth or the divine—then precisely I can become like the divine and yet still never be the divine because my love of God will endlessly stretch me toward the divine in the continual production of distance just by virtue of betrothal to the divine becoming possible.

## THE EXISTENTIAL MEANING OF THE DIVINE NAMES

What is indicated here is a re-reading of the meaning of τὸ ἀγαθόν that I proposed in chapter 4. The yoke that Plato describes is never assembled, because I am always stretching after God, who is that which will never allow a higher yoking together. *Summum bonum* therefore could be understood, not as a name for God that discloses God's essence, but rather my everlasting stretching, turning, toward which simultaneously is a beckoning and a never being completed. Such an understanding of the highest good could never be metaphysical, although it is developed out of it, and always accounts for the danger of the collapse back into metaphysics that it represents, because as soon as the yoke is assembled, that is, as soon as I think of God as *summum in semetipso bonum*, i.e., as highest good without including in this thinking the fact that it is *I* who think it, and so attempting to think

God as highest good apart from creation or world, then what God as *summum bonum* has to give me in its naming collapses into metaphysics and renders God a thing or being or object.

Michael Baur demonstrates a further important consequence of Heidegger's phenomenology of care as it relates to Aquinas. In a detailed argument, he traces the common origin of Aquinas's notion of intellection and Heidegger's positing of the insubstantiality of *Dasein*. In this he is only following comments of Heidegger's to which I have already drawn attention, although he does not explicitly say this. Baur interprets Heidegger's understanding of the knowing of *Dasein* and Aquinas's understanding of the human knower as having a common inspiration, Aristotle. It is precisely the *immateriality* of Aquinas's understanding of the human knower that Baur draws attention to and shows how close it is to Heidegger's understanding of the structure of *Dasein* as care and as temporality.[16] He adds: "It is because of the knower's high degree of immateriality and self-subsistence that the knower does not regard the other (i.e., whatever is alien to it) as simply 'other'. . . On the level of intellectual cognition, the intellect withstands and overcomes the alien-character of other beings, not by destroying the other in its otherness, but by preserving the other in its otherness. The intellect does this by *becoming* the other. Because of its greater degree of immateriality, the intellect can become the other while still remaining itself".[17] This is correct if becoming here is a figure for taking into care.

It is necessary here to make an important point that Baur overlooks: the intellect remains itself only insofar as it retains its structure as knower, that is, as capable of intellection. It remains itself even as determined out of what it knows. The significance of this cannot be underplayed. The question arises, the question St. Catherine herself brings before us, *what* does the knower know? *What* the knower knows will determine *how* the knower will *be*.

Baur does not fail, however, to draw attention to the other most important point here: Heidegger's closeness to Aquinas is entirely different from Heidegger's distance from Thomism. Moreover his remarks go to the very heart of the issues I have brought to the fore. He says:

---

16. Baur, M., *Heidegger and Aquinas on the Self as Substance* (1996), p. 329. "Aquinas' Aristotelian background leads him to view the human knower as that kind of substance which exhibits such a high degree of immateriality that it retains no entitative obstinacy of its own, and thus is a sheer openness of the kind that Heidegger describes."

17. Baur, M., *Heidegger and Aquinas on the Self as Substance* (1996), p. 331.

I believe that a Heideggerian reading of Aquinas can unlock and release some of the existential-ontological possibilities of Aquinas' rich thought. For too long, many of these possibilities have been overlooked and even repressed by certain currents in neo-Thomism which seek to turn Aquinas' thought into a set of techniques for the purpose of combatting what some fear to be the incipient nihilism of contemporary philosophy. If we have learned anything from Heidegger, however, we should realize that such attempts to fasten onto the ontic presence of rigid techniques only play into the hands of nihilism itself.[18]

What does it mean that the essence of being-human *never* reaches the place of God? The human essence never reaches it, because it is always reaching out for it. The self is the horizon where God is revealed, but every revelation is a failure, a falling short of God. Such a revelation always strives forward into silence, as the place where all distance is overcome (because all giving of things is a speaking, and speaking thereby produces difference—so that overcoming speaking is at the same time overcoming distance), and yet is forced, gabbling, back on itself, only to struggle back into silence. It is for this reason that the prayer of silence is the deepest form of prayer. Heidegger's atheism, taken in this sense, means to overcome speaking *of* God. Theology, as the science of reflection on faith, is therefore always to be overcome, to be exceeded, to be abandoned, only for the need of it to arise again.

A similar understanding of the name of God as *summum ens* could be suggested as was proposed for the name of *summum bonum*. In chapter 6 I indicated how, for pseudo-Dionysius, God 'is' beyond being. Normally Dionysius's continued use of the verb 'to be' in these contexts of speaking of beyond-being is understood to have stretched language to its limit, to have exceeded what can be said and yet still have need of speaking. This does not do Dionysius justice: the 'is' denotes me in my being: the self that is bringing itself into relation with God. Such an 'is' in its 'how' will always denote to what extent and that I am always included in and excluded from God. If God does not exist, because God exceeds existence, and I am yet in some sense included in the essence of God by this 'is', then what is at issue is not God's existence as independent from me, but rather the distance between us, and that God always lies ahead of me, in the future. God exists, as far as I am concerned with God. This does not mean God depends on my existence, but rather that it is only within my exis-

---

18. Baur, M., *Heidegger and Aquinas on the Self as Substance* (1996), p. 336.

tence, the ontological difference that I am, that I can know God, and insofar as I do, God exists. God exists means I have taken into account the question of my own being with regard to God. This is exactly the resolution of Heidegger's enigmatic comments I have already considered from the *Einleitung* to the lecture *Was ist Metaphysik?* that God is, but does not exist.

The critical term for pseudo-Dionysius is ὑπερ-, beyond. How does ὑπερ- differ from μετα-, the beyond that indicates the supersensory realm of metaphysics? Ὑπερ- indicates relation, the being-betrothed of my-self to God. Central to this being-related is the self-experience of betrothal I have shown to be at work in thinking and knowing. *Summum ens* does not denote a or the or even the highest name of God; rather, it denotes my ecstatic entering into the place of the divine. If the description of this ecstasis preserves within it the original articulation of place in the cosmos, the *uppermost* that denotes the place of the divine in the ancient cosmos, highest can also mean latest, as most turned out to the future, the place from where the future springs, the eschaton. The word eschaton, if it bears within it the Christian relation to time, is also as τό ἔσχατον, for Aristotle, the outermost of the heavens, and so ties together highest and latest, the last, or *Letzte*, of Heidegger's own naming of God. Betrothal, articulated through love, is the ever-closening that simultaneously preserves my ever-distance from God. The divine names, in this reading, must always thereby be made mine. They can never stand on their own, but must be owned by me, in prayer, in the vibrant life of the sacraments to which I must constantly return to be renewed, in my repeated return to the Scriptures, in my tending to my neighbor—The practices of faith, devoid of all metaphysical necessity. To be carried out devoid of necessity means here to be carried out in love.

What is the significance of Martin Heidegger's atheism? In the first place, Heidegger remains firmly within the Western tradition to which he repeatedly returns and on which his work meditates. For Heidegger, this tradition remains a Christian one, although he refuses to acknowledge it confessionally or within the terms of *die Kirchenlehre*, Church Doctrine. His philosophical atheism is simultaneously this remaining within and refusing the institutional claims of the tradition. Second, Heidegger indicates a return to the open immediacy of the moment, that place which is the site of redemption. Redemption in this sense is always particularized: there is never a general or universal redemption that would devalue everything called into the presence of God, but every particular redemption takes place as always within a world, always-related to the whole of being-human, being-together-with others. Third, Heidegger, in indicating a way out of theology construed as metaphysics, returns theology to its task of reflecting on and preparing for the faithful proclamation of salvation. In short, theology is always soteriology and never metaphysics.

It is for this reason that Heidegger's confrontation with Aquinas is important: not because it brings Heidegger into conformity with Aquinas, thereby ratifying him as trustworthy or genuinely theological or better yet, Thomist, but rather furthering the recovery of a reading of Aquinas in particular, and the breadth of the medieval tradition more generally, not as a metaphysics, but rather as a soteriology.

Underlying my argument has been a barely articulated Christology. There is not space, and this is not the space, for that Christology to be worked out and discussed. That such a Christology is orthodox is, I believe, a requirement of the understanding I have undertaken. Phenomenology says nothing of Christ, which means in no sense does it determine the essence of Christ in advance of Jesus the Christ's advent, crucifixion, and resurrection. In the undertaking of such a Christology, phenomenology, as I have already indicated, quite properly might act as an ontological corrective to the truth that Christ's ontic being as Jesus is. Here I have been strictly concerned with how and to what extent Heidegger's work opens up or closes off a Christian, theological undertaking. It should by now be entirely clear that I do not believe Heidegger's work is hostile to or destructive of faith or the theologian's task, though it reinvokes the sharpest requirements of the theologians' self-perspicacity and discipline in what and how he might speak. Quite the opposite from hostility, an adequate engagement with Heidegger can inform and fructify future theological thinking to the deepest extent.

Heidegger's work remains within the province of his theological origins, to the extent that, as I have implied but not (for reasons of space and to remain faithful to the task I set myself) fully disclosed, it provides for a way of thinking theologically that has often been called mystical: the theology, for instance, of divine union implied in the works of St. Gregory of Nyssa (in particular the *Life of Moses*), Eckhart, and St. Catherine of Siena, to name only three. In this, I suspect, it is Heidegger's own faith, piety, and life that speak. To say any more than this would be speculative at best, gossip at worst.

## HEIDEGGER'S LOVE

There are two places in the work of the later Heidegger which speak of love and which can be read as demonstrating the position for which I have argued.

Only one has been translated into English. Taken together, they unfold Heidegger's entire later view of theology and reveal his significance for contemporary theological thinking. The first is from *Nietzsches Wort 'Gott ist tot'*, from 1943.[19] The second is from a 1944 lecture series entitled *Heraklit*.[20]

The first text comes from Heidegger's extensive consideration of Nietzsche's proclamation that God is dead. He contrasts the collapse of the supersensory world with the world in which, according to Nietzsche's metaphysics, the will to power now holds sway. The supersensory world no longer supports life; it has become dead. He notes:

> There will be Christian faith here and there. But the love holding sway in that world is not the effectively working (realizing) and operating principle of what now occurs.[21]

I have already noted in chapter 4 the importance of Heidegger's use of the verb *geschehen*, "occur," rather than *sich ereignen*, "events-itself." In this sentence the use of the verb "occurs" indicates that what now holds sway is distanced from things; it (as the will to power) produces things only in terms of subjectivity. Heidegger confirms this later in the text. Similarly, there is the immediate connection of any understanding of love with Christian faith, albeit negatively. The love indicated by the supersensory no longer holds sway. What love does hold sway? The implication is none, but rather, there is a way of thinking through the meaning of love which both overcomes (Christian) faith in a supersensory world and the distancing lovelessness of nihilism in the will to power. Such a love might also be Christian, but it is to do with how being is thought, as I have already indicated from the passage from the *Humanismusbrief*. Heidegger then indicates the need for faith's determination to unfaith, an understanding already indicated in his work:

> God is still not a living God if we persist in trying to master the real without taking God's reality seriously and calling it into question beforehand, and when we persist in this without pondering whether

---

19. *Nietzsches Wort 'Gott ist Tot'* (*Holzwege* [GA5]), pp. 253–255.
20. From *Logik: Heraklits Lehre vom Logos* (GA55), pp. 207–213.
21. *Nietzsches Wort 'Gott ist Tot'* in *Holzwege* (GA5), p. 254. "Christlicher Glaube wird da und dort sein. Aber die in solcher Welt waltende Liebe ist nicht das wirkend-wirksame Prinzip dessen, was jetzt geschieht."

man and woman have so matured for the essence into which, from out
of being, he and she are being drawn, that he and she may withstand
and surmount that destining genuinely from out of his and her essence
and not do so with the sham help (*Scheinhilfe*) of mere expedients.[22]

The *Scheinhilfe*—literally, apparent-assistance—is precisely the appeal to an
immovable, supersensory world as would be defined by a Christian philosophy: what Heidegger proposes is dynamic and living—it *moves*. Living, here,
however, must be understood in the context of Nietzsche's definition of life;
it refers to human life, not the life of God, of which nothing which pertains
to the essence of God can and need be said. Heidegger's whole critique of
the ancient theology, the realm of the supersensory and without-death
(ἀθάνατος) is unable to bring God to life in a human existence. There is,
however, a way of God being life-filled, of human existence vigorously dy-
namized in the divine. Such a way is a *way*, a maturing toward that to which
the human essence is called. This calling is from out of being, which means,
belonging to no supersensory realm; it belongs to the worlding of world, the
place that being emplaces, the ontological difference. How is such a God to be
put into question *from out of being*, except through placing myself into question? To take God seriously is to seek to move in the direction of God, that
moving which is an ecstasis, a being turned out to the future, which has no
return, no expectation of a return, and is therefore never completed, never
fulfilled, never reduced to a 'now', a particular being or thing.

Ecstatically to turn out toward God is to seek to become the essence of
God, because here it is *my* essence that is in question, as in essencing I attempt to know God and so knowing, become God. This knowing is always
factical, always from out of being, for how else could it be? Here the full
meaning of facticity is disclosed. There is no knowing I could undertake
which did not also include the finitude of my being. Facticity just and only,
means knowing, to be authentic knowing, is always mine. It could never 'be'
other, which means all other realms of knowing are *scheinbar*, mere appearances and illusions. How are they illusory? They are those kinds of illusion

22. *Nietzsches Wort 'Gott ist Tot'* in *Holzwege* (GA5), p. 254. "Gott ist nicht ein lebendi-
ger Gott, wenn wir weiter versuchen, das Wirkliche zu meistern, ohne zuvor seine
Wirklichkeit ernst in die Frage zu nehmen, ohne zu bedenken, ob der Mensch dem Wesen,
in das er aus dem Sein her hineingerissen wird, so zugereift ist, daß er dieses Geschick aus
seinem Wesen und nicht mit der Scheinhilfe bloßer Maßnahmen übersteht."

where my 'I' is hidden from myself, and so returns to me as alienated, an object, othered to the extent that my presence in them is effaced and forgotten. Aristotle's theology is this effacement, my effacement from the divine.

It is precisely because Heidegger has suggested that 'I' could *become* the essence of God, that he proceeds in the next two paragraphs to illustrate how the essence of God can never be thought out of being. The first is through Nietzsche's proclamation of the death of God. I can never become the essence of God through the will to power. This gives rise to a misunderstanding: in the devaluation of the uppermost values, surely man and woman supplant God and stand in the place of God? Is this not the intended meaning of Nietzsche's declaration through Zarathustra: "*Dead are all gods: now we will that overman live!*"?[23]

Heidegger says that to take God seriously is to be called from out of being into the divine essence. How does he himself understand this? The answer is in the second paragraph, answering the implied misunderstanding. He says:

> One could believe, were one thinking crassly, that this pronouncement says that dominion over all that is, is passing from God to man, or, even more crassly, that Nietzsche puts man in the place of God. Those who believe thus do not, of course, think in a very godly way about the divine essence. Never can man put himself in the place of God, because the essence of man never reaches the essential realm belonging to God.[24]

For Heidegger, man and woman never reach the essential realm of God, which *is the very striving for it*. God always beckons me further, outer, to this essential realm which I can never reach. This being-beckoned and stretching-out-for is precisely that way in which I transcend—am ecstatic for, toward, God, in the way described earlier. The alternative to this, the

---

23. *Nietzsches Wort 'Gott ist Tot'* in *Holzwege* (GA5), p. 255, quoting the first part of *Also sprach Zarathustra* (*Friedrich Nietzsche* [1999], IV, p. 102). "*'Tot sind alle Götter: nun wollen wir, daß der Übermensch lebe!'*" (Heidegger's italics).

24. *Nietzsches Wort 'Gott ist Tot'* in *Holzwege* (GA5), p. 255. "Man könnte grob denkend meinen, das Wort sage, die Herrschaft über das Seiende gehe von Gott an den Menschen über oder, noch gröber gemeint, Nietzsche setze an die Stelle Gottes den Menschen. Die es so meinen, denken allerdings wenig göttlich von Gottes Wesen. Nie kann sich der Mensch an die Stelle Gottes setzen, weil das Wesen des Menschen den Wesensbereich Gottes nie erreicht."

way of appearances and false realms, Heidegger assures us, a place proper to overman as that one who occurs out of the will to power and as willing, is "subjectness".[25]

It is *Dasein* as the overcoming of the subject-object distinction and in its knowing and moving that can take seriously the realm proper to God. This moving, into which things enter and pass away, which means into which and from which *Dasein* properly (self-ownedly) is entered and is withdrawn, can move me toward the divine essence. Such a moving offers me the possibility of knowing the divine essence and simultaneously never allows me to accede to it. God is known through God's effects, of which (for myself) I am the first. Unless I am self-included in this knowing, I know nothing of God. This self-inclusion occurs and can only be an event of faith. It can never occur through mere scientific thought, mere philosophy, mere reason alone.

The second passage I want to examine briefly, and in which Heidegger mentions love, is different in character, though no less important. It takes up from where this first one leaves off. It is in the summary of a lecture on logic. Heidegger considers the nature of logic as a thinking about thinking, Aristotle's name for the divine. He observes that what is at issue is reflection and abstraction, as a being bent back of the self upon the self. The being bent back belongs to the originary temporality of *Dasein.* Such a bending back already, therefore, speaks out of the forgetfulness of being, since to be bent back upon the self and yet be unaware of it immediately suggests concealment of the self from the self, in exactly the way that, with regard to both Aristotle and Plato I have suggested that the metaphysical idea of God occurs at all.

Heidegger asks a fundamental question concerning this *Reflexion:*

But has man already escaped *Reflexion* when he for example thinks in a Christly way of his God, or has he just accommodated himself in his own certainty of salvation? What if the power of self-reflection of subjectivity had only been unleashed into the modern world-epoch and cemented within it through (among other things) this type of self-concern and way of self-*Reflexion?* Then Christianity, which is one of the essential reasons for the coming about of modern technology due to the τέχνη-like thought of creation (seen metaphysically) which it believes and teaches, would play an essential role in the development of the rule of self-*Reflexion* of subjectivity, so that precisely Christianity is incapable of overcoming this *Reflexion.*[26]

What Heidegger poses is a duplicity, which contains within it a negative formulation of exactly the theology of salvation I have indicated, albeit as a sketch, that his thinking points toward. Simultaneously, in its duplicitous formulation, Heidegger *negatively* suggests what the individual Christian might think and *positively* asks whether in fact something quite other has occurred. He asks, has the Christian who thinks toward God overcome *Reflexion*, or rather (i.e., is it not the case) that he or she desires a certainty of salvation, which would be a metaphysical determination of that form of the willing of the *ens certum*, the subject? The terms Heidegger uses to describe the unfolding of this subjectivity all indicate the perspective he has in mind: self-concernedness, self-reflection, and in the previous paragraph "bent back on the self; egocentric; *to be self-seeking*".[27] To be Christian, to think toward God, would have to be self-abandoning, to expect no return to the self but an endless openness toward God. Such a being open to God is so difficult that it collapses into subjectivity, into the ordinary everyday ruling thinking of the alienative world. It is this which characterizes nihilism, that it is precisely a self-concernedness that never exceeds the self (a failure of transcending as a failure of knowing and so coming close to any being in its being).

It is only in the overcoming of this being bent back on the self in which Heidegger speaks of love. He takes a line of Hölderlin's: "Who thinks the

---

26. *Heraklit* (GA55), p. 209. "Ist der Mensch aber schon der Reflexion entgangen, wenn er z. B. als Christ an seinen Gott denkt, oder richtet er sich dabei gerade nur auf seine eigene Heilssicherheit ein? Wie, wenn erst mit durch diese Art der Selbstbekümmerung und durch diese Form der Selbstbegegnung die Macht der Selbstreflexion der Subjektivität in die moderne Weltgeschichte losgelassen und darin verfestigt worden wäre. Dann hätte das Christentum, das zufolge des in ihm geglaubten und gelehrten τέχνη-haften Schöpfungsgedankens, metaphysisch gesehen, auch mit einer der wesentlichen Gründe ist für die Heraufkunft der modernen Technik, an der Ausbildung der Herrschaft der Selbstreflexion der Subjektivität einen wesentlichen Anteil, so daß gerade das Christentum zur Überwindung dieser Reflexion nichts vermag."

27. *Heraklit* (GA55), p. 208. "Sichzurückbiegen . . . ichsüchtig . . . *selbstsüchtig zu sein*" (author's italics). Heidegger culminates this list with the final definition of subjectivity that he also uses in the lecture course *Einleitung in die Philosophie: Denken und Dichten* (*Nietzsche* [GA50]), p. 111: "sich auf sich selbst stellende Subjekt".

deepest, loves the most living".[28] This thinking the deepest, he argues, is not a thinking, which, having thought, stops and returns to itself, but rather, *as* the thinking of the deepest remains with the thought. What he is articulating is the recovery of the holding together of the two temporal determinations that were lost in the rising up of metaphysics, the thought of being and the thought of becoming, as a simultaneity. *This* is love: to think and turn into the thought of what is thought as it appears and passes by.

Such a thinking holds all together in its thought; it is the thinking and saying of the many of the one (τὸ ὂν λέγεται πολλαχῶς).[29] This thinking thinks *through* time:

> The more purely man has thought, the more decidedly has he reached the path of thinking and continues to be a thinker; just as only the one who has seen rightly, can see at all. Strange, how here the end is actually the beginning.[30]

It is a thinking in which the end gives the beginning and the beginning discloses the end. Indeed, such a beginning is only possible because (in a sense) the end is already in view and has been attained. Such a thinking (exactly as posed in the *Humanismusbrief*) is simultaneously a loving, a being most open toward things in order that they co-disclose themselves and me to myself. It is *this* thinking which, negatively posed, might think toward God, for the Christian. It remains only to say that the Christian who desires to think toward God desires to be like Christ.

These two passages contain, I would argue, a fully thought-through theology of a special kind, a theology that, because it constantly poses the nothing against God as revealing what it might be to think of God again, is characterized by a refusal, because to say other would be to attain the realm proper to God, which men and women may never attain, and yet may be called into.

---

28. *Heraklit* (GA55), p. 211. "Wer das Tiefste gedacht, liebt das Lebendigste."

29. Aristotle, *Metaphysics*, VI, 11 (1026a33). "Being is said in many ways." (See chapter 6).

30. *Heraklit* (GA55), p. 212. "Je reiner der Mensch nur gedacht hat, je entschiedener ist er auf den Weg des Denkens gelangt, und bleibt er ein Denkender; genauso wie derjenige, der recht gesehen hat, erst sieht. Seltsam, wie hier das Ende erst der eigentliche Beginn ist.

## Conclusion

In conclusion, therefore, how can I, as a Christian believer and theologian, understand that Heidegger might invite me to understand what he means by atheism? God is not a being like the human being, *Dasein:* God does not in this sense exist. More importantly, God is not a being at all, in the sense that God does not fall within being except insofar as God chooses to (above all in the person of Jesus Christ). In this sense, nothing can be said of the existence of God. If nothing can be said, then *the* nothing is also to be said of the existence of God, which means that the question of 'who' God is recovers itself and is recovered through turning into nihilism and understanding from within what it means to proclaim God is dead. It is for this reason that Zarathustra is of paramount importance in the saying of nothing of God. Nietzsche's riddles, first of the shepherd into whose mouth the black snake of nihilism has crawled, and second of the doorway, are figures for a return to a more original and renewed experience of God. Is Zarathustra therefore really Christian? Zarathustra is the voice of the discovery of radical, individualistic atheism. How, therefore, could Zarathustra be Christian? The question is better put as: what kind of Christianity does Zarathustra denounce? Moreover, *as* the one who provides the way back for me to rediscover, non-metaphysically, my embodiment, Zarathustra is solely a non-embodied figure. How do you baptize a figure? Zarathustra says *the* nothing of God. As one who turns in to nihilism, as a discovery that being is itself a radical, individualistic, atheism: as one, therefore who stands within the ontological difference as a coming to the self (which phenomenology yields), as *this* one, I discover myself to be in a place, the *there* of there-being.

The site for God, Heidegger tells me, may remain empty, or it may be filled. However, every filling of the site collapses, and so every *ecstasis* toward God both reveals who God is and falls short of God and denies God, because it collapses into objectness. The site, which is the place where *I* may say something of God, leaves me only with some *thing.* All speaking of the filling of this site, in this sense, is both open to the experience of God and fails to say anything of God. To say anything of God in this way is simultaneously to say nothing of God, not even to come close to who the God is, and yet to be pulled toward God. To say anything of God (even to say some-*thing* which must then be exceeded and denied) I must return again and again to how God is to be known. The scriptures, the sacraments, the faith of my neighbor, and my love of her and him are places where God can be known: in these places, through my being (and my being Christ-like), God comes to *be*. Above all, and belonging to all of these, is prayer. The highest and deepest and most demanding prayer is to enter into silence. To say nothing, that God might speak. To say nothing, that no objects, no thing, nothing intervenes between God and me, God and the soul (understanding soul here in no supersensory, but an entirely immaterial, sense). Every entry into this silence collapses, into words, into the speaking, the babbling that being is. This silence is therefore one to which I must return again and again. What I describe are not techniques of saying something, or even nothing, of God, but a way, a path, which, God-given, is a being underway to God. To come to myself means I both discover my separation from God, and I become open to who the God is. To come to myself requires that I exceed myself: to come to myself means to seek union with God, to abandon the self I have become for the sake of what else I might divinely myself become. To come to my-self and seek union with God demands, at every step along the path, that I say nothing of God. This could be taken within Heidegger's atheism: indeed, this would be a holy atheism.

# The Reply to the Third Question at the Seminar in Zurich, 1951[1]

*Third Question:* May being and God be posited as identical?

*Heidegger:* I am asked this question almost every fortnight, because it (understandably) disconcerts theologians, and because it relates to the Europeanization of history, which already began in the Middle Ages, through Aristotle's and Plato's penetration into theology, specifically the New Testament. This is a process whose immensity cannot be over-estimated. I have asked an old Jesuit friend of mine to show me the place in Thomas Aquinas where he says what '*esse*' specifically means and what the proposition means that says '*Deus est suum esse*'. I have to this day received no answer. —

God and being is not identical. (If Rickert suggests that the concept 'being' might be too loaded, this is because he understood being in the very restricted sense of reality in distinction to values.) Being and God are not identical, and I would never attempt to think the essence of God through being. Some of you perhaps know that I came out of theology, and that I harbor an old love for it and that I have a certain understanding of it. If I were yet to write a theology—to which I sometimes feel inclined—then the word 'being' would not be allowed to occur in it.

Faith has no need of the thinking of being. If faith has recourse to it, it is already not faith. Luther understood this. Even in his own church this appears to be forgotten. I think very modestly about being with regard to its use to think the essence of God. Of being, there is nothing

---

1. *Seminare* (GA15), p. 436f.

here of impact. I believe that being can never be thought as the ground and essence of God, but that nevertheless the experience and manifestness of God, insofar as they meet with humanity, eventuate in the dimension of being, which in no way signifies that being might be regarded as a possible predicate for God. On this point one would have to establish wholly new distinctions and delimitations

*Dritte Frage:* Dürfen Sein und Gott identisch gesetzt werden?

*Heidegger:* Diese Frage wird mir fast alle vierzehn Tage gestellt, weil sie die Theologen (begreiflicherweise) beunruhigt, und weil sie zusammenhängt mit der Europäisierung der Geschichte, die schon im Mittelalter beginnt, nämlich dadurch, daß Aristoteles und Plato in die Theologie eingedrungen sind, respektive in das Neue Testament. Das ist ein Prozeß, den man sich gar nicht ungeheuer genug vorstellen kann. Ich habe einen mir wohlgesinnten Jesuiten gebeten, mir die Stellen bei Thomas von Aquin zu zeigen, wo gesagt sei, was 'esse' eigentlich bedeute und was der Satz besage: *Deus est suum esse.* Ich habe bis heute noch keine Antwort.—

Gott und Sein ist nicht identisch. (Wenn Rickert meint, der Begriff 'Sein' sei zu sehr belastet, so darum, weil er Sein im ganz engen Sinn von Wirklichkeit im Unterschied zu den Werten versteht.) Sein und Gott sind nicht identisch, und ich würde niemals versuchen, das Wesen Gottes durch das Sein zu denken. Einige wissen vielleicht, daß ich von der Theologie herkomme und ihr noch eine alte Liebe bewahrt habe und einiges davon verstehe. Wenn ich noch eine Theologie schreiben würde, wozu es mich manchmal reizt, dann dürfte in ihr das Wort 'Sein' nicht vorkommen.

Der Glaube hat das Denken des Seins nicht nötig. Wenn er das braucht, ist er schon nicht mehr Glaube. Das hat Luther verstanden. Sogar in seiner eigenen Kirche scheint man das zu vergessen. Ich denke über das Sein im Hinblick auf seine Eignung, das Wesen Gottes theologisch zu denken, sehr bescheiden. Mit dem Sein ist hier nichts auszurichten. Ich glaube, daß das Sein niemals als Grund und Wesen von Gott gedacht werden kann, daß aber gleichwohl die Erfahrung Gottes und seiner Offenbarkeit (sofern sie dem Menschen begegnet) in der Dimension des Seins sich ereignet, was niemals besagt, das Sein könne als mögliches Prädikat für Gott gelten. Hier braucht es ganz neue Unterscheidungen und Abgrenzungen.

# Glossary of Greek Terms

| | | |
|---|---|---|
| ἀεί | aei | ever, the eternal |
| ἀγαθόν | agathon | the good, the serviceable |
| αἴσθησις | aisthesis | sensation, immediate knowledge |
| ἀλήθεια | aletheia | truth |
| ἀληθεύειν | aletheuein | making-true |
| ἀθάνατος | athanatos | without-death, immortal |
| ἀριθμὸς | arithmos | number |
| ἀρχή | arche | origin |
| δαιμόνιον | daimonion | demonic |
| ἐπιστήμη | episteme | science |
| ἕν | hen | unity, the 'one' |
| εἶναι | einai | being |
| εἶδος | eidos | form; the look or face of a thing |
| ἔρως | eros | desire, attraction |
| θαυμάζειν | thaumazein | wonder |
| θεά | thea | goddess |
| θέα | thea | look |
| θεῖον | theion | the divine |
| θεολογία | theologia | theology |
| θεωρεῖν | theorein | contemplation |
| ἰδέα | idea | idea |

| κίνησις | kinesis | movement |
|---|---|---|
| λεγεῖν | legein | speaking |
| λόγος | logos | speech |
| μεταβαλλεῖν | metaballein | change |
| μοῖρα | moira | fate |
| μορφή | morphe | form |
| νοῦς | nous | knowledge as such |
| νοεῖν | noein | knowing, intellection |
| Ὀκεανός | Okeanos | the name of the the "mighty river" in Homer, an intimation of the divine |
| ὄν | on | (a) being |
| οὐσία | ousia | substance |
| πρᾶξις | praxis | whatever is concerned with the movable |
| πόιησις | poiesis | creativity |
| πόλις | polis | people |
| σοφία | sophia | wisdom |
| τέχνη | techne | art |
| τόπος | topos | place |
| φίλια | filia | love, belonging |
| φύσις | physis | nature |
| φρόνησις | phronesis | 'practical wisdom' |
| ψεῦδος | pseudos | the false |
| ψυχή | psyche | the soul |

# Bibliography

WORKS BY MARTIN HEIDEGGER

Texts referred to are from the *Gesamtausgabe* of Heidegger's works, indicated in footnotes by the letters GA and the volume number. Where no volume number is recorded, the text referred is not, or not yet, in the *Gesamtausgabe*. I have usually indicated English translations where they exist. There are a number of texts which, although assigned a *Gesamtausgabe* volume number and published under license in separate (subscription) editions by Klostermann, also exist in *Einzelausgabe* editions by either Klostermann (Frankfurt), Neske Verlag (Tübingen), or Niemeyer (Pfullingen). I have indicated the use of these *Einzelausgabe* editions with †.

## Martin Heidegger—*Gesamtausgabe*

Gesamtausgabe 1, *Frühe Schriften*, von Herrmann, Friedrich-Wilhelm (ed.), Frankfurt, Klostermann, 1978. First published as *Frühe Schriften*, Frankfurt, Klostermann, 1972.

> *Vorwort.* Inaugural address, 1957. First published in *Jahreshefte der Heidelberger Akademie der Wissenschaften 1957/58*, Heidelberg, 1959. Translated by Siegfried, Hans, as "A Recollection (1957)" in *Man and World*, no. 3 (1970).

> *Die Lehre vom Urteil im Psychologismus* (1914).

> *Die Kategorien- und Bedeutungslehre des Duns Scotus* (Habilitationsschrift, 1916). Translated by Robbins, Harold J., as "Duns Scotus's Theory of the Categories and of Meaning by Martin Heidegger," unpublished Ph.D. thesis, DePaul University, Illinois, 1978.

> *Der Zeitbegriff in der Geschichtswissenshaft* (1916). Translated by Taylor, Harry S., and Uffelman, Hans W., as "The Concept of Time in the Science of History" in *Journal of the British Society for Phenomenology*, vol. 9 (1978).

†Gesamtausgabe 2, *Sein und Zeit*, Niemeyer, Tübingen, 1993 [17th ed.] (von Herrmann, Friedrich-Wilhelm [ed.], Frankfurt, Klostermann, 1977.)

*Sein und Zeit*, Tübingen, Niemeyer, 1927. First published in the *Jahrbuch für Philosophie* 1927. Translated by Macquarrie, John, and Robinson, Edward, as *Being and Time*, London, SCM Press, 1962, and by Stambaugh, Joan, under the same title, New York, SUNY, 1996.

Gesamtausgabe 3, *Kant und das Problem der Metaphysik*, von Herrmann, Friedrich-Wilhelm (ed.), Frankfurt, Klostermann, 1991.

Based on a series of lectures given at Marburg in the winter semester of 1927/28 and published separately as volume 25 of the *Gesamtausgabe* (see below). First published as "Kant und das Problem der Metaphysik" in *Max Scheler zum Gedächtnis*, Friedrich Cohen Verlag, Bonn, 1929. Fourth, altered edition Frankfurt, Klostermann, 1973. Fifth (expanded) edition 1991 as vol. 3 of the *Gesamtausgabe*. Translated twice under the same title, *Kant and the Problem of Metaphysics:* (1) based on the 1950 second edition by Churchill, James S., Bloomington, Indiana University Press, 1962; and (2) based on the 1973 fourth, enlarged, edition by Taft, Richard, Bloomington, Indiana University Press, 1990.

Gesamtausgabe 4, *Erläuterungen zu Hölderlins Dichtung* (1936–1968), Frankfurt, Klostermann, 1991.

*Hölderlin und das Wesen der Dichtung* (1936). Lecture given in Rome.

*Heimkunft/An die Verwandten* (1943). Lecture given at Freiburg. Translated by Scott, Douglas, as "Hölderlin and the Essence of Poetry" and "Remembrance of the Poet" in Werner, Brock (ed.), *Existence and Being*, Chicago, Regnery, 1949.

Gesamtausgabe 5, *Holzwege*, von Herrmann, Friedrich-Wilhelm (ed.), Frankfurt, Klostermann, 1977. First published as *Holzwege*, Frankfurt, Klostermann, 1950.

*Der Ursprung der Kunstwerkes* (1935/36). Translated by Hofstadter, Albert (ed.), as "The Origin of the Work of Art" in *Poetry, Language, Thought*, New York, Harper & Row, 1971.

*Die Zeit des Weltbildes* (1938). Translated by Lovitt, William (ed.), as "The Age of the World Picture" in *The Question Concerning Technology*, New York, Harper & Row, 1977.

*Hegels Begriff der Erfahrung* (1942/43). Translated by Gray, Glenn J., as *Hegel's Concept of Experience*, New York, Harper & Row, 1970.

*Nietzsches Wort 'Gott ist tot'* (1943). Translated by Lovitt, William (ed.), as "The Word of Nietzsche: 'God Is Dead'" in *The Question Concerning Technology*.

*Wozu Dichter?* (1946). Translated by Hofstadter, Albert (ed.), as "What Are Poets For?" in *Poetry, Language, Thought*.

*Der Spruch des Anaximander* (1946). Translated by Krell, David F., as "The Anaximander Fragment" in Krell, David F. and Capuzzi, Frank (eds.) *Early Greek Thinking,* New York, Harper & Row, 1975.

†Gesamtausgabe 6.1, *Nietzsche* I, Pfullingen, Neske, 1961

*Der Wille zur Macht als Kunst.* Freiburg, winter semester 1936/37. Translated by Krell, David F. (ed.), as "The Will to Power as Art" in *Nietzsche by Martin Heidegger,* four vols., New York, Harper & Row, 1979, vol. 1.

*Die ewige Wiederkehr des Gleichen.* Freiburg, summer semester 1937. Translated by Krell, David F. (ed.), as "The Eternal Recurrence of the Same" in *Nietzsche by Martin Heidegger,* vol. 2.

*Der Wille zur Macht als Erkenntnis.* Freiburg, summer semester, 1939. Translated by Krell, David F. (ed.), as "The Will to Power as Knowledge" in *Nietzsche by Martin Heidegger,* vol. 3.

†Gesamtausgabe 6.2, *Nietzsche* II, Pfullingen, Neske, 1961

*Die ewige Wiederkehr des Gleichen und der Wille zur Macht.* The two concluding lectures to all three lecture courses, written in 1939 but not delivered. Translated by Krell, David F. (ed.), as "The Eternal Recurrence of the Same and the Will to Power" in *Nietzsche by Martin Heidegger,* vol. 3.

*Der europäische Nihilismus.* Freiburg, first trimester, 1940. Translated by Krell, David F. (ed.), as "European Nihilism" in *Nietzsche by Martin Heidegger,* vol. 4.

*Die seinsgeschichtliche Bestimmung des Nihilismus.* An essay composed during the years 1944–46. Translated by Krell, David F. (ed.), as "Nihilism as Determined by the History of Being" in *Nietzsche by Heidegger,* vol. 4.

*Die Metaphysik als Geschichte des Seins.* Essay, 1941. Translated by Stambaugh, Joan (ed.), as "Metaphysics as History of Being" in *The End of Philosophy,* New York, Harper & Row, 1973.

*Entwürfe zur Geschichte des Seins als Metaphysik.* Essay, 1941. Translated by Stambaugh, Joan (ed.), as "Sketches for a History of Being as Metaphysics" in *The End of Philosophy.*

*Die Erinnerung in die Metaphysik.* Essay, 1941. Translated by Stambaugh, Joan (ed.), as "Recollection of Metaphysics" in *The End of Philosophy.*

†Gesamtausgabe 7, *Vorträge und Aufsätze. 1936–53,* Pfullingen, Neske, 1954.

*Die Frage nach der Technik.* Originally published in *Die Technik und die Kehre,* Pfullingen, Neske, 1962. Based on the 1949 lecture entitled *Das Ge-stell* in the series *Einblick in das—Was ist?* (see *Gesamtausgabe* vol. 79 below). Translated by Lovitt, William (ed.), as "The Question Concerning Technology" in *The Question Concerning Technology,* New York, Harper & Row, 1977.

*Wissenschaft und Besinnung.* Given to a small circle in Munich in 1953. Translated by Lovitt, William (ed.), as "Science and Reflection" in *The Question Concerning Technology.*

*Überwindung der Metaphysik.* Translated by Stambaugh Joan (ed.), as "Overcoming Metaphysics" in *The End of Philosophy*, New York, Harper & Row, 1973.

*Wer ist Nietzsches Zarathustra?* Lecture given at the Bremen Club in 1953. Translated by Krell, David F. (ed.), as "Who Is Nietzsche's Zarathustra?" in *Nietzsche by Martin Heidegger*, four vols., New York, Harper & Row, 1979, vol. 2.

*Was heißt Denken?* Lecture broadcast on Bavarian Radio in 1952 and first printed in Moras J., and Paeschke H. (eds.), *Zeitschrift 'Merkur'*, vol. 6 (1952). Translated by Wieck F. D., and Gray J. G., as "What Calls for Thinking" in Krell, David F. (ed.), *Basic Writings: Martin Heidegger*, New York, Harper and Row 1977.

*Bauen Wohnen Denken.* Lecture, given in the series *Darmstädter Gespräche II*, series title *Mensch und Raum* and published by the series editors, *Neue Darmstädter Verlagsanstalt*, Darmstadt, 1952. Translated by Hofstadter, Albert, as "Building Dwelling Thinking" in Krell, David F. (ed.), *Basic Writings: Martin Heidegger.*

*Das Ding.* One of the series of four lectures given at the Bremen Club under the title *Einblick in das—Was ist?* with an epilogue *Ein Brief an einen jungen Studenten* (see *Gesamtausgabe* vol. 79, below). Translated by Hofstadter, Albert (ed.), as "The Thing" in *Poetry, Language, Thought*, New York, Harper and Row, 1971.

*. . . dichterisch wohnet der Mensch . . .* Given in 1951 in Bühlerhöhe. First published in Höllerer, W. and Bender Hans (eds.), *Akzente*, booklet 1, Bühlerhöhe, 1954. Translated by Hofstadter, Albert (ed.), as "'. . . Poetically Man Dwells. . .'" in *Poetry, Language, Thought.*

*Logos.* A contribution to the *Festschrift* for Hans Jantzen edited by Bauch, Kurt, Berlin, 1951, and given as a lecture to the Bremen Club in the same year. Translated by Krell, David F., as "Logos (Heraclitus, Fragment B 50)" in Krell, David F., and Capuzzi, Frank (eds.), *Early Greek Thinking*, New York, Harper and Row, 1975.

*Moira.* An undelivered section of the 1951/52 lecture series *Was heißt Denken*, Tübingen, Niemeyer, 1954 (see *Gesamtausgabe* vol. 8 below). Translated by Capuzzi, Frank, as "Moira (Parmenides VIII, 34–41)" in Krell, David F., and Capuzzi, Frank (eds.), *Early Greek Thinking.*

*Aletheia.* Originally a contribution to the *Festschrift* for the 350th anniversary celebrations of the *Humanistischen Gymnasiums in Konstanz* and first prepared but undelivered for a lecture series on Heraclitus in 1943. First published in a separate volume by Pfullingen, Neske, 1959. Translated by Capuzzi, Frank, as "Aletheia (Heraclitus, Fragment B 16)" in Krell, David F., and Capuzzi, Frank (eds.), *Early Greek Thinking.*

†Gesamtausgabe 8, *Was heißt Denken?,* Tübingen, Niemeyer, 1954. Lectures given at Freiburg, winter semester 1951–52. Translated by Gray, John G., and Wieck, F. D., as *What is Called Thinking?* New York, Harper, 1972.

Gesamtausgabe 9, *Wegmarken,* von Hermann, Friedrich-Wilhelm (ed.), Frankfurt, Klostermann, 1976. 1919–61. First published as *Wegmarken,* Frankfurt, Klostermann, 1967. Translated by McNeill, William (ed.), *Pathmarks,* New York, Cambridge University Press, 1998.

*Anmerkungen zu Karl Jaspers 'Psychologie der Weltanschauungen'* written between 1919 and 1921 and sent to Karl Jaspers. Translated by van Buren, John, as "Comments on Karl Jaspers' Psychology of Worldviews (1919/21)," in *Pathmarks.*

*Phänomenologie und Theologie.* Lecture given in Tübingen in 1927 and again in Marburg in 1928. First published in *Archives de Philosophie,* vol. 32 (1969), together with a French translation. Subsequently published separately as *Phänomenologie und Theologie,* Frankfurt, Klostermann, 1970. First translated by Hart, J., and Maraldo, J. C. (eds.), as "Phenomenology and Theology" in *The Piety of Thinking,* Bloomington, Indiana University Press, 1976. Reprinted in a revised form in *Pathmarks.*

*Aus der letzten Marburger Vorlesung.* First published in *Zeit und Geschichte,* a *Festschrift* for Rudolf Bultmann, Siebeck, P. (ed.), Tübingen, Mohr, 1964. Translated by Robinson, E., as "From the Last Marburg Lecture Course" in Robinson, E. (ed.), *The Future of Our Religious Past: Essays in Honor of Rudolf Bultmann,* New York, Harper and Row, 1969. Retranslated by McNeill, William, as "From the Last Marburg Lecture Course" in *Pathmarks* as an adaptation of part of the translation undertaken by Heim, M. in *The Metaphysical Foundations of Logic;* see *Gesamtausgabe* vol. 26 below.

*Was ist Metaphysik?* Inaugural lecture given at Freiburg in 1929. First published as *Was ist Metaphysik?,* Bonn, Cohen Verlag, 1929. The fourth edition was published in Frankfurt, Klostermann, 1943, together with a postscript (see below). Fifth (1949) edition included an introduction (see below). First translated by Hull, R. F. C., and Crick, Alan, as "What Is Metaphysics?" (including the postscript) in Brock, Werner (ed.), *Existence and Being,* Chicago, Regnery, 1949. Subsequently translated as "What Is Metaphysics?" in Krell, David F. (ed.), *Basic Writings: Martin Heidegger,* San Francisco, Harper Collins, 1977. Revised translation by Krell, David F., and McNeill, William, in *Pathmarks.*

*Vom Wesen des Grundes.* First published as a contribution to the *Festschrift* for Edmund Husserl's 70th birthday in *Ergänzungsband zum Jahrbuch für Philosophie und Phänomenologie Forschung,* Halle, 1929, and simultaneously on its own as *Vom Wesen des Grundes,* Halle (Saale), Niemeyer, 1929. The third and subsequent editions were published in Frankfurt, Klostermann, 1949 and thereafter. Translated by Malick, Tom, as *The Essence of Reasons* (bilingual edition), Illinois, Evanston, 1969. Retranslated by McNeill, William, as "On the Essence of Ground" in *Pathmarks.*

*Vom Wesen der Wahrheit.* An often-repeated lecture from 1930. First published as *Vom Wesen der Wahrheit,* Frankfurt, Vittorio Klostermann, 1943. First translated by Hull, R. F. C., and Crick, Alan, as "On the Essence of Truth" in Brock, Werner (ed.) *Existence and Being.* Subsequently translated by Krell, David F. (ed.), as "On the Essence of Truth" in *Basic Writings: Martin Heidegger.*

*Platons Lehre von der Wahrheit.* From a Freiburg lecture course, winter semester 1930/31 (see *Gesamtausgabe* vol. 34, below). First published as *Geistige Überlieferung,* Berlin, 1942. Subsequently in *Platons Lehre von der Wahrheit mit einem Brief über den Humanismus,* Bern, Francke, 1947. Translated by Barlow, J., and Lohner, E., as "Plato's Doctrine of Truth" in Barnett, W., and Aiken, H. (eds.), *Philosophy in the 20th Century,* New York, 1962. Retranslated by Sheehan, Thomas J., S.J., and McNeill, William, as "Plato's Doctrine of Truth" in *Pathmarks.*

*Vom Wesen und Begriff der* Φύσις, *Aristoteles Physik B, 1.* Unpublished composition from 1939. First published in *Il Pensiero,* vol. 3, nos. 2 and 3, Milan, 1958. Translated by Sheehan, Thomas J., S.J., as "On the Being and Conception of Physics: Aristotle's Physics B 1," in *Man and World,* no. 9 (1976).

*Nachwort zu Was ist Metaphysik?* See *Was ist Metaphysik?* above. Translated by Hull, R. F. C., and Crick, Alan, at the end of "What Is Metaphysics?" in Brock, Werner (ed.) *Existence and Being:* retranslated by McNeill, William, as "Postscript to 'What Is Metaphysics?'" in *Pathmarks.*

*Brief über den Humanismus.* First published with the subtitle *Brief an Jean Beaufret,* Paris, 1946. Republished in Grassi, E., and Szilasi, W. (eds.), *Platons Lehre von der Wahrheit mit einem Brief über den Humanismus* in *Reihe Probleme und Hinweise,* 3d ed., Bern, 1975. Translated by Barlow, J., and Lohner, E. (eds.), as "Letter on Humanism" in *Philosophy in the 20th Century.* Republished as "Letter on 'Humanism'" in *Pathmarks.*

*Einleitung zu Was ist Metaphysik? (Der Rückgang in den Grund der Metaphysik).* See *Was ist Metaphysik?* above. Translated as "The Way Back into the Ground of Metaphysics: Introduction to the lecture Was ist Metaphysik ? (1929) — Introduction to the 5th Edition" in Kaufman, Walter (ed.), *Existentialism from Dostojiwski to Sartre,* New York, Fontana, 1957. Republished as "Introduction to 'What Is Metaphysics?'" in *Pathmarks.*

*Zur Seinsfrage.* Originally published as *Über 'die Linie'* in a *Festschrift* for Ernst Jünger, *Freundschaftliche Begegnungen: Festschrift zum 60. Geburtstag,* Frankfurt, Klostermann, 1955. Published separately as *Über 'die Linie',* Frankfurt, Klostermann, 1956. Translated by Kluback, T., and Wilde, J.T., as *The Question of Being* (bilingual edition), New York, Twayne, 1958. Retranslated by McNeill, William, as "On the Question of Being" in *Pathmarks.*

*Hegel und die Griechen.* Lecture, given at the Heidelberger Akademie der Wissenschaften in 1958. First published as a contribution to the *Festschrift* for Hans-Georg Gadamer on his 60th birthday, *Die Gegenwart der Griechen im neueren Denken,* Tübingen, Mohr, 1960. Translated by Sallis, J., and McNeill, William, as "Hegel and the Greeks" in *Pathmarks.*

*Kants These über das Sein.* Originally published as a contribution to the *Festschrift* for Erik Wolf on his 60th birthday as *Existenz und Ordnung* in Würtenberger, T., Maihofer, W., and Hollerbach, A. (eds.), *Festschrift für Erich Wolf zum 60 Geburtstag,* Frankfurt, Klostermann, 1962; also published separately in Frankfurt, Vittorio Klostermann, 1963. Translated by Klein, T., and Pohl, W., as "Kant's Thesis about Being" in *The Southwestern Journal of Philosophy,* vol. 4 (1973). Reprinted in *Pathmarks.*

Gesamtausgabe 10, *Der Satz vom Grund,* Jaeger, Petra (ed.), Frankfurt, Klostermann, 1997. Lectures given in Freiburg, winter semester 1955/56; the final (extended) lecture was given in Vienna and to the Bremen Club in 1956. Translated by Lilly, R., as *The Principle of Reason,* Bloomington, Indiana University Press, 1991.

†Gesamtausgabe 11, *Identität und Differenz,* Pfullingen, Neske, 1957. Translated by Stambaugh, Joan (ed.), as *Identity and Difference* in a bilingual edition, New York, Harper Torchbooks, 1969.

*Der Satz der Identität.* Freiburg lecture, 1957. Translated as *The Principle of Identity.*

*Die onto-theo-logische Verfassung der Metaphysik.* Reworked from a Freiburg seminar on Hegel's *Science of Logic* of the winter semester 1956/57. Translated as *The Ontotheological Constitution of Metaphysics.*

†Gesamtausgabe 12, *Unterwegs zur Sprache,* Pfullingen, Neske, 1965. [Frankfurt, Klostermann, 1985]. Lectures from 1950–59. Translated by Hertz, Peter D. (ed.), as *On the Way to Language,* San Francisco, Harper, 1982.

*Die Sprache,* lecture, Bühlerhöhe, 1950. Translated by Hofstadter, Albert (ed.), as "Language" in *Poetry, Language, Thought,* New York, Harper, 1971.

*Die Sprache im Gedicht.* First published as "Georg Trakl: Eine Erörterung seines Gedichtes" in *Merkur,* no. 61, 1953. Translated by Hertz, Peter D.(ed.), as "Language in the Poem: A Discussion on George Trakl's Poetic Work" in *On the Way to Language.*

*Aus einem Gespräch von der Sprache.* The 1953/54 text of a conversation between a Japanese professor and the author. Translated by Hertz, Peter D. (ed.), as "A Dialogue on Language" in *On the Way to Language.*

*Das Wesen der Sprache.* Three Freiburg lectures from December 1957 and January 1958. Translated by Hertz, Peter D. (ed.), as "The Nature of Language" in *On the Way to Language.*

*Das Wort.* Vienna lecture, 1958. Translated by Stambaugh, Joan, as "Words" in Hertz, Peter D. (ed.), *On the Way to Language.*

*Der Weg zur Sprache.* Lecture given in Munich and Berlin in 1959 under the title *Die Sprache.* First published in the fourth series of *Gestalt und Gedanke,* Podewils, C. (ed.), 1959. Translated by Hertz, Peter D. (ed.), as "The Way to Language" in *On the Way to Language.*

Gesamtausgabe 13, *Aus der Erfahrung des Denkens,* Heidegger, Hermann (ed.), Frankfurt, Klostermann, 1983. 1910–76. [Cf. *Denkerfahrungen,* Frankfurt, Klostermann, 1985]

*Abraham a Sankta Clara.* First published in *Allgemeine Rundschau,* Munich, 1910.

*Frühe Gedichte.* 1910–1916. Variously published in minor journals.

*Schöpferische Landschaft: Warum bleiben wir in der Provinz?* Originally written in the autumn of 1933 and broadcast on Berlin Radio. A version was published in 1934 in *Die Freiburger Tagespost.* Republished in *Nachlese zu Heidegger* by Schneeburger, Guido (ed.), Bern, 1962. Translated by Sheehan, Thomas J., S. J., as "Why Do I Stay in the Provinces?" in *Listening, Journal of Religion and Culture,* vol. 5 (1977); reprinted in *Heidegger the Man and the Thinker,* Sheehan, Thomas J., S. J. (ed.), Chicago, Precedent, 1981.

*Wege zur Aussprache.* Originally published in the *Jahrbuch* of the city of Freiburg, vol.1, *Alemannenland,* Kerber, F. (ed.), Stuttgart, Engelhorns, 1937. Republished in *Nachlese zu Heidegger.*

*Winke.* Privately published in Meßkirch, Heuberg-Druckerei, 1941.

*Chorlied aus der Antigone des Sophokles.* Privately published in 1943 on the occasion of Elfride Heidegger's 50th birthday.

*Zur Erörterung der Gelassenheit.* Written in 1944 and 1945. First published as *Gelassenheit,* Pfullingen, Neske, 1959. Translated by Anderson, J. M., and Freund, E. H., as *Discourse on Thinking,* Harper & Row, New York, 1966.

*Aus der Erfahrung des Denkens.* Written in 1947 and published privately. Published as *Aus der Erfahrung des Denkens,* Pfullingen, Neske, 1954. Translated by Hofstadter, Albert, as "The Thinker as Poet" in *Poetry, Language, Thought,* Harper & Row, New York, 1971.

*Der Feldweg* (1949). First published privately under the title *Der Zuspruch des Feldwegs* in *Sonntagsblatt,* no. 43 (1949) and as *Der Feldweg* in *Wort und Wahrheit,* Vienna, 1950. Republished with supporting photographs, Frankfurt, Klostermann, 1953.

*Holzwege ('Dem künftigen Menschen . . .').* First published in the newspaper *Die Welt,* 26 September 1949.

*Zu einem Vers von Mörike.* A 1951 exchange of letters between Heidegger and Emil Steiger. First published in *Trivium,* vol. 9 (1951).

*Was heißt Lesen?* First published in Munich, Ehrenwirth, 1954.

*Vom Geheimnis des Glockenturms.* Written in 1954 and published in *Martin Heidegger, zum 80. Geburtstag von seiner Heimatstadt Meßkirch,* Frankfurt, Klostermann, 1969.

*Für das Langenharder Hebelbuch.* First published in *Der Altvater* in the *Lahrer Zeitung,* 12th year, p. 48, December 1954.

*Über die Sixtina.* Published in Putscher, M., *Raphaels Sixtinische Madonna— Das Werk und seine Wirkung,* Tübingen, 1955.

*Die Sprache Johann Peter Hebels.* A contribution to *Der Lichtgang,* 5th year, Book 7, Freiburg, 1955.

*Begegnungen mit Ortega y Gasset,* a contribution to a *Zeitschrift* in honor of Ortega y Gasset, translated into Spanish and published in *Clavileno,* the journal of the *Asociación Internacional de Hispanismo,* 7th year, no. 39 (1956).

*Hebel—der Hausfreund.* First published in Pfullingen, Neske, 1957.

*Aufzeichnungen aus der Werkstatt.* Published on the occasion of Heidegger's 70th birthday in the *Neue Zürcher Zeitung,* 26 September 1959.

*Sprache und Heimat.* 1960 lecture, published in a *Festschrift* for Carl J. Burckhardt, Munich, Callwey, 1960.

*Über Igor Stravinsky.* First published in the *Zeitschrift für Neue Musik 'Melos',* 29th year, vol. 6 (1962).

*Für René Char.* First published in facsimile under the general title "Hommage à Georges Braque" in *Derrière le Miroir,* nos. 144–146, Paris, Maeght Editeur, 1964.

*Adalbert Stifters 'Eisgeschichte'.* First published in *Wirkendes Wort,* Schweizerische Bibliophilen-Gesellschaft, Zurich, 1964.

*Wink in das Gewesen.* A contribution to a *Festschrift* for the publisher Vittorio Klostermann, *Vittorio Klostermann zum 29.12.1976,* Frankfurt, Weisbecker, 1976.

*Die Kunst und der Raum.* 1964 lecture. First privately published in an edition of 150, then as *Die Kunst und der Raum: L'art et l'espace,* St. Gallen, Erker-Verlag, 1969. Translated by Seibert, Charles, as "Art and Space" in *Man and World,* no. 6 (1973).

*Zeichen.* First published in the newspaper *Neue Zürcher Zeitung,* 21 September 1969.

*Gedachtes.* First published in French and English in *L'Herne—René Char,* Fourcade, Dominique (ed.), Paris, Éditions de l'Herne, 1971. Translated by Hoeller, Keith, as "Gedachtes" (bilingual edition) in *Philosophy Today,* vol. 20 (1976).

*Das Wohnen des Menschen.* First (privately) published as a contribution to a *Festschrift* for Gustav Hillard Steinbömer on the occasion of his 90th birthday in *Hesperus,* Hamburg, Hans Christians, 1971.

*Rimbaud.* Written in 1972 and first published as a contribution in *Archives des lettres Modernes,* vol. 160 as "Aujourd'hui, Rimbaud . . .," with a French translation, Paris, 1976.

*Sprache.* Written in 1972 and first published with a French translation by Roger Munier in *Argile,* Paris 1973. Translated by Sheehan, Thomas J., S.J., as "Language" in *Philosophy Today,* vol. 20 (1976).

*Der Fehl heiliger Namen.* Written in 1974 as a gift to the Freiburg novelist Hugo Friedrich. First published with a French translation by Roger Munier and Philippe Lacoue-Labarthe as "Le défaut de noms sacrés" in *Contre toute attente* vol. 2/3, spring/summer 1981.

*Fridolin Wiplingers letzter Besuch.* Written in 1974 and delivered on Vienna Radio. Published as a tribute in the posthumous edition of *Metaphysik* by Wiplinger, Fridolin, Kampits, Peter (ed.), Freiburg, Munich, and Vienna 1976.

*Erhart Kästner zum Gedächtnis.* First published as an introduction to *Erhart Kästner—Leben und Werk in Daten und Bildern,* Frankfurt, Insel-Taschenbuch no. 386, 1975.

*Grußwort von Martin Heidegger.* Letter written the day before Heidegger's death to Bernhard Welte and first published in *Ehrenbürgerfeier Professor Dr. Bernhard Welte,* Stadt Meßkirch, p. 17, 1978.

†Gesamtausgabe 14, *Zur Sache des Denkens,* Tübingen Max Niemeyer Verlag, 1969. Translated by Stambaugh, Joan (ed.), as *On Time and Being,* San Francisco, Harper Torchbooks, 1972.

*Zeit und Sein.* Freiburg seminar 1962. Translated as "Time and Being" in *On Time and Being* First published in *L'endurance de la pensée,* Paris, 1968.

*Protokoll zu einem Seminar über den Vortrag 'Zeit und Sein'/Stichwortartiges Inhaltsverzeichnis.* Translated as "Summary of a Seminar on the Lecture 'Time and Being'" in *On Time and Being.*

*Das Ende der Philosophie und die Aufgabe des Denkens.* Translated as "The End of Philosophy and the Task of Thinking" in *On Time and Being.* First published in French in *Hermann Niemeyer zum 80. Geburtstag,* Paris, 1963.

Gesamtausgabe 15, *Seminare,* Ochwadt, Curd (ed.), Frankfurt, Klostermann, 1986.

*Martin Heidegger—Eugen Fink: Heraklit.* Seminar, winter semester 1966/67. First published as *Martin Heidegger—Eugen Fink: Heraklit,* Frankfurt, Klostermann, 1970. Translated by Seibert, Charles, as *Heraclitus Seminar,* Tuscaloosa, University of Alabama Press, 1979.

*Vier Seminare.* Seminars at Le Thor; 1966, 1968, 1969; and Zähringen 1973. First published as *Vier Seminare,* Frankfurt, Klostermann, 1977.

*Zürcher Seminar.* From a seminar in Zurich in 1951. First published as *Vortragsausschuß der Studentschaft der Universität Zürich,* Zurich, 1952.

Gesamtausgabe 16, *Reden und andere Zeugnisse eines Lebensweges,* Heidegger, Hermann (ed.), Frankfurt, Klostermann, 2000.

1. *Per mortem ad vitam (Gedanken über* Jörgensens *'Lebenslüge und Lebenswahrheit')* (March 1910).

5. *Zur philosophischen Orientierung für Akademiker* (March 1911).

6. Zimmerman, O. S. J., *Das Gottesbedürfnis* (May 1911).

9. *Religionspsychologie und Unterbewußtsein* (March 1912).

10. Gredt, Jos, O. S. B., *Elementa Philosophic Aristotelico-Thomistcae* (March 1912).

15. *Lebenslauf (Zur Habilitation* 1915).

17. *Vita* (1922).

253. *Spiegel-Gespräch mit Martin Heidegger* (September 1966). A corrected and expanded version of the article originally published in *Der Spiegel,* 31 May 1976. The *Spiegel* published text is translated as "The Spiegel Interview" in *Martin Heidegger and National Socialism—Questions and Answers.*

Gesamtausgabe 19, *Platon: Sophistes,* Schüßler, Ingeborg (ed.), Frankfurt, Klostermann, 1992. Marburg lecture course, winter semester 1924/25. Translated by Rojcewicz, Richard, and Schuwer, André, as *Plato's Sophist,* Bloomington, Indiana University Press, 1997.

Gesamtausgabe 20, *Prolegomena zur Geschichte des Zeitbegriffs*, Jaeger, Petra (ed.), Frankfurt, Klostermann, 1979. Marburg lecture course, summer semester 1925. Translated by Kisiel, Theodore, as *History of the Concept of Time, Prolegomena*, Bloomington, Indiana University Press, 1985.

Gesamtausgabe 21, *Logik: Die Frage nach der Wahrheit*, Biemel, Walter (ed.), Frankfurt, Klostermann, 1976. Marburg lecture course, winter semester 1925/26.

Gesamtausgabe 24, *Die Grundprobleme der Phänomenologie*, von Herrmann, Friedrich-Wilhelm (ed.), Frankfurt, Klostermann, 1989. Marburg, summer semester 1927. Translated by Hofstadter, Albert, as *The Basic Problems of Phenomenology*, Bloomington, Indiana University Press, 1982 (revised 1988).

Gesamtausgabe 25, *Phänomenologische Interpretation von Kants Kritik der reinen Vernunft*, Görland, Ingtraud (ed.), Frankfurt, Klostermann, 1977. Marburg lecture course, winter semester 1927/28. Translated by Emad, Parvis, and Maly, Kenneth, as *Phenomenological Interpretation of Kant's Critique of Pure Reason*, Bloomington, Indiana University Press, 1997.

Gesamtausgabe 26, *Metaphysische Anfangsgründe der Logik im Ausgang von Leibniz*, Klaus Held (ed.), Frankfurt, Klostermann, 1978. Marburg lecture course, summer semester 1928. Translated by Heim, Michael, as *The Metaphysical Foundations of Logic*, Bloomington, Indiana University Press, 1984.

Gesamtausgabe 27, *Einleitung in die Philosophie*, Saame, Otto, and Saame-Speidel, Ina (eds.), Frankfurt, Klostermann, 1996. Freiburg lecture course, winter semester 1928/29.

Gesamtausgabe 28, *Der Deutsche Idealismus (Fichte, Hegel, Schelling) und die philosophische Problemlage der Gegenwart*, Strube, Claudius (ed.), Frankfurt, Klostermann, 1997. Freiburg lecture course, summer semester 1929.

Gesamtausgabe 29/30, *Die Grundbegriffe der Metaphysik: Welt, Endlichkeit, Einsamkeit*, von Herrmann, Friedrich-Wilhelm (ed.), Frankfurt, Klostermann, 1992. Freiburg lecture course, winter semester 1929/30. Translated by McNeill, William, and Walker, Nicholas, as *The Fundamental Concepts of Metaphysics — World, Finitude, Solitude*, Bloomington, Indiana University Press, 1995.

Gesamtausgabe 31, *Vom Wesen der Menschlichen Freiheit*, Tietjen, Harmut (ed.), Frankfurt, Klostermann, 1994 (1982). Freiburg lecture course, summer semester 1930.

Gesamtausgabe 32, *Hegels Phänomenologie des Geistes*, Görland, Ingtraud (ed.), Frankfurt, Klostermann, 1980. Freiburg lecture course, winter semester 1930/31. Translated by Emad, Parvis and Maly, Kenneth, as *Hegel's Phenomenology of Spirit*, Bloomington, Indiana University Press, 1988.

Gesamtausgabe 33, *Aristoteles: Metaphysik Θ 1–3—Vom Wesen und Wirklichkeit der Kraft*, Hüni, Heinrich (ed.), Frankfurt, Klostermann, 1981. Freiburg lecture course, summer semester 1931. Translated by Brogan, Walter and Warnek, Peter, as *Aristotle's Metaphysics Θ 1–3 On the Essence and Actuality of Force*, Bloomington, Indiana University Press, 1995.

Gesamtausgabe 34, *Vom Wesen der Wahrheit. Zu Platons Höhlengleichnis und Theätet*, Mörchen, Hermann (ed.), Frankfurt, Klostermann, 1988. Freiburg lecture course, winter semester 1931/32.

Gesamtausgabe 39, *Hölderlins Hymnen 'Germanien' und 'Der Rhein'*, Ziegler, Susanne (ed.), Frankfurt, Klostermann, 1980. Freiburg lecture course, winter semester 1934/35.

†Gesamtausgabe 40, *Einführung in die Metaphysik*, [Jaeger, Petra (ed.), Frankfurt, Klostermann, 1983]. Freiburg lecture course, summer semester 1935. First published as *Einführung in die Metaphysik*, Tübingen, Niemeyer, 1953. Translated by Manheim, Ralph, as *An Introduction to Metaphysics*, New Haven, Yale University Press, 1959; and by Fried, Gregory, and Polt, Richard, as *Introduction to Metaphysics*, New Haven, Yale University Press, 2000.

†Gesamtausgabe 41, *Die Frage nach dem Ding: Zu Kants Lehre von den transzendentalen Grundsätzen*, [Jaeger, Petra (ed.), Frankfurt, Klostermann, 1984]. Freiburg lecture course, winter semester 1935/36. First published as *Die Frage nach dem Ding*, Tübingen, Niemeyer, 1962. Translated by Barton, W. B., and Deutsch, Vera, as *What Is a Thing*, Illinois, Regnery, 1967.

Gesamtausgabe 42, *Schelling: Vom Wesen der menschlichen Freiheit (1809)*, Schüßl, Ingrid (ed.), Frankfurt, Klostermann, 1988. Freiburg lecture course, summer semester 1936. First published as *Schellings Abhandlung über das Wesen der Menschlichen Freiheit (1809)*, Tübingen, Niemeyer, 1971. Translated by Stambaugh, Joan, as *Schelling's Treatise on the Essence of Human Freedom*, Athens, Ohio University Press, 1985.

Gesamtausgabe 45, *Grundfragen der Philosophie: Ausgewählte 'Probleme' der 'Logik'*, von Herrmann, Friedrich-Wilhelm (ed.), Frankfurt, Klostermann, 1984. Freiburg lecture course, winter semester 1937/38. Translated by Rojcewicz, Richard, and Schuwer, André, ?? *Basic Questions of Philosophy—Selected 'Problems' of 'Logic'*, Bloomington, Indiana University Press, 1994.

Gesamtausgabe 49, *Die Metaphysik des deutschen Idealismus*, Seubold, Günter (ed.), Frankfurt, Klostermann, 1991. Freiburg lecture course, first trimester, 1941; Freiburg seminar, summer semester 1941.

Gesamtausgabe 50, *1. Nietzsches Metaphysik. 2. Einleitung in die Philosophie—Denken und Dichten*, Jaeger, Petra (ed.), Frankfurt, Klostermann, 1990. Freiburg lecture course, winter semester 1941/42; and interrupted Freiburg lectures, winter semester 1944/45.

Gesamtausgabe 51, *Grundbegriffe*, Jaeger, Petra (ed.), Frankfurt, Klostermann, 1981. Freiburg lecture course, summer semester 1941. Translated by Aylesworth, Gary E., as *Basic Concepts*, Bloomington, Indiana University Press, 1993.

Gesamtausgabe 52, *Hölderlins Hymne 'Andenken'*, Ochwadt, Curd (ed.), Frankfurt, Klostermann, 1982. Freiburg lecture course, winter semester 1941/42.

Gesamtausgabe 53, *Hölderlins Hymne 'Der Ister'*, Biemel, Walter (ed.), Frankfurt, Klostermann, 1984. Freiburg lecture course, summer semester 1942. Translated by McNeill, William, and Davis, Julia, as *Hölderlin's Hymn 'The Ister'*, Bloomington, Indiana University Press, 1996.

Gesamtausgabe 54, *Parmenides*, Frings, Manfred S. (ed.), Frankfurt, Klostermann, 1982. Freiburg lecture course, winter semester 1942. Translated by Schuwer, André, and Rojcewicz, Richard, as *Parmenides*, Bloomington, Indiana University Press, 1992.

Gesamtausgabe 55, *Heraklit. Der Anfang des abendländischen Denkens; Logik: Heraklits Lehre vom Logos*, Frings, Manfred S. (ed.), Frankfurt, Klostermann, 1979. Freiburg lecture courses; summer semester 1943, and summer semester 1944.

Gesamtausgabe 56/57, *Zur Bestimmung der Philosophie*, Heimbüchel, Bernd (ed.), Frankfurt, Klostermann, 1987. Freiburg lectures: *Kriegsnotsemester* (war emergency semester) 1919 and summer semester 1919. Translated by Sadler, Ted, as *Toward the Definition of Philosophy*, London, Athlone, 2000.

Gesamtausgabe 58, *Grundprobleme der Phänomenologie (1919/20)*, Gander, Hans-Helmuth (ed.), Frankfurt, Klostermann, 1993. Freiburg lecture course, winter semester 1919/20.

Gesamtausgabe 59, *Phänomenologie der Anschauung und des Ausdrucks. Theorie der philosophischen Begriffsbildung*, Strube, Claudius (ed.) Frankfurt, Klostermann, 1993.

Gesamtausgabe 60, *Phänomenologie des religiösen Lebens*, Jung, Matthias, Regehly, Thomas, and Strube, Claudius (eds.), Thomas, Frankfurt, Klostermann, 1995. Freiburg lecture course, winter semester 1920/21.

Gesamtausgabe 61, *Phänomenologische Interpretationen zu Aristoteles: Einführung in die phänomenologische Forschung*, Bröcker, Walter, and Bröcker-Oltmans, Käte (eds.), Frankfurt, Klostermann, 1985. Freiburg lecture course, winter semester 1921/22.

Gesamtausgabe 63, *Ontologie (Hermeneutik der Faktizität)*, Bröcker-Oltmans, Käte (ed.), Frankfurt, Klostermann, 1985. Freiburg lecture course, summer semester 1923. Translated by van Buren, John, as *Ontology—The Hermeneutics of Facticity*, Bloomington, Indiana University Press, 1999.

†Gesamtausgabe 64, *Der Begriff der Zeit*, Tübingen, Niemeyer, 1989. A lecture delivered to the Marburg Theology Society, 1924. Translated by McNeill, William, as *The Concept of Time* in a bilingual edition, Oxford, Blackwell, 1992.

Gesamtausgabe 65, *Beiträge zur Philosophie (Vom Ereignis)*, von Herrmann, Friedrich- Wilhelm (ed.), Frankfurt, Klostermann, 1989. Original (and incomplete) text worked out between 1936 and 1938. Translated by Emad, Parvis, and Maly, Kenneth, as *Contributions to Philosophy (from Enowning)*, Bloomington, Indiana University Press, 1999.

Gesamtausgabe 66, *Besinnung*, Herrmann, Friedrich-Wilhelm (ed.), Frankfurt, Klostermann, 1997.

Gesamtausgabe 67, *Metaphysik und Nihilismus: 1. Die Überwindung der Metaphysik (1938/39); 2. Das Wesen der Nihilismus (1946–48)*, Friedrich, Hans-Joachim (ed.), Frankfurt, Klostermann, 1999.

Gesamtausgabe 69, *Die Geschichte des Seyns*, Trawny, Peter (ed.), Frankfurt, Klostermann, 1997.

Gesamtausgabe 77, *Feldweg-Gespräche*, Schüßler, Ingrid (ed.), Frankfurt, Klostermann 1995. Imaginary conversations, 1944/45.

Gesamtausgabe 79, *Bremer und Freiburger Vorträge: 1. Einblick in das was ist; 2. Grundsätze des Denkens*, Jaeger, Petra (ed.), Frankfurt, Klostermann, 1994.

The lectures given under the title *Einblick in das was ist* were first given at the Bremen Club in 1949 and 1950. The lectures were entitled *Das Ge-stell, Die Kehre, Das Ding*, and *Die Gefahr. Das Ge-stell* was later republished in substantially altered form as *Die Frage nach der Technik* first in *Die Technik und die Kehre* (Pfullingen, Neske, 1962), and subsequently in *Vorträge und Aufsätze* (see Gesamtausgabe 7 above). *Die Kehre* was published in *Die Technik und die Kehre* in virtually unaltered form and translated by William Lovitt in *The Question Concerning Technology* (see Gesamtausgabe 7 above). *Das Ding* was also published in *Vorträge und Aufsätze* combined with the introduction to the *Einblick* series but otherwise largely unaltered. *Die Gefahr* was not published in any earlier form.

## Other Works by Martin Heidegger

In a number of cases works listed here are also in preparation to be published in the *Gesamtausgabe* at a later date.

*Briefwechsel 1926–1963*, Biemel, Walter, and Saner, Hans (eds.), Munich, Piper, 1985 (between Heidegger and Karl Jaspers).
Letter to Pastor W. D. Zimmermann, dated 30 June 1968, in response to a request to contribute to an edited volume. In private hands.

*Martin Heidegger im Gespräch*, ed. Wisser, Richard, Munich, Alber, 1970. First broadcast on German television. Translated as "Martin Heidegger in Conversation with Richard Wisser" in *Martin Heidegger and National Socialism—Questions and Answers.*

*Phänomenologische Interpretationen zu Aristoteles (Anzeige der hermeneutischen Situation)*, Lessing, Hans-Ulrich (ed.) in *Dilthey-Jahrbuch für Philosophie und Geschichte der Geisteswissenschaften*, vol. 6, Göttingen, Vandenhoeck und Ruprecht, 1989. Translated by Baur, Michael, as "Phenomenological Interpretations with Respect to Aristotle: Indication of the Hermeneutical Situation" in *Man and World*, no. 25 (1992).

*Das Realitätsproblem in der modernen Philosophie* in the *Philosophisches Jahrbuch der Görresgesellschaft*, vol. 25 (1912). Translated by Bossert, Philip, J., as "The Problem of Reality in Modern Philosophy" in the *Journal of the British Society for Phenomenology*, vol. 4 (1973).

*Die Selbstbehauptung der deutschen Universität. Das Rektorat 1933/34, Tatsachen und Gedanken.* Rectorial inaugural lecture, 1933, and handwritten manuscript 1945. Frankfurt, Klostermann, 1983. Translated by Harries, Karsten, in collaboration with Heidegger, Hermann, as "Preface to the Rectorial Address (Hermann Heidegger), The Self-Assertion of the German University," and "The Rectorate 1933/34: Facts and Thoughts" in *Review of Metaphysics*, vol. 38 (1985). Reprinted in Neske, Günther, and Kettering, Emil (eds.), *Martin Heidegger and National Socialism—Questions and Answers*, New York, Paragon, 1990.

*Über den Humanismus (Sonderausgabe)*, Frankfurt, Klostermann, 1949. For translations, see Gesamtausgabe 9, *Wegmarken.*

*Was ist das—die Philosophie?* Pfullingen, Neske, 1956. Translated by Kluback, W., as *What Is Philosophy?*, bilingual English/German edition, Plymouth, England, Vision, 1989.

## WORKS BY OTHER AUTHORS

Angelus Silesius, *Cherubinischer Wandersmann (Kritische Ausgabe)*, Stuttgart, Reclam, 1985. Translated by Shrady, M., in an abridged edition as *The Cherubinic Wanderer* in *The Classics of Western Spirituality*, New York, Paulist Press, 1986.

Aquinas, St. Thomas, *De Ente et Essentia*, Rome, Marietti, 1957. Translated by Maurer, Armand, as *On Being and Essence*, Toronto, Pontifical Institute of Medieval Studies, 1949.

———, *Quaestiones Disputatae: de Veritate* (2 vols.), Rome, Marietti, 1965.

———, *Sancti Thomae Super Librum de Causis Expositio*, Fribourg, Société Philosophique, 1954. Translated by Guagliardo, Vincent A, Hess, Charles R., Taylor, Richard C., as *Commentary on the Book of Causes*, Washington, D. C., Catholic University of America Press, 1996.

————, *Summa Contra Gentiles*, Paris, Marietti, 1967. Translated by Pegis, C., as *Summa Contra Gentiles* (5 vols.), Notre Dame, University of Notre Dame Press, 1975.

————, *Summa Theologiae*, Rome, Marietti, 1962. Translated by Shapcote, L. OP, as *Summa Theologica*, Oxford, Blackfriars, 1924.

Arendt, Hannah, "Martin Heidegger ist achtzig Jahre alt" in *Merkur*, vol. 10 (1969). Translated by Hofstadter, Albert, as "Martin Heidegger at Eighty," in Neske, Günther, and Kettering, Emil (eds.), *Martin Heidegger and National Socialism* (see above and below).

Aristotle, *Metaphysics* (2 vols.), translated by Tredennick, Hugh, Cambridge, Harvard University Press (Loeb), 1933.

————, *Nicomachean Ethics*, translated by Rackham, H., Cambridge, Harvard University Press (Loeb), 1934.

————, *On the Soul*, translated by Hett, W.S., Cambridge, Harvard University Press (Loeb), 1936.

————, *Physics* (2 vols.), translated by Wicksteed, P.H., and Cornford, F., Cambridge, Harvard University Press (Loeb), 1934.

Bailiff, J., "Truth and Power: Martin Heidegger" in *Man and World*, no. 20 (1987).

von Balthasar, Cardinal Hans Urs, *Herrlichkeit: Eine theologische Ästhetik*, vol. 3.1, *Im Raum der Metaphysik;* vol. 3.2, *Neuzeit*, Einsiedeln, Johannes Verlag, 1965. Translated by Davies, O., Louth, A., McNeil, B., C.R.V., and Riches, J., as *The Glory of the Lord*, vol. 5, *The Realm of Metaphysics in the Modern Age*, Edinburgh, T & T Clark, 1991.

————, *Karl Barth: Darstellung und Deutung seiner Theologie*, Cologne, Hegner, 1951. Translated by Oakes, E., S.J., as *The Theology of Karl Barth*, San Francisco, Ignatius Press, 1991.

Bambach, C.R., *Heidegger, Dilthey, and the Crisis of Historicism*, London, Cornell University Press, 1995.

Baur, Michael, "Heidegger and Aquinas on the Self as Substance," *American Catholic Philosophical Quarterly*, vol. 52 (1996).

Beaufret, J., "En chemin avec Heidegger" in Haar, M. (ed.), *Cahier de l'Herne: Heidegger*, Paris, Éditions de l'Herne, 1983.

Bernasconi, Robert, "The Greatness of the Work of Art" in Risser, James (ed.), *Heidegger toward the Turn*, Albany, SUNY Press, 1999.

————, *Heidegger in Question: The Art of Existing*, Atlantic Highlands, N.J., Humanities Press, 1993.

————, *The Question of Language in Heidegger's History of Being*, London, Macmillan, 1984.

Biemel, Walter, *Heidegger and Metaphysics* in Sheehan, Thomas J., S.J. (ed.), *Heidegger: The Man and the Thinker*, Chicago, Precedent, 1981.

————, "Heideggers Deutung des Heiligen bei Hölderlin" in *Theologische Forschung*, vol. 58 (1976).

Bockmühl, K., *The Unreal God of Modern Theology : Bultmann, Barth, and the Theology of Atheism: A Call to Recovering the Truth of God's Reality*, Colorado Springs, Colo., Helmers & Howard, 1988.

Bonsor, Jack Arthur, *Rahner, Heidegger, and Truth: Karl Rahner's Notion of Christian Truth, The Influence of Heidegger*, Lanham, Md., University Press of America, 1987.

Booth, Edward, O. P., *Aristotelian Aporetic Ontology in Islamic and Christian Thinkers*, Cambridge, Cambridge University Press, 1983.

Bouckärt, L., "Ontology and Ethics: Reflections on Lévinas' Critique of Heidegger" in *International Philosophical Quarterly*, vol. 10 (1970).

Buckley, Michael J., S. J., *At the Origins of Modern Atheism*, New Haven, Yale University Press, 1987.

Bultmann, R. K., "Replies" in Kegley, C. W. (ed.), *The Theology of Rudolf Bultmann*, New York, Harper & Row, 1966.

van Buren, John, "The Ethics of Formale Anzeige in Heidegger" in *American Catholic Philosophical Quarterly*, vol. 69 (1995).

——, *The Young Heidegger: Rumor of the Hidden King*, Bloomington, Indiana University Press, 1994.

Cajetan, Cardinal de Vio, *de Nominum Analogia*, P. N. Dammit (ed.), Rome, 1934 (Cf. Hering, P. H., Rome 1952) (1506, 1511). Translated by Bushinski, E. A., and Koren, H. J., as *The Analogy of Names and the Concept of Being*, Pittsburgh, Duquesne University Press, 1953.

Caputo, John, *Demythologizing Heidegger*, Bloomington, Indiana University Press, 1993.

——, "Fundamental Themes in Meister Eckhart's Mysticism" in *The Thomist*, vol. 42 (1978).

——, *Heidegger and Aquinas*, New York, Fordham University Press, 1982.

——, "Heidegger and Theology," in Guignon C. (ed.), *The Cambridge Companion to Heidegger*, Cambridge, Cambridge University Press, 1993.

——, "Heidegger's Dif-ference and the Distinction between Esse and Ens in St Thomas" in *International Philosophical Quarterly*, vol. 20 (1980).

——, *The Mystical Element in Heidegger's Thought*, Athens, Ohio University Press, 1978.

——, "The Nothingness of the Intellect in Meister Eckhart's Parisian Questions" in *The Thomist*, vol. 39 (1975).

——, "Phenomenology, Mysticism and the *Grammatica Speculativa:* A Study of Heidegger's Habilitationsschrift" in the *Journal of the British Society for Phenomenology*, vol. 5 (1974).

——, "The Poverty of Thought: A Reflection on Heidegger and Eckhart" in *Heidegger: The Man and the Thinker*, Sheehan, Thomas J., S. J. (ed.), Chicago, Precedent, 1981.

——, "The Problem of Being in Heidegger and the Scholastics" in *The Thomist*, vol. 41 (1977).

Casper, Bernhard, "Martin Heidegger und die Theologische Fakultät Freiburg 1909–1923" in *Kirche am Oberrhein: Festschrift für Wolfgang Müller*, Bäumer, R., Suso Frank, K., and Ott, H. (eds.), *Freiburger Diözesan Archiv*, no. 100 (1980).

Catherine of Siena, *Dialogo della serafica Vergine et Sposa di Christo S. Catherina da Siena*, Venice, Giacomo Conciti, 1589. Modern edition *Santa Caterina di Siena: Dialogo della divina provvidenza*, Taurisano, P. Innocenzo (ed.), Rome, Ferrari, 1947. Translated by Noffke, Suzanne OP, as *St. Catherine of Siena: The Dialogue* in *The Classics of Western Spirituality*, London, Paulist Press, 1980.

Clarke, Samuel (Vailati, E. [ed.]), *A Demonstration of the Being and Attributes of God and Other Writings*, Cambridge, Cambridge University Press, 1998. First published in 1704.

Connell, George, "Against Idolatry: Heidegger and Natural Theology" in Westphal, Merold (ed.), *Postmodern Philosophy and Christian Thought*, Bloomington, Indiana University Press, 1999.

Corngold, Stanley, *The Fate of the Self: German Writers, and French Theory*, New York, Columbia University Press, 1986.

Courtine, Jean-François, *Suárez et le système de la métaphysique*, Paris, Presses Universitaires de France, 1990.

Coxon, A. H., *The Fragments of Parmenides*, Maastricht, Van Gorcum, 1986. Although Coxon has his own schema for the ordering of the fragments, I have retained the Diels-Kranz schema which Heidegger used.

Crownfield, David, "The Question of God: Thinking after Heidegger" in *Philosophy Today*, vol. 40 (1996).

Deely, J, "The Situation of Heidegger in the Tradition of Christian Philosophy" in *The Thomist*, vol. 31 (1967).

Deleuze, Gilles, *Nietzsche et la philosophie*, Paris, Presses Universitaires de France, 1962. Translated by Tomlinson, H., as *Nietzsche and Philosophy*, London, Athlone, 1983.

Derrida, Jacques, "Comment ne pas parler: Dénégations" in *Psyché: Inventions de l'autre*, Paris, Galilée, 1987. Translated by Coward, H., and Foshay, T. (eds.), as "How to Avoid Speaking—Denials" in *Derrida and Negative Theology*, Albany, SUNY, 1992.

———, *De l'esprit: Heidegger et la question*, Paris, Galilée, 1987. Translated by Bennington, G., and Bowlby, R., as *Of Spirit*, Chicago, University of Chicago Press, 1989.

———, "Of an Apocalyptic Tone Newly Adopted in Philosophy" in *Derrida and Negative Theology*, Coward, H., and Foshay, T. (eds.), Albany, SUNY, 1992. Original (French) text in the proceedings of a conference in Cerisy-la-Salle entitled *'Les fins de l'homme.' A partir du travail de Jacques Derrida* and published as *Les fins de l'homme*, Paris, Galilée, 1981.

Descartes, René, *Œuvres publiées*, eds. Adam, Charles, and Tannery, Paul, vols. 1–12, Paris, Vrin, 1996 (1965).

————, *Meditationes de prima philosophia* in *Œuvres de Descartes,* vol. 7.

Des Chene, Dennis, *Physiologia: Natural Philosophy in Late Aristotelian and Cartesian Thought,* Ithaca, Cornell University Press, 1996.

Dinkler, E. (ed.), "Martin Heidegger und die Marburger Theologie" in *Zeit und Geschichte—Dankesgabe an Rudolf Bultmann zum 80. Geburtstag,* Tübingen, Mohr, 1964.

Dreyfus, Hubert, L., "Mixing Interpretation, Religion, and Politics: Heidegger's High Risk Thinking," Center for Hermeneutical Studies, Colloquy 61, Berkeley, University of California Press, 1992.

Eckhart, *Werke* (Largier, N. [ed.]), 2 vols., Frankfurt, Deutscher Klassiker Verlag, 1993.

————*The Book of Benedictus, Counsels on Discernment* and *On Detachment* are translated by Colledge, Edmund, and McGinn, Bernard (eds.), in *Meister Eckhart: The Essential Sermons, Commentaries, Treatises, and Defense,* New York, Paulist Press, 1981.

————Latin sermons 4, 6, 25, 29, 45, 49, the *Commentary on the Book of Exodus* and selections from the *Commentary on the Book of Wisdom, Lectures on Ecclesiasticus* and the *Commentary on the Gospel of St. John* translated by McGinn, Bernard (ed.), in *Meister Eckhart, Teacher and Preacher,* New York, Paulist Press, 1986.

————Latin sermons 24, 29, 40, 47, translated by Davies, Oliver (ed.), in *Meister Eckhart, Selected Writings,* Harmondsworth, Penguin, 1994.

————*Quaestiones Parisiensis* and *Prologi* translated by Maurer, A., in *Master Eckhart: Parisian Questions and Prologues,* Toronto, Pontifical Institute of Mediaeval Studies, 1974.

————The complete German works are translated by Walshe, M. O'C., in *Meister Eckhart: Sermons & Treatises* (3 vols.), Shaftesbury, Element, 1987.

Farías, Victor, *Heidegger et la nazisme,* Paris, Éditions Vernier, translated by Benaroch, M., and Gras, J.-B. (eds.), as *Heidegger und der Nationalsozialismus,* Frankfurt, Fischer, 1989. The German edition is an expanded and corrected version of a French and Spanish original and is therefore the more authoritative of any of the editions with which Farías has been directly concerned. The English edition translated by Margolis, J., and Rockmore, T. (eds.), *Heidegger and Nazism,* Philadelphia, Temple University Press, 1989, with a foreword, appears to be a version of the less accurate original.

————, "Reply to Jacques Derrida" in *El Pais,* 19 November 1987.

Fehér, István, "Heidegger's Postwar Turn: The Emergence of the Hermeneutic Viewpoint of His Philosophy and the Idea of 'Destruktion' on the Way to *Being and Time*" in *Philosophy Today,* vol. 40 (1996).

————, "Heidegger's Understanding of the Atheism of Philosophy" in *American Catholic Philosophical Quarterly,* vol. 49 (1995). See also the expanded version published under a similar title: "Heidegger's Understanding of the Atheism of Philosophy: Philosophy, Theology, and Religion on his Way to *Being and Time*" in *Existentia:* ΜΕΛΕΤΑΙ ΣΟΦΙΑΣ, Szeged, Budapest, vols. 6–7, fasc. 1–4 (1996–97).

Gadamer, Hans-Georg, *Heidegger und die hermeneutische Philosophie*, Freiburg, Alber, 1983.

———, *Heidegger's Wege*, Tübingen, Mohr, 1983. Translated by Stanley, J. W., as *Heidegger's Ways*, Albany, SUNY, 1994.

———, "Wilhelm Dilthey nach 150 Jahren (Zwischen Romantik und Positivismus): Ein Diskussionsbeitrag" in Orth, E. W. (ed.), *Dilthey und die Philosophie der Gegenwart*, Freiburg, Alber, 1985.

Gall, Robert, *Beyond Theism and Atheism: Heidegger's Significance for Religious Thinking*, Dordrecht, Nijhoff, 1987.

———, "The Divine in Heidegger and Tragedy" (misprinted as "Beyond Tragedy"), *Philosophy Today*, vol. 29 (1985).

———, "Toward a Tragic Theology," *Journal of Literature and Theology*, no. 7 (1993).

de Gandillac, M. and de Towarnicki, A., "Deux documents sur Heidegger" in *Les Temps Modernes*, vol. 1 (1946).

Gillespie, Michael A., *Nihilism before Nietzsche*, Chicago, University of Chicago Press, 1995.

Godzieba, Anthony, "Prolegomena to a Catholic Theology of God between Heidegger and Postmodernity" in *Heythrop Journal*, vol. 40 (1999).

Grondin, Jean, *Le tournant dans la pensée de Martin Heidegger*, Paris, Presses Universitaires de France, 1987.

Haar, M. "Critical Remarks on Heidegger's Reading of Nietzsche" in Macann, C. (ed.), *Critical Heidegger*, London, Routledge, 1996 [1995].

Habermas, Jürgen, "Mit Heidegger gegen Heidegger denken: Zur Veröffentlichung von Vorlesungen aus dem Jahre 1935" in *Frankfurter Allgemeine Zeitung* 25 July 1953. Reprinted in *Habermas: Philosophisch-politische Profile* (enlarged edition), Frankfurt, Suhrkamp, 1981.

Hart, Kevin [Derrida, Jacques], "Introduction to and Excerpt from How to Avoid Speaking" (see also Derrida, Jacques, "Comment ne pas parler—Dénégations" above) in Ward, Graham (ed.), *The Postmodern God—A Theological Reader*, Oxford, Blackwell, 1997.

Hegel, G. W. F. (Jaeschke, Walter [ed.]), *Vorlesungen über die Philosophie der Religion*, 1–3, Hamburg, Felix Meiner Verlag, 1993–95. Translated by Hodgson, Peter G. (ed.), as *Lectures on the Philosophy of Religion*, vols. 1–3, Berkeley, University of California Press, 1985–88.

von Herrmann, Friedrich-Wilhelm, *Subjekt und Dasein: Interpretationen zu 'Sein und Zeit'*, Frankfurt, Klostermann, 1985.

Hiley, David R; Bohman, James; Shusterman, Richard, *The Interpretive Turn: Philosophy, Science, Culture*, Ithaca, Cornell University Press, 1992.

Hurd, Robert L., "Heidegger and Aquinas: A Rahnerian Bridge" in *Philosophy Today*, vol. 28 (1984).

Husserl, E. (Strasser, S. [ed.], *Husserliana: Edmund Husserl Gesammelte Werke*, Nijhoff, The Hague, 1963–
— *Cartesianische Meditationen und Pariser Vorträge*, vol. 1 (1963). Translated by Cairns, D., as *Cartesian Meditations: An Introduction to Phenomenology*, Nijhoff, The Hague, 1960.
Ihde, Don (ed.), "Deromanticizing Heidegger" in *Postphenomenology: Essays in the Postmodern Context*, Evanston, Northwestern University Press, 1993.
Imhof, Paul, and Biallowons, Hubert (eds.), *Karl Rahner im Gespräch*, 2 vols., Munich, Kösel, 1983. Translated by Egan, Harvey D., as *Karl Rahner in Dialogue*, New York, Crossroad, 1986.
Janowski, Zbigniew, *Cartesian Theodicy: Descartes' Quest for Certitude*, Kluwer Academic Publishers, Dordrecht, 2000.
Jaspers, Karl, *Philosophische Autobiographie*, Munich, Piper, 1977.
Pope John XXII, Bull *In Agro Dominico* translated by Colledge, Edmund, and McGinn, Bernard (eds.) in *Meister Eckhart: The Essential Sermons, Commentaries, Treatises, and Defense* in *The Classics of Western Spirituality*, New York, Paulist Press, 1981.
Pope John Paul II, *Fides et Ratio*, Vatican, Libreria Editrice Vaticana, 1998. Translated in Hemming, Laurence P., and Parsons, Susan Frank (eds.), *Restoring Faith in Reason*, London, SCM Press, 2002.
Jonas, Hans, "Heidegger and Theology" in *Review of Metaphysics*, vol. 18 (1964).
Jones, J. D., "A Non-Entitative Understanding of Being and Unity: Heidegger and Neoplatonism" in *Dionysius*, vol. 6 (1982).
———, "The Ontological Difference for St. Thomas and Pseudo-Dionysius" in *Dionysius*, vol. 4 (1980).
Jünger, Ernst, *Der Arbeiter—Herrschaft und Gestalt* in *Werke*, vol. 6, Stuttgart, Klett, 1964. First published in Hamburg, Hanseatische Verlagsanstalt, 1932.
———, *Die totale Mobilmachung* in *Werke*, vol. 5, Stuttgart, Klett, 1960. First published in *Krieg und Krieger*, edited by the author, Hamburg, Hanseatische Verlagsanstalt, 1930.
———, *Über die Linie*, in *Werke*, vol. 5, Stuttgart, Klett, 1960. First published in *Martin Heidegger zum 60. Geburtstag*, Frankfurt, Klostermann, 1950.
Kant, Immanuel, *Kritik der reinen Vernunft*, Stuttgart, Reclam, 1966. Translated by Kemp-Smith, Norman, as *Critique of Pure Reason*, Oxford, Clarendon Press, 1929.
——— (Adickes E. [ed. and arr.]), *Opus Postumum*, Berlin, Kantstudien Ergänzung, 1920. Translated by Förster, Eckart, and Rosen, Michael, as *Opus Postumum*, Cambridge, Cambridge University Press, 1993.
Kaufmann, Walter, *Nietzsche—Philosopher, Psychologist, Antichrist*, Princeton, Princeton University Press, 1974.
Kearney, Richard, *Between Kant and Heidegger: The Modern Question of Being*, in O'Rourke, Fran (ed.), *At the Heart of the Real*, Dublin, Irish Academic Press, 1992.

Kearney, Richard, and O'Leary, Joseph. S. (eds.), *Heidegger et la Question de Dieu*, Paris, Grasset, 1980.

Kerr, Fergus, O. P., "Aquinas after Marion" in *New Blackfriars*, vol. 76 (1995).

———, *Immortal Longings*, Notre Dame, University of Notre Dame Press, 1997.

Kisiel, Theodore, *The Genesis of Heidegger's Being and Time*, Berkeley, University of California Press, 1993.

———, "Das Kriegsnotsemester 1919: Heideggers Durchbruch zur hermeneutischen Phänomenologie" in *Philosophisches Jahrbuch*, no. 99 (1992).

Kovacs, G., *The Question of God in Heidegger's Phenomenology*, Evanston, Northwestern University Press, 1990.

Lacoue-Labarthe, Philippe, *La fiction du Politique*, Paris, Christian Bourgois, 1987. Translated by Turner, C., as *Heidegger, Art, and Politics*, Oxford, Blackwell, 1990.

Lafont, Ghislain, *Dieu, le temps, et l'être*, Paris, Cerf, 1986. Translated by Maluf, L., as *God, Time, and Being*, Petersham, Massachusetts, St Bede's, 1992.

Langiulli, Nino, *The Existentialist Tradition*, New York, Doubleday, 1971.

von Leibniz, Gottfried Wilhelm, Robinet, André (ed.), *Principes de la Nature et de la Grâce; Principes de la Philosophie ou Monadologie*, Presses Universitaires de France, Paris, 1954. Translated by Morris, Mary, and Parkinson, G. H. R. (ed.) in *Leibniz: Philosiophical Writings*, London, Everyman, 1995 (1973).

Lehmann, Cardinal Karl, "Christliche Geschichtserfahrung und ontologische Frage beim jungen Heidegger," in Pöggeler, O. (ed.), *Heidegger: Perspektiven zur Deutung seines Werkes*, Athenäum Taschenbücher, Königstein, 1984.

Lotz, Johannes B., *Martin Heidegger und Thomas von Aquin: Mensch, Zeit, Sein*, Freiburg, Herder, 1975.

Löwith, Karl, *Heideggers Kehre* in *Die Neue Rundschau*, Frankfurt, Fischer, 1951.

———, "The Historical Background of European Nihilism," in Levison, Arnold (ed.), *Nature, History and Existentialism*, Evanston, Northwestern University Press, 1966.

———, "Les implications politiques de la philosophie de l'existence chez Heidegger" in *Les Temps Modernes*, vol. 2 (1946). Translated by Wolin, Richard (ed.), as "The Political Implications of Heidegger's Existentialism" in *The Heidegger Controversy*, Cambridge, MIT Press, 1993 (2nd ed.).

———, *Mein Leben in Deutschland vor und nach 1933: Ein Bericht*, Stuttgart, Metzler, 1986. Translated by King, Elizabeth, as *My Life in Germany Before and After 1933—A Report*, London, Athlone, 1994.

———, "Réponse à A. de Waelhens" in *Les Temps Modernes*, vol. 4 (1947/48).

Löwith, Karl, *Sämtliche Schriften*, vols. 1–8, Stuttgart, Metzler, 1981–88.

—*Heidegger—Denker in dürftiger Zeit*, in *Die Neue Rundschau*, vol. 1 (1984). First published in Frankfurt (Fischer Verlag) in 1952. Published as a single volume under the same title in Göttingen (Vandenhoeck und Ruprecht) in 1953. Reworked and republished under the same title in Stuttgart (Metzler) in 1960. Translated by Wolin, Richard (ed.), as "Heidegger:

Thinker in a Destitute Time" in *Martin Heidegger and European Nihilism*, New York, Columbia University Press, 1995. The translation is of the 1960 (Metzler) edition.

—*Von Hegel zu Nietzsche: Der revolutionäre Bruch im Denken d. 19. Jahrhunderts* in *Sämtliche Schriften*, vol. 2 (1988). Translated by Green, R., as *From Hegel to Nietzsche: The Revolution in Nineteenth-Century Thought*, Garden City, N.Y., Doubleday, 1964.

—*Heidegger: Problem and Background of Existentialism*, vol. 8 (1984).

—*Heideggers Vorlesungen über Nietzsche*, vol. 8 (1984).

—*M. Heidegger und F. Rosenzweig. Ein Nachtrag zu Sein und Zeit*, vol. 8 (1984). Translated by Levison, Arnold (ed.), as "M. Heidegger and F. Rosenzweig: A Postscript to *Being and Time*" in *Nature, History, and Existentialism*, Evanston, Northwestern University Press, 1966. First published in English as "M. Heidegger and F. Rosenzweig, or Temporality and Eternity" in *Philosophy and Phenomenological Research*, vol. 3 (1942).

McCool, Gerald A. (ed.), *A Rahner Reader*, London, Darton, Longmann, and Todd, 1975.

Macquarrie, John, *An Existentialist Theology; A Comparison of Heidegger and Bultmann*, New York, Macmillan, 1955.

———, *Heidegger and Christianity*, London, SCM Press, 1994. Originally given as the Hensley-Henson lectures in Faculty of Theology at the University of Oxford, 1993–94.

———, *Martin Heidegger* in the series *Makers of Modern Theology*, London, Lutterworth, 1968.

———, "Philosophy and Theology in Bultmann's Thought" in Kegley, C. W. (ed.), *The Theology of Rudolf Bultmann*, New York, Harper & Row, 1966.

Manning, Robert John Scheffler, "The Cries of Others and Heidegger's Ear: Remarks on the Agriculture Remark" in Milchman, Alan, and Rosenberg, Alan (eds.), *Martin Heidegger and the Holocaust*, Atlantic Highlands, N.J., Humanities Press, 1996.

Manstetten, Reiner, *Esse est Deus: Meister Eckharts christologische Versöhnung von Philosophie und Religion und ihre Ursprünge in der Tradition des Abendlandes*, Freiburg, Alber, 1993.

Marion, Jean-Luc, *La Croisée du visible*, Paris, Presses Universitaires de France, 1996.

———, *Dieu sans l'être: Hors-texte*, Paris, Arthème, 1982. Translated by Carlson, Thomas A., as *God Without Being*, Chicago, University of Chicago Press, 1991.

———, *L'Idole et la distance*, Paris, Grasset & Fasquelle, 1977.

———, "Métaphysique et phénoménologie: Une relève pour la théologie" in *Bulletin de Littérature Ecclésiastique*, Paris, BLE, 1993. Translated by McGeoch, Angus, as "Metaphysics and Phenomenology: A Summary for Theologians" in Ward, Graham (ed.), *The Postmodern God: A Theological Reader*, Oxford, Blackwell, 1997.

———, "Saint Thomas d'Aquin et l'onto-théo-logie" in *Revue Thomiste*, vol. 95 (1995).

————, "The Saturated Phenomenon" in *Philosophy Today,* vol. 40 (1996).

Masson, Robert, "Rahner and Heidegger: Being, Hearing, and God" in *The Thomist,* vol. 37 (1973).

Milbank, John, "Intensities" in *Modern Theology,* vol. 15 (1999).

————, "Only Theology Overcomes Metaphysics" in *New Blackfriars,* vol. 76 (1995).

Minder, R., Faye, J.-P. and Patri, A., "À propos de Heidegger" in *Critique,* no. 237 (1967).

Moss, David, "Jean-Luc Marion" in *New Blackfriars,* vol. 74 (1993).

Newton, Sir Isaac, *Philosophiae Naturalis Principia Mathematica,* Koyré, Alexander, and Cohen, I. Bernard (eds.), Cambridge, Cambridge University Press, 1972. Translated by Cohen, I. Bernard, and Whitman, Anne, as *Isaac Newton: The Principia: Mathematical Principles of Natural Philosophy,* Berkeley, University of California Press, 1999.

Nietzsche, Friedrich (Colli, Giorgio, and Montinari, Mazzino [eds.]), *Friedrich Nietzsche: Kritische Studienausgabe,* Berlin, de Gruyter, 1999 (1968), vols. 1–15.

—*Menschliches Allzumenschliches,* vol. 2. Translated by Hollingdale, R. J., as *Human, All Too Human,* Cambridge, Cambridge University Press, 1986.

—*Die fröhliche Wissenschaft,* vol. 3. Translated by Kaufmann, Walter, as *The Gay Science,* New York, Random House, 1974.

—*Also sprach Zarathustra,* vol. 4. Translated by Kaufmann, Walter (ed.), as *Thus Spoke Zarathustra* in *The Portable Nietzsche,* Harmondsworth, London, Penguin, 1976.

—*Jenseits von Gut und Böse,* vol. 5. Translated by Levy, O., as *Beyond Good and Evil,* Edinburgh, Foulis, 1909.

—*Zur Genealogie der Moral,* vol. 5. Translated by Ansell-Pearson, Keith, as *On the Genealogy of Morality,* Cambridge, Cambridge University Press, 1994.

————, *Der Wille zur Macht,* material ordered by Gast, Peter, and Förster-Nietzsche, Elizabeth, in a reworked edition, Stuttgart, Kröner, 1930. First published Stuttgart, 1921. The edition cited is the 1996 Kröner (13th) edition. Translated by Kaufman, Walter, and Hollingdale, R. J., as *The Will to Power,* New York, Random House, 1967.

Olafson, Frederick A., *Heidegger and the Philosophy of Mind,* New Haven, Yale University Press, 1978.

————, "The Unity of Heidegger's Thought" in Guignon, Charles (ed.), *The Cambridge Companion to Heidegger,* Cambridge, Cambridge University Press, 1993.

O'Rourke, Fran, *Pseudo-Dionysius and the Metaphysics of Aquinas,* Leiden, E. J. Brill, 1992.

O'Rourke, Fran (ed.), "The Gift of Being: Heidegger and Aquinas" in *At the Heart of the Real,* Dublin, Irish Academic Press, 1992.

Ott, Heinrich, *Denken und Sein: Der Weg Martin Heideggers und der Weg der Theologie,* Zurich, EVZ-Verlag, 1959.

———, "Heidegger's Catholic Origins" in *American Catholic Philosophical Quarterly*, vol. 69 (1995).

———, *Martin Heidegger: Unterwegs zu seiner Biographie*, Frankfurt, Campus Verlag, 1988. Translated by Blunden, A., as *Martin Heidegger: A Political Life*, London, Harper Collins, 1993.

Petzet, H. W., "Antwort: Martin Heidegger im Gespräch" in *Martin Heidegger und der Nationalsozialismus*, Halle, Neske, 1988. Translated by Harries, Karsten, as "Afterthoughts on the Spiegel Interview" in Neske, Günther, and Kettering, Emil (eds.), *Martin Heidegger and National Socialism*, New York, Paragon House, 1990.

———, *Auf einen Stern zugehen: Begegnungen und Gespräch mit Martin Heidegger, 1929–1976*, Frankfurt, Frankfurter Societäts-Verlag, 1983. Translated by Emad, Parvis, and Maly, Kenneth, in a slightly reworked edition, as *Encounters and Dialogues with Martin Heidegger 1929–1976*, Chicago, University of Chicago Press, 1993.

Philipse, Herman, *Heidegger's Philosophy of Being: A Critical Interpretation*, Princeton, Princeton University Press, 1998.

Plato, *Gorgias*, translated by Lamb, W. R. M., in *Lysis, Symposium, Gorgias*, Cambridge, Harvard University Press (Loeb), 1925.

———, *Republic* (2 vols.), translated by Shorey, Paul, Cambridge, Harvard University Press (Loeb), 1935.

———, *Theaetetus: Sophist*, translated by North, Fowler Harold, Cambridge, Harvard University Press (Loeb), 1921.

Pöggeler, Otto, *Der Denkweg Martin Heideggers*, Pfullingen, Neske, 1963. Translated by Magurshak, D., and Barber, S., as *Martin Heidegger's Way of Thinking*, Atlantic Highlands, N. J., Humanities Press, 1987.

———, *Neue Wege mit Heidegger*, Freiburg, Alber Verlag, 1992. Translated by Bailiff, John, as *The Paths of Heidegger's Life and Thought*, Atlantic Highlands, N. J., Humanities Press, 1997.

Powell, R., "Has Heidegger Destroyed Metaphysics?" in *Listening*, vol. 2 (1967).

———, "The Late Heidegger's Omission of The Ontico-Ontological Structure of Dasein" in Sallis, John (ed.), *Heidegger and the Path of Thinking*, Pittsburgh, Duquesne University Press, 1970.

Przywara, Erich, *Analogia Entis*, Einsiedeln, Johannes Verlag, 1962 (1926).

Pseudo-Dionysius, *Corpus Dionysiacum*, Berlin, de Gruyter, 1990. Translated by Luibheid, C., as *Pseudo-Dionysius: The Complete Works* in *The Classics of Western Spirituality*, New York, Paulist Press, 1987.

Rahner, Karl, S. J., *Geist in Welt*, Munich, Kösel, 1957. Translated by Dych, William, S. J., as *Spirit in the World*, London, Herder, 1968.

——— (Metz, Johann B. [ed.]), *Hörer des Wortes: Zur Grundlegung einer Religionsphilosophie*, Munich, Kösel, 1963. First published in 1941. Translated by Richards, Michael, as *Hearers of the Word*, London, Herder, 1969.

———, "Introduction au concept de philosophie existentiale chez Heidegger" in *Recherche de science religieuses,* vol. 30 (1939). Translated by Tallon, A., as "The Concept of Existential Philosophy in Heidegger" in *Philosophy Today,* vol. 13 (1969). The original German text has been lost.

———, "The Theology of the Symbol" in *Theological Investigations,* vol. 4, London, Darton, Longmann, and Todd, 1966.

Richardson, William J., S.J., "Heidegger and Aristotle" in *Heythrop Journal,* vol. 5 (1964).

———, *Heidegger: Through Phenomenology to Thought,* Dordrecht, Martinus Nijhoff, 1963.

———, "Heidegger's Way through Phenomenology to the Thinking of Being" in Sheehan, Thomas J., S.J. (ed.), *Heidegger: The Man and the Thinker,* Chicago, Precedent, 1981.

Risser, James (ed.), *Heidegger toward the Turn,* Albany, SUNY Press, 1999.

Robinson, James McConkey, and Cobb, J. B. (eds.), *The Later Heidegger and Theology,* New York, Harper & Row, 1963.

Rockmore, Tom, *Heidegger and French Philosophy: Humanism, Antihumanism, and Being,* London, Routledge, 1995.

———, *On Heidegger's Nazism and Philosophy,* London, Harvester/Wheatsheaf, 1993.

Sadler, Ted, *Heidegger and Aristotle: The Question of Being,* Athlone, London, 1996.

Safranski, Rüdiger, *Ein Meister aus Deutschland,* Munich, Hanser, 1994. Translated by Osers, Ewald, as *Martin Heidegger: Between Good and Evil,* Cambridge, Harvard University Press, 1998.

Sallis, J. (ed.), *Reading Heidegger: Commemorations,* Bloomington, Indiana University Press, 1993.

Schaeffler, Richard, *Frömmigkeit des Denkens? Martin Heidegger und die katholische Theologie,* Darmstadt, Wissenschaftliche Buchgesellschaft, 1978.

Schelling, Friedrich Wilhelm, *Über das Wesen der menschlichen Freiheit,* Reclam, Stuttgart, 1964.

Secada, George, *Cartesian Metaphysics: The Scholastic Origins of Modern Philosophy* Cambridge, Cambridge University Press, 2000.

Shanley, Brian J., O. P., "St. Thomas Aquinas, Onto-Theology and Marion," in *The Thomist,* vol. 60 (1996).

Sheehan, Thomas J., S.J., "Das Gewesen" in *Existentia:* ΜΕΛΕΤΑΙ ΣΟΦΙΑΣ, Szeged, Budapest, vol. 6–7, fasc. 1–4 (1996–97).

———, *Karl Rahner, the Philosophical Foundations,* Athens, Ohio University Press, 1987.

———, "Notes on a Lovers'Quarrel: Heidegger and Aquinas," in *Listening,* vol. 9 (1974).

Sluga, H., *Heidegger's Crisis: Philosophy and Politics in Nazi Germany,* Cambridge, Harvard University Press, 1993.

Smith, Gregory Bruce, *Nietzsche, Heidegger, and the Transition to Postmodernity*, Chicago, University of Chicago Press, 1996.

Tallon, Andrew, "Personal Becoming: Karl Rahner's Christian Anthropology," in *The Thomist*, vol. 43 (1979).

Thiselton, Anthony. C., *The Two Horizons: Heidegger and New Testament Hermeneutics*, Grand Rapids, Eerdmans, 1980.

te Velde, Rudi A., *Participation and Substantiality in Thomas Aquinas*, Leiden, E. J. Brill, 1995.

Vycinas, V., *Earth and Gods: The Theology of Martin Heidegger*, The Hague, Nijhoff, 1961.

de Waelhens, A., "La philosophie de Heidegger et le nazisme," in *Les Temps Modernes*, vol. 4 (1947/48).

———, "Réponse à cette réponse" in *Les Temps Modernes*, vol. 4 (1947/48).

Ward, Graham, *Cities of God*, London, Routledge, 2000.

———, "Introducing Jean-Luc Marion" in *New Blackfriars*, vol. 76 (1995).

Ward, James F., *Heidegger's Political Thinking*, Amherst, University of Massachusetts Press, 1995.

Welte, Bernard, "The Question of God in the Thought of Heidegger," in *Philosophy Today*, vol. 26 (1982).

Westphal, Merold, "Overcoming Onto-theology" in Caputo, John, and Scanlon, Michael (eds.), *God, the Gift, and Postmodernism*, Bloomington, Indiana University Press, 1999.

Young, Julian, *Heidegger, Philosophy, Nazism*, Cambridge, Cambridge University Press, 1997.

Zimmerman, Michael E., "The Death of God at Auschwitz?" in Milchman, Alan, and Rosenberg, Alan (eds.), *Martin Heidegger and the Holocaust*, Atlantic Highlands, N. J., Humanities Press, 1996.

———, *Eclipse of the Self: The Development of Heidegger's Concept of Authenticity*, Athens, Ohio University Press, 1981.

———, *Heidegger's Confrontation with Modernity: Technology, Politics, Art*, Bloomington, Indiana University Press, 1990.

# Index